Global Bearings

An Introduction to the Politics
of International Order

by

Jeremy Penna
Tobias Lemke

Branton Press

Branton Press is an independent publishing house located in northern Delaware focusing on basic, vintage, and critical editions of works of fiction, poetry, and drama. We also publish original work by new and established authors. This is our first ever textbook in our "Pathways" Series.

Global Bearings: An Introduction to the Politics of International Order
Printed in the United States of America
Newark, Delaware
Copyright © 2021 Jeremy Penna
All rights reserved.
ISBN-13: 978-1-950299-04-1

Library of Congress Control Number:

To Abdulkadir Tanis, Wahmeedh Sabri, Yara, Abheer, Enoch, Zeyu, Joseph, Kim, Mia, Adam, & this semester's King of Study

PART I: INTERNATIONAL ORDER OVER TIME

PART II: THEORY

PART III: ISSUES

Aknowledgements

We owe the largest debt of gratitude to those students who made teaching global politics both a joy and a challenge. There are too many to name, but a quick hopscotching through recent memory lands on Kim, Zeyu, Enoch, Adam, Phil, Jinwei, Danny, and Winston as inquisitive, energetic and dedicated scholars who were always a pleasure to have in class. A special nod also to Joseph who said one of the best things I've ever heard in the classroom, "We all agree that America is pandemonium, but who is its Lucifer?"

At a more practical level, I'm grateful to Brianna Martinez for invaluable help prepping the glossary; Sarah Baird, for early help with templates; and Henry John Temple, 3rd Viscount Palmerston, for being a handsome cat & a very fine Snapchat distraction.

This book is for all of you.

Preface

This book (like much both in the political world and the regular old world) was born out of that happy congress of necessity and accident. Necessity in that we were becoming frustrated with the textbooks that we had been using, which, it seemed to us, asked too much of the students. The books weren't bad per se. But they were, too often, academics speaking to other academics, grad students to grad students, initiates to initiates. They would unwind sentences like, "the agency of political actors is structured by both claimed and implicit identities," without explaining what "agency" means or "structured" or giving enough background to a philosophical tradition which our students, with some exceptions, were not born understanding. We needed something just a bit more foundational, a text that would allow students to get their bearings and would show them where the shores were before sailing out on the wide sea of discourse. Accident because in the process of making handouts, lecture notes, supplementary readings, assessments, and rubrics we found we had a textbook before we knew it.

This book does not assume any background in politics and does not take for granted the sort of generalized understanding of culture that used to be termed "common knowledge." We've had university students with no idea what World War II was, ones who maintained the European Union and the Soviet Union were the same thing, and ones who thought Americans colonized England rather than vice-versa. Though grumpy professors sometimes like to blame students for being unprepared, most of the time it isn't their fault. Universities in the twenty-first century are full of students who professors never used to expect: international students from non-western countries, first-generation students from BIPOC communities, students with penchants for art or engineering but none for the soft sciences, etc. They simply have different experiences. We have learned to be suspicious, therefore, of the idea that there is a common frame of reference for large historical events like (say) the French Revolution. In the western canon, events like these, after all, are not simply "historical events" but, rather, history-shaping symbolic events. They occupy a certain space in our minds, add a certain texture to our language and form part of the blocks with which we construct the world. Realizing that this varies widely across cultures, we have decided to introduce historical landmarks with a great deal of patience and contextualization. We recognize that this slows the pace of the book down, and that we might be accused of having a too basic approach. True enough. Still, we'd prefer to have a book that students can read and understand before class and then add on the nuance and complexity during lecture as needed rather than have a book that students don't get a lot out of and then having to use lecture to walk back and simplify. We feel that what we occasionally lose in depth and academic tone, we gain by making this book accessible to a wider segment of the student population. The purpose of a textbook is to teach, after all, and we believe that the best method is to meet the students where they are rather than hoping they meet us where we are.

Thematically, this book is divided into three sections: history, theory, and issues. The problem is that global politics isn't so neatly segmented. Everything happens all at once. A strictly chronological organization will become conceptually blurry. The 17th century, after all, saw the wars of religion, the enlightenment, the voyages of discovery, the birth of capitalism, the Columbian exchange, and dozens of other important but seemingly unrelated occurences. Saying "the 17th century" doesn't help much. Similarly, conceptual organization necessitates jumping around in time in a way that can sometimes induce vertigo. The tradition of liberalism really begins in the west during the British Civil War. If we start then, we could teach it all the way through to the present day. But then we'd have to jump back a few hundred years to teach the next concept (Marxism, say) in a backing-and-forthing which might prove more than a little eccentric. There really is no perfect way to integrate history, concepts, and issues, and all we can do is hope the present organization of the book is concrete enough to allow students to have a sense of discrete units while malleable enough to allow instructors to make those units bend in whatever ways seem interesting. The relatively short chapter-lengths, to that end, were designed to allow multiple options for course design. For example, instructors might choose to teach a historical event, a related theory, and an issue all in the same week: (for example, by bundling together the World War I, realism, and nationalism chapters). Or they might choose to begin with issues and then work backward into history. Or they might choose to throw out a whole section altogether. We believe the structure of the book allows for that kind of imaginative rearrangement.

Of course, we don't doubt that whatever instructors pick this up will be frustrated by some things, disappointed by others, maybe even infuriated now and again. They'll wind up making supplementary materials, handouts, extra readings, and assessments, and, maybe, before long, in whatever congress of accident and necessity, have a book of their own. Fine with us. This book is another brick in the wall (not the wall itself), and we hope students and teachers will take it for what it is, get out of it what they can, and use it for whatever wall-brickings or wall-scalings are in their future. This is what it means to be part of a community of scholars, and taking part in a cooperative enterprise which it would not be wrong to call an institution.

PART I: INTERNATIONAL ORDERS THROUGH TIME

The opening section introduces the historical background necessary for understanding contemporary global politics. After defining basic vocabulary and concepts, we take a brief tour through western history, highlighting the events which have been instrumental in establishing the structure of international relations. We start with the collapse of the Roman Empire and then proceed rapidly through the Wars of Religion, the Peace of Westphalia, and the Atlantic Revolutions, illustrating how those events gave rise to different norms of **sovereignty**. We then discuss **The Great Divergence** in two phases: first describing the consequences of the **Voyages of Discovery** in the 16th century and then the **Age of Imperialism** in the 19th century which established the dominance of the West. We briefly examine the period of the **Great Powers**, focusing on how different forms of nationalism led to the **First Great War**. Then we slow down quite a bit, unpacking the justifications for and the goals of the **Liberal International Order (LIO)** which followed World War I. We explore the drastic changes in the LIO that resulted from the outbreak of World War II, the establishment of the United Nations, decolonization and the containment policies of the Cold War. Finally, we explore the challenges confronting the LIO which have arisen in the past twenty years, highlighting America's problematic leadership in the context of a polarized world.

Key starting Concepts	**Key Events**
• Politics	• Fall of Roman Empire
• Power	• Protestant Reformation
• Institutions	• Enlightenment
• Sovereignty	• Voyages of Discovery
• Legtimacy	• Industrial Revolution
• International Order	• World War I & II
• Secularism	• Decolonization
• Imperialism	• Cold War
• Hegemony	• 9/11 War on Terror

CHAPTER 1: POLITICS, POWER, AND INSTITUTIONS

Overview

This chapter introduces the basic vocabulary of political science. The following terms will appear over and over again throughout this book:

- Politics
- Nation-state
- Authority
- Political Actor
- Legitimacy
- Power
- Institution

Getting Started: What is Politics?

No matter what country you're from, you probably have some idea of what **politics** is and how it works. What does the word mean to you? It might be helpful, before starting out, to take a moment and jot down a brief definition of your own:

I define politics as_____

If you're from the United States, you probably wrote something about the Democratic and the Republican parties and the politicians who compete for votes in regular elections. If you're from China, you might have mentioned the Chinese Communist Party and National People's Congress. If you're from Saudi Arabia, you might have thought of the House of Saud and the various ministries appointed by the royal family. Definitions of politics are **relative**. They vary among people situated in different places and times. The political order of the ancient Roman Empire, for example, was quite different from that of modern day Brazil. Yet politics has been unmistakably present in all cultures. Whether you notice it or not, politics is present in your life right now. Where you live, who you are, what you happen to be doing with your life are all connected, in some way, to political forces.

Can we give a general definition of politics? One which can be applied to all cultures and moments? The political scientist Harold Laswell thought so. He put it simply when he proclaimed that politics is a **process of social organization** which describes "**who gets what, when, and how.**" In other words, politics decides

1. **Who** the members of a community are.
   (Example: A community may be large, like a nation-state, or small, like a town.)
2. **What** rights and duties the members have.
   (Example: They may have the *right* to equal treatment before the law and the *duty* to work.)
3. **When** political decisions are to be made.
   (Example: There may be a yearly schedule of political events).
4. **How** decisions are to be carried out.
   (Example: The king may give a command. Or there may be a vote. Or a negotiation).

This "who, what, when, and how" does not occur once and for all (with, say, a treaty or a constitution) but occurs over time, is ongoing and may be renegotiated in the future. You can think of it as a long conversation among many individuals, all of whom belong to the community in some way. This conversation might include the relatively *loud* voices of the wealthy and powerful, **the privileged few.** Small in number, they often make the rules that everyone else has to follow. The conversation might include the relatively *quieter* voices of those who live under those rules and bear their consequences. The masses, the poor, the working class, the private citizens, or, **the many**: these individuals make up the vast majority of the community.

Throughout history, most if not all communities have included members of these two groups. Sometimes, as in the case of a **monarchy** or an **oligarchy**, it's the few that seem to do all the talking. Sometimes, as in the case of a **republic**, the many seem to have more of a voice. In all cases, however, their conversation makes up the **discourse** through which the political community organizes itself.

Key Questions: What you need to know.

- According to Laswell, what is politics?
- Do politics look the same everywhere? How might they differ?
- What is important about the word "process?"
- What is meant by "discourse?" Why is it important?
- What is the relationship between "the few" and "the many?"

Questions for Reflection

1. In your own country, what defines the "who, what, when, and how" of politics?

- Who:

- What:

- When:

- How:

Political Actors

When we say "community," your first instinct might be to think of *countries*--the United States, China, Russia, Japan. We tend to think that everyone *has* a country in the same way that everyone has a name. However, communities have been organized in many different ways over history, and the idea of a country is a relatively recent construction. You might have heard, for example, of the Native American **tribes** that hunted and farmed in North and South America before the coming of the Europeans. Or of the Arabic **clans** such as the Quraysh who wandered with their herds on the Arabic peninsula. Or the medieval European **principalities** and **monarchies** in which a king or queen governed from one castle wall to another. Or the **empires,** like ancient Rome, in which some powerful Cesar dominated a number of smaller vassal states.

As for the countries that exist today, in one sense the definition is obvious. It is so ingrained in our culture that everyone "knows" what the word means. Political scientists, however, argue that the idea of a country raises certain questions. What makes a country a country? Is it a place on a map? A piece of land with soldiers around it? A group of culturally connected people? Because of the difficulty of answering these questions, political scientists tend to prefer the more precise term **"nation-state."** This term reflects an important distinction: namely, there is a difference between, on the one hand, a group of *people* who have been bound together, over time, by a common language, culture, territory, and collection of traditions; and, on the hand, the *organizations of power* which formalize the relations among them. On the one hand, there are the men and women who live somewhere, socialize, sing songs, write poems, and pass on their values to their children. On the other hand, there are the "official organizations" that surround those individuals: the banks, schools, courts, and offices. The "nation" part of the term "nation-state" refers to the people and their common identity; the "state" part refers to those organizations by which they order their societies. Altogether, "nation-state" describes the interdependence of the two elements.

Nation (people)	State (Institutions of Power)
Language	Legal System
Religion	Beurocracies
Culture	Legislative Assemblies
Territory	Military
Relationships	Written Contracts

Key Question: What you need to know
- Why is the term "nation-state" preferable to the term "country?"
- What does the "nation" part of nation-state refer to? What does the "state" part refer to?

Question for Discussion:

Think of your own nation-state. What reflects the nation? What reflects the state?

Finally, although nation-states are undeniably important, modern global politics is by no means limited to them. Indeed, the world is characterized by **multiplicity**, the simultaneous existence of many competing political forces. The World Bank, for example, is not a nation-state, but it nonetheless is influential in the "who, what, when, and how" of the political process. In the modern world, it is fairly easy to name many organizations and entities which likewise have political power. You might think of transnational companies, political parties, private militia groups, religious organizations, and, in certain cases, individual human beings. Political scientists refer to these as **political actors**. In rather obvious terms, a political actor is anything that might act politically.

Power

As political actors interact with one another, they make choices about how to organize their communities. When these choices are made, some interests are affirmed while others are denied. Actors say "yes" to some things and "no" to others. While there can be general consensus, there

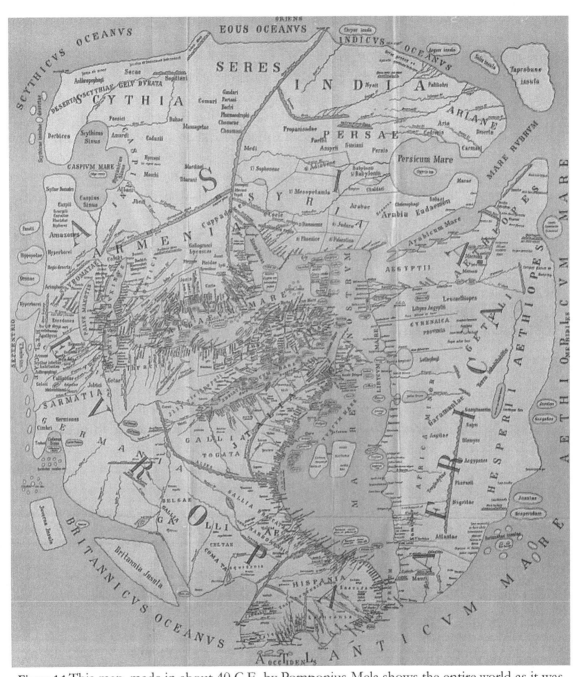

Figure 1.1 This map, made in about 40 C.E. by Pomponius Mela shows the entire world as it was understood thousands of years ago. Though there were "regions" these would not have been understood as "countries." The idea of a country, which we will explore later in this textbook, developed gradually in early modern Europe (1600-1800 C.E.) and would have seemed strange to many living before our era.

can also be sharp disagreement. This disagreement can sometimes be so intense that it can lead to violence. Why do political actors take things to such bloody extremes? The answer is that politics almost always involves questions of power.

Power is a slippery concept and political scientists do not always agree on how to define, measure, and analyze it. For our purpose it is useful to start with a very simple definition: **the ability to make people do things they otherwise would not do.** If your parents tell you to come home by 10:00 PM and you agree (even though you would like to stay out longer), it is because your parents have a certain amount of power over you. Power has many sources and can work in a variety of ways. The German sociologist **Max Weber** (1864 - 1920) explained the operation of power in terms of three different *sources of authority*. According to Weber power can be understood as deriving from:

- **Traditional authority:** Authority that comes from long-established cultural practice and customs.
- **Charismatic authority:** Authority that comes from the personal characteristics and influence of powerful leaders.
- **Rational authority:** Authority that comes from laws, institutions, rules or "standards."

Weber studied different societies throughout history to explain how these forms of authority were exercised and how they affected the development of politics across time and space. For most of history, Weber found, power was connected to traditional and charismatic forms of authority. Only more recently, in the more open and civic-minded societies of the late 18th and 19th centuries did power become increasingly grounded in rational authority. Weber believed that the evidence for the rise of rational authority could be found in the growing number of **political constitutions** that *restricted* the power of individual rulers and made clear guidelines for the exercise of authority.

(**Figure 1.2**)
Constitution: a legal agreement restricting the power of rulers and setting conditions for the exercise of authority.

Power: the ability to make someone do something that they otherwise would not do.

Max Weber: German sociologist. Identified three sources of authority.

One of the most important points to take away from Weber's work is the realization that power does not *have to* involve the threat of force or violence. Often political power often enjoys a high level of acceptance by the members of a community. When power is accepted in this way we refer to it as **legitimate** power..

At the same time, this does not mean, of course, that power *never* involves force. You are probably aware of the fact that power and authority are often backed up by a police or military presence. We refer to this kind of power as **coercive** in nature. Occasionally, the line between coercion and legitimacy is not always so clear. When the police knock at your door and ask you to open it, do you follow their instructions because you believe it is the "right thing to do" (legitimacy) or because you are worried that if you do not they might use violence to come into your house (coercion)? Weber combined the ideas of legitimate and coercive power when he argued that in most modern societies the state enjoys the **monopoly of the legitimate use of violence**. That is, the state is allowed to use force (i.e. the police and the military) while private actors, including citizens are not.

Key Questions: What you need to know

- What are the different ways of thinking about power and authority? According to Weber where does authority come from?
- What is the difference between legitimate and coercive authority?

Violence

This connection between authority and violence, between coercion and power, explains the reason why politics has often been a bloody affair. It is difficult to write the political history of any people without mentioning, on nearly every page, wars and the consequences of wars. Violence casts a long shadow over even times of peace. Even if you have lived in a relatively safe country during a peaceful era, you no doubt have learned about the wars your country has fought. You have also likely observed that politics, even when it does not include outright violence, can be a cause of social division, moral outrage, and even hatred. The philosopher Carl von Clausewitz has famously remarked that **"war is a continuation of politics by other means."** Turning his aphorism around allows us to rephrase it: "politics can continue into war." Or, more reductively, politics can be a nasty business.

Indeed, certain political scientists have gone so far as to argue that almost all politics reduces to bullying and oppression, a large-scale fist-fight among competitive actors. Others take a more moderate stance and point out that many of the questions of politics—questions of administrative-planning or trade, for example—concern the **public good** or the establishment of **social justice**. They consist, for the most part, of deliberations among reasonable people of good will attempting to do what is best for the communities in which they live. We will explore this debate more fully in later chapters, and, for now, it may be best to put the matter somewhat ambivalently and admit that politics, like much in our lives, is complex and can reflect both the best and the worst in human nature.

Institutions

When it comes to the exercise of power, there are occasions when political actors may choose one course of action for no clearly defined reason. The majority of the time, however, power is exercised according to certain legitimate and accepted patterns called **norms**. One assumption about norms is that they are related to **law**, written agreements establishing, in contractual terms, the actions which society requires or prohibits. Another assumption is that they come from the **government,** the people who make and enforce the laws. Both laws and governments have existed for as long as men and women have had societies, and the analysis of them opens up a host of complex questions. How are laws made? How is consent achieved? Do laws and governments create norms or merely describe the cultural assumptions which lie behind them?

Pondering these questions leads us away from the narrow terms "law" and "government" and toward the broader, more flexible term **institution**. Roughly speaking, an institution is the way in which a society shapes behavior and creates trust. In every society, multiple institutions exist and form relationships (or "correspondences") with one another. Institutions may be visualized as a series of interlocking rings, beginning with the smallest and most personal and proceeding outward to the largest and most abstract. For example, we can imagine the institutions of society as beginning with "the family" and proceeding outward to "the peer group," the "school," the "place of worship," the "workplace," and the "state." In all of these institutions behavior is regulated to create a standard of what is "normal and acceptable." The institution encourages the individual to engage in patterns of behavior which recur again and again. In this way, institutions help to form the **structures** through which individuals are given their cultural education (their "programming") and rendered serviceable members of a society.

Question for discussion: In your view, what *norms* does each institution help establish?

- The family

- The school

- The place of worship

- The marketplace

- The state

Institutions encompass and reinforce one another

Figure 1.3

In sum, though politics can be quite relative (varying according to time and place), there are certain features that all forms of politics have in common. First, all politics are fundamentally *processes* of social organization. They reflect the way that political actors negotiate the structure of their communities. Secondly, these negotiations involve *power*, the ability to make people do what they otherwise wouldn't. At times, this power is coercive; at times legitimate. In general the use of power stems from *authority* (whether traditional, charismatic, or rational). Last but not least, the exercise of power is visible in *institutions*: the organizations, formal and informal, through which communities establish norms. So far, all of the terms that we have discussed have been abstract and general. We will begin to explore how these ideas actually work in the real world in the following chapter.

Summing Up: Key Chapter Points

1. Politics pervades all forms of social organization. A helpful definition of politics is a process which organizes "who gets what, when, and how" in society.
2. The study of global politics goes beyond the country and concerns the relationships between different political actors.
3. Political actors can be "anything that acts politically" from an individual human being to a state.
4. Political actors can exercise power through different forms of authority.
5. The ways which societies regularize behavior are reflected in institutions.
6. Institutions are political in that they provide the "cultural programming" that allows individuals to be serviceable members of their societies.

CHAPTER 2: INTERNATIONAL ORDERS AND THE BIRTH OF HISTORY

Overview

This chapter begins with a definition of "international order" and a brief description of the three main types of international order:

- War
- Trade
- Diplomacy

We then discuss the invention of agriculture as a "starting point" of political history, paying specific attention to the growth of sedentary populations and the invention of "kingship." The chapter concludes with a discussion of the different types of cultural patterns reflected in international orders throughout history.

Moving beyond the State: International Orders

We ended the last chapter with a brief discussion of institutions and gave as examples the family, the school, the place of worship, the workplace, the market, and the state. For the most part, these institutions operate "inside" of our political communities. Indeed, from time to time, we are all tempted to think that the state (or the country) is the boundary of politics, the limit where institutions end. However, these familiar institutions, so-called **domestic institutions,** are only a small part of the political system. Our state, (whether America, China, Saudi Arabia, or any other country) does not exist in isolation but in a dynamic system of interaction and negotiation. For that reason, **international institutions**, institutions which operate in more than one state, are an essential part of global politics. There is often an invisible overlap between domestic and international institutions. A government, for example, might decide to use a certain currency, and that currency might affect international trade. The impacts on trade might affect the economies in both countries, which might lead to new political leaders taking power. And so on. This overlap, these chains of causes and effects, are part of what is meant by the term **international order**. At the most basic level, an international order is simply the forms of exchange among the global political actors that recognize one another as independent. To put this in simpler language, it is the way "global interaction" happens, the many **transactions** that take place between countries, institutions, and actors around the world. Though, in theory, countless forms of such interaction are possible, historically the three most common forms have been **war, trade,** and **diplomacy**. We will talk about each more fully in later chapters. For now, a brief description of each type will allow us to get our bearings:

- **War:** We tend to think of war as a form of dis-order. However, historically war has served a paradoxically constructive purpose. It has brought diverse political communities together. It has eliminated old states and established new ones. It has led to long-standing alliances and relationships. Finally, it has often been underneath the establishment of powerful international institutions from the Roman Empire to the United Nations.

- **Trade:** As a human institution, trade is probably as old as language. It establishes the ideas of "fairness" and "reciprocity" that bind communities together. Historically, it has been the basis for international cooperation, interdependence, and trust. As trade becomes more complex, international institutions become necessary in order to create norms for the exchange of goods and services.

- **Diplomacy:** At its most basic level, diplomacy is the way different international political actors make mutual decisions. Sometimes diplomacy can be *direct*: for example, when two heads of state meet one-on-one to negotiate a treaty. Sometimes, it can be *indirect,* for example, when a third-party or a diplomat conducts negotiations on behalf of a country. Most often, diplomacy is a combination of direct and indirect forms of negotiation.

When exchanges (related to war, trade, and diplomacy) happen over and over again, in roughly the same way, we refer to them as *regularized*. Studying international orders means understanding why they have become regularized (or deregularaized) and how, as they have done so, interactions have changed. Regularized international orders have existed throughout history. The Roman Empire, for example, was such an international order. The Warring States period of China was a different type of international order. We are all living in an international order right now: the **modern liberal international order**.

Key Questions: What you need to know

- What is the difference between a domestic and international institution?
- What is an international order?

Farming, Surplus, and Hierarchy: the Birth of Civilization

The *exact* historical beginnings of international order are unknown. Our best guess is that international order began roughly 7,000 years ago in ancient Sumer, when a growing number of people settled in the region and began to farm the land in and around the Tigris and Euphrates rivers. What caused this increase in farming activity is not clear. It is possible the inhabitants of the region learned how to farm gradually. Or it is possible that people migrating northwards from the Arabian Peninsula brought farming techniques with them. Others suggest that a melting of the northern ice sheets allowed animal herds to move out of the region, which forced local communities to look for alternative sources of food, like wild grains growing in the river plains. What matters is that during this time we can see a growing number of people focusing on the year-long planting and tending of crops. The result was an increase in full-time village life.

Figure 2.1 Civilization began bettween the Tigris and Euphrates rivers

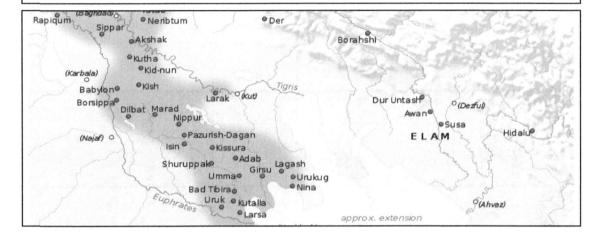

Living in a village with enough food meant that people started to have more children. The populations of the villages began to grow steadily as a result. Over time, these village communities grew into medium-sized towns and then into larger cities with up to 50,000 inhabitants. These communities provided several straightforward benefits. Most obviously, there was a consistent generation of food surpluses. What could be done with the extra food? Many things: first, surpluses encouraged the development of institutions of trade. Trade, in turn, created diplomatic relationships among communities of mutual interest and led to the expansion of the ways these communities shared benefits and burdens. Trade routes were established, and, with them, technologies for transportation and communication: roads, bridges, chariots, wagons. Second, communities were able to feed and equip large armies which not only defended them from attack but also enabled the conquest of larger territories. We see the beginning of larger and larger empires beginning in this period. Third, social complexity increased, leading to hierarchies which divided manual and administrative tasks. The various non-farmers in the community--tool-makers, weavers, carpenters, leather-workers--needed fair access to food and agriculture resources too. In order to better manage the increased social complexity, a new form of politics developed during this period: **kingship,** the concentration of political authority in the hands of one leader with near absolute power. This new system reorganized in the relationships between people, their land and their leader, gradually substituting the more or less egalitarian model of tribalism with the increasingly heirarchical model of monarchy.

Nomadic communities: (Figs **2.2-2.3** below) Before the invention of agriculture, communities travelled from place to place hunting and gathering resources. Though lacking cities, many nomadic communites thrive and certain ones, such as the Bedoins, communities continued a nomadic lifestyle well into the twentieth century.

Sedentary communities: (Figs **2.4-2.5** below) With the invention of agriculture, communities settled down and built cities. The earliest sedentary communities were in ancient Sumer. The below is a Sumerian temple from roughly 2000 BCE. Alulim (below) was recorded in the ancient Sumerian "king list" as the first king of Sumer.

Land Rights

The development of farming also coincided with a more abstract political development: the creation of an interest in the ownership and use of land. By and large, nomadic societies did not have a particularly intricate system of land-rights. What mattered were the resources in the land—which, once taken, made the land useless. To put it simply, nomadic societies cared about where the deer and the fruit trees were. The existence of agriculture, however, made the land itself, the definite location upon which people lived, an essential form of property. This led to the growth of a legal tradition in order to secure and to protect its ownership. Property lines were marked with barriers, registered with magistrates who enforced the rights and protected the power of the owners. Over time, the ownership of land by individual families led to a concentration of wealth and privilege in the hands of an elite few.

Ancient Rome was made possible by agricultural development

(**Fig 2.6**) The hot, dry summers allowed for the cultivation of wheat, olives, and grapes, calorie-dense staples, which could support a large population. The Romans had developed a significant degree of agricultural advancement, had written complex manuals on the science of farming, and had developed roads in order to supply armies.

(**Fig 2.7**) Property boundaries were marked with fortified walls (called *limes*) and registered with magistrates who enforced the rights and oversaw the transfer between recognized landowners. Ownership of land by individual families led to an extraordinary concentration of wealth and privilege by elite patricians.

Key Questions: What you need to know

- When, where, and why did interational order develop?
- What is the importance of the development of agriculture?

Types of International Order

Though all international orders have developed out of the same cultural root (the invention of farming), it does not follow that all international orders are of the same type. Over the past 10,000 years, many international orders have come and gone. Two points of comparison are particularly interesting in classifying the different kinds of international order:

- The **distribution of power** among the political units that belong to an international order
- The **cultural make-up** of these political units.

For example, an international order can have a high concentration of power in which one actor controls the behavior of many lesser "powers." We usually refer to this as an **Empire** or **hegemonic** order. The Roman Empire is perhaps the most well-known example of such an order, in which political authority, concentrated in Rome, extended over almost all of Europe and North Africa. In contrast, there can be an international order in which power is distributed equally among two or more states. We may call this a "**balance of power**" system. In the Warring States period of China, for instance, several large states existed, side by side, in rough military and economic equilibrium. In terms of culture and ideology, we can have orders in which many of the actors share a common set of values and beliefs: i.e. **cultural homogeneity**: Pre-modern Europe (500-1500 CE) for example, was distinguished by a shared belief that rulers derived their authority through their close connection to God and the Roman Catholic Church. Conversely, we may encounter international orders in which actors identify with a broad range of cultural, ideological, and religious groups: i.e. **cultural heterogeneity**. For example, the international order during the time of the Crusades (1095-1571 CE) included a wide spectrum of religious, ideological, and linguistic differences. The table on the following page summarizes some of the various types of international orders that have existed throughout history.

Key Questions: What you need to know

- How do international orders differ?
- What are the four "types" of international order?
- What type of international order do we seem to be living in now?

This, then, for our purposes, was the beginning. Over the course of the following chapters we will study the development of international order and politics through time until we arrive at the present day. Obviously, it is impossible for us, as we tell the stories of these international orders, to give a thorough account of *everything* that has happened over such a large span of time. In addition, as members of a broadly European culture, we admit in advance that our focus will largely be **Eurocentric**. It will focus, in general, on the way international orders look from the perspective of "the west." The historical events which we will present, therefore, will be limited, in both scope and perspective. Nonetheless, they are the ones we regard as having radically changed the international

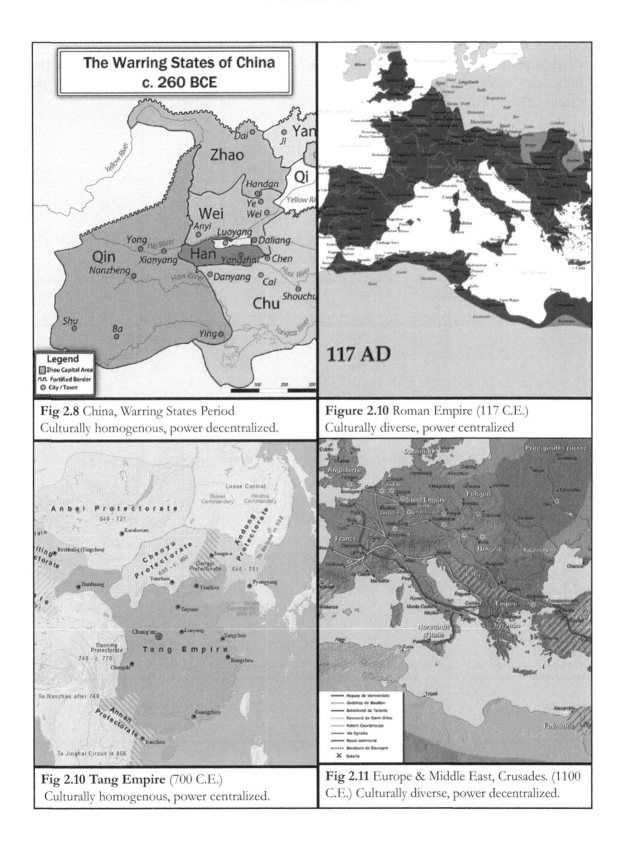

Fig 2.8 China, Warring States Period
Culturally homogenous, power decentralized.

Figure 2.10 Roman Empire (117 C.E.)
Culturally diverse, power centralized

Fig 2.10 Tang Empire (700 C.E.)
Culturally homogenous, power centralized.

Fig 2.11 Europe & Middle East, Crusades. (1100
C.E.) Culturally diverse, power decentralized.

orders of their time and place. They have altered the ways that political communities are imagined, what institutions exist within them, and how they interact with one another. Though our story is oversimplified, and leaves out a great deal, it provides basic landmarks which are necessary to start thinking about contemporary politics.

Summing Up: Key Chapter Points

1. An international order is defined by regularized forms of exchange among political actors who recognize each other as independent.
2. The three most common types of international order are war, trad, and diplomacy.
3. Political scientists regard "the beginning of history" as the invention of agriculture and the subsequent establishment of sedentary communities.
4. The establishment of agriculture created surplus, trade, hierarchy, kingship, and institutions of land-rights.
5. International order can vary according to cultural make-up and the distribution of power.

CHAPTER 3: THE FALL OF ROME,
CATHOLICISM AND THE REFORMATION (496-1517)

Overview

This chapter begins with the fall of the western Roman Empire and the subsequent political **fragmentation** of Western Europe. During this time the **Catholic Church** became a major unifying force in European politics. As the dominant institution of its time, the church played important religious, social, economic, and political roles. As you read, pay particular attention to

- The relationship between the church and state ("divine right of kings")
- The problems with such a relationship for both parties.

The chapter concludes with a brief description of the **Protestant Reformation** and an analysis of why this so traumatic for European political institutions.

Fall of Rome

We can start the story of international relations with the story of two rather solitary men: one of them a king, one of them a monk. The solitary king, **Romulus Augustus,** was placed on the throne when he was just 15 years old. Calling him a "king" is a little silly. Calling him an "emperor" is sillier. As we mentioned in the last chapter, Rome once was a great power in the ancient world, in control of nearly half of Europe. But by 475 C.E., it was falling apart. The city of Rome was no longer the capital. After a series of military losses, the Romans relocated it to Ravenna, in the swamps to the north. The territory of Western Roman Empire was only a shadow of what it had been. At its height, it extended for thousands of miles: Britain to Northern Africa to present-day Turkey. By the fifth century, however, the "empire" only amounted to the Italian Peninsula and parts of Gaul.

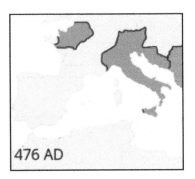

476 AD

(Fig 3.1) The Western Roman Empire in 476 C.E. Compare this to the map in the previous chapter. The "decline" of Rome was due to many factors: the economic strain of managing a large territory, the political instability created by rival factions, and the growing power of the many non-Roman peoples, particularly to the north.

Even this small territory, however, would not last. In 476 C.E., a Germanic army officer named **Odoacer** launched a rebellion, captured Ravenna and took Romulus hostage. Though he could have killed the young man, he decided, instead, to keep him under house arrest in *Castel dell'Ovo* ("the castle of the egg") a small fort out in the water only accessible by bridge. Romulus was still king and his face still appeared on Roman coins, but, in reality, he was a prisoner. He lived out his days in the castle, the last Roman Emperor.

(Fig 3.2) Romulus Augustus on Roman coin.	**(Fig 3.3)** Castel dell 'Ovo

What happened to the territory which the Romans once ruled? By the time Romulus was deposed, it had become **fragmented** into dozens of small kingdoms, each representing various tribes and ethnic groups. There were the Britons, the Angles, and the Saxons in present-day England. There were the Frisians, the Franks, and the Burgundians in what we could now call France. You can see a map of the various kingdoms below. The power of the kings who ruled these kingdoms was often insecure, and the borders would often shift. Nonetheless, political power was significantly more decentralized than it had been in the days of the Empire. The miniature kingdoms below represent, in many ways, the seeds of the European countries that exist today.

Key Vocabulary

Fragmentation: The breaking up of larger political units into smaller ones. The end of the Roman empire saw the political fragmentation of Europe.

Key Questions: What you need to know

- What happened after the fall of the Western Roman Empire?
- Why was this important?

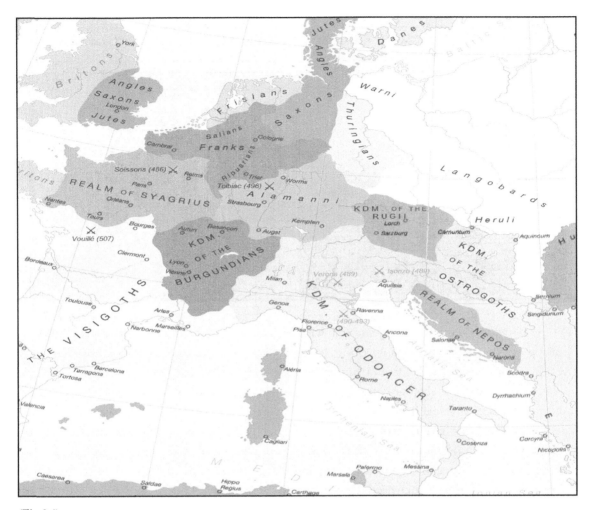

(Fig 3.4)

Rise of the Monastery system

Our second solitary man enjoyed, it might be said, a somewhat more fortunate form of isolation. **Benedict of Nursia** was from a wealthy family in central Italy when he was sent to Rome as a teenager to study. He gradually became unhappy with life in Rome: the crowds, the corruption, the disorganization. Benedict, a pious young man and a serious student, wanted to find a place where he could live a simple life of meditation and discipline. In the year 500 C.E., he and a group of like-minded students went south of Rome, into the hills, and eventually established a private villa in Monte Cassino. This would become the first **Benedictine monastery,** a secluded religious community where the "monks" dedicated themselves to *ora et labora,* prayer and work. The work part of their day included farming, caring for the sick, and, perhaps most importantly, making books. Each day, they copied texts, producing high-quality decorative manuscripts.

| (Fig 3.5) Monastery at Monte Cassino | (Fig 3.6) Monk copying manuscript |

During Benedict's life and in the years following his death, Benedictine monasteries spread across Europe as other Christians followed the "rule of Benedict." Often for religious reasons, many wealthy families donated lands and money to the monasteries, and over time, the monasteries became, in addition to religious communities, cultural centers with large churches, farms, schools, and marketplaces attached to them.

What does this have to do with politics? In general, the spread of monasteries through Europe served two important political functions. First, it allowed the Christian religion, in the form of the **Catholic Church**, to continue to expand. After its founding in the early 1st century C.E., Christianity had gradually increased its influence in the Roman Empire. Though the religion was officially illegal, (at least at first) it spread throughout Europe and North Africa in small, highly dedicated churches and congregations. In the year 313, a rather unlikely event occured: the Emperor Constantine reported that he had seen a vision of a cross emblazoned with the words, "By this sign, conquer." Soon after, he passed the **Edict of Milan**, ending state persecution of Christians and allowing them to worship openly. In 380, the three co-emperors Theodosius I, Gratian, and Valentinian II passed the **Edict of Thessalonica**, which made Christianity the "official religion of the Empire."

At the time of the Edict, perhaps 20 percent of Europeans were Christians. Many in Europe, particularly in the Germanic areas and in present-day England, had never heard of Christianity. After Benedict's death, however, Pope Gregory I launched a series of missions (the so-called **Gregorian Missions**) designed to convert the remaining non-Christians in Europe and to harmonize the organization of the church. The extensive church **hierarchy** (see diagram) allowed for the effective supervision of monasteries. The monks adopted a strategy of converting the wealthiest nobles first, believing that, over time, those nobles would shape the broader cultures of their kingdoms. Monasteries educated the children of the most affluent families, becoming sources of learning, culture, and literacy. As a result, within a few generations, Christianity was widely prevalent in Europe.

(Fig 3.7) Church Hierarchy	**(Fig 3.8)** Diagram of Benedictine monastery

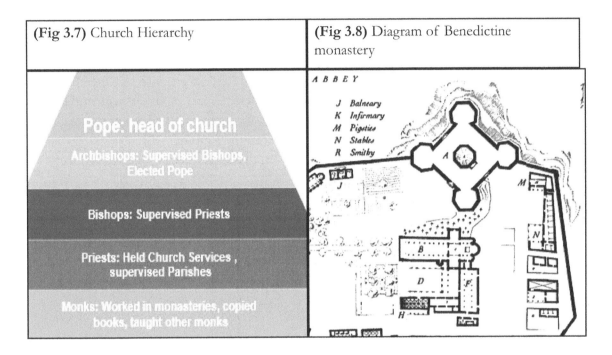

The second political function is related to social administration. The talent of the monks for book-making and record-keeping made them useful to the various governments that succeeded the empire. They wrote in Latin, the old imperial language, which continued as an official tongue of diplomacy and discourse. Over time the monks began to copy not only religious texts but also legal documents, historical chronicles, and occasionally secular works of literature. They developed into major libraries and, in many cases, these libraries expanded into affiliated universities. It is no exaggeration to say that, if you could read and write in the middle ages in Europe, you were, in all probability, in a monastery. The monasteries, in other words, became the keepers of cultural memory. As their importance in this regard increased, so did their wealth and influence. Though the Roman Empire had fallen and its old territories had become politically fragmented, the monasteries that crisscrossed Europe, in a way, continued the many of the old administrative practices. In this sense, they provided cohesion and integration to the disparate and often hostile kingdoms that rose out of the ashes of the empire. If the various kingdoms were the bones and muscles of Europe, you can think of Christianity, administered through the Catholic Church, as the blood vessels that flowed between them.

Putting these two points together, we can simply say that the Catholic Church, after the fall of the Roman Empire, organized through monasteries and churches, became the *dominant institution* in

Europe. Not only was it a *religious* institution--providing the spiritual and philosophical framework that structured the inner lives of believers--but it was also

- a *social* institution: a place people went to interact with their friends and neighbors
- an *educational* institution: the place where people learned to read and write
- a *legal* nstitution, the place where baptisms and marriages and funerals and transfers of property were legitimized.
- An *economic* institution: the place that collected "tithes" (taxes) and was therefore often responsible for much of the "poor relief" and social welfare of the ancient world.
- And last but not least, an *international* institution: forming the broader network that joined the various independent kingdoms that succeeded the Empire.

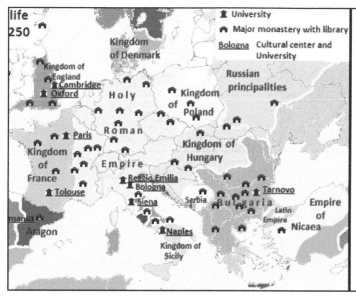

(Fig 3.9)

Monasteries and affiliated Catholic universities were present in all the major cities of Europe during the middle ages. Not only were these important institutions of social cohesion, but they also continued many of the administrative functions of the Roman empire. The dominance of the Catholic church can be visualized in terms of a supra-national institution.

Key Questions: What you need to know

- What were the two political functions of Catholic monasteries?
- In what ways were monasteries a "continuation" of the Roman empire?
- In what ways was the Catholic Church the "dominant institution" of ancient Europe?

Protestant Reformation and Wars of Religion

The Catholic Church was supreme in Europe for over 1000 years. One question you might have is: what about the kings and queens? Didn't they have a great deal of power? How did they fit into the

Catholic system of administration? There are many ways to answer this question, but perhaps the simplest is to argue that Europeans, at the time, would have recognized two types of power. The authority of the Catholic Church would have been regarded as **spiritual power**: power centered on religion and the social institutions and practices which religion helped organize. The authority of kings, on the other hand, was **temporal power**: power over the material resources of the land and people which they ruled.

Theoretically, temporal power was distinct from spiritual power, yet, in reality there was frequent overlap between the two realms. As the Catholic Church continued to spread and to establish churches, monasteries, and schools across Europe, it came to control no small amount of land and revenue. In fact, by the middle of the 11th century, the Catholic Church was, by far, the largest landowner in Europe. The church collected a 10% tithe on nearly all members (and many Europeans donated more than this) making it also the wealthiest institution in Europe. Not only that, but it could have significant political influence on the affairs within the individual kingdoms. The Pope could appoint bishops and priests anywhere he wanted to, could advise kings on religious policy, and could use his influence to negotiate agreements.

For centuries, the kings and the churches had shared power in a kind of delicate balance. There were moments of hostility and violent struggles, (as, for example, when Henry IV launched a small, but failed rebellion against the authority of the Pope in 1073) but, in general, the kings protected and helped to maintain the churches, while the churches, in turn, legitimized the kings. In much of Europe, kings went to Rome in order to be crowned by the Pope. Though the ceremony was often only symbolic, it allowed both the king and the Pope to acknowledge their alliance and assert their authority over their different realms. In this way, the relationship was mutually affirming. The king could say that he ruled by **divine right**—the will of God (or God's middleman, at least), and the Pope could say that every king in the world was, at least in spiritual matters, submissive to his authority.

Charlamagne is crowned by Pope Leo III. The kings were regarded as subservient to the church in spiritual matters. In return, the popes acknowledged the authority of the kings in temporal matters.

Divine Right: Belief, common in much of Europe, that the authority of the king came from God.

Key Questions: What you need to know

- What was the relationship between "the kings" and "the church?"
- How was this relationship mutually supportive?
- What was meant by the "divine right of kings?"

The alliance between the temporal and spiritual powers of Europe, however, began to be sharply fragmented in the year 1517. Angered by what he perceived as corruption and hypocrisy within the Catholic Church, a young monk named Martin Luther famously nailed his 95 theses (or theological points) to the church door in Wittenberg, Germany. In doing so, he started the **Protestant Reformation**—a religious split in Christianity which, in a few short years, would divide the faith into Catholic traditionalists and Protestant reformers.

Like most events in Europe at the time, this split can be attributed to both religious and political causes. On the religious side of things, there were many who believed that the Catholic Church had grown greedy, corrupt, and hypocritical, for example by selling **indulgences** (or religious forgiveness) for a profit. Many believed that the church, pursuing money and influence, had lost its way and had perverted the spirit of Christianity. On the political side, Protestantism appealed to many monarchs who viewed it as an opportunity to take more control over their institutions. In 1525, just eight years after Martin Luther nailed his theses to the church door in Wittenberg, **Albert of Prussia** converted to Lutheranism, becoming, in so doing, the first Protestant prince in Europe. His Duchy of Prussia, though technically part of the larger **Holy Roman Empire**, was the first independent European state to be ruled by a Protestant monarch. Other nearby European states followed. In addition to whatever theological reasons may have persuaded European princes to convert, the importance of power and sovereignty cannot be overstated. Monarchs who converted to Protestantism, in general, relished the financial and administrative control that came with increased oversight over their churches. No longer would policy on religious matters be decided by Catholic leaders in Rome. No longer could the Pope claim a transcendent authority to interfere with matters of state. Monarchs themselves could oversee the churches of their own territories.

A gain in institutional power for the king, though, meant a *loss* in such power for Catholicism. In 1534, Henry VIII, the King of England, converted to Protestantism. His **act of supremacy** established himself as the "supreme head" of the churches in England. In the years that followed, in a series of acts that became known as the **suppression of the monasteries,** he dissolved the 900 monasteries in England, confiscating their funds, destroying many of their buildings, and executing many Catholic leaders. It was a revolutionary act, and it was by no means limited to England. Other kings, dissatisfied with Rome and, in many cases, eager to control the functions of religion themselves, likewise repossessed Catholic churches and monasteries. The Catholic parishes, and their affiliated monasteries, which had enjoyed enormous privileges for over 1000 years, suddenly, in Protestant territories, came to be regarded as unwelcome, heretical, and invasive institutions.

What was the result? War. Beginning in the years following the reformation and continuing into the early 18th century, the states in Europe fought one battle after another. More than 30 extended military conflicts connected to conflicts between Catholics and Protestants, engulfed Europe for close to one hundred and fifty years. Collectively, these wars are referred to as the **wars of religion**. Despite this name, it would be naive, however, to say that the wars were only about how to worship God. More broadly, the wars were about power and **sovereignty**, about who has the right to control institutions. Deciding this question, as bloody as it was, proved instrumental in shaping the idea of the nation-state that we have today. We will learn about the consequences of these wars in the following chapter.

Key Questions: What you need to know

- What was the Protestant Reformation? Why was it so significant?
- Besides religion, what motivated monarchs to convert to become Protestant?
- Why were the wars that followed the Protestant Reformation "not only" about religion?

Questions for Reflection:

The Catholic Church was the dominant institution in medieval Europe. Is there an equivalent today?

Think about:

What are some of the major institutions that "unify" diverse political actors both in your country and worldwide?

What are the advantages to having a single dominant institution?

What are the disadvantages?

How do institutions change? Have you witnessed any big changes in the major institutions of your country during your lifetime?

(Fig 3.11) King Henry VIII (1491-1547): In his "Act of Supremacy," Henry broke from the Catholic Church and declared that the king is the "supreme head" of the church.

(Fig 3.12) The Ruins of Roche Abbey in England: the monastery, along with 900 others in England, was dissolved.

(Fig 3.13) Religious divions in Europe 1600 C.E. following reformation

Summing Up: Key Chapter Points

1. The collapse of the Roman Empire led to the fragmentation of Europe into many competitive kingdoms.

2. The establishment of the monastery system helped to "unify" Europe through the Catholic Church.

3. In Europe of the Middle Ages, power was shared between the kings and the representatives of the Roman Catholic Church. The system of the Divine Right of Kings was challenged by the Protestant Reformation.

4. Many European monarchs converted to Protestantism in an effort to gain more control over their institutions.

5. This struggle over religious and institutional power led to the period in European history marked by the "Wars of Religion."

CHAPTER 4: THE WARS OF RELIGION
AND EARLY STATE BUILDING (1517-1648)

This chapter tells the story of the **Wars of Religion**, the most devastating period of time in Early Modern Europe. As you read, consider:

- Besides religion, what were the wars "about?"
- What was the significance of the **Peace of Westphalia**?
- In what ways did the wars contribute to the development of the state?

The chapter includes a discussion of the development of the norm of **territorial sovereignty**, the notion that a state is identified with a certain territory, within which the government has absolute right to administer its affairs.

Territory and sovereignty

At the end of the last chapter, we mentioned **Albert of Prussia**, the first Protestant prince of Europe. Albert was the ruler of the "Duchy of Prussia," a small state in the **Holy Roman Empire**. The Holy Roman Empire (not to be confused with the Roman Empire) was a loose association of hundreds of semi-independent territories: some no larger than individual cities located, roughly, in present-day Germany. Though the territories, under the system of **feudalism** then prevalent in Europe, were *technically* ruled by one elected "emperor" (in this case Charles V), in reality, power was significantly decentralized. Individual princes had fairly absolute control over their states, and the emperor had a limited ability to "rule" against the wishes of the princes. The map below (fig 4.1) shows the disunified nature of the empire in the 16th century.

Questions for discussion

What does the map below remind you of?

Why do you suppose power was so decentralized in the Holy Roman Empire?

What does soverignty mean?

During the period of Catholic dominance in Europe, what determined sovereignty?

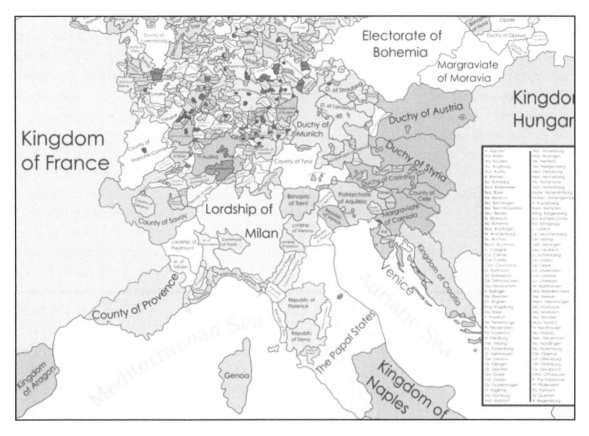

After Prince Albert's conversion, many other princes and rulers in the Holy Roman Empire also became Protestant, some for religious reasons, others because they wanted greater control over their institutions. If they no longer had to listen to the Pope, they would increase their own power and strengthen their **territorial sovereignty**, control over their land, without external interference.

Key Vocabulary

Territorial Sovereignty: The idea that political authority extends over a certain area of land. Within that land the government has supreme legal authority. Political actors outside of that land, those in other land, have no right to meddle with external affairs.

By 1531, these Protestant rulers had joined together in the **Schmalkaldic League**, a military alliance designed to protect their religious rights from the Catholic states in the Empire. For the next fifteen years, the League struggled with various Catholic powers in a series of small-scale wars and battles. In the map at the end of the preceding chapter, you can see the religious divisions of the HRE during this period.

In 1555, the Empire negotiated an end to the violence with the **Peace of Augsburg**. The treaty established the principle of *cuius regio eius religio* (Latin for "whose realm, his religion"). Put simply, each ruler in the Holy Roman Empire had the right to establish the religion for his people. Anyone who didn't like the religion of the prince was expected to move to another part of the Empire. Princes were not allowed to interfere in the churches outside of their kingdoms. The treaty, in other words, *attempted* to articulate the principle of terretorial sovereignty based on the government rather than the church.

Though the Peace of Augsburg led to a temporary easing of tensions, the effects would be short-lived. For one thing, the treaty only recognized the rights of one type of Protestant: the Lutherans. In the years since Martin Luther had launched his protest, a number of other reformers and dissidents had also broken away from Catholicism. One of the larger groups, the followers of John Calvin, became particularly numerous in Geneva and the Netherlands. Calvinists were not given any official recognition or toleration in the Peace of Augsburg. Secondly, it was rather naive to expect all of the people in the Holy Roman Empire to simply relocate to religiously-friendly territories. What would happen, after all, if a Prince happened to convert from Catholicism to Protestantism *after* his people had relocated? The expectation of religious uniformity was highly unrealistic. Last but not least, the Peace of Augsburg only applied to the states within the Holy Roman Empire. It had no effect on the other major European powers: England, France, Spain, and Portugal, all of whom suffered from religious divides during the 16th and 17th centuries. Wars quickly broke out in (and between) those countries as political leaders fought over which religion the people would follow.

War	Actors	Outcome
Dutch Revolt 1566–1648	Catholic Spain and HRE allies vs Holland and England.	Continues until Peace of Westphalia. 700,000 casualties.
British Conquest of Ireland 1529-1603, 1640-1652	Protestant Britain launches a series of campaigns against Catholic Ireland.	Continues through British Restoration. 600,000 casualties.
French Wars of Religion 1562-1598	Catholic French leaders drive Protestant Heugonots from the country.	Ends with Edict of Nantes. Perhaps as many as 4,000,000 dead.
30 Years War 1618-1648	Catholic vs Protestant states in Holy Roman Empire.	Ends with Peace of Westphalia. 12,000,000 possibly killed.
Hessian Wars 1567-1648	House of Hesse vs House of Hesse-Cassel in Holy Roman Empire	Ends with Peace of Westphalia. Perhaps 1,000,000 killed.

Fig 4.3 Painting of the **St. Bartholomew's Day Massacre**. Catholic mobs across France killed as many as 10,000 Protestant Huguenots on August 24, 1572. The Wars of Religion saw violence in Europe which, in many cases, would not be equaled until Wolrd War I.

Fig 4.4 In one of the most famous events of the wars of religion (the "Defenestration of Prague") a group of Protestants from the state of Bohemia hurled the Catholic messengers of Frederic II out of the window of Hradcany Castle. Miraculously, the messengers survived the fall.

This would be the most violent period of European history until the first World War. In France, the Catholic kings launched a series of campaigns against the so-called **Huguenots** (Calvinist Protestants) in the east. Between 1562 and 1598, Catholic and Protestant groups in France fought for control of their communities, with Catholics, in general, getting the upper hand. Over the course of the French religious wars, they drove the Huguenots out of the country and committed a number of notorious massacres. One of the most well known was the **St. Bartholomew's Day Massacre** in which Catholic mobs around Paris killed roughly 10,000 Protestants, wiping out entire villages and executing many religious leaders. The Protestants, of course, could be just as brutal. When the Protestant Henry VIII of England suppressed the British monasteries, his soldiers killed and arrested countless Catholic priests, monks, and scholars. For the next hundred years, the Protestant kings and queens of England sent troops into Catholic Ireland, killing as many as 600,000 Irish Catholics in a campaign that has been frequently described as a genocide.

The Wars of Religion, affected every corner of Europe. In Italy there were the **Habsburg–Valois Wars.** In the Low Countries, there were the Anglo-Dutch Wars and the Dutch revolts. In France, there were the wars with the Huguenots. In Spain, there was the 1588 **Spanish Armada,** an attempt to invade England in order to restore Catholic leaders to the throne. Finally, in the Holy Roman Empire, there was the **30 Years War.** Beginning in 1618, this war proved so bloody that as many as one-third of the people in the Holy Roman Empire may have been killed.

The Peace of Westphalia: End or Rest-stop?

Most textbooks will tell you that these wars "ended" in 1648 with a treaty known as the **Peace of Westphalia**. The treaty, named after the region in Northwest Germany where the treaties were negotiated and signed, consisted of two relatively similar treaties: the Treaty of Münster and the Treaty of Osnabrück. The Kingdom of Sweden, a powerful Protestant state, participated in the negotiations in Osnabrück, along with a delegation from France, an important Catholic power. These treaties reestablished agreement in the Peace of Augsburg (*cuius regio, eius religio*), giving princes "territorial superiority in all matters ecclesiastical as well as political." European monarchs had the right to choose the religion of their territories and conclude treaties both between themselves and with foreign powers outside of the empire. The treaties also rejected the Pope's claim of a "supranational" religious authority to interfere in affairs of state. In so doing, the argument runs, the Peace of Westphalia fully established **territorial sovereignty** across Europe. Often called **"Westphalian sovereignty"** for this very reason, this had the effect of "fixing" the European borders in more or less agreed-upon locations. Within those borders, the government would have absolute authority to rule, without interference, over its land. This would prove decisive in the politics of the late 17th century and would continue to shape international orders into the present day. After all, every country in the world, as we understand it now, is synonymous with a "place on a map," a location within which the government is regarded as supreme.

This "Westphalian story" is, unfortunately, a bit of an oversimplification. First of all, though it is true that the Peace of Westphalia did much to relieve the religious tensions in Europe and though it is true that it did settle certain questions related to borders and authority, it would be a incorrect to argue that the Peace of Westphalia either "ended" the wars of religion or "established" territorial sovereignty. For one thing, the idea that rulers had full authority over their territory had actually been articulated previously (in the 1534 Preamble to the English Statute of Appeals, for example, as well as in the Peace of Augsburg). In some respects, the treaties of 1648 actually *limited* the power of German princes to make final decisions over important religious and territorial questions. For example, princes that changed their religion could not change the religion of their subjects but had to respect the minority rights of their populations. In addition, many kingdoms did not achieve full sovereignty in 1648. Sweden and France were awarded fiefdoms (rights to control land) over territories that were formerly under imperial control, yet, at the same time, the Swedish king became a vassal of the Holy Roman Emperor. Finally, despite the fact that the Peace of Westphalia seemed to establish a form of religious toleration, religious strife continued to be a major source of European conflict after 1648. For example, only forty years later, in the **Glorious Revolution**, the protestant William of Orange invaded England, on religious grounds, to take the throne from the Cathlolic James II.

Therefore, rather than assuming that territorial sovereignty "began" at Westphalia, it is more useful to think of it as having developed as a result of a long and drawn out process that transformed European politics over centuries. During this time, the idea that political power was connected to a ruler's ability to control his land gained general acceptance and became part of European international law. But this did not happen all at once."This process was slow--negotiation by negotiation, norm by norm,--a "development" rather than a "revolution."

Key Questions: What you need to know
- What was the Holy Roman Empire?
- What was the Peace of Augsburg?
- Why were there so many wars following the Protestant Reformation?
- Besides "religion," what else were the belligerents fighting over?

(Fig 4.7) Peace of Westphalia

Taxes in war and peace: early state-building

Besides the Peace of Westphalia, what else shaped this process? It is often surprising to learn that, for all of its destructive power, war itself can often have a progressive effect on institutions. The wars of religion during the 16th and 17th centuries (besides, of course, leaving a tragic number of people dead) were instrumental in the process of establishing sovereign, fixed, independent states. In order to understand how this is possible, consider a basic question: how are wars conducted? What do states need in order to fight them? The most obvious answer, of course, is *people:* a lot of people, all willing to kill and die for a cause. These people, in order to be an effective fighting force, have to be organized, equipped, clothed, sheltered, and fed. This takes an enormous amount of money. The most conventional way for states to get money is, of course, through taxation. Taxes can be

- Collections on transfers of goods and capital (**payments on flows)**
- Collections on land and property (**payments on stocks),**
- Collections on income (**income taxes)**.

Collecting taxes requires the government to be more highly organized. This includes the ongoing surveillance of the economy and the development of specialized staff for evaluation and collection. During the period of the wars of religion (as during all periods of war), the governments of the various states across Europe began to increase their abilities to exact revenue from their populations. Though taxation did not become efficient until after the wars ended, the necessity for money to fund the wars was instrumental in setting the process in motion.

In addition, the governments sought to raise revenue from other sources. The **voyages of discovery** (which we discuss more thoroughly in the following chapters) were intended to increase the wealth of European kingdoms through international trade and colonial development. In addition the **establishment of banking**, which began, in most states, in the 17th century, established a connection between government wealth and private wealth" European monarchs would borrow money from the various aristocrats in their kingdoms, not only increasing available funds but also strengthening the connection between the central government and the powerful elites.

These efforts to increase revenue through taxation, trade, and borrowing were not only important during the wars of religion but also continued during the (slightly) more peaceful years that followed Westphalia. As this process continued, European monarchs and their governments were able to more effectively centralize power: not only increasing their ability to defend their territory from outside threats but also reducing the influence of competitive actors within their states: such as the church or the local lords. To put it more simply, European monarchs, in order to survive in the dangerous and competitive world of almost constant warfare, accumulated money and resources, and, as they did so, solidified their control over their land.

Key Questions: What you need to know
- How did the wars of religion help European leaders increase their control over their territory?
- What different forms of taxes are there?
- Besides taxation, how else did European leaders attempt to raise revenue?

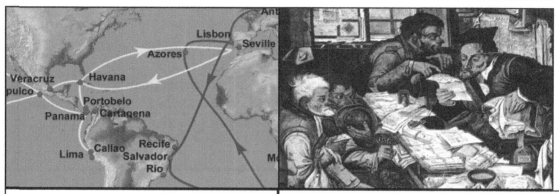

(Fig 4.8) The Voyages of Discovery.

(Fig 4.9) Peter Brughel's "The Tax Office."

(Fig 4.10) In 1694, William III borrowed 1.2 million pounds from Scottish creditors. The establishment of modern banking connected public and private interests.

Summing Up: Key Chapter Points

1) After the Protestant Reformation, Europe was engulfed in war during a 150 year period known as the "wars of religion."
2) The wars pitted Catholic states against Protestant states in an effort to determine which religion the people would follow.
3) These wars were instrumental in the gradual development of "territorial sovereignty," the idea that the government has absolute control over its land.
4) An important treaty was the Peace of Westphalia (1648), which is often credited with establishing the norm of territorial sovereignty in Europe.
5) In fact, territorial sovereignty was a much more gradual development.
6) The wars of religion required significant amounts of revenue. In order to raise money, the European states gradually increased their ability to tax their subjects.

CHAPTER 5: ENLIGHTENMENT
SECULARISM, AND THE GROWTH OF THE NATION (1648-1688)

Overview

This chapter explains the way the church began to lose some of its influence following the Wars of Religion. The rise of **secularism** is attributed to

- The beginning of **the enlightenment**
- The growing popularity of **deism** among the educated classes.
- New technology, such as the development of the **printing press** and a growing interest in mechanics.

The chapter concludes with a discussion of the **British Civil War** and the birth of the **liberal tradition** as Enlightenment thinkers began to challenge norms of sovereignty.

By the time the **Peace of Westphalia** put a nominal end to the Wars of Religion, Europe was simply exhausted. Whether they liked it or not, Catholics and Protestants had to recognize each other's existence. It was during this time that some of the earliest **liberal philosophers** began advocating for increased religious freedom. In 1688, **John Locke** wrote *A Letter Concerning Toleration,* arguing for the separation of religion from "civil society." As he put it: "The commonwealth seems to me to be a society of men constituted only for the procuring...of civil interests. Civil interests I call life, liberty, health... possession of outward things, such as money, lands, houses, furniture, and the like."

Locke imagined "civil society as a kind of religiously-neutral domain: where individuals could cooperate and interact with regard to "outward things." This idea coincides with the birth of **secularism,** the gradual decline in the power of the church and the growth of a more religiously tolerant public space. Locke's argument for the establishment of a secular domain resulted from his awareness of the disaster that had resulted from 150 years of war, and the social consequences that result when governments attempt to control those whom they consider "heretics."

Key Question: What you need to know

- What did Locke mean by "civil society?"
- Why was it important?
- Is our society now "secular?" Does it matter?

(Fig 5.1) John Locke's **Letter Concerning Toleration** would argue for limited government and religious freedom.

(Fig 5.2) In 1688, the British Parliament signed the "**Toleration Act**" granting religious freedom to some minority Christians.

The enlightenment and the birth of "rational" authority

At the time that Locke was writing his *Letter Concerning Toleration*, broader changes were occuring in European society that were making church institutions less total, pervasive, and ubiquitous in European life. Secularism happened slowly, yet, little by little, institutional changes began to create a gap between the church and the individual. In addition to exhaustion over the wars of religion, secularism is related to several other factors.

First, in the 16th and 17th centuries, an explosive growth in the progress of scientific, philosophical, and cultural disciplines took place. Fields as diverse as agriculture, navigation, medicine, physics, and literature entered a period of flourishing, despite the devastation of the recent wars. This period of growth, known as **the enlightenment**, was enabled by the spread throughout Europe of increasingly productive technologies for producing texts. The **printing press**, invented in Germany in 1453, was utilized more and more widely, leading to the increasingly rapid dissemination of information and ideas. Prior to the invention of the printing press, the monasteries (see chapter 3) were, for all intents and purposes, the only places where book-making occurred. By the 16th century, though, anyone with Gutenberg's device could mass produce texts cheaply and distribute them widely. It is no exaggeration to say that the Protestant Reformation itself could not have occurred without the widely printed pamphlets, tracts, and treatises written by religious dissenters. By the end of the Wars of Religion, the use of the printing press had expanded beyond religious texts to include literature, recipe books, works of philosophical speculation, and the first weekly newspapers. The possibility for the rapid exchange of ideas brought about the **decentralization of information** which, in turn, led to the growth of the sciences and humanities. Literacy began to spread beyond the walls of the monasteries and to reach many of the people at large.

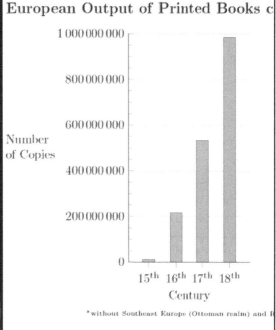

European Output of Printed Books c

Number of Copies

1 000 000 000
800 000 000
600 000 000
400 000 000
200 000 000
0

15th 16th 17th 18th
Century

*without Southeast Europe (Ottoman realm) and R

(Fig 5.3) The development of newspapers after the Wars of Religion was crucial to the decentralization of knowledge.	(Fig 5.4) Copies of Printed Books from the 15th to the 18th centuries

This rapid spread of ideas contributed to the declining power of the church as the *only* dominant social and political institution in Europe. Though the church would remain essential (at least to the majority of ordinary Europeans), increased secularization occurred among elites and intellectuals for whom "reason" seemed to do a better job of explaining the world than dogma or revelation. In 1666, Isaac Newton developed his theory of gravity and then, in 1687, published *Principia* (Principles) which articulated his three famous laws of motion. If, as Newton argued, the motion of any physical object can be predicted through laws, then it seems that much in the world can be understood without explicit reference to the supernatural. Though Newton himself was a devout Christian, many intellectuals of the time used his and similar ideas in order to critique the Christian traditionalism which had dominated Europe for centuries. Toward the end of the 17th and the beginning of the 18th century, there were numerous books and pamphlets arguing that the world was best apprehended through ideas and reasons and not through divine revelation. Nicolas Malebranch's *The Search After Truth* in 1674; John Toland's *Christianity Not Mysterious* in 1699; and William Wollaston's *The Religion of Nature* in 1722 reached a wide audience of educated Europeans due to the spread of information enabled by the printing press. As a result, more and more intellectuals moved away from traditional Christianity and towards **natural religion**. Many became

deists, believers in an impersonal "watchmaker" god who did not miraculously intervene in human affairs, who governed through ordinary nature. To these new thinkers, the world became, to borrow Max Weber's term, **"disenchanted,"** imagined in terms of impersonal forces rather than divine presences.

This change in belief accompanied a change in institutions. For hundreds of years, European universities had had one purpose: the training of men for the priesthood. As science developed and secularism increased, they began to focus more on academic subjects: law, philosophy, mathematics, engineering, geography--the beginnings of the sorts of majors we see at universities today. Their purpose became less to polish leaders and more to educate experts. As these ideas continued to spread through Europe (through printing technology and other factors), the institutional powerbrokers of European culture gradually became synonymous less with the clerical order of priests and pastors and not with the allies of royal families but with the educated and specialized intelligentsia who emerged from the universities.

Key Vocabulary

Disenchantment: Max Weber's term for the world imagined in terms of impersonal forces and material laws.

Secularism: The loss in church power that began to occur during the enlightenment along with the gradual establishment of a more "religion-free" social space.

Key Questions: What you need to know

- What was "the enlightenment?"
- In what respects did the enlightenment lead to the "disenchantment" of European culture?
- What institutions changed during the enlightenment?

Industry, Production, and Expertise

The enlightenment, and the process of secularization that accompanied it, would be a major contributing factor to two important developments that would transform Europe in the following centuries. The first, and most obvious, was improved technology. One of the immediate consequences of Newton's laws of motion was an increased interest in the field of **mechanics**, the study of objects in motion, necessary for the making of machines. European workshops, under the influence of university-trained experts, began producing new (albeit rudimentary) machines: in 1656, the pendulum clock; in 1675, the pocketwatch; in 1680, the gunpowder engine; in 1712 the Newcomen **steam engine**. This last, allowing individuals to release the steam-energy stored in simple bricks of coal, is often taken to mark the "official start" of the **industrial revolution**, a period of rapid growth in technology and economic productivity. Again, the prevalence of printing technology allowed these new ideas to reach wide audiences, allowing scientists, professional and amateur, to experiment on their own, make new models, improvements, and replicas.

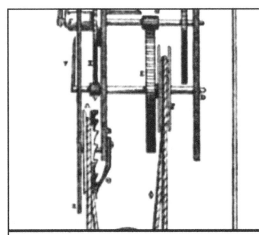

(Fig 5.5) Gears in an early "**pendulum clock**" (1656). Improvements in time-keeping allowed for increased organization during the period of bureaucratization during the early Industrial Revolution.

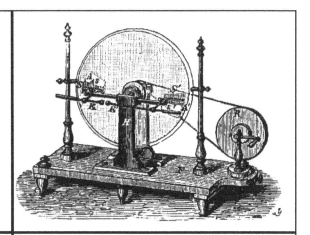

(Fig 5.6) An early "**electricity generation**" device (1663) used friction and glass to make sparks. The device had little practical value but encouraged interest in electric phenomena.

Enlightened Politics: Popular Sovereignty

Just as enlightenment thinkers had challenged traditional religious authority, so too did they begin questioning political authority. As science advanced in Europe, as ideas spread rapidly, as more and more people became literate, thinkers began to be critical of the traditional forms of political power. Why does the king get to be the king? Why should we pay a tax to support his army? Or a tithe to his church? What do we get in return? To some extent, these questions simply reflect the ordinary curiosity and critique which thinkers have always engaged in. However, it is no coincidence that they began to be asked with more urgency in the enlightenment. Ever since the wars of religion, after all, European governments had been extracting more tax revenue from their populations and states were becoming increasingly powerful. The argument of those who questioned the government was simple: if the government wanted to increase the power of the state to manage society, those most affected by these decisions should have a say in them. It is an argument, in other words, based on **consent**. Power exercised without permission often seems random, unfair, and arbitrary. In general, the more strongly such power is exercised, the unhappier people become.

One of the first places where these questions became important was in England. Toward the end of the Wars of Religion, in 1641, the English King Charles I, like many monarchs in

Europe, found himself in desperate need of money to continue to finance his government. British **Parliament**, at the time, consisted of the representatives of the most powerful and wealthy families. Though the Parliament was hardly "democratic" in our understanding of the word today, they saw themselves as spokesmen for the people. When King Charles I attempted to increase taxes, Parliament resisted. When the king tried to raise taxes without their permission, they rallied military support against him. From 1642-1649, England was engulfed in three civil wars, pitting the supporters of the king, known as **royalists** against the supporters of Parliament, known as **parliamentarians**.

(Fig 5.7) **King Charles I** angered many of his people by attempting to raise taxes without consent of the people.	The British **Parliament**, though not "democratic" by today's standards, believed that the king's powers were not absolute and that he had to respect their wishes.

In 1649, after a decisive victory, the parliamentarians seized power and executed Charles I. For several years, the shape of England's new government seemed uncertain, with some arguing that parliament should rule with absolute power and others arguing for more democratic reforms. One historically interesting group, the **Levellers** (see chapter 14), called for civil rights, democratically elected governments, and broad social freedoms. Others, such as the group of religious reformers, **the Puritans**, advocated for a kind of half-republican, half-theocratic sort of government. Viewing the established English church as corrupt, they hoped to institute a stricter, more rigorously Protestant national church which would purify British Christianity from Catholic influence.

Eventually, after a series of power-struggles, **Oliver Cromwell,** a Puritan, instituted a military dictatorship known as **the Protectorate**. Though the period saw some "republican" reforms, in general, it was authoritarian one, with harsh suppression of political opponents, strict limitations of freedom, and the constant potential for violence. Eleven years later, in 1660, Charles II, son of the executed king, returned to the throne and restored the monarchy in series of counter-revolutions known as the **Restoration**. Though Charles II did his best to keep the peace, British politics remained tumultuous. As was the case with the Wars of Religion, the people were deeply divided into opposing spiritual camps: the Puritans on one side, the defenders of the established church on the other, and, playing no insignificant role, a sizable Catholic minority.

One especially difficult issue involved who would succeed Charles II to the throne. His brother, the next in line, James II, was Catholic, a fact which worried many of the English nobles, Anglican and Puritan alike. Over 100 years since Henry VIII had become Protestant (see chapter 4), many in England were now afraid of the possibility of a Catholic King. Among many British at the time, Catholicism was associated with authoritarianism and dogmatism, a king who insisted on "divine right" and refused to listen to his subjects.

This period of political chaos was finally brought to an end in 1688 with the **Glorious Revolution**. Supporters of King Charles II's Protestant great-nephew **William of Orange** and his wife **Mary II**, succeeded in bringing the two to the throne in a bloodless coup. Yet, this did mean simply swapping one authoritarian leader for another. As part of the agreement that brought William and Mary to the throne, the pair agreed to respect the **Bill of Rights**. This document, drafted the year before, made explicit rules about who could be king, defined the limits of royal power, and based political legitimacy on the consent of parliament. It also listed a series of rights, such as the right to free speech and the right to bear arms, that any king or queen had to respect. In other words, the document marked the beginning of **constitutional government** in England, authority which was based not on the will of a powerful person but on the rule of written laws..

The 1688 Bill of Rights, furthermore, was only one example of a broader revolution in political thought that grew out of the enlightenment. Just as enlightenment thinkers had challenged the absolute power of the church, stressing reason rather than tradition so too did they begin to question the absolute power of the monarch. Thinkers like John Locke, who we mentioned at the beginning of this chapter, argued that a king or a queen has no "natural right" to rule. They may happen to have power, but the only thing that makes that power legitimate, in civil society, is the **free consent of the people.** Indeed, five years before the Bill of Rights was instituted, Locke had written *On Government,* an influential treatise making the argument that government is only justified when it is based on the permission of those who are ruled. This notion, many have argued, is one of the earliest significant articulations of the principle of **popular sovereignty**: simply put, that power comes from the people.

It would be inaccurate to say that, with the Glorious Revolution, this principle was *established* in Europe. Far from it. Every country in Europe was still, more or less, a monarchy, and, even in England, despite the advent of constitutional order, power was still largely in the hands of the royal family and the wealthy, land-owning nobles. Nonetheless, popular sovereignty, at least as an idea, traces its birth to this period of history, and, as we will see, led to decisive consequences for both Europe and the world before long.

(Fig 5.9) The English **Bill of Rights** is one of the earliest examples of "constitutional government" in Europe. The Bill put limits on the authority of the monarch, required the consent of Parliament for taxation, and enumerated basic rights that no king or queen could take away. Though England was far from a democracy, the Bill of Rights, and the ideas of popular sovereignty associated with it, would prove highly influential in the American and French Revolutions of the following century.

Summing Up: Key Chapter Points

1) Following the Peace of Westphalia, Europe entered an age of scientific advancement and secularization known as the Enlightenment.

2) One effect of the Enlightenment was the decreased power of the church, an event known as **secularization**.

3) As a result of secularization, universities became more focused on training "experts" than priests. Increased economic production and led to the birth of bureaucracies.

4) Just as people began to question the authority of the church, so too they began to question established political orders

5) The Civil War in England gave rise to the principle of "constitutional government," based on the rule of law rather than the whim of the king.

6) Constitutional government coincided with the birth of the idea of popular sovereignty: the notion that political power comes from "the people."

CHAPTER 6: THE VOYAGES OF DISCOVERY (PART I 1492-1756)

Overview

This chapter tells the story of the **Voyages of Discovery**, focusing particularly on:

- The motivations for the voyages
- The early economic and political advantages gained by western states as a result of the voyages
- The way the voyages shaped institutions back in Europe.

Itconcludes with an examination of four important political consequences:

- The price revolution
- The birth of capitalism
- The Columbian exchange
- The development of new social relationships.

Thus far we have been considering the world from the perspective of **the West,** looking through the eyes of Europeans. In chapter 1, we mentioned the problem of **Eurocentrism,** the tendency to emphasize European perspectives while ignoring those of other peoples and nations. Why is Eurocentrism a problem? One reason is that it limits our understanding of history. Another is that it reflects an imbalance in the modern world. On the latter point, you are likely aware that Western nations own and consume much more than everyone else. Political scientists have referred to this imbalance in a number of ways. Most often it has been referred to as the imbalance between **the West** and **the non-West.** During the Cold War, it was described in terms of "**the first world, the second world, and the third world.**" Many currently label it as the divide between **the global north** (North America, Canada, Australia, and Europe) and the **global south** (China, India, Africa, South America).

Whatever you call it, (in this chapter we'll use "the west/ the non-west") economic figures reveal a striking gap. The GDP of the United States, for example, at over 20 trillion dollars, is more than five times greater than the GDP of *all* of Africa and South America combined, despite the larger populations in those regions. Data reflecting standards of living likewise show a gulf between the haves and the have-nots. The income of many American and European companies, for example, (like Apple, Microsoft, and Walmart) exceeds that of entire nations in the developing world. What is the historical cause for this imbalance? Before we go on, it might be helpful for you to take a moment and think about what you consider the cause is and whether or not we should regard this as a problem.

Key Vocabulary

Global North: The wealthy and developed countries of North America, the EU, and some parts of Southeast Asia

Global South: The poorer and less developed countries of South America, Africa, and Asia

Fig 6.1

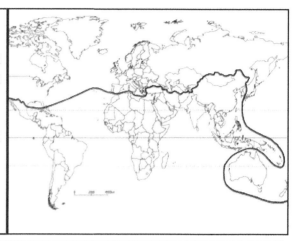

Questions for Discussion

1. In your opinion, what is the cause of the dramatic level of global inequality?
2. What, if anything, ought to be done about it?
3. Is global inequality as big a problem as domestic inequality?

The answers that political scientists give to this question are complex, and the subject has occasioned much debate. However, the majority of historians agree that there were several decisive developments, over the past centuries, leading to this system of global inequality. In the previous chapters, in fact, we have already discussed two of them:

- **Industrialization:** In the wake of the enlightenment, Europeans learned how to derive energy from machines, leading to an increase in production.
- **State Building:** European states grew more centralized and powerful due to the pressures of warfare. Increased tax revenue, expanded bureaucracies, and the growth of "experts" led to states that were well-organized and efficient.

It can be argued, however, that industrialization and state-building are only enabling factors in the global dominance of the west. In order to truly understand how Europe conquered the world we need to go back in time and discuss something which, to this point, we have only hinted at: **colonies** and **empires**: the way that Europeans, starting in the 15th century, went travelling the globe, establishing economic and political control far from their homelands. In this chapter, we will take a tour through Europe's early colonial history, briefly telling the stories of America, Asia and Africa and explaining the consequences of these expeditions.

The Search for the New Silk Road: Early Factors

The early European explorers, in general, were motivated by three factors:

- **Trade**: the desire to sell European goods abroad and bring back "exotic" goods to Europe.
- **Conversion:** the desire to spread the Christian faith.
- **Settlement**: the desire to make a "new home," in part to escape difficult conditions in Europe (push factors) and in part to take advantage of perceived opportunities elsewhere (pull factors)

Of the three, trade, by far, was the most significant, particularly early on. The wealth of India and China (particularly for silk and spices) had been known since the middle ages. For hundreds of years, European traders had made the long trip from Constantinople (modern day Istanbul) to India along the famous **silk road**, a trading route that connected important centers of commerce in the ancient world. However, in 1453 the **Ottoman Empire**, a powerful and rapidly expanding state in the middle east, began closing the route to non-Muslim merchants. It blocked major roads and demanded heavy tolls from European traders who sought to pass through. As a result, Europeans began looking for a way around the Ottoman Empire, attempting to make their way to India by sea.

To do so, they sailed out in two directions: with the Portuguese heading south and east, along the coast of Africa; and Spain heading west, across the Atlantic Ocean. Both Portugal and Spain were well-equipped to attempt such a journey, having powerful navies, wealthy monarchies, and advanced ports at the westernmost tip of Europe. In addition, advances in maritime technology (such as the magnetic compass and the carrack ship) as well as navigation techniques made long sea voyages increasingly more feasible. These voyages inaugurated the so-called **Age of Discovery**, a period of wide-ranging exploration, mercantilism, and diplomacy which increased global connection.

In addition to the technological factors which made the Age of Discovery possible, a certain amount of dumb luck played a role as well. When **Christopher Columbus** sought financing from the Portuguese monarchy to attempt to sail west to India, he was ridiculed and dismissed. For generations, American schoolchildren have learned that the Portuguese scientists told Columbus that the word was flat and that, if he went west, he would simply fall off the edge and be devoured by dragons, but nothing could be further from the truth. What the Portuguese told him was the world was *big*. Accurate knowledge of the world's circumference had been common knowledge, among educated Europeans for over 1000 years. Surely any effort to reach India over the Atlantic would fail disastrously, as the sailors would run out of provisions long before reaching a hospitable port. Nonetheless, Columbus, who was convinced of his mathematical calculations, persisted in his determination and was eventually financed by Isabella of Spain. When he set sail from Palos

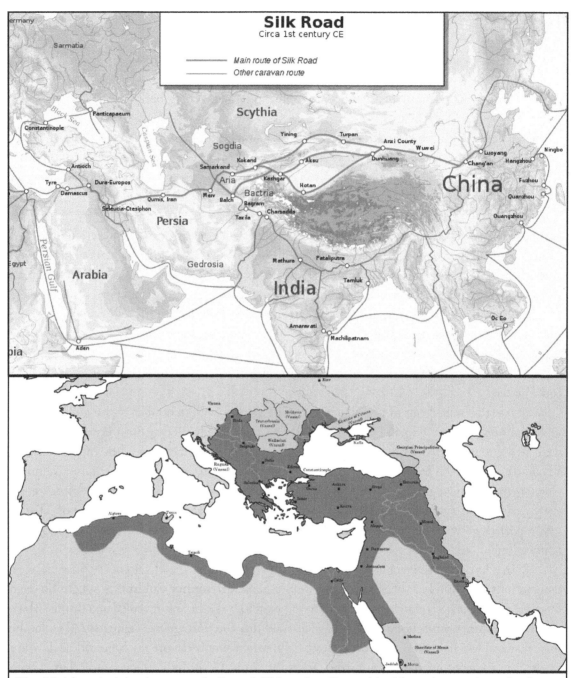

Fig 6.2 (above). A land route to India and China, the silk road had been in use since the days of the Roman Empire. It connected Paris to Byzantium to Beijing.

Fig 6.3 (below). The expansion of the Ottoman Empire in the 16th century blocked the Silk Road to non-Muslim traders.

de la Frontera with his three ships, most European scientists were certain that he would never return. He probably shouldn't have. In one of the great historical instances of "fortune favors the foolhardy," Columbus and his men were saved by the enormous stroke of luck: there happened to be a huge continent in between Spain and Calcutta.

Columbus's discovery of America in 1492 presented Spain with a problem. They had run into a continent "in the way," one they were never looking for and which they did not particularly want. For decades, the Spanish searched the new world, improvising, without any intention of settling down, trying to make the geographical inconvenience they had encountered pay off. By the 1520's, after a number of years of fruitless (and expensive) wandering, they had succeeded. In 1521, Hernan Cortes conquered the Aztec Empire, overthrowing powerful civilizations, and appropriating the sizable gold and silver coffers of Tenochtitlan. In 1545, the Spanish established the **Potosi silver mines** in present-day Argentina, which, along with other mines in South America, quickly began to produce large quantities of the precious metal. By the middle of the 16th century, in fact, more than three quarters of the global quantity of silver was mined by Spain in South America. In addition, agricultural settlements called **encomiendas**, many of which employed native Americans as slaves, harvested commodities (such as corn and tobacco) which would be sold back in Europe. As a result, within fifty years of Columbus's first voyages, Spain came to control the largest empire and perhaps the wealthiest one in the history of the world.

(Fig 6.4) Representation of the Aztec capital of Tenochtitlan (~1521). Destroyed by the Spanish, it was one of the most impressive cities in the Americas.	**(Fig 6.5)** The new world proved to be rich in silver. By the middle of the 16th century, Spain controlled more than 3/4ths of the global silver supply.

Key Questions: What you need to know
- What motivated Europe's early voyages of discovery?
- In what ways was Colombus's "discovery" of America ironic?
- How did Spain profit from the New World?

As news of Spain's conquests spread throughout Europe, the other governments in the old world were eager to catch up. With motivations partly economic, partly competitive, partly a result of sheer curiosity, Portugal, France, Holland, and England all launched exploratory journeys across the Atlantic. The French, seeking a **northwest passage** through to India, established trading outposts in present-day Canada, engaging in a profitable fur trade with the indigenous tribes. (A noteworthy historical detail is the fact that cold weather in Europe, in the period known as the "little ice-age," entailed a high demand for beaver-skin fur). The Dutch did the same thing, a little farther south, establishing fur trading outposts and small settlements in present day New York and Massachusetts. The Portuguese landed down in Brazil, importing large numbers of slaves from West Africa in order to work in sugarcane plantations, and eventually discovering significant quantities of gold, which, toward the end of the 17th century, caused the **Brazillian Gold Rush**.

While France, Holland, and Portugal, therefore, were largely driven by trade, England presented a different and in many ways much more significant story. Colonists from England, unlike those from the other European countries, often went to the New World with the express purpose to *settle*. In the 1580's, when England sent its first exploratory parties across the sea, a number of factors in England made migration highly desirable. The population of England was growing rapidly. Economic challenges brought about by inflation (more on this later) had increased the cost of living. Finally, the **wars of religion** (Chapter 4) had imposed difficult conditions on many dissenting Protestant minorities, such as Calvinists. In 1585, when Ralph Lane established the first British colony at Roanoke, his party contained 17 women and a number of children. Though the Roanoke colony failed, the 1609 Jamestown colony and the 1620 Plymouth colony likewise contained women, and the later colonies in New England even more. The presence of women allowed the British colonists to focus on deliberate "community-building" in ways that the other European powers had neglected. As a result, the British colonies gradually developed stronger political organization and a more thoroughly integrated and permanent colonial culture than the other European settlements, for whom community was a secondary concern. **(Fig 6.6/6.7)**

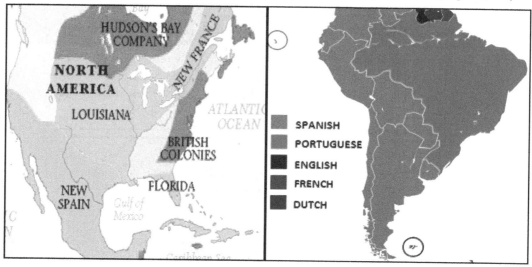

East and West: Trading Post Empires and the Opening of Asia

The Europeans who came upon the New World had gone west, looking for India. What about the ones who had gone east? While the early Spanish *conquistadors* were making their way through South America, the Portuguese, in the late 15th and early 16th centuries, were undertaking a series of equally earth-changing voyages in the other direction. The map below **(Fig 6.8)** shows the scope of the early Portuguese explorations, which proceeded along the coast of western Africa before turning north into east Asia.

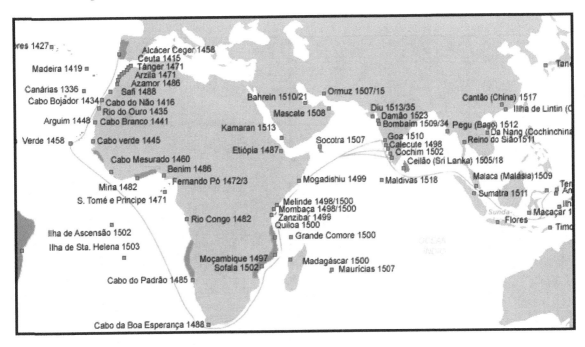

The Portugueuse voyages of exploration, in general, had two major impacts on the development of global politics in the 16th and 17th centuries: the first having to do with the rapid growth of the **African slave trade** and the second having to do with the re-opening and expansion of trade with the far east.

As the Portuguese sailed down Africa, they began to trade with some of the larger tribes and kingdoms along the western coast. Most notably the Kongo, the Mande and the Gbe peoples established early relationships with Portuguese merchants. Slave labor had long been present in these cultures: sometimes as a result of warfare, sometimes as a result of crime, sometimes as a result of traditional hierarchies. When Portuguese merchants came, offering firearms, textiles, rum, and other goods, the African traders, not having their own manufactured goods to trade in return, would offer slaves as a kind of currency. The Kingdom of the Kongo, in particular, established a close rapport with Portuguese, with the royal family converting to Christianity in the early 1500's. The Kongo, with a robust military equipped with European muskets, became an early source of slaves for Portugal. As the Kongo leaders went waging war (with European firearms) to acquire more slaves, they were able to become a political force in western Africa, but at the expense of seriously damaging the African social order, wreaking demographic havoc on much of the African population, and impairing social development for generations to come.

As demand for labor increased, particularly in the new settlements in South America, thousands of slaves were captured, sold to European traders, and shipped across the Atlantic in slave ships. This brutal practice, which cost the lives of many during the **middle passage** increasingly intertwined slave labor with the colonial economies and led to the institutionalization of race based slavery in both north and south America and parts of Europe.

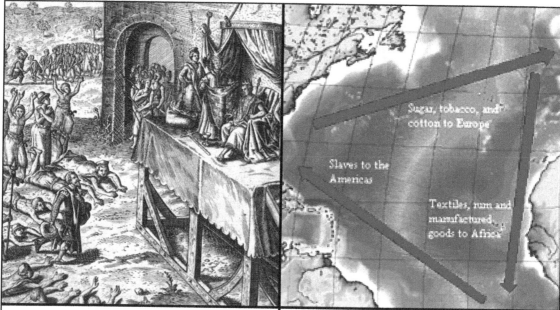

(Fig 6.10) Portuguese Merchants Presenting themselves before **King of the Kongo**: European goods and weapons initially helped the Kongo to expand its power, but, over the long run, the Atlantic Slave Trade would have a devestating effect of Africa.

(Fig 6.11) The so-called **Triangle Trade** which sent slaves to the Americas, raw materials to Europe and manufactured goods to Africa. The slave-trade was heavily intertwined in the global economy.

The second impact of the Portuguese voyages, the opening of Asia, would have consequences which, if less immediately grotesque, would prove, in the long term, just as momentous for political and economic institutions. As the Portuguese made their way east to India and China, they built trading outpost after trading outpost in order to secure their supply lines. Other European countries, the British the French, and the Dutch followed along the "new silk road" building outposts of their own, usually not far from those of the Portuguese. Though, at first, the idea of "trade" seems constructive and friendly, in actuality these trading outposts shortly evolved into heavily guarded command centers from which the Europeans launched attacks and retreated in defense while engaging in the competitive "gang warfare" of militarized capitalism. When the Europeans arrived in the east what they encountered was not a placid and stable open market but a competitive arena in which rival merchants, rebel clans, and power-seeking warlords sought to protect their interests. Skirmishes were not uncommon and even large scale massacres occurred with some regularity. The Europeans, using musket and cannon to their advantage, often engaged in trade practices which would perhaps be more accurately labeled acts of piracy. The Portuguese, to take only one example, established a kind of naval blockade around its outposts, refusing to let other merchant ships pass without the *cartaz* (pass) which they sold at a profit to restrict access to ports. The Dutch and the British recruited sizable mercenary armies among the native populations and used local power politics to their advantage by lending men and equipment to factions in local wars. In 1661, the British East India Company received permission from King Charles II to arm ships with cannons and to make war against all non-christian people in the region. **(Fig 6.12)**

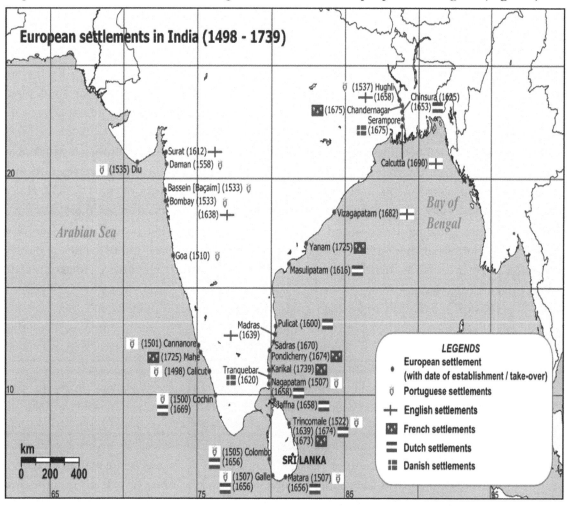

Within a few decades of the Portuguese voyages, Europeans had established a long belt of formidable outposts. The Portuguese had outposts in western India and southeast Asia. The French had bases in Indochina, Southern India, Laos, and Cambodia. The British had garrisons in eastern India, Australia, Hong Kong, and Samoa. Finally, the Spanish had forces in the Philippines and parts of Taiwan. The result is what some have referred to as **trading post empires**. Though, unlike in America, the Europeans were unable to project power into the interior of Africa, India, or China, their posts gave them control of the ports and, in so doing, allowed them to significantly influence the local economies. These outposts, furthermore, would prove to be efficient launchpads for the eventual military expeditions of the late 18th and 19th centuries through which Europe, particularly Great Britain, would tighten its control over the East.

Silver, Sickness, Stock, Savagery: Impacts of the early Voyages of Discovery

Taking a step back, how can we describe the impact of the early European voyages of discovery? In the long term, the effects have been countless, but, to begin with a simple overview, we can identify economic, ecological, institutional, and social consequences.

Economic Impacts: The Voyages of Discovery were initially motivated by trade. By the end of the 17th century the new trade routes that had been established sent economic shockwaves through almost every aspect of the global economy. Perhaps the most immediate impact was the sudden effect of inflation due to the discovery of large quantities of silver in Argentina and then in the Philippines (conquered by Spain in 1571). This increase in currency, combined with the influx of new products from the far east (such as silk and porcelain) led to the **price revolution** in Europe, in which costs for common goods rose, during the 17th century, over 500%. The effects were particularly noticeable in Spain, which controlled, by far, the majority of the global silver and gold supply. Although inflation put a strain on the domestic industries of many European nations, and, during this period, a wider gap began to emerge between the rich and the poor, it also created great economic opportunity for adventurists and entrepreneurs. A growing **middle class** of merchants, financiers and go-betweens appeared in European cities in the 17th century. This new class of economic actors would eventually gain significant political influence, wresting power away from the traditional sources of authority: the monarchy and the nobles. The urban and increasingly literate (chapter 5) middle classes, the **bourgeoisie,** would play a large role in the liberal revolutions of the 18th century.

The influx of gold and silver would also have economic consequences on the far east. Since Europeans had few products which (at least in the 18th century) could be sold in China and India, silver became a kind of standard currency in global trade. China, in particular, established a trade surplus with Europe, accumulating an enormous quantity of silver which would enrich the Qing Dynasty, which, by the end of the 18th century was at least as wealthy as any nation in Europe. Japan also saw substantial economic growth. It was a key importer of European firearms, enlarging its military which would allow it to centralize political control during the Edo period.

Institutional impacts This economic expansion transformed institutions of trade and logistics. The price revolution in the European economy led to the establishment of **modern banking** systems, which helped to regulate currencies and which funded both public and private projects. As we mentioned in Chapter 4, banks often became political actors, lending money to the state and helping with the surveillance of the economy. In addition to banks, another modern financial institution was the development of joint stock companies and stock exchanges. In order to mitigate the risk of long sea voyages, merchants became investment partners, with multiple stakeholders acquiring shares in an overseas venture. Large-scale **capitalism** might be said to have originated as a part of this process. It only led to the beginning of the sort of stock market we have today but also allowed for the massive incorporation of private capital. To take the most famous example, the British East India Company, a jointly owned corporation quickly became one of the most powerful political entities in the world, with a large army of mercenaries and governors which served as de facto heads of many distant outposts. Economic power and political power became intertwined like never before.

(Fig 6.13) Engraving of the **Amsterdam stock exchange**. The Voyages of Discovery led to the development of new institutions of trade and investment. These instiutions were important in the growth of **capitalism** in Europe.	**(Fig 6.14)** The **British East India Company**, acquired significant political power in India, ruling extensive territory in a manner not unlike a nation-state. The growth of private power would be an essential component of the age of imperialism.

Ecological Impacts It was not only money and goods which were being exchangat this point in time. The voyages of discovery led to massive ecological changes which would affect the entire world. As sailors traversed the planet, they brought with them crops, flowers, animals, and viruses which would lead to an enormous disruption in native ecosystems. In the so-called **Colombian exchange**, Europeans introduced to the New World sugar, bananas, olives, bees, and, most tragically, many infectious diseases to which native Americans had little immunity. They also brought back to the New World tobacco, tomatoes, potatoes and corn. While it may at first seem that ecological changes have little to do with politics, this is not the case. The smallpox virus, to take the most dramatic example, introduced to the New World by Europeans, led to a devastating pandemic killed perhaps 50 percent of the indigenous inhabitants of the Americas and precipitated the collapse of the Inca and Mayan civilizations. The Colombian exchange transformed markets, disrupted agriculture in both the old and new worlds, and consequently transformed many of the micro economies that depended on the old ecosystems.

Columbian Exchange

Introduced to New World (list not inclusive)	Introduced to Europe (list not inclusive)
Animals: • Cat • Donkey • Horse • Pig • Rabbit	**Animals:** • Alpaca • Llama • Parrot • Turkey • Guinea Pig
Plants: • Apple • Apricot • Banana • Basil • Coffee • Lettuce • Onion • Pea • Peach • Pear	**Plants:** • Avacado • Black cherry • Brazil Nut • Cashew • Cotton • Pumpkin • Peanut • Pecan • Potato • Tomato
Diseases: • Gonnorhea • Small pox	**Diseases:** • Chagas Disease • Syphillis

Social Impacts Last and perhaps most importantly, the voyages of discovery created new global social relationships which complex issues related to identity and culture. The Europeans and the indigenous inhabitants of the Americas went from existing in two separate and independent political orders from being inextricably linked in a way that was problematic for both peoples. The indigenous inhabitants, within a few generations became marginalized in their own homeland, as the European language, religion, and social institutions became dominant. Over time the indigenous inhabitants would be almost entirely displaced to the periphery of the political order. In addition, due to the Atlantic Slave Trade, a new race-based system would become prevalent in the Americas, with chattel slavery becoming an institution which would form an intractable part of the social order for over two hundred years. The African kingdoms (such as the Kongo) who sold slaves to the Europeans would find their societies destabilized as the influx of firearms and the outflow of working-age men would lead to population crises and warfare which would seriously damage the entirety of the African continent.

These things, of course, were not merely political or economic questions but moral ones, issues of humanity which would eventually loom large in European consciousness. From the very beginning no small number of Europeans were troubled by the brutality of slavery and the treatment of the indigenous inhabitants of the Americas. European churches, for instance, often sent large missions to the Americas, Africa, and the far east. Although it is debatable whether the effort to convert the non-christian inhabitants to Christianity (thereby destroying indigenous beliefs) was morally justified, it is undeniable that religious missions were in many cases motivated by European concerns for the welfare of peoples, which, 200 years before, no one had known existed. For good or for ill, people in the Americas and Africa and Asia became part of European moral consciousness.

This list, of course, is an oversimplification, the totality of effects of the early Voyages of Discovery could probably not be exhaustively covered by an entire library of books. For now, though, it is important to recognize that the shifts in the global political order, instituted by the Voyages of Discovery, made for a new world in more ways than one and set into motion many of the changes which have created the interconnected global village of today.

Key Questions: What you need to know

- What was the significance of eastern "trading posts?"
- Why should we not describe the European presence in the east as "free trade?"
- What were the causes of the slave trade?
- How did the "price revolution" come about?
- What was the significance of "stock exchanges?"
- What were the ecological impacts of the voyages of discovery?
- What new social relationships came from the voyages of discovery?

Summing Up: Key Chapter Points

1) The problem of Eurocentrism reflects a modern imbalance of power in which western nations continue to own and consume more than anyone else.

2) The story of how Europe conquered the world began in the 15th century with the Voyages of Discovery.

3) When they landed in America the Spanish claimed a continent they did not particularly want. Their early explorations were motivated by financial concerns in an effort to make the discovery pay off.

4) Unlike the Spanish and French, the British often came to the New World to settle, leading to better community-building.

5) In the East the Portutguese, followed by the British, French, and Spanish set up a series of trading posts. The militarization of these posts led to trading post empires.

6) The early Voyages of Discovery resulted in enormous economic, institutional, ecological and social impacts.

CHAPTER 7: THE AGE OF REVOLUTIONS (1688-1848)

Overview

This chapter examines both the economic and political revolutions that occured in the 17th and early 18th century. On the economic side of things, the industrial revolution continued its progress leading to

- The harnessing of steam technology
- Advances in textiles, medicine, and logistics
- The continued growth of bureaucracies.

The political side of things is marked by the birth of popular sovereignty in the wake of the Atlantic Revolutions. These revolutions would transform Europe, greatly reducing the power of the traditional royal houses and leading to the development of the modern nation-state.

Enlightenment Continued: Inventions and Organization

When we left off with European domestic politics, at the end of Chapter 5, things seemed to be looking bright. The **Wars of Religion** had (mostly) come to an end. Great Britain had developed its first constitutional government with the **Glorious Revolution** bringing stability to the monarchy. The **enlightenment** had brought Europe into a new age of reason, with philosophers challenging their culture's dogmas and scientists making important discoveries in physics, navigation, and mechanics. The economic transformations of the age of discovery had led to the rapid development of institutions of capitalism: from banks, to stock markets, to supply lines and, with them, increasingly advanced bureaucracies for supervising and regulating economic activity. Civilization, it seemed, was making good progress.

To a certain degree, this optimistic view of the period is correct. There was a great deal of social and economic development in the late 17th and early 18th century, as **the first phase of the industrial revolution** slowly began to pick up steam. In Chapter 5, we mentioned early experiments in mechanics with the clock, the friction generator, and Newcomen's steam engine. As the century advanced, progress accelerated with scientists continuing to share their discoveries with one another through increasingly effective printing and publishing. The chart on the following page documents some of the more groundbreaking discoveries of the period.

Question for discussion

Can an age be good and bad at once? What accounts for "progress" amid social upheaval?

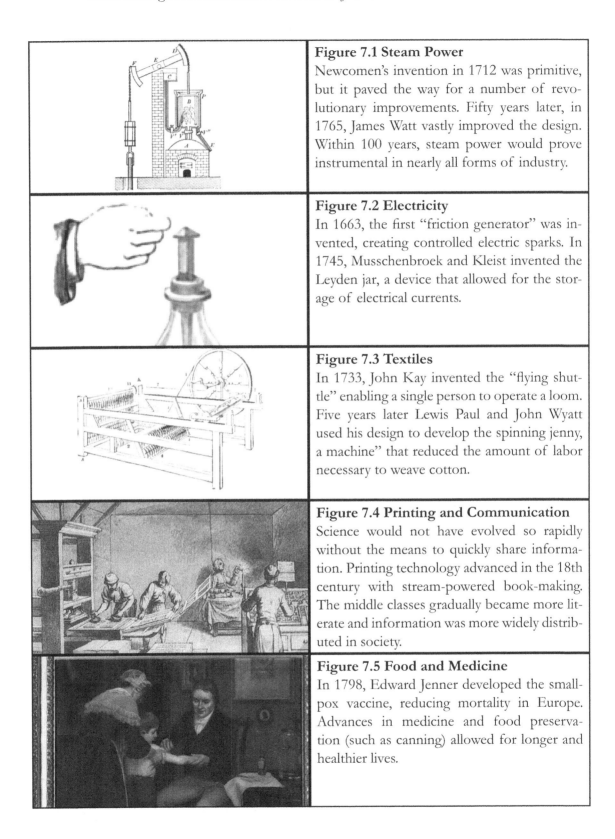

Figure 7.1 Steam Power
Newcomen's invention in 1712 was primitive, but it paved the way for a number of revolutionary improvements. Fifty years later, in 1765, James Watt vastly improved the design. Within 100 years, steam power would prove instrumental in nearly all forms of industry.

Figure 7.2 Electricity
In 1663, the first "friction generator" was invented, creating controlled electric sparks. In 1745, Musschenbroek and Kleist invented the Leyden jar, a device that allowed for the storage of electrical currents.

Figure 7.3 Textiles
In 1733, John Kay invented the "flying shuttle" enabling a single person to operate a loom. Five years later Lewis Paul and John Wyatt used his design to develop the spinning jenny, a machine" that reduced the amount of labor necessary to weave cotton.

Figure 7.4 Printing and Communication
Science would not have evolved so rapidly without the means to quickly share information. Printing technology advanced in the 18th century with stream-powered book-making. The middle classes gradually became more literate and information was more widely distributed in society.

Figure 7.5 Food and Medicine
In 1798, Edward Jenner developed the smallpox vaccine, reducing mortality in Europe. Advances in medicine and food preservation (such as canning) allowed for longer and healthier lives.

As machines led to increased production, Europe began, gradually, to need better organization. Schools and universities continued to expand, with a greater emphasis placed on both method and critique. During this time, we see the further expansion of **bureaucracies** to manage both political and economic affairs. Specialized offices were led by experts who helped forge hierarchies of workers. Training, expertise, supervision, and rules helped form new social relationships based on the needs of labor. Though bureaucracies would not become completely pervasive in Europe until later in the 19th century (with the rise of factories), the early industrial revolution would create the conditions which made them necessary. Later on, the sociologist Max Weber (see chapter 1) would analyze the growth of bureaucracies, arguing that they allowed for more wide-reaching state-power.

Max Weber's elements of bureaucracy			
Specialization: Tasks are carried out by specialists who have learned how to do a specific task in an efficient way.	**Rules:** Rules are objective and impersonal. They apply to all workers equally.	**Hierarchies:** Overseers are responsible for their employees. There are multiple levels of supervision.	**Merit:** Career advancement is based on talent and achievement.

Key Questions: What you need to know

- What was the industrial revolution? How was it connected to the enlightenment?
- How did the industrial revolution lead to growth in bureaucracy?
- How might the industrial revolution connect to the voyages of discovery?

New Wars, Old Problems

Though science was making good progress at the time, it would be wrong to say that it was an age of peace and prosperity. True, things calmed down a bit after the Peace of Westphalia, but within a few generations the old belligerents were once again shedding blood. While the wars of the 17th century, by and large, were about religion, those in the 18th century were about power in cruder and more earthly forms. Since the decline of the Catholic church as a unifying, supre-national institution, sovereignty in Europe had become increasingly divided among competitive **royal houses,** the families of kings and queens, which often controlled territory in multiple countries at once.

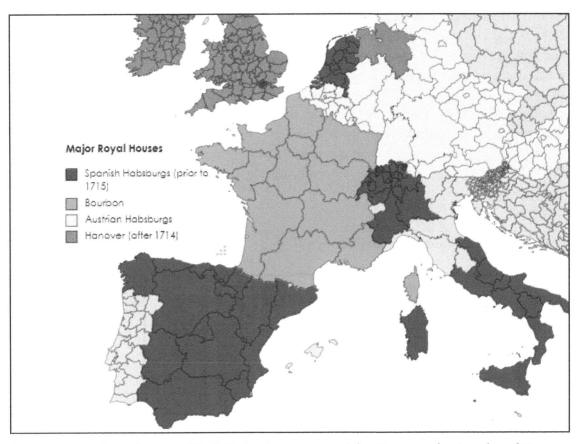

Major Royal Houses

- Spanish Habsburgs (prior to 1715)
- Bourbon
- Austrian Habsburgs
- Hanover (after 1714)

As can be seen from the map, **(Fig 7.6)** the dominant royal families owned quite a bit of Europe. The famous **House of Habsburg** (though divided into two branches) had all of Spain, bits of Italy, and a good chunk of present day Germany. The **House of Bourbon** had France, and, after the **War of the Spanish Succession**, would succeed in taking Spain from the Habsburgs. Following the succession of George I, Hanover had England, Ireland, and parts of present-day northern Germany.

There are two important things to remember about these dynasties. The first is that, with few exceptions, their claims were regarded as absolute, at least within their own territories. It is true (as we learned in Chapter 5), that England had adopted the beginnings of constitutional government following the Glorious Revolution, but England's constitution was hardly democratic. Nowhere else in Europe (with the possible exception of Sweden) was the right of the king to rule seriously challenged. The royal families relied upon a vast system of aristocratic connections and social hierarchies to maintain influence over their institutions. With the power of the church weakening, territorial sovereignty, the control of land, was more or less synonymous with the "king's realm." The people who lived on that land were regarded as subjects to the monarch. Though the king might have wanted to take care of his people and make them happy, in reality, they had little "right" to demand to be treated well.

	**Figure 7.7** **War of Spanish Succession** (1701-1714) Holy Roman Empire, Habsburg Spain, Dutch Republic, Great Britain, Prussia, Portugal, and Savoy VS Bourbon Spain, Bavaria, France.	A pan-European conflict, the War of Spanish Succession saw 500,000 soldiers killed on both sides. The outcome of the war proved to be a major loss for the Spanish Habsburgs with control of Spain falling to the House of Bourbon. The Peace of Utrecht redrew borders of many European territories and led to more solidified teritorial sovereignty.
	Figure 7.8 **War of the Austrian Succession** (1740-1748) France, Prussian, Spain, Saxony, & Sweden VS House of Habsburg, Great Britain, Russia, Dutch Republic	At the end of the fighting, the House of Habsburg maintained control of Austria, but both sides lost nearly 500,000 soldiers. Prussia became a dominant state in the HRE, which would hace consequences for the development of Germany. A new system of alliances, known as the "Diplomatic Revolution" rebalanced power in Europe.
	**Figure 7.9** **Seven Years War** (1756-1763) Great Britain, Portugal, Prussia VS France, House of Habsburg, Russia, Spain, and Sweden	One of the first truly "global wars," the Seven Years War featured fighting that spread to India, North America, and Africa. The militarization of the east was an important causal factor in the development of broader empires. The war was enormously expensive for all European powers and left England in the end as the major global hegemon.

The second important point is that these dynasties were fiercely competitive. They fought for wealth, prestige, and, of course, the right to control territory. As such, the years 1700 to 1764 saw three major wars:(see table). All of these wars were related, in some way, to issues of which royal family was permitted to control what.

Fracture and Revolution: The Birth of Popular Sovereignty

Wars, of course, have consequences. As we discussed in Chapter 4, one of the most obvious consequences of war is cost. In addition to tragic loss of life, war requires governments to centralize money and resources. The major countries in Europe--England, Spain, France, and the Holy Roman Empire--had fought three major wars between 1700 and 1763. They had spent almost as much time at war as at peace. Though scientific and economic progress helped offset some of the cost of these wars, on the whole, each of these governments (and their royal leaders) found themselves in difficult financial circumstances. They knew they had to raise more money, but the civilian population, after decades of fighting, often didn't have a lot of money to spare. Imagine yourself as a farmer or a merchant or an artisan in late 18th century Europe. In all likelihood, you had known your country to be at war your whole life. Chances are, you had lost a brother or a son in the fighting (or at least knew someone who had). Would you be eager to see your taxes go up? How would you likely have felt about the king or queen?

Great Britain attempted to solve this problem by taking advantage of its colonies. From the perspective of Britain, the colonists in North America benefited from being part of the English empire, yet they contributed too little to its maintenance. The Seven Year War, in particular, had been fought, partly, defending the North American colonies from the French in Canada. It was only fair, Britain reasoned, to have the Americans pay their fair share in taxes. From 1765-1775, Britain levied tax after tax, (most famously, the Tea Tax and the Stamp Tax) meeting fierce resistance from the unwilling colonists.

To the Americans, after all, the argument of the British crown carried little weight. Why should those in North America have to obey the mandates of King George III, who sat on a throne more than six thousand miles away, and who ruled with a parliament that Americans were not permitted to send members to? What connection did the king have to the American colonies? What gave him the right to administer affairs in a land he had never set foot in? If these ideas sound familiar, you may recall the opponents of the British King Charles I used much of the same reasoning in the years preceding the Glorious Revolution. The American rebels were, in fact, building on a tradition of British **liberalism** which had developed, under much different circumstances, 100 years before.

In 1776, after a series of skirmishes between the British soldiers and local militias, the American Continental Congress sent to King George III the **Declaration of Independence**, a document founding the United States as an independent country. At the very beginning of the document, in a passage many American schoolchildren are required to learn by heart, is a sentence defining the terms of political legitimacy: "We hold these truths to be self-evident: that all men are created equal, that they are endowed by their creator with certain unalienable rights; that, among these are life, liberty, and the pursuit of happiness; **that to secure these rights governments are instituted among men, deriving their just power from the consent of the governed.**" The last clause in that sentence articulates what has since been termed popular sovereignty: the idea that the people—not the kings, not the churches—are the source of political power. As Benjamin Franklin, one of the fathers of the American republic phrased it, "In free governments, the rulers are the servants, and the people their superiors and sovereigns."

A few years later, inspired, in no small part, by the American Revolution, the French rose up on largely the same principles. In certain details, the stories are almost identical. In desperate financial straits after the 18th century's costly wars (including, ironically, supporting the American War of Independence) the French Louis the XVI and the aristocratic rulers of the *ancien regime* needed to raise funds. To do so, they levied high taxes against the French Third Estate: the commoners that made up over 95 percent of the total population. The combination of high taxes and a bad series of harvests led to social unrest and a sense among the French population that the king and the ruling class only cared about their own privileges. In June of 1789, the Third Estate elected the **National Assembly,** a group of statesmen who were charged with representing the will of the people. The next month, supporters of the National Assembly stormed the Bastille Prison and, after killing several of the guards, seized the weapons from the prison's armory. In August of the same year, the National Assembly approved the **Declaration of the Rights of Man and the Citizen**. Following the language of the Declaration of Independence rather closely in places, the French Declaration of the Rights of Man asserted "The principle of all sovereignty resides essentially in the nation [the people]. No body nor individual may exercise any authority which does not proceed directly from the nation [the people]."

Key Questions: What you need to know

- What is popular sovereignty?
- What was the cause of the American and French revolutions?
- What connection do you see between "the Enlightenment" and revolution?

In the following years, one revolution followed in another. South America followed North America, as Mexico, Venezuela, Bolivia, Brazil and many other countries gained their independence from Spain and Portugal. Back in Europe, French armies led by **Napoleon Bonepart** went west, exporting the new ideas as they went. Though Napoleon himself was an emperor (having seized power in a counter-revolution), he nonetheless was influenced by the national ideals of popular sovereignty. In each area that Napoleon conquered, he attempted to establish a government based on the people rather than the kings. The **Napoleonic Code** spread through Europe, reforming the old aristocratic order. To many in Europe, it was obvious that the dominance of the royal houses was coming to an end and a new wave of republicanism was on its way in. Between 1800 and 1848, political actors across European society asked their governments to share power with a broader slice of the population and to represent the interest of the nation, rather than that of a small group of privileged individuals. Though these revolutions were not always immediately successful they were instrumental in bringing about a change of thinking in western politics. Key to this change of thinking was the idea that arbitrary authority, based on royal blood or aristocratic privilege is unacceptable, and that the people have a right to assert their control over the state, by revolution if necessary. Equality before the law, constitutional law, and popular representation would become the cornerstones of acceptable power.

These revolutions had another important consequence. The growth of popular sovereignty would begin a process through which individuals, over time, would more and more come to identify with the nations in which they lived. Prior to the revolutions, people were "subjects" to a king. Afterwards, little by little, they came to regard themselves as "citizens" of a country. No longer was the state to be imagined as a majestic authority towering above the masses who were expected by the supernatural order to obey it. Rather, it became the image of the people themselves, their collective unity. The benefits of the state were no longer understood in terms of the charity of divinely appointed rulers. Rather, they were the **natural rights** due to all citizens. With these rights, furthermore, came duties: forms of civic participation, desires to maintain the nation which represents "us." To put it simply, the establishment of popular sovereignty helped to give rise to **nationalism**, a bond of identification between people and their state.

Conclusion

In sum, the years between the Peace of Westphalia and Age of Revolutions was a period of growth and reform. The Enlightenment, and the secularization which accompanied it, led to a weakening of the power of the church and an increase in rational authority. This, in turn, proved to be contributing factors to the beginning of the industrial revolution which not only led to an increase in economic production but also the birth of rational bureaucracies. As this process unfolded, political thinkers began to advocate for popular sovereignty, eventually transforming the norms of legitimacy during the Age of Revolutions. This led to an increase in nationalization: the closer identification between "the country" and "the people." Along with territorial sovereignty (which we discussed in chapter 4), popular sovereignty has been crucial in the modern understanding of politics. Every nation in the world today understands itself as a definite territory in which the government has the authority to rule, free from outside interference, and every government insists that it represents the will of the people .Both of these principles will be interrogated more fully in later chapters. For now, it is enough to assert that they are two of the pillars on which the architecture of contemporary global politics indisputably rests.

The Age of Revolutions: 1775-1848

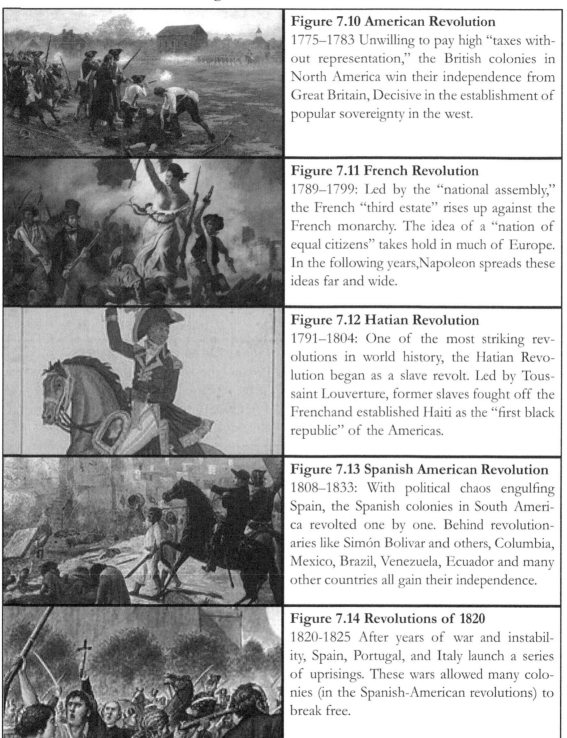

Figure 7.10 American Revolution
1775–1783 Unwilling to pay high "taxes without representation," the British colonies in North America win their independence from Great Britain, Decisive in the establishment of popular sovereignty in the west.

Figure 7.11 French Revolution
1789–1799: Led by the "national assembly," the French "third estate" rises up against the French monarchy. The idea of a "nation of equal citizens" takes hold in much of Europe. In the following years, Napoleon spreads these ideas far and wide.

Figure 7.12 Hatian Revolution
1791–1804: One of the most striking revolutions in world history, the Hatian Revolution began as a slave revolt. Led by Toussaint Louverture, former slaves fought off the Frenchand established Haiti as the "first black republic" of the Americas.

Figure 7.13 Spanish American Revolution
1808–1833: With political chaos engulfing Spain, the Spanish colonies in South America revolted one by one. Behind revolutionaries like Simón Bolivar and others, Columbia, Mexico, Brazil, Venezuela, Ecuador and many other countries all gain their independence.

Figure 7.14 Revolutions of 1820
1820-1825 After years of war and instability, Spain, Portugal, and Italy launch a series of uprisings. These wars allowed many colonies (in the Spanish-American revolutions) to break free.

Figure 7.15 Belgian Revoluton
1830-1831 Prior to 1831, Belgium had been a part of the United Netherlands. Supported by the French, the French-speaking Belgian people rose up and established Belgium as an independent, French-speaking and Catholic republic.

Figure 7.16 Liberal Wars
1828–1834: The Liberal Wars in Portugal pitted the old against the new. Those who wanted a "liberal constitutional monarchy" defeated the "conservatives" who favored a return to the system of an "absolute" king or queen. The wars led to several important constitutional changes in Portugal.

Figure 7.17 Revolutions of 1848
Perhaps the most important historical event of the 19th century, the 1848 revolutions were a series of (mostly failed) liberal uprisings in Germany, France, Poland, Russia, Austria, and many other countries. The revolutionaries advocated for greater power to people and an end to many monarchic customs.

Differences at a glance: Territorial vs Popular Sovereignty	
Territorial Sovereignty	**Popular Sovereignty**
• Established at Peace of Westphalia • Government has a right to rule its territory. • Territories are regarded as legimately fixed • States defend territories with force • Territories become "power containers."	• Established following Atlantic Revolutions • The people are the source of legitimacy. • Constitutions and equality before the law • Bonds people and their state • Citizens have rights and duties .

Summing up: Key Chapter Points

1) Following the Enlightenment, scientists and engineers made great progress in steam, textiles, medicine, and transportation. This marks the first phase of the industrial revolution.

2) Three major wars of the mid 18th century (The War of the Spanish Succession, The War of the Austrian Succession, and the Seven Years War) put enormous strains on Europe's governments.

3) Following efforts by European monarchs to raise taxes, revolutions broke out, first in North America, then in France, and then in much of the rest of the west.

4) These revolutions rested on liberal principles which developed during the Enlightenment, particularly the idea that legitimate government depends on consent of the people.

5) As a consequence of these revolutions, the norm of popular sovereignty was established in the west.

CHAPTER 8: THE AGE OF EMPIRE (PART II 1756-1900)

Overview

This chapter examines the "domination of the west" that occured during the latter half of the 18th century. In particular, we discuss

- The role of the Seven Years War in militarizing the East
- The gradual conquest of India leading to the British raj
- The Opium Wars and the imposition of the "unequal treaties."
- The Scramble for Africa and the highwater mark of European imperialism.

We then discuss the different causes of European dominance. We pay particular attention to:

- Ideologies of dominance
- The belief in the standard of civilization and the goal of bettering the rest of the world

The chapter concludes with a discussion of anticolonialism and the significant moral questions that Europe's dominance gave rise to.

We began chapter 6 by pointing out the issue of **Eurocentrism** and asking the question "how did Europe conquer the world?" By the middle of the 18th century, European nations had laid the groundwork for future hegemony: establishing colonies in North America and trading outposts along the coast of Africa and in the far East. Yet, no reasonable person before the year 1800 could have argued that Europe had achieved global dominance. True, Europe was rapidly developing. The first phase of the **Industrial Revolution** was well underway. European states, due to the influence of the enlightenment, were becoming increasingly rational and bureaucratized, allowing governments to extract more revenue and resources from their populations. Years and years of warfare (during and after the Wars of Religion) had caused European states to develop organized and deadly military forces.

Question for discussion

Besides military and economic dominance, what else might Eurocentrism be caused by? What other factors give rise to the idea that Europe is the "center" of the world?

Nonetheless, non-western powers were not far behind. Consider the following chart (**8.1**):

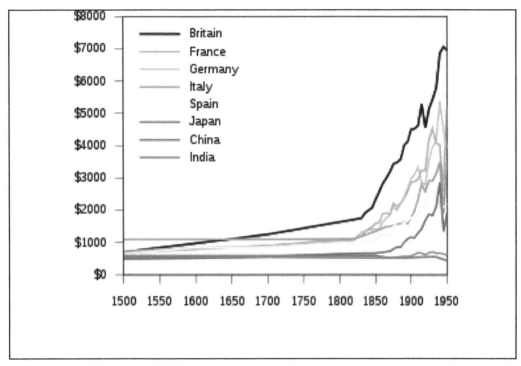

As can be seen, until the year 1800 or so, western and non-western powers were about equal. China, in the year 1800, accounted for about 33 percent of global GDP, while Europe and the United States accounted for 34 percent. By some measures, the non-west enjoyed significant advantages over the west. Western traders, returning to Europe, were often in awe about the marvels of China and India: the palaces, the monuments, the achievements in art, literature, and music. At the peak of the Qing Dynasty, China controlled well over ten million square kilometers and had amassed the largest supply of silver in the world. The Indian Mughal Empire, likewise, represented to many Europeans one of the pinnacles of civilization. Under the leadership of the various Islamic Shahs, the empire's economy, culture, and institutions flourished. Some of the most impressive "wonders of the world" such as the Taj Mahal and the Shalamar Gardens, were completed during the period.

However, jump ahead to the year 1900 and it's quite a different story. At the turn of the century, China's share of global GDP was only 6 percent, India's 2 percent, while that of the United States and Europe was over 80 percent. China and India, once kingdoms of great power and prestige, were filled with a kind of poverty and disorder which had been unimaginable in previous centuries. One-hundred years is an eyeblink in human history. What happened, in such a short period of time to shift the balance of power so decisively?

Surprisingly enough, one of the most important events in tipping the global balance of power was the **Seven Years War (1756-1763)** which we discussed a bit in our last chapter. The origins of the conflict are arcane: tensions between Austria, Prussia, Britain and France over succession to the Austrian throne and territorial disputes in the New World between French Canada and the British colonies. Nonetheless, the consequences would be explosive. Within a year of the outbreak, the fighting had spread far outside of Europe. The British East India Company allied with the British government and launched a series of raids against French and Spanish outposts in India and West Africa. In response, the French entered into an alliance with the **Mughal Empire** who were eager to check British expansion. The Mughals, unfortunately, sided with the wrong European power. One year into the conflict, in 1757, the forces from the British East India Company won a decisive victory over French and Mughal forces in the Battle of Plassey. The victory, effectively, put the entire region of Bengal under British control.

The fighting between the British, French, and Indians during the Seven Years War not only had immediate military consequences but also led to a continuous entanglement of Great Britain in Indian political affairs. Throughout the history of India, the Hindu majority was often in fierce competition with the Muslim ruling class and vice versa. Various warlords and tribal leaders launched rebellions, and, as they did, both the rulers and the rebels often solicited European help. During the Seven Years War, and for many years after, British armies began fighting side by side with these warlords in order to influence Indian political power in ways which they believed were to their advantage. In 1775, the East India Company, with nearly 100,000 soldiers, intervened in an internal conflict with the Maratha Empire (the successor to the Mughal Empire) in what became known as the First Anglo-Maratha War. Between 1775 and 1800, the British and the Maratha Empire would fight back and forth a total of four wars during which the British helped Indian rulers who they favored, and, in so doing, solidified their military domination over much of the northeast. In short, what began as "trading posts" quickly, during the Seven Years War and after, became highly militarized "bases" of an increasingly dominating occupation.

The question of how this made the Indians feel is hardly worth asking. Little by little, battle by battle, they saw their control and sovereignty ceded to Great Britain. Not only did the British East India Company control significant territory along the coast (see following map), but they also began "importing" their own institutions. They set up British style schools, marketplaces, and "factories." Political and economic control gradually passed into the hands of either the English or those Indians who had received an "English-style" education.

Key Vocabulary

British East India Company: The large private company which established numerous British trading outposts along the eastern coast of India in the 17th and 18th centuries. They gradually increased their power, and, by the 19th century controlled significant territory and revenue throughout the subcontinent.

Tensions boiled over in 1857. After years of skirmishes between the local population and company mercenaries, full-scale war broke out. **The Indian Rebellion of 1857** saw forces from the former Mughal empire, private civilians and local "sepoys" rise up against company rule. The war went disastrously for the Indians. The East India Company, with a large contingent of well-armed British troops won a decisive victory and, in so doing, gained control of virtually all of India. The behavior of the company, however, generated a good deal of shock back in Europe. In village after village, British mercenaries exacted revenge for the rebellion through mass-executions, destruction of food supplies, rape and enslavement. As a result of the rebellion, the British government decided it was too chaotic to allow a private company to rule a continent by itself. In 1858, the British Crown passed the Government of India Act which essentially annexed India from the company and placed it under British crown rule. In the decades that followed, the period of the so-called **British Raj** (1858-1947) saw the British establishing the Indian Civil Service, building government offices throughout the country and assuming complete political authority.

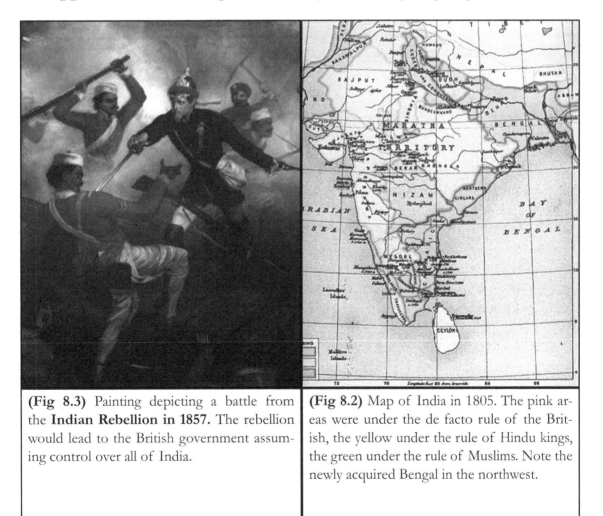

(Fig 8.3) Painting depicting a battle from the **Indian Rebellion in 1857.** The rebellion would lead to the British government assuming control over all of India.

(Fig 8.2) Map of India in 1805. The pink areas were under the de facto rule of the British, the yellow under the rule of Hindu kings, the green under the rule of Muslims. Note the newly acquired Bengal in the northwest.

The Start of the "Century of Humiliation": The Opium Wars

Britain's militarization of its outposts during the conquest of India would have significant effects on the rest of the East. For many years the British had used their bases in India to trade with the Qing Dynasty, and, for much of that period, the Qing had enjoyed a significant trade surplus with Britain. The Chinese, with a thriving and largely self-sufficient economy, had no need for British manufactured goods. The only currency the Chinese would accept from the British was silver (much of it mined in South America: see chapter 6). Treasure-chests flowed into the Qing coffers, a fact which concerned not only Britain but all of Europe, who feared a Chinese monopoly on the silver supply. Economic power began to shift, however, in the early 19th century when British opium, almost exclusively harvested in India, began to take hold in China. Opium was lucrative for the British, but the addictive drug proved destructive to the social fabric of Chinese society. The Qing dynasty had passed multiple edicts banning the sale and use of opium, but British merchants continued to smuggle the drug into the south of China. Finally, in 1839, outraged by continual British smuggling and concerned by the erosion of the Chinese silver surplus, the Chinese official Lin Zexu ordered troops to seize all British opium in the port-city of Canton (Guangzhou). Nearly 2 million pounds of opium was confiscated and thrown into the sea.

Though the seizure of the British opium may have been a moral victory for the Chinese, the fallout would be tragic. Eager both for revenge and for the resumption of the opium trade, the British, under the expansionist Prime Minister **Lord Pomerston**, sent the most powerful navy in the world to the Chinese harbors. Though the Qing economy was highly advanced, the Chinese had failed to modernize their military. The British navy, with large ships equipped with multiple cannon and congreve rockets, easily destroyed the out-of-date "junk ships" in use by the Chinese navy. The war was over in less than a year. And though the Chinese would launch a series of rebellions: (most notably the **second opium war** (1856-1860) and the **Boxer rebellion** (1899)), the power of the Qing Dynasty would never be the same. The British forced the Chinese to accept a series of treaties, known as the **unequal treaties**, which had the effect of crippling Chinese international trade and giving European powers almost total domination of a series of **treaty ports**. Among the largest concessions of the unequal treaties, China was forced

- To open its ports to unrestricted British trade.
- To surrender the island of Hong Kong to Britain
- To pay British war expenses
- To grant British soldiers "immunity" for any crimes committed in China.

Though the Qing Dynasty was to remain in power, the Opium Wars and the unequal treaties would be destabilizing to the Chinese political order. Chinese GDP and standard of living fell, and, before long. This period of misery which would reach its peak when the Japanese invaded (and nearly conquered) China in 1935, is referred to as the century of humiliation.

Britain's Empire and Conquest

(Fig 8.4) Lord Palmsterston, Prime Minister of Great Britain from 1830-1865, oversaw the height of Britain's expansion.

(Fig 8.5) The ruins of the Summer Palace in Beijing, destroyed during the second Opium War.

(Fig 8.6) Explorer James Cook lands in Botony Bay in 1770. The British would increase their control over Australia and New Zealand throughout the late 18th and 19th centuries.

(Fig 8.7) During the Australian Frontier Wars, which raged continuously during the 19th century, the British killed and displaced the indigenous tribes that had lived in the continent for thousands of years.

The Peak of Pax Britannica and The Scramble For Africa

After their annexation of India and their defeat of China in the Opium Wars, Great Britain had come to rule the most extensive empire in the world. In addition to India and Hong Kong, they had scooped up dozens of small islands in South East Asia and the Pacific: Ceylon, New Guinea, Fiji, Tonga. After first establishing a penal colony in Australia in 1788, they gradually expanded their control, leading exploratory and military expeditions throughout the continent. By 1842, they had established six semi-independent colonies, which, 60 years later, would be united into the **Federation of Australia**. Much of the colonization of these areas was violent with the British displacing the Maori and other tribes that had lived in the South Pacific for thousands of years.

The final piece in the Pax Britannica, Britain's great global empire, would be Africa. Though the Europeans had had coastal settlements in Africa since the days of the Portugeuse traders (see last chapter), they had never managed to push into the interior. The climate was too inhospitable, the African kingdoms (such the Kongo and the Ashanti) were too militaristic and highly organized. Perhaps most importantly, they didn't see the point. While China and India possessed luxury, consumer goods such as silk, spices, porcelain, and tea, Africa, so it was believed, lacked the sort of valuables which could be profitable in the European market (see Atlantic Slave Trade in last chapter).

European attitudes towards Africa began to change in the mid-19th century. Newfound European interest in Africa was chiefly due to four factors:

The decline of the Ottoman Empire: At its height, the Ottoman Empire (which, recall from our last chapter, first blocked the "silk road") stretched from central Asia to the gates of Vienna, along the north African coast all the way to Spain. However, by the 1830s, the Sultan's authority over his dominions was weakening and the state was nearing bankruptcy. The Russian Tsar Nicholas I allegedly referred to the Ottoman Empire as the "Sick Man of Europe," and more than once, the European powers suggested carving up the empire among themselves. Those plans became a reality in 1830 when France invaded Algiers, in Northern Africa, and established a permanent colony there. France's expansion into North and West Africa pressured other European powers to expand their own colonial control into the continent.

The Suez Canal: For hundreds of years, the only way to get from Europe to Asia had been down along the coast of Africa and along the Cape of Good Hope. In 1859, British and French engineers (again, moving into territory abandoned by the Ottomans) began construction on the "Suez Canal" which would link the Mediterranean Sea to the Arabian Sea through the Nile River. The project was intensive and would bring men, materials, and money flowing into Egypt. France and Britain quickly came into conflict over the project and the 1882 **Anglo-Egyptian War** saw Britain take control over the canal (and most of the rest of Egypt). The importance of the Suez Canal to global commerce again increased European interest in the continent.

Improved technology: Much European reluctance to explore and colonize central Africa had been due to its inhospitable climate and militarized populace. As industrialization continued in Europe, new technology enabled explorers and colonists to overcome these obstacles. The second phase of the industrial revolution, which saw the development of railroads, steamships, and the telegraph, vastly improved logistics. This enabled quick transport from the coast to the interior. The discovery of quinine, as a treatment for malaria, enabled explorers to survive in the humid, mosquito-infested swamps along the Congo. Finally, the continual improvement of military technology, such as the Maxim gun (an early machine gun) allowed European armies to achieve decisive victories over native tribes, even with relatively small armies.

The need for raw materials: Perhaps most significantly, as industrialization continued to expand, there was a rapid increase in demand for consumer products. Manufacturing these consumer products required a greater and greater need for raw materials: materials that, by and large, could not be found in Europe. Examples of this are endless (tin, copper, steel, oil, etc), but one of the most instructive, as it pertains to Africa, is the need for rubber. When Joyh Lloyd Dunlop invented the pneumatic tire in 1887 (making it much easier to ride bicycles), demand for rubber products soared. As a result, European industrialists scoured Africa searching for the valuable commodity. The domination of early African colonies, such as the Congo Free State was fueled by the need for rubber and similar materials.

Taken together, these four factors made up the motivations for the so-called Scramble for Africa during which European powers entered and colonized virtually all of the continent. After the Berlin Conference in 1885, the Europeans essentially agreed to "divide" the territory among themselves. Though they did so without (much) fighting among themselves, the Scramble for Africa was marked by persistent warfare with the African tribes and kingdoms. The British alone fought no fewer than twenty wars during the Scramble for Africa, destroying the traditional orders and bringing the African population into a condition of political subjection. **(Fig 8.17)**

Questions for Discussion

• How are the four factors that led to Europe's colonization of Africa related to one another?

• Though the inter-continental slave trade had been made illegal by the mid-19th century, its after-effects were still apparent throughout the world. How so? How might 200 years of slavery have weakened the African continent?

• What do you make of European powers "dividing up" Africa at the conference of Berlin? What does that tell you about how they saw the world?

Colonialism and Anticolonialism

(Fig 8.9) The Conquest of Algeria not only marked the decline of the Ottoman Empire, but also a new European interest in Africa.

(Fig 8.10) The opening of the Suez Canal would transform maritime commerce and lead to the domination of Egypt by Britain.

(Fig 8.12) The Maxim fired 11 bullets per second. The British poet Hillaire Belloc described the dominance of the Maxim gun in a sardonic couplet: "Whatever happens we have got/ The Maxim gun and they have not.

(Fig 8.16) John Lloyd Dunlop on a bicycle. The invention of the pneumatic tire created huge demand for rubber, which, in turn spurred the colonization of the Congo.

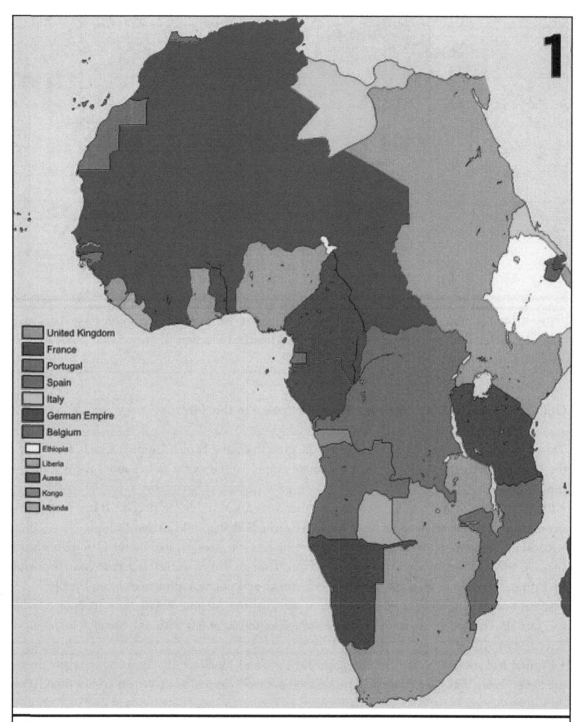

Fig 8.17 After the Scramble for Africa, virtually the entire continent was under European control by the turn of the century. note the large areas held by Great Britain (pink) and France (dark blue).

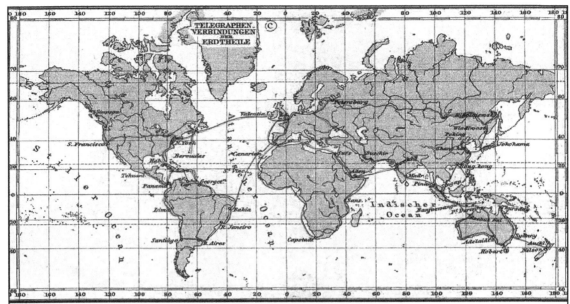

(Fig 8.14) Telegraph lines (red) linked North America, Europe, Africa, South East Asia, and Australia. The invention of the telegraph in 1844, marked the start of the second phase of the industrial revolution.

Old Powers decline: New Powers find their "place in the Sun"

Thus far, we have been largely considering the growth of the British Empire: which, throughout the 19th century, grew to be the most dominant empire in the world. What about the rest of Europe?

• **The Ottoman Empire**, as we have already mentioned, was in serious decline. It had lost control over much of its old territory in Northern Africa, the Balkans, and Eastern Europe.

• **Russia** had begun to expand to the south in much of the area vacated by the Ottoman Empire such as Albania, Bosnia, Serbia, and Montenegro. Though Russia would have little control outside of Europe, it began to gradually increase its territory and political influence within Europe.

• **Spain and Portugal** were also in decline. Following the Atlantic Revolutions (chapter 5), they had lost almost all of their territory in the Americas and were left with only small colonies along the coast of Africa.

• **France** had lost its North American possessions and much of its Asian possessions due to the Seven Years War. Nonetheless, it had gained control over much of North and Central Africa during the Scramble for Africa and maintained its colony in Indochina (present day Vietnam).

• **Germany**, after uniting under Otto Von Bismark, (chapter 5) was proving to be a key player in Africa, establishing several colonies in central Africa. After a slow start, it had industrialized rapidly and was quickly developing one of the most efficient land-militaries in Europe.

Yet, outside of Europe, there was a new imperial power on the horizon. **The United States**, though long viewed as behind Europe, was growing fast. In 1803, Napoleon, unable to afford France's colonial holdings in the New World, had sold Louisiana Territory to Thomas Jefferson and the United States for only fifteen million dollars. In 1848, America would grow even more when it defeated Mexico in the Mexican-American war, annexing the territories between Texas and California. In 1866, it bought Alaska from Russia, and, in 1893, annexed Hawaii from the indigenous Polynesian people who had long ruled the island. Five years later, America defeated Spain in the **Spanish-American War** acquiring the Philippines, Puerto Rico, Guam, and Cuba.

America's aggressive expansion during the 19th century was fueled by energetically nationalist politics. The ideal of **"manifest destiny"** reflected the belief that America was destined to settle and develop the land between the Atlantic and Pacific oceans. A swelling population, caused by rapid industrialization which brought immigrants to work in the factories of New York and Boston spilled toward the midwest and California. As white settlers went into the frontier, they forcibly displaced native populations, fighting a series of "wars of pacification." **The Indian Removal Act of 1830** was the first of several official laws forcing Native Americans out of their homelands. Meanwhile the Homestead Act of 1862 encouraged European settlers to go west and build farms and settlements on the newly acquired land.

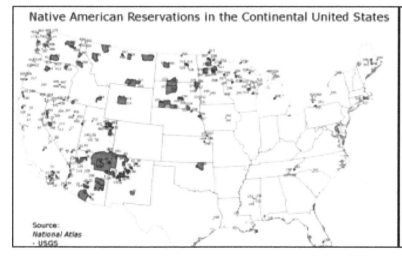

Native American Reservations In the Continental United States

Source: National Atlas - USGS

(Fig 8.18) Following various "Indian Removal Acts" in the 19th century, the indigenous peoples of the United States were moved to a number of "reservations" in the west. Though nominally independent, the people on the reservations remain culturally and economically marginalized.

But Why? The Ideologies of Dominance

Taken together, the colonial possession of Europe and those of the United States) included almost 60 percent of the world's population by the turn of the century. What explained this drive towards increasing colonial expansion and territorial control? Certainly, as we have been emphasizing, economic motives played an important role: mercantilism, profit-seeking, opportunism. The rise of large and centralized nation-states and the development of industrial capitalism created new pressures on governments to sustain economic growth and development. Budding industries required not only access to a steady supply of cheap raw materials but new markets in which industrial goods could be sold. Accumulating capital needed to be invested somewhere and colonies provided a prime target for moving excess capital out of the country.

Yet there was more to the story than just economics. Political, social, and moral points of view developed in Europe alongside imperialism, providing both justifications and criticisms of the European project. In general, European attitudes about seizing territory so far from their homeland, during the 19th century, can be divided into three ideological points of view.

Standard of Civilization

First, there were those who regarded colonialism as a noble, even philanthropic endeavour. To these proponents of imperialism, the presence of European government in Asia and Africa was beneficial to the colonized peoples, bringing economic progress, technology and free trade. Such philanthropists pointed to cultural advantages, such as the introduction of modern education, abolition of slavery, and the introduction of modern medicine. They spoke of "spiritual enlightenment" due to the spread of Christianity. The process of building empires, to those who viewed colonialism in these terms, was not one of greedy territorial acquisition but of the selfless pursuit of global advancement. In the words of Rudyard Kipling, it was the **white man's burden** to bring civilization to peoples who had been trapped in darkness and barbarity. Imperialism was an act of tiresome but necessary charity through which the rest of the world would be brought up to the European **standard of civilization**.

Scientific Racism

Though such a view may seem condescending to us, it was perhaps more humane than that of other European imperialists. Many at the time regarded Europe's conquests over the colonies not as an effort to "improve" or "civilize" them but simply as the natural right of a superior people to rule over an inferior one. The nineteenth century saw the rise of what since has been termed **scientific racism**, the effort to establish European superiority on the grounds of biology. For example, the American biologist Samuel Morton helped to found the pseudosciences of craniology and phrenology, efforts to rank the intelligence of other races based on measurements of their skulls. The idea of innate European superiority was widespread during the age of colonialism and did much, in the minds of its proponents, to explain the necessity of the empires.

> **Key Questions: What you need to know:**
>
> • What was the difference between the "standard of civilization" and "scientific racism?"
> • What accounted for the moral backlash against colonialism in the late 19th century?

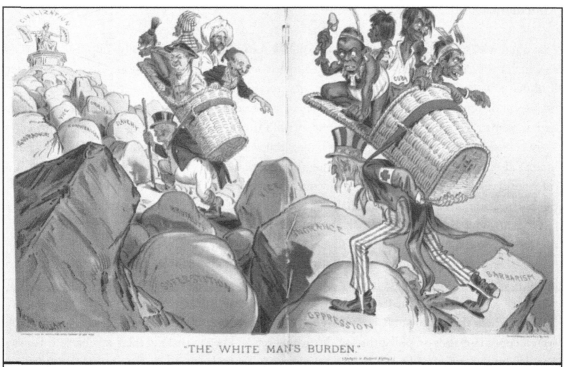

"THE WHITE MAN'S BURDEN."

(Fig 8.19) The White Man's Burden: A cartoon from 1899 depicting America and Great Britain carrying the "barbaric" peoples of the world up a mountain to "civilization." The two figures climb over stones reading "oppression, superstition, ignorance, brutality, and vice."

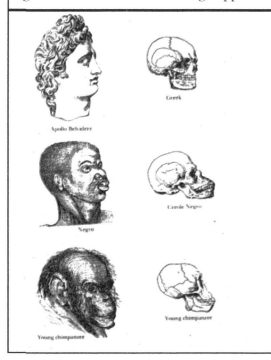

(**Fig 8.20**) Scientific Racism: This illustration, from the 1854 *Types of Mankind* exemplifies the 19th century preoccupation with "Scientific Racism." The book argued that the indegenous inhabitants of Africa were a unique species "a step up" from chimpanzees but a step down from the ancient Greeks. Scientific racists supported their claims with evidence from skull measurements. The scientific reports have been since debunked as "pseudo-science. Unlike those who believed that non-white people would be brought up to European standards of civilization, scientific racists held that such progress was impossible due to the innate biological differences between western and non-western peoples.

Anticolonialism

Last but not least, there was a sizable group of Europeans and Americans who opposed the cruelty to which the colonized had been subjected and advocated for their liberation. The rise of **anticolonialism**, which intensified during the last quarter of the nineteenth century, owed to something of a spirit of reform in Europe during the age. By the mid-19th century, most countries in Europe had abolished the slave trade (and America would do the same, following a Civil War, in 1866). New laws designed to protect factory workers, child-laborers, women and the elderly reflected an increased concern from standards of living, human rights, and the common good. This spirit of reform was energized by technologies of communication which made the conditions of colonized peoples apparent to a broader public. There are numerous examples of this, but, perhaps the most significant is the widespread backlash against Belgian **King Leopold II** when news reports of his oppression of the inhabitants of the Congo came to light in Europe.

Leopold had privately established the so-called "**Congo Free State**" in 1885, which had become economically important due to the demand for rubber. Belgium established trading outposts or "stations" along the Congo river, arguing that these stations would benefit the Congolese by giving them the opportunity to acquire the benefits of free trade, medicine, and education. Despite Leopold's claims of philanthropy, disturbing reports began making their way back to Europe. Shocked missionaries told tales of slaughter, mutilation, and slavery. Technological advancements made these reports both widely available and credible. The photographs of **Alice Seeley Harris**, in the 1890's, for example, provided indisputable evidence of Belgian barbarity and represent one of the first instances of activist photography. In 1904, Roger Casement's **Congo Reports** appeared in England detailing Belgian colonial practice. These reports led to significant moral outrage throughout Europe and called into question the supposed beneficence of the imperialists. Anti-colonial societies sprang up across Europe and America. Around the same time, scholars like John Hobson published books arguing that the European presence in Asia and Africa was based not on philanthropic generosity but on pure, economic greed. As the voices of anti-colonialists gradually began to be heard in European politics, they helped to create and popularize ideas of colonial liberation and national self determination, the principles that all peoples should have the right, without interference, to shape their own destinies.

Despite the moral force of these arguments, they nonetheless remained minority opinions into the 20th century. The major European powers, benefiting economically and politically from their global dominion, had little desire to relinquish control over their vast empires. For them to begin to open their fists would require more than a few disturbing news reports. It would require two cataclysms, visiting on the European powers traumas which were as violent and disruptive as those which they had visited upon the colonies.

(Fig 8.21) King Leopold of Belgium (1900) was remembered as one of the great villains of his time due to the barbarity of the Belgian-controlled "Congo Free State."

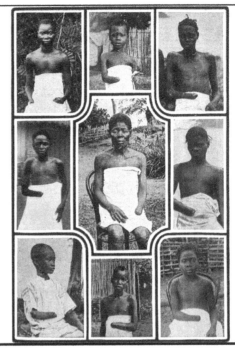

(Fig 8.22) Early photographs (1900) of mutilated Congolese generated moral outrage in Europe and called into question the supposed benevolence of imperialism.

Summing Up: Key Chapter Points

1. The modern world is divided between the developed "west" and the less developed "non-west."
2. The origin of this inequality is in the 19th century age of empires.
3. In the age of empires, European powers asserted their control over much of the non-European world.
4. Some Europeans justified colonialism on the grounds of philanthropy, others on innate superiority, while still others opposed it for moral reasons.
5. The opposition to colonialism led to ideas of colonial liberation and national self determination which would become crucial in 20th century international orders.

CHAPTER 9: THE GREAT POWERS & TOTAL WAR (1900-1945)

Overview

This chapter begins with the period of "great power" competition that preceded World War I. In particular we examine:

• The growth of nationalism (state supporting, state opposing, liberal, convservative)
• The military competition and complicated network of alliances that established fault lines across Europe.

After outline the story of World War I, we discuss **Wilsonian idealism** and the ideas of free trade, interdependence, and national self determination embodied in the **League of Nations**. We then discuss the failure of these ideas in practice citing

- **German Revanchism**
- **Weak international governance**
- **The rise of fascism**
- **Great Depression**

Whose Nation? Whose Nationalism?

Imagine living at the very beginning of the 20th century. How would you have felt about the world you lived in? The answer probably would depend on who you were and where you came from. If you were a middle-class Englishman living in London you might have felt a deep sense of pride in what your country had achieved. Queen Victoria's British Empire stretched all across the globe, with land in India, China, Africa and the West Indies. "The sun never sets on the British Empire" was a common saying at the time. Maybe you would have felt great satisfaction with your government and supported its rule. In such a case, we could describe the nature of your feelings as nationalist. More precisely, this would have been a form of state-supporting nationalism; a strong attachment to your nation and a commitment to the power of your government. During the early years of the twentieth century, many Europeans felt precisely this way, pleased with their empires and impressed with the powerful armies and navies that stretched around the world.

But suppose you had been born just 200 miles away, in Ireland. You would still be a citizen of the British empire, but you might have felt a bit different about its legitimacy. You might have believed that England was a bully and an oppressor, dominating other lands and denying other people popular sovereignty. Or suppose you were an Indian living under British rule in Delhi. You might have felt, as Mahatma Ghandi did, that the English were an "invading" force with no right to the territory they occupied. In either case you might have identified strongly with your "people" (the Irish people or the Indian people) but not with the state which ruled you. In this case you would still be a nationalist, but you would be a **state opposing nationalist**, someone who, though identifying with a nation, expresses opposition to the ruling state. Some state-opposing nationalists may seek to reform those institutions or separate from them entirely. Others may want to unify with different countries. Historically, conflicts between state supporting nationalists and state opposing nationalists have led to significant political turbulence.

Key Vocabulary

State Supporting Nationalism: Loyalty to and identification with a particular "people" accompanied with support of the institutions of state power which govern them. State supporting nationalism occasionally seeks to strengthen the power of the state or to "purify" it from the intrusion of "outsiders."

State Opposing Nationalism: Loyalty to and identification with a particular "people" accompanied by opposition to the institutions of state power which govern them. State opposing nationalism may seek to reform the state or separate from it. Occasionally, it may seek to unify with another nation-state or to form a new nation-state.

| **(Fig 9.1)** Queen Victoria (1819-1901): Monarch at the height of the British Empire. | **(Fig 9.2)** Mahatma Ghandi (1869-1948): Leader of the Indian independence movement. |

Either sort of nationalism--state-supporting or state-opposing--reflects an important development in political thinking. Though we may take it for granted that people "naturally" identify with a nation, this has not always been the case. In chapter 7, we mentioned the importance of the Age of Revolutions in which the principle of popular sovereignty spread through both Europe and the New World. One consequence of these revolutions, as we mentioned, was the idea that people stopped regarding themselves as simply passive "subjects" of a king and began to think of themselves as active "citizens" of a nation, citizens with rights and responsibilities. After the establishment of this idea, few politicians would be successful without portraying themselves as representing the nation and its people.

Early demands for national representation often went in hand with demands for the extension of rights, the period before 1848 is one in which **liberal nationalism** dominated politics. Liberal nationalists fought not only for the independence of their countries but ideas such as universal suffrage (voting) republicanism, and democracy. Later in the 19th century, however, many of Europe's conservative elites began to realize that nationalism represented a force that could be used to pursue their own interests and strengthen their own power. Using the language of nationalism to rally the people, these **conservative nationalists** saw the nation as something they could "use" to centralize the authority of the state. One representative of this new form of conservative nationalism was **Otto von Bismarck**. At the time, Germany, like Italy, was not yet a unified nation-state but split into many smaller states, some of them not much bigger than medium-sized towns. Bismarck, was a leading conservative politician in the second largest state in Germany: the Kingdom of Prussia. During the German revolutions of 1848, Bismarck had fought successfully against the liberal nationalists' plans to create a unified German nation-state with a constitution that would limit the power of the Prussian King, Wilhelm IV. Now that the revolution was over and the liberal nationalists defeated, Bismarck wanted to use the appeal of nationalism to make Prussia the dominant state not just in Germany, but in all of Europe. To do this, he rallied public opinion in Prussia and the other German states behind the idea of unifying Germany into one powerful nation-state under Prussian leadership. Then he led Prussia into a series of short but decisive wars against Denmark in 1864, Austria in 1866, and France in 1870. After securing sufficient public support at home and asserting its power abroad, Prussia, transformed into the German Empire in 1871 became one of the largest and most powerful states in Europe.

Key Vocabulary:

Liberal Nationalism: Emphasizes civil rights and liberties for the national community.

Conservative Nationalism: A form of nationalism that tends to emphasize the power and authority of the state.

Nationalization: The transfer of the institutions of the state to the entire community.

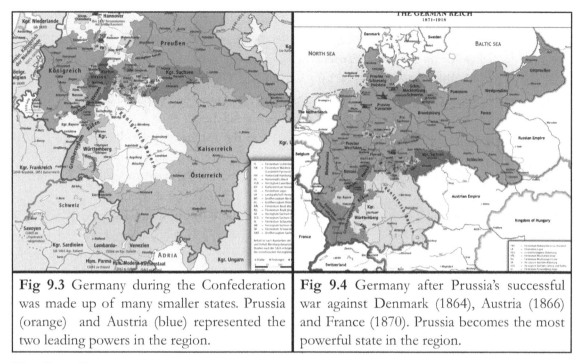

| **Fig 9.3** Germany during the Confederation was made up of many smaller states. Prussia (orange) and Austria (blue) represented the two leading powers in the region. | **Fig 9.4** Germany after Prussia's successful war against Denmark (1864), Austria (1866) and France (1870). Prussia becomes the most powerful state in the region. |

The Great Powers

Otto Von Bismark's establishment of a nationalized Germany reflected a broader global order dominated by great powers which ruled over almost the entire globe. **Great Britain** remained first among them with the largest empire in the world, the largest economy and the sea's most formidable navy. By the beginning of the twentieth century, it had developed a new battleship called the dreadnought. With iron armor, swivelling guns, and long-range torpedoes, the dreadnought was an unprecedented weapon and solidified Great Britain's leadership over the oceans. On the continent, however, Bismark's **Germany** was not far behind. It had enormous industrial capacities and a highly organized and modern military. After Britain built its dreadnought, Germany began to expand its own navy, building dreadnought models and inventing the deadly underwater submarine known as the U-boat. **The Ango-German Arms Race** saw the rapid growth of both the German and the British militaries as the two powers competed for European preeminence.

| **Fig 9.5** British dreadnaught | **Fig 9.6** German U-boat |

France, though it had once been, in the days of Napoleon I the largest power in Europe, found itself in roughly third place. It had a large empire, particularly in Africa, but it lacked either the navy of Britain or the industrial capacity of Germany. Losing the Franco-Prussian war meant that it had to cede the lands of Alceste and Lorraine to Germany. The humiliation of this loss made France increasingly bitter towards Germany, and it established an alliance first with Russia and then with Britain in an effort to restrict its powerful neighbor.

Russia, though it had not yet industrialized to the extent of the other powers, was by far the largest country in Europe, with a sizable military and imperial ambitions to unite all of the Slavic peoples in the east. Tsar Nicholas II ruled over 40% of all the territory in Europe, from the northern Pacific all the way down to the borders of modern day Afghanistan.

Impeding Russia's ambition, however, was the **Austro-Hungarian Empire**. The second largest country in Europe, Austria Hungary possessed a powerful economy, having developed a highly modern electrical industry. On the basis of common language and culture, it had also forged a close alliance with Germany to its north. It exercised control over much of the Balkan region, an area which Russia regarded as historically its own.

Last and in many least was the declining **Ottoman Empire**. The so-called "sick man of Europe," the Ottoman Empire had been in serious financial and political trouble since the 1870's. Though it maintained nominal control over lands in northern Africa and the Balkans, it lacked the ability to oversee its empire. This created a power-vacuum, and the Germans, Austro-Hungarians and Russians all vied for control of the old Ottoman territories.

Key Questions: What you need to know

• What is the difference between "state supporting" and "state opposing" nationalism?
• What was the international order like at the turn of the century?
• What was noteworthy about the rise of a unified Germany?
• Besides "power" what else was the period of competition among the great powers about?

Key Vocabulary

Great Powers: Great Britain, Germany, France, Russia, Austria-Hungary, and the Ottoman Empire. The Great Powers dominated Europe and much of the globe.

Franco-Prussian War: In 1870, Prussia (soon to be Germany) defeated France and seized the territories of Alceste and Lorraine. This defeat humiliated France and made it eager to attack Germany at the beginning of World War I.

Anglo-German Arms Race: Great Britain and Germany greatly expanded their militaries, particularly their navies in competition with one another for European dominance.

Allied Powers	Strengths	Weaknesses
	Great Britain • Economic powerhouse • Largest Navy in the world	• Slowing industrialization. • Empire necessitated significant expenditure.
	France • Second largest empire • Industrialized.	• Lost Franco-Prussian war • Economy slowing .
	Russia • Largest nation in Europe. • Large military in the west.	• Lack of industrialization. • Political instability.
Central Powers	**Strengths**	**Weaknesses**
	Germany • Most heavily industrialized country in Europe. • Large ground forces • Unified leadership	• Few imperial colonies. • Navy weaker than Britain's. • Target of French and British hostility.
	Austria Hungary • Heavily industrialized • Close alliance with Germany	• Political instability in Balkan region. • Lack of support among multi-ethnic population.
	Ottoman Empire •One of the largest and oldest empires in Europe. • Large population base.	• Poor control over empire • Economically weak. • The "sick man of Europe.

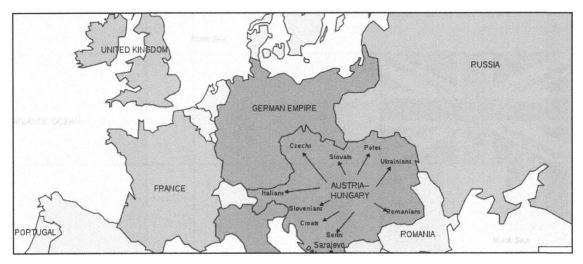

(Fig 9.7) Map of Europe, 1914. (Fig 9.8) Assassination of Franz Ferdinand

Following the **Assination of Archduke Franz Ferdinand** by Serbian nationalists, the government of Austria-Hungary gave Serbia a list of ultimatums with which it was impossible to comply. Though Serbia attempted to resolve the problem diplomatically, Austria Hungary was determined to punish the small nation and to expand into the Balkans. The tension in the Balkans is only one example of the Great Powers' struggle over the territory and political influence which formed in the power vacuum following the decline of the Ottoman Empire.

World War I: the beginning of the end of empires

In 1908, Austria-Hungary annexed the small territories of Bosnia and Herzegovina from the Ottoman Empire. Austria-Hungary had always been a multi-ethnic empire, whose inhabitants included Germans, Italians, Serbians, Bosnians, Ukrainians, Greeks, Slovenians, and Poles. Though Germany, who saw the annexation as an opportunity to limit Russia's influence in the east, supported the move, the act infuriated almost everyone else in Europe. Russia saw it as an infringement on its sphere of influence. Britain and France saw it as destabilizing to the balance of power. The small independent nation of Serbia viewed it as a threat to its own safety. Last but not least, the Bosnians, tired of imperial rule and hoping either to establish their own independence, or else to unify with Serbia, viewed it as an oppressive denial of their right to national self-determination. Though Germany was able to negotiate with the other great powers and thus (temporarily) forestall war, tensions and resentments continued to grow.

Six years later, in June of 1914, two members of a nationalist group, called "Young Bosnia," (a state-opposing nationalist group) ambushed and assassinated the **Archduke of Austria-Hungary.** The Young Bosnians favored the break-up of the Austro-Hungarian empire and the unification of the Serbian, Bosnian, and Yugoslavian ethnic groups into independent states. The Archduke was the heir to the Austro-Hungarian throne and was therefore one of the most important members of the royal family. The political consequences were swift and severe. The Austro-Hungarian empire blamed Serbia for the attack, and, after presenting Serbia with a list of political demands, mobilized its army, and declared war in July. Serbia activated its alliance with Russia, and Russia, long suspicious of Austro-Hungarian expansion in the Balkans, declared war on Austria-Hungary in response. Austria-Hungary, in turn, activated its alliance with Germany, and Germany declared war on Russia. France, long bitter towards Germany and eager to reclaim the lost territories of Alceste and Lorraine, declared War on Germany. The Ottoman Empire joined the war on the German side, making up the **central powers**, while England joined the war on the French side, making up the **allied power**s. Not only was the war fought in and around the home territory of those nations, but it also spread to the colonial outposts and the trading routes that connected them, making the scope of the conflict truly worldwide.

Though, from our perspective, the assination of the Archduke may seem like a small spark to set off such a large explosion, to those living at the time the outbreak of war would have seemed inevitable. The European international order had been in a state of tension for decades. The great powers of Europe, in both implicit and explicit competition with one another, after engaging in a military arms race and forming a complex network of interlocking political blocs, had created a balance of power which was extremely precarious. Enormous militaries were locked in a perpetual state of rivalry and mistrust. Austria-Hungary's declaration of war, therefore, though the most proximate cause of World War I, cannot be said to be the ultimate cause. In a way it was simply the last straw, breaking a peace which had long been fragile and causing the hostile energies long present in the world system to be released.

New Ordeals, New Orders

It is beyond our scope in this book to tell the story of World War I in even a superficial way. The strategic campaigns, the fierce battles, the deadly trenches, the expansion of warfare to the sea and the skies: all of this, instrumental to history, requires a much more complete treatment than we have space to offer. Our concern is not with the specific events of the war but with the way those events changed the international order. To that end, we limit ourselves to four facts about World War I which shaped political conditions which emerged in the following decades and have continued to make an impact on global politics.

First, World War I was the first **total war** in modern history. In the combatant countries, every aspect of the state, the entire population and all of the resources, were engaged, in some way, in the war effort. Second, the totality of the war reshaped many domestic political institutions. Women, for the first time in the twentieth century, entered the workforce in large numbers and gained an increase in political rights and economic power as a result. Third, the effects of the **industrial revolution** on war proved unexpected and tragic. The machine gun, poison gas, the submarine, the fighter plane, the tank: all of these revolutionized military tactics and increased suffering. Casualties in single battles of World War I often exceeded those of entire campaigns in prior wars. Finally, the war proved culturally traumatic to the broader European psyche. By 1918, 40 million Europeans had either been killed or wounded, a casualty rate, which, if confined to one country, would have exceeded the entire population of any nation in Europe. This trauma led to a critical reexamination of many European institutions. Art, literature, and philosophy entered a period rebellion and uncertainty. "The age of innocence" had come to an end.

Wilsonian Idealism

The examination of conscience which began towards the end of World War I centered on one basic question: "What went wrong and how do we prevent it from happening again?" The American president Woodrow Wilson had his own answer. According to Wilson, the chief cause of the war had been colonialism and imperialism. Wilson's activism, which marked the United States' first major entrance into European politics after decades of isolationism, offered a critique of the 19th century. The great powers, according to Wilson, with their formidable and competitive militaries had made the world a dangerous place. As he put in a speech to the American Congress in 1917:

> "This war had its roots in the disregard of the rights of small nations and of nationalities which lacked the union and the force to make good their claim to determine their own allegiances and their own forms of political life. Covenants must now be entered into which will render such things impossible for the future; and those covenants must be backed by the united force of all the nations that love justice and are willing to maintain it at any cost."

Wilson, in other words, believed that the solution was **national self-determination**: giving all nations the freedom to form their own states and shape their own destinies. According to Wislon, there had to be "an impartial adjustment to all colonial claims." If nations were given popular sovereignty rather than being, in his words, "handed about from one sovereignty to another,", then the political anger which had led to the assassination of Franz Ferdinand would be avoided. The great powers would be forced to respect the rights of all independent peoples. What Wilson argued for, in other words, was an extension of legitimate authority, of freely-chosen governments, throughout the world.

World War I: Four Consequences

(Fig 9.9) **Total War**: mobilization of entire population and resources. The whole nation contributed to the war effort.

(Fig 9.10) **New weapons** such as the machine gun and poison gas led to higher casualties than ever before.

(Fig 9.11) **Women** entered the workforce in large numbers. The expansion of women's rights such as suffrage, divorce, and property ownership owes in large part to the need for labor in World War I.

(Fig 9.12) An end of innocence: John Sargeant's Gassed. Much of the west entered a period of cultural cycnicism and self-doubt. Art, literature, film, and theater became significantly darker.

October 1908	**Bosnian Crisis:** Austria-Hungary annexes Bosnia
June 1914	Assassination of Archduke Franz Ferdinand by Serbian nationalists.
July-August 1914	Austria-Hungary declares war on Serbia. Russia, Germany, France, and Britain quickly join in the war.
May 1915	Sinking of passenger ship Lusitania. German submarine warfare targets "neutral" shipping lanes. Italy declares war on Austria-Hungary.
February 1916	Battle of Verdun begins. The longest and bloodiest battle of the war, it would leave more than 700,000 killed and wounded.
July 1916	Battle of the Somme begins. Sustaining enormous casualties, the allied armies achieved little against the complex and heavily fortified German trenches.
April 1917	America enters the war on the side of the Allies.
December 1917	Following the **Bolshevik Revolution**, Russia exits the war, negotiating a separate peace with Germany.
January 1918	Wilson presents his "**14 points** for Peace" to the US Congress.
November 1918	The Central Powers surrender. The **Treaty of Versailles**, based on Wilson's, would shape the global international order for the next two decades.

Key Questions: What you need to know

- How did World War I begin?
- Why was the assassination of Archduke Franz Ferdinand not the "ultimate" cause?
- How did nationalism contribute to the outbreak of World War I
- How did World War I affect the domestic institutions of Europe? (4 ways).

How was this to be achieved? Wilson believed the only way that the rights of small nations could be respected was through consensus with all of the nations of the world joining together in a **"democratic association"** in order to protect peace. This association, which he called the **League of Nations**, would be a kind of world government and would ensure peace by binding states in cooperative institutions. If problems were to arise, the League would solve them through global arbitration and diplomacy. In order to strengthen cooperative ties between states, Wilson advocated for free trade, an opening of the seas and ports for unrestricted commerce. Trade, according to Wilson, would create economic interdependence and allow for mutual interest to replace competition in international affairs. Wilson called these proposals for peace his **Fourteen Points**: fourteen policy prescriptions intended to create a lasting peace in Europe. These fourteen, however, in effect, can be summarized in terms of three broad themes: national self-determination, global diplomacy, and economic interdependence.

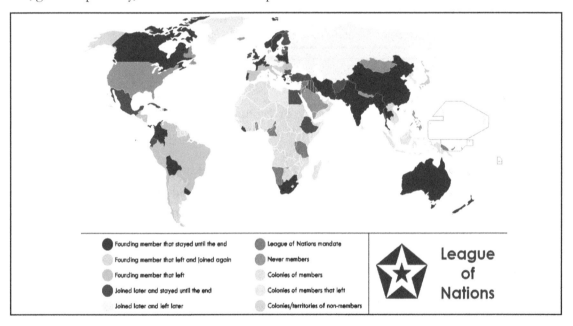

When the Central Powers finally surrendered and the **Versailles Treaty** was instituted in 1918, Wilson's Fourteen Points were instrumental in structuring the terms. Many nations in Europe which had been part of the Austro-Hungarian or Ottoman empires were granted national self-determination. Notably, Poland, Yugoslavia, Latvia, Romania, Armenia, Georgia, Greece and Egypt all became independent states. Though national self-determination did not extend to France and England's colonized holdings in Africa and the far East, independence movements in those territories gained strength and there was a gradual increase in regional autonomy and home rule. The League of Nations was established in January of 1920, and, though the United States (notoriously) refused to join, it was hoped that diplomacy would replace military conflict. There were a series of treaties: the **Washington Naval Treaty,** in 1922, attempted to end arms races (like the Anglo-German arms race) by setting limits on the navies of the Great Powers. Each nation would only be allowed a certain number of battleships, cruisers, destroyers, and submarines--each nation in proportion to each other. **The Locarno Treaty** in 1925 set post-war borders in an effort to ensure peace between Germany and newly independent Poland. **The Kellog-Briand** pact in 1928 officially "outlawed war" and mandated that diplomacy be used to solve international agreements. Finally, there was an effort to increase free trade, particularly along contested waterways. The years after the establishment of the Versailles Treaty were marked by widespread idealism among many political thinkers. It was hoped that a rational, cooperative, and democratic order would end wars once and for all.

Key Vocabulary

National Self-determination: the right of each national group to have its own state
Economic interdependence: A relationship of mutual self interest based on trade.

What Went Wrong

Of course we know happened next. A decade of economic growth and (relative) peace followed by the Great Depression and the outbreak of World War II. The First World War had devastated Europe--40 million killed and wounded--yet the Second World War would bring destruction on an even greater and more unimaginable scale: 85 million dead, likely as many wounded, civilian populations decimated, cities bombed to powder, death-camps and genocide. An unprecedented catastrophe, **World War II** would come to an end with two nuclear blasts each consuming an entire city in an eyeblink. The world had every reason to avoid such a calamity and it was in its power to do so. What happened? How was history allowed to repeat itself?

Answering that question has filled entire libraries with books, and it is unlikely that anyone knows for sure. In general, however, political theorists have identified three problems in Wilson's plan which created conditions for the Second World War.

• **Economic Problems and Revanchism:** Though Wilson had recognized the importance of free trade and economic interdependence, the allied powers failed to ensure global prosperity. Weakened by the economic toll of the war, the allies were determined to punish Germany for the destruction it had caused and to make the Germans pay reparations for the allied war costs. The notorious "Article 231" of The Treaty of Versailles forced Germany to assume all responsibility and required payments which strained the economic capacity of the defeated country. These reparations not only led to a great deal of suffering on the part of the German people but also contributed to what since has been termed **German revanchism**: a deep-seated feeling of humiliation and bitterness toward the allies and a desire for revenge. After the **Great Depression** further weakened the global economy, an outraged and desperate population turned to **Fascism** and Adolf Hitler in an effort to reclaim Germany's autonomy and rebuild its prior strength. In short, the Versailles Treaty failed to anticipate the ways that domestic economic insecurity, particularly among the losing states, could plant the seeds for future violence.

• **Lack of Legitimacy of the League of Nations**: Though the intentions behind the League of Nations were good, the association suffered from the very beginning from a perceived lack of legitimacy. Wilson failed to persuade congress to allow America to join the League--a failure which weakened its authority in the eyes of many in the international community. The League had neither the power nor the consensus to enforce its decrees. In 1931, when Japan attacked the Chinese coast and, in 1935, when Italy attacked Ethiopia, the League, though largely opposed, was powerless to prevent the aggression or to bring about the arbitration needed to prevent violence.

• **Neglecting the East**: Wilson had realized that imperial aggression was a key cause in World War I. Yet, his notion of such aggression was Eurocentric, based on Europe's history of expansion and empire building. Europe's leaders failed to anticipate the consequences of a rising Japan, which had stayed clear of World War I. Europe was caught off guard when Japan, seeking the same imperial strength which Europe had sought in the 19th century, began expanding into surrounding island chains and conquering the east coast of China.

• **Rise of Fascism**: Due to the economic stress of the **Great Depression**, a new kind of politics emerged in the 1930's. Emphasizing military strength, traditional national myths, and racial purity, the fascist leaders of the 1930's promised to make their countries powerful and proud.

(Figs 9.13-9.17) Adolf Hitler, Germany; Hirohito, Japan; Benito Mussolini, Italy; Francisco Franco: Spain

Into the 1930's the architects of the Versailles treaty remained in denial about their failures. In 1931, Japan invaded Manchuria. The League of Nations timorously condemned the aggression but could do nothing more. Japan, in response, simply withdrew from the League. In 1937, Japan began an invasion of the rest of China. In 1933, Adolph Hitler seized dictatorial powers in Germany, blaming Jews and communists for Germany's downfall, and vowing to restore Germany to its former glory. Britain and France were unable to stop him. In 1935, Italy invaded Ethiopia. The Ethiopian King Haile Selassie pleaded with the League for protection. The League passed a few ineffectual economic sanctions and allowed the invasion to continue. In March of 1938, Hitler, having remilitarized the Rhineland, annexed Austria. In response, the rest of Europe adopted a policy of appeasement, allowing the expansion in the hopes that it would satisfy German aggression and prevent war. In September of the same year, Germany annexed the Sudetenland from Czechoslovakia, and Neville Chamberlain, then Prime Minister of Britain, signed the Munich Agreement, effectively assenting to Hitler's demands and legitimizing German expansion. Only a year after that, Hilter, seeking to consolidate all of the German-speaking areas of Poland, sent tanks blitzing into Warsaw. It was only then that England and France realized that they had no choice but to fight. If Hitler was allowed to take Poland, then the entire principle of national self-determination, the central thesis of the Fourteen Points, was doomed. A child born in Europe in the year that the League of Nations was established would be eighteen years old in 1939, in all likelihood one among the millions of young conscripts destined to play a part in the world's next great tragedy.

October 1929	Crash of the stock markets sends the world into the **Great Depression.**
September 1931	Seeking to expand its sphere of influence and grow into a world power, Japan invades Manchuria.
March 1933	Adolph Hitler seizes control of German parliament (Reichstag). He embarks on a policy of centralization and remilitarization.
September 1939	Germany invades and annexes Poland. France and Britain, in turn, declare war on Germany.
June 1942	The allies begin a bombing campaign over Germany. Allied air raids would eventually reduce much of the German interior to rubble.
July 1943	Allied troops begin invasion of Italy
July 1944	Allied troops take Rome and land on the beaches of Normandy

July 1945	Conference in Bretton Woods Massachusetts establishes new economic institutions for the post-war international order.
May 1945	After a year of losses in both the east and west, Germany surrenders unconditionally to the allies and the Soviet Union.
August 1945	The United States drops nuclear bombs on Hiroshima and Nagasaki, forcing Japan to surrender.

Summing Up: Key Chapter Points

1) At the beginning of the 20th century, the world was dominated by huge European powers. Within these powers were ideologies of nationalism: both state-supporting and state-opposing.
2) The tensions between these nationalistic ideas, along with years of precarious military competition, led to the outbreak of World War I following the assassination of Franz Ferdinand.
3) World War I was the first "total war" in the twentieth century, martialing the entire population and all of the resources of the combatants and changing domestic political institutions.
4) The end of World War I, with the Treaty of Versailles, sought to establish peace by implementing many of the ideas in Woodrow Wilson's "14 Points."
5) Chief among these ideas were national self-determination, the League of Nations, and economic interdependence.
6) Ultimately the idealistic aspirations of the Treaty of Versailles were never achieved due to economic and political flaws in the agreement.

CHAPTER 10: ANOTHER TRY AT PEACE

This chapter explains the theory and development of the modern post-war **liberal international order**. Specifically, we focus on:

- The way the Allies attempted to improve on the Versailles arrangement
- **National self-determination, free trade**, and **collective security**
- The **United Nations** and how it differed from the **League of Nations.**

In addition, we discuss the growth of a new economic perspective in the 1940's, **Keynesian economics** and explain

- The birth of the modern **welfare state**
- The provisions of the **Bretton Woods system**
- The attempts to avoid the **beggar thy neighbor politics** of the 1920's

World War II was both a human and an institutional tragedy. The human tragedy is reflected in the widespread suffering of the violence itself. If World War I had marked the beginning of industrialized warfare (machine guns, tanks, planes, and submarines) World War II showed the capacity of technology to unleash even greater destruction. Aircraft carriers crossed the seas bringing hundreds of bombers and fighters to far-away targets. Incendiary bombs unleashed fires over heavily populated areas. And at the end of the war, the nuclear warhead, the most deadly device ever used in battle, destroyed two entire cities in an instant. Never before had ordinary civilians--women, children, and the elderly--been so vulnerable to attack.

The devastation of World War II, however, was not simply a function of technological advances. Human cruelty, for reasons which will always remain mysterious, was manifested in atrocities which continue to loom large in historical memory. In China, three-hundred thousand civilians were killed in the Japanese **massacre of Nanjing.** In Russia, more than 95% of the civilians of Stalingrad perished in the year-long siege of the city. In Germany and Poland, the moral calamity of the **holocaust** claimed the lives of over six million Jews, Gypsies, disabled individuals, and political dissidents in concentration camps.

Neither were the Allied Powers guiltless of war crimes of their own. There was the fire-bombings of Tokyo and of Dresden in which the Allies killed nearly two hundred thousand non-combatants. In the early years of the post-war occupation, records report over 10,000 sexual assaults by allied soldiers of civilian women in France and Germany. In 1955, the American writer John Berryman, looking back on the destruction of World War II, famously referred to the 20th century as "the sickening century." And, a decade later, the Nobel Laureate Seamus Heaney summed it up this way: "history resembles an abattoir."

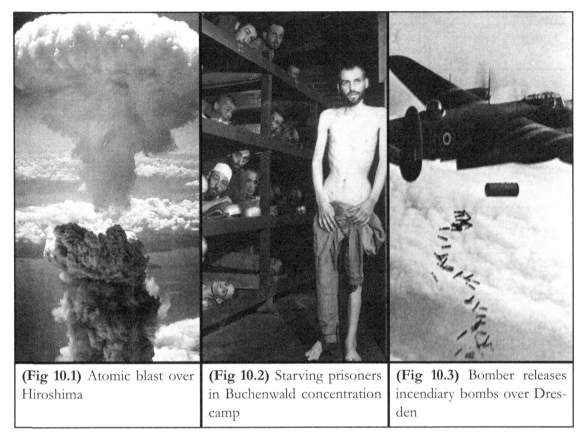

| **(Fig 10.1)** Atomic blast over Hiroshima | **(Fig 10.2)** Starving prisoners in Buchenwald concentration camp | **(Fig 10.3)** Bomber releases incendiary bombs over Dresden |

Underlying the human tragedy was deep institutional dysfunction. The Treaty of Versailles, though deliberately crafted to produce lasting harmony, had achieved the exact opposite result. The best and most idealistic efforts had proven futile. Certain political philosophers, who called themselves **realists**, pointed out that such treaties had failed over and over again in human history. Dating back to the Peace of Westphalia, there had been countless international agreements attempting to forge peace among rival states. Yet each time, almost before the ink was dry, another war had broken out. Peace, the realists proclaimed, has never lasted long in human history and it never will.

Questions for Discussion

What explains the incredible amount of human cruelty during World War II? Technology? Human nature? Desire for revenge? Something more subtle?

Do you think World War II could have been prevented with better instituions? Why or why not?

If yes, how could the post World War I institutions have been better structured?

International Agreements: An exercise in futility?

Treaty	Promise
1648 Peace of Westphalia	Territorial sovereignty established. States allow monarchs to choose the religion of their states.
1815 Congress of Vienna	After the Napoleonic Wars, the borders of Europe are redrawn to create a balance of power.
1878 Congress of Berlin	Attempts to settle the dispute among the Great Powers over the Balkans.
1899 Hague Conventions	Establishes the "Permanent Court of Arbitration" to avoid conflicts through trials. Rules for the treatment of prisoners and noncombatants.
1918 Versailles Treaty	Ends World War I. Attempts to establish an international order based on democracy, national self-determination, and free trade.
1921 Washington Naval Treaty	Promise made among major military powers to limit the sizes of their navies in order to ensure the balance of power.
1925 Lacarno Treaty	Germany agrees to accept new international borders. European powers promise never to go to war with each other.
1928 Kellogg-Briand Pact	Pledge made among nearly all major world powers promising not to attempt to solve international disputes through war.

Question for Discussion

Choose one of the major international treaties listed above. Do a bit of research on your own. What can you find out about it? Why do you think war continually breaks out despite promises to resolve disputes peacefully?

Before World War II had ended, the leaders of the Allied Powers were contemplating this problem and trying to determine how they could improve on the Versailles Treaty. What lessons could be learned from the failures of the 1930s: the economic misery and aggressive violence that dominated the decade? This question was particularly important to politicians in the United States. President Roosevelt and his colleagues knew that their country would emerge from the war as the greatest power on earth and they were determined to assert American leadership in global politics. Unlike their predecessors after 1919, there would be no avoiding the responsibilities of leadership necessary to create a more stable international economic order and to prevent the resurgence of German or Japanese power. In August of 1941, Winston Churchill and Franklin D. Roosevelt met (maybe prematurely) to discuss the structure of the post-war international order. The document they drafted, known as the **Atlantic Charter**, reflected their belief that, although the Versailles

Treaty had failed, much of it had not been wrong in principle. National self-determination, free trade, and democratic consensus were all good ideas, even if institutions had been unable to make them work. The Atlantic Charter, to that end, affirmed the commitment of Great Britain and the United States to the core tenets of Woodrow Wilson's vision. In particular, the countries emphasized four key points:

• **An end to territorial expansion**: "Their countries seek no aggrandizement, territorial or other...and desire to see no territorial changes that do not accord with the freely expressed wishes of the peoples concerned."

• **National self-determination:** "They respect the right of all peoples to choose the form of government under which they will live; and they wish to see sovereign rights and self government restored to those who have been forcibly deprived of them."

• **Economic Stability:** "They desire to bring about the fullest collaboration between all nations in the economic field with the object of securing, for all, improved labor standards, economic advancement and social security."

• **Disarmament:** "They believe that all of the nations of the world, for realistic as well as spiritual reasons, must come to the abandonment of the use of force... They believe, pending the establishment of a wider and permanent system of general security, that the disarmament of such nations is essential."

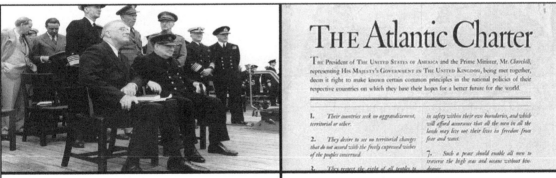

(Fig 10.4) FDR and Winston Churchill in 1941	(Fig 10.5) The Atlantic Charter

Key Questions: What you need to know

• What is the Atlantic Charter and what principles did it reaffirm?
• Do you notice anything differences between it and the 14 points?

A New Economic Perspective?

Though the language of the Atlantic Charter echoed that of Wilson's 14 Points, it differed slightly in its economic emphasis. For Wilson, **economic interdependence** was to be achieved through free trade. If countries were at liberty to trade with one another, economic collaboration, trust, and prosperity would result. A shift in thinking had occurred, however, in the years following the Great Depression. Faced with mass domestic poverty, political leaders in Europe and the United States had concluded that free-market capitalism was insufficient for economic stability. The government, they argued, had to regulate markets in order to ensure full employment and a fair distribution of wealth. Influenced by the economist **John Maynard Keynes**, these political leaders helped to create the modern **welfare state**, in which the government would intervene in the economy to ensure social security. Government-funded poverty-relief measures, regulatory institutions, and social insurance systems sprang into existence, one noteworthy example being in the United States with Roosevelt's **New Deal** programs.

(Fig 10.6) John Manyard Keynes: British economist who argued for increased government spending to support the economy in times of crisis.	**(Fig 10.7)** New Deal Poster advertising the Social Security program. The 1930's saw the birth of the modern "welfare state."

One potential unintended consequence of a government-regulated (or "mixed") economy, however, was the possibility of unhealthy international competition. Political leaders would be tempted to gain an advantage for their own nations at the expense of others. For instance, they would be tempted to create high tariffs to impede the shipment of foreign goods or to manipulate their nation's currency to improve the price of their exports. Such policies, known as **beggar-thy-neighbor** policies, tend to create an antagonistic economic order in which rivals seek relative gains while ignoring the potential for greater prosperity through cooperation. In the 1930's, beggar-thy-neighbor policies became common among the major powers of the world, with each government attempting to "fix" the economic woes of their own countries by "beggaring" others. For example, in the United States, during the 1930's, tariffs on imported goods reached nearly 60% during the 1930's. Such efforts, of course, only backfired and led to a worsening of the crisis.

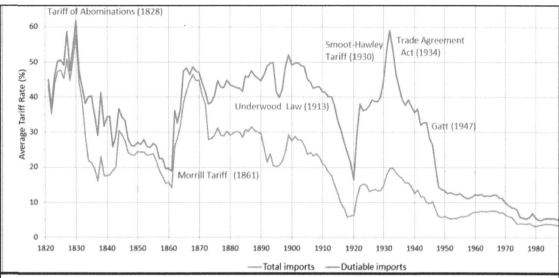

(Fig 10.8) Chart showing average tariff rates in the United States from 1821-206. Note the large spike in the 1930's followed by the drop following Bretton Woods (next page).

Key Vocab

John Maynard Keynes: British economist. Beginning in the 1930's, his ideas became highly influential in establishing an economic order in which the government was responsible for intervening in markets.

Welfare state: a system in which the government attempts to ensure full employment and economic stability through anti-poverty and regulatory measures.

Beggar-thy-neighbor policies: economic policies in which one country seeks economic advantages at the expense of another.

The leaders of the Allied Powers recognized that these policies had helped create the conditions for World War II and understood that they would have to end if the post-war international order would have any chance of succeeding. In July of 1944, three years after the Atlantic Charter was signed, the representatives of 44 allied nations met in **Bretton Woods**, New Hampshire to discuss the best way to create economic stability after the war. The agreement, which marked the beginning of the so-called Bretton Woods System, emphasized the importance of ensuring both a robust welfare system, on the one hand, and free trade on the other. In order to achieve this balance, the Bretton Woods agreement created two major institutions designed to promote both public investment and international cooperation:

• **The International Bank For Reconstruction and Development (IBRD)**: An international bank offering loans to countries for post-war rebuilding and anti-poverty measures. The IBDR would allow countries to invest in their own economies without resorting to economic isolationism.

• **The International Monetary Fund (IMF)**: An institution designed to regulate currency in order to prevent manipulation and other beggar-thy-neighbor policies. Nations would be required to link their currency to the United States dollar, which, in turn, would be pegged to gold at a fixed rate. This would prevent countries from arbitrarily changing the value of their currency.

In addition to these two institutions, the Bretton Woods Conference created a large framework of economic measures designed to ensure that the new collaboration between nations would be long-term. Taken altogether, the Bretton Woods agreement marked the beginning of a "rule-based" international economic order.

Key Questions: What you need to know

• What was the purpose in creating the institutions of the Bretton Woods system?
• Why was economic collaboration so important?
• What were the allied powers hoping to avoid?

New Nations, United

The Allied Powers still had one major set of problems to figure out. How would national self-determination be achieved? What would prevent large countries from bullying and dominating weaker ones? How would expansionist aggression (like the Japanese invasion of Manchuria, the Italian invasion of Ethiopia, and the German annexation of Czechoslovakia) be avoided? The League of Nations had been a failure. Was it worth trying to improve upon it or should the whole idea of "global governance" be scrapped?

The Allied Powers answered these questions over the course of three separate conferences. In 1943, as a part of the **Moscow Conference,** the Allies declared their belief in the necessity of an international organization to replace the league of nations, writing,

"[We] recognize the necessity of establishing at the earliest practicable date a general international organization based on the **principle of the sovereign equality** of all peace-loving states, and open to membership by all such states, large and small, for the maintenance of international peace and security."

A month after the Bretton Woods Conference, in August of 1944, the Allied Powers met in Dumberton Oaks, near Washington, and agreed upon the rough framework of what would become the United Nations. In particular, they decided that the organization would include

- **A General Assembly**: in which representatives of all the nations would gather together to deliberate and vote.
- **A Security Council:** made up of the most powerful nations who would be responsible for using their military might to maintain the peace and prevent conflicts
- **An International Court of Justice**: to settle disputes between nations which might otherwise lead to war
- **A Secretariat:** responsible for organizing meetings and drawing the attention of the General Assembly to international problems.

| **(Fig 10.9)** Churchill, Roosevelt, and Stalin | **(Fig 10.10)** Dumberton Oaks Mansion |

Finally, a year later, in San Francisco, just one month after the end of World War II, the Charter of the **United Nations** was complete. Forty eight nations signed the agreement formally establishing the United Nations and agreeing upon its rules. In addition to the organizational structure which had been outlined in Dumberton Oaks, the final version of the charter included a lengthy list of procedural arrangements, checks and balances.

The United Nations differed from the League of Nations in four significant ways. First, it was given significantly more power. While the League of Nations attempted to ban warfare as a means of resolving disputes, it had little means for actually enforcing this ban. The Security Council of the United Nations, by comparison, was permitted to actively keep the peace by, if necessary, ordering direct military intervention by all member nations. Second, the United Nations Charter included a significant preamble concerning **human rights.** It wasn't enough to simply "pacify" the relationships between states, as the League had attempted to do. Rather, the United Nations claimed a responsibility to ensure the basic rights and welfare of the citizens living within those states. Respect for individual life and dignity would be just as important as national sovereignty. Third, the United Nations took a more active role in national **self-determination** and decolonization than the League had. Disputed territories in the aftermath of World War II were divided into administrative regions and then, through international deliberation, given **popular sovereignty.** Last but by no means least, the United Nations included the participation of the United States, both as a founding state and a key security-council member. America had refused to join the League of Nations, and the world knew the United Nations would likewise be destined to fail without its support. By 1945, America had become the most powerful country in the world, both economically and militarily. Though it had a long tradition of isolationism, or reluctance to enter into international affairs, the attack on Pearl Harbor and the story of World War II had convinced American politicians that the fate of America was tied up in the fate of the community of nations at large. Not only would America join the United Nations but it would assume a central leadership position.

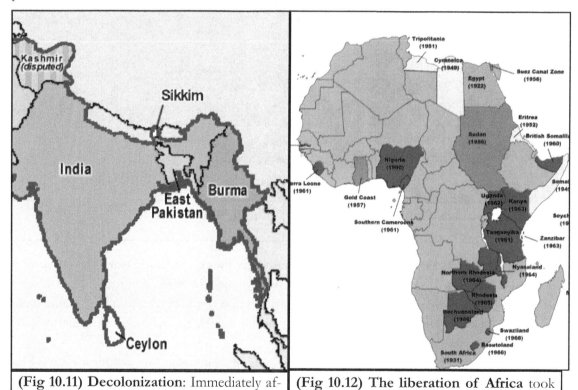

| **(Fig 10.11) Decolonization:** Immediately after WWII, the British empire left India, creating four new independent states. (See chapter 13) | **(Fig 10.12) The liberation of Africa** took somewhat longer. But, by the 1960's, the British and French empires also granted its colonies in Africa independence. |

In sum, the United Nations and the Bretton Woods institutions would be the two pillars of the post-war international order, or, what has since been called the modern **liberal international order** (LIO). With the former designed to ensure global peace and the latter designed to ensure economic stability, the two pillars would attempt to create a rule-based system of trust and cooperation. Following World War II, many of the new "decolonized" countries would join the LIO. It was hoped that the global order would be free and democratic, with the rights of small nations respected, avoiding the militaristic and imperialistic politics of the Great Powers period. Though political leaders were not as optimistic in 1945 as they had been in 1918, they were not altogether cynical either. The United Nations and the Bretton Woods system did seem to offer significant improvements over the Versailles model. It seemed possible that peace could be established and maintained. Then again, the "sickening century," in Berryman's words, was only half over.

Key Conferences of World War II

Atlantic Conference (June 1941)	Great Britain and the United States reaffirm their commitment to national self-determination, economic progress, peace and disarmament.
Third Moscow Conference (October 1943)	Allied Powers affirm their belief in the necessity of an international organization to replace the League of Nations.
Bretton Woods Conference (July 1944)	Allied Powers establish institutions to ensure free and fair trade while supporting full employment.
Dumberton Oaks Conference (August 1944)	Allied Powers establish the organizational structure of the United Nations.
Yalta Conference (February 1945)	The United States, Great Britain, and the Soviet Union make preliminary plans for post-war Germany.
United Nations Conference (April 1945)	The United Nations Charter is ratified
Potsdam Conference (July 1945)	The United States, Great Britain and the Soviet Union decide upon the partition of Germany and the fate of occupied territories. The Soviet Union promises to allow free and fair elections in the territories under its control.

Summing Up, Key Chapter Points:

1) World War II was a humanitarian and institutional tragedy, with unprecedented loss of life and an obvious failure of institutions designed to keep the peace.
2) Before the war had ended, the Allied Powers had reaffirmed their commitment to national self-determination, economic interdependence, and democracy.

3) The Bretton Woods Conference attempted to create a stable economic system balancing the need for a welfare state with the need for free trade. It was particularly concerned with ending the "beggar-thy-neighbor" policies of the 1930's.

4) The United Nations attempted to improve upon the League of Nations by empowering the security council and making broader provisions to protect human rights.

5) Taken together, the United Nations and the Bretton Woods system are two of the major pillars of the "modern liberal international order," the post World War II effort to ensure peace through rules and collaboration.

CHAPTER 11: THE COLD WAR

Overview

This chapter tells the story of the Cold War and explains how the military tensions during the period challenged the idealism of the Liberal International Order. In particular, we examine

• The reason that Russia and the West mistrusted each other prior to World War II
• The outbreak of the Cold War, resulting from the violation of the terms of the Yalta and Potsdam conferences
• The cultural dimensions of the Cold War, as reflected in the two **red scares**
• The broader global effects of the Truman doctrine and containment

We then discuss the various proxy wars and the periods of military escalation and detente in the 1960's and 1970's. The chapter concludes with an explanation of the reasons the Cold War ended:

• Russia's overextended empire and inefficient economic system
• Ghorbachev's **glastnost and perestroika** reforms
• The replacement of the **Brezhnev doctrine** with the **Sinatra doctrine**
• **The Autumn of nations**

In 1906, the Spanish-American philosopher George Santayana said, **"Those who do not learn history are doomed to repeat it."** It was a saying the founders of the liberal international order believed they had taken to heart. They remembered the failures which had led to the Second World War and believed they had learned from them: with a stronger international community, better economic oversight, and a more rigorous commitment to peace. Nonetheless, only a few short years after the establishment of the United Nations, the world was again on the brink of catastrophe. The two largest superpowers in the world, the United States and the Soviet Union, seemed determined to destroy each other. In February of 1946, USSR leader Joseph Stalin announced that war with the west was "inevitable." Given the existence of nuclear weapons, such a war would have threatened not only the nations involved but perhaps life on earth itself. Eighty years after Santayana uttered his famous adage, the literary critic Steven Helmling quipped in response, "History is doomed to repeat itself, whether we learn its lessons or not."

Of course, we know that things didn't turn out as badly as they could have. The United States and the Soviet Union did, in fact, avoid *direct* war. Nonetheless, over the next 45 years, they engaged in military competition, political **brinkmanship**, and confrontation in several **proxy wars**. This period of history, known as the **Cold War,** created some of the most dangerous conditions the world has ever known. In 1947, scientists at the *Bulletin of Atomic Scientists* created a

"**Doomsday Clock**" to measure how close humanity was to total annihilation. The clock, which measured the likelihood of nuclear and environmental catastrophe, would indicate "doomsday" if it were to ever reach midnight. Though doomsday never came, there were periods during the Cold War in which the clock was only two minutes away.

Doomsday Clock: Close to Midnight?

11:53 (1947)	Original setting of the Doomsday Clock. Each "minute" was meant to correspond to a specific level of crisis.
11:55 (1953)	United States and Soviet Union each test "hydrogen bombs."
11:58 (1960)	Before the Cuban Missile Crisis, relations between the US and Soviet Union deteriorate.
11:48 (1963)	US and Soviet Union agree to limit nuclear testing.
11:57 (1984)	Tensions between the US and Soviet Union increase as Ronald Reagan insists on increased military spending.
11:43(1991)	New arms deal signed as Cold War winds down.

The Beginning

Even before World War II ended the Soviet Union and western Europe had been uneasy with one another. The differences were partially cultural, partially political. Culturally, Russia had long been somewhat misplaced in Europe. The Russian language belonged to a different branch than the other European languages and used a different alphabet. The Russian Orthodox Church belonged to neither mainstream Protestant nor Catholic Christianity. The major Russian cities were far to the east, across forests and tundra, away from the major European metropolises of Paris, London, Berlin, and Rome. Finally, Russia had been slow to industrialize and was therefore viewed as culturally and economically backward.

The political differences became striking in 1917 following the **Communist Revolution**. Unable to endure the impoverished conditions in Russia during the first World War and blaming the Russian royal family for the country's woes, Vladimir Lenin and his **Bolshevik Party** overthrew the government and established a "Soviet Republic." Soon, the "Republic" had expanded to include several other quasi-independent states (such as the Ukraine, Belarus, Latvia, and Estonia) and had thus become the Union of Soviet Socialist Republics (USSR). In many respects, the USSR was the political, economic, and cultural opposite of the western powers of Europe and the United States. While the western powers featured market economies, democratically elected leaders, and broad civil freedoms, the USSR had a **command economy**, a single-party government, and state limitations on speech, press and religion. For this reason, the western powers viewed the USSR as tyrannical and believed communism to be a threat to "the democratic way of life."

In 1918, the United States, Britain, France, Italy, and several other allied nations sent nearly 200,000 soldiers into Russia in an attempt to support the "White" or anti-commuunist side in the Russian Civil War. The invasion was ineffective and confirmed, to Russia's new communist government, that the west was not to be trusted. Meanwhile, Lenin had imperialistic leanings of his own. In 1919, he helped establish the **Communist International** which pledged "to struggle by all available means, including armed force, for the overthrow of the international bourgeoisie and the creation of an international Soviet republic." In response, the United States developed several domestic anti-communist measures designed to discredit the Soviet Union and limit the popularity of communism at home and abroad. For example, during the period of time known as the **"first red scare"** (1918-1921), Woodrow Wilson passed the **Espionage and Sedition Acts**. Ostensibly designed to prevent spying on behalf of Germany, the laws essentially made it illegal to support any form of communism. Eugene Debs, the Socialist Candidate for president, was sent to prison where--in an unprecedented oddity in American politics--he received almost 4% of the vote. Meanwhile, the **Committee for Public Information** published anti-communist books and magazines in order to portray communism as an evil and anti-American philosophy. Anti-communism was nearly as strong in Europe. France established *la Ligue Internationale Anti-Communiste* (National Anti-Communist League), and in Great Britain, Winston Churchill distinguished himself as a fervent opponent of the Soviet Union, famously vowing to "strangle the infant Bolshevism in its cradle." The Soviet Union, of course, recognized this hostility and feared the danger which their powerful western neighbors posed to their new government. Therefore, before World War II even began, the Soviet Union and the west regarded one another with mutual distrust.

Key Vocabulary

Brinksmanship: The act of taking a political policy to dangerous limits.
Proxy War: An indirect war in which two larger nations arm and support smaller nations who then fight one another on their behalf.
Cold War: The period of military competition, brinksmanship, and indirect conflict between the United States and Soviet Union that lasted between 1946 and 1990.

(Fig 11.1) American troops in Vladivostok in 1918. The US had invaded on behalf of anti-communists during the Russian civil War.

(Fig 11.2) 1877 British propaganda poster depicting Russia an octopus devouring the rest of Europe.

Fig 11.3 American anti-communist book from 1947. Fear of a communist revolution in the United States was intense during the two "red scares."

(Fig 11.4) Pamphlet during the second "red scare" accusing communists of having infiltrated the entertainment industry.

Questions for Discussion

What accounted for the fervent anti-communism among the western powers before World War II? Fear? Incompatible political philosophies? Something more complex?

Can you think of any similar political fears in the west today?

Early on in World War II, anti-Russian fears briefly intensified. It looked, at first, like the Soviet Union and Germany might join forces. In 1939, Stalin and Hilter signed a "nonaggression pact" promising not to attack one another and dividing the newly conquered Poland between them. It was only after Hitler broke the pact and invaded Russia that Stalin's allegiances switched. For a few years, the United States, Great Britain, and Russia were able to put their common differences aside in order to battle their mutual enemy. Franklin D. Roosevelt sent military aid to Soviet Union, and, though an anti-communist, Churchill sent Stalin British intelligence and famously quipped, "If Hitler were to invade hell, I would put in a good word for Lucifer in the House of Commons." The American government put up pro-Russian posters, featuring a smiling Russian soldier over the words *"This man is a Russian. He is your friend. He fights for freedom!"* The Russians, likewise, welcomed the allied invasion of Germany, which helped relieve pressure on their soldiers in the east (though they suspected Britain and America had delayed their attack in order to weaken their forces). All through World War II, the three allied powers remained reliable partners: not only battling Germany and Japan but also, away from the battlefield, negotiating the structure of the institutions that would form the post-war international order.

Almost immediately after World War II ended, however, the relationship began to deteriorate again. Problems began with a broken promise. During the Yalta and Potsdam conferences of 1944, the Allied powers agreed on policies for the European territories that would soon be liberated from Germany. After the war, they would give the territories national self-determination and supervise free and fair elections. Stalin, at first, agreed to this idea and announced that he would move Russian troops back east as soon as the elections were over. Yet when it was time for the elections to be held, Stalin's soldiers stayed put. In the past twenty years, Russia had been invaded twice from the west, each time with devastating consequences. In World War II, Russia had suffered more casualties than all other allied countries, and it was largely through the Russian sacrifice that the war was won. Stalin believed he needed the new territories as a buffer against potential future aggression. At first, the Soviet Union pretended to hold elections, yet it quickly became clear that Russia was determined to remain in control. Certain territories, such as Georgia, Armenia, Ukraine, and Lithuania were reabsorbed directly into the USSR. Others, such as Poland, East Germany, Hungary, Czechoslovakia, Romania, and Bulgaria quickly became Soveit **satellite**

states, nominally independent, but, in fact, largely under control of the USSR communist party.

Key Vocabulary

First Red Scare (1918-1921): Following the communist revolution in Russia, the United States enacted a series of anti-communist policies at home. These anti-communist measures parrelled those of other countries in Europe.

Satellite State: The communist countries to the west of the Soviet Union. Though not "officially" part of the USSR, they formed a security "buffer" against the west and were largely under Soviet control.

Iron Curtain: Winston Churchill's term for the Soviet presence in Europe. According to Churchill, the Soviet Union would establish a tyrannical presence across Europe.

This broken promise immediately alarmed Great Britain and the United States. At the time, the Soviet Union had the largest army in Europe. Its ground-forces out-numbered those of the United States and Great Britain by almost a 3-1 ratio. It did not take long, faced with this perceived threat, for the United States and Great Britain to return to their anti-communist ways. In March of 1946, Winston Churchill delivered a speech to Westminster College in Missouri in which he called the Soviet presence an **iron curtain**. He claimed that Moscow was determined to establish a police state across Europe, occupying nation after nation and ruling them dictatorially. Russian historians have long claimed that this speech marked the "official beginning" of the Cold War.

Containment and Rising Tensions: 1946-1962

The western response to Stalin's refusal to withdraw his armies consisted of military, economic, and political actions. These counter-measures, led by the United States, defined the policy known as **containment** or **The Truman Doctrine**. The goal of this policy was to prevent the spread of communism as an ideology and limit Soviet influence. The first actions of the containment strategy occurred far away from either the United States or the Soviet Union, in the Mediterranean, the Middle East, and Asia, areas which had been somewhat removed from the main frontlines of World War II and which had yet to come decisively under either American or Soviet spheres of influence. In late 1945, for example, in what became known as the **Iran Crisis,** the United States gave military and political support to the anti-communist Shah (king) of Iran and helped him to expel Soviet forces occupying northern Iran. The following year, the United States gave military and economic aid to the anti-communist side of the **Greek Civil War**, and, in Turkey, sent warships to help blockade the Turkish straits from Soviet ships.

Key Early Events in Cold War

Began	Event	Outcome
Novemeber 1945	**Iran Crisis**	U.S. puts political and military pressure on Soviet Union to withdraw of Soviet armies from northern Iran.
March 1946	**Greek Civil War**	U.S. gives miliary and economic aid to the Greek National Government, the anti-communist side of the Greek civil war.
August 1946	**Turkish Straits Crisis**	U.S. sends warships to protect Turkish shipping routes from Soviet aggression.

Key Questions: What you need to know

• How did the Cold War begin and where were the earliest conflicts?
• What were the economic, military, and cultural considerations of the early cold war?

The most significant measures of the early containment strategy, however, occurred in Asia. At the conclusion of World War II, China quickly resumed a decades-long civil war between the nationalist Kuomintang, led by Chiang Kai-Shek and the Communist Party of China, led by Mao Zedong. The United States gave significant support to the Kuomintang, supplying military equipment and sending over 400 million dollars of economic aid to Shek's armies. The Soviet Union gave corresponding help to the communist side, and, eventually, after a series of decisive victories in southern China, the communist leader Mao Zedong prevailed driving the nationalist armies to the island of Taiwan. It was here, near the narrow strait of water that separates Taiwan from mainland China, that the United States positioned several battleships in order to prevent the Communist Party from unifying all of China under communist rule. Until 1972, the United States refused to recognize Communist Party as the legitimate government of China, giving its United Nations security council seat to Taiwan.

The bloodiest confrontation in Asia between communism and anti-communism, however, would come in Korea, which, at the end of WWII, had been divided between communist north and the nationalist south. In 1950, with military equipment supplied by the Soviet Union, the north invaded the south, taking the capital of Seoul, and driving the South Korean armies to a tiny defensive position in Pusan. Unwilling to allow another country in Asia to fall under communist control, the United States sent 300,000 soldiers to South Korea--making a surprise landing at Incheon and pushing the North Korean armies back to the Chinese border. The Chinese responded with a counter-invasion, as over a million Chinese soldiers poured south of the Yalu river, forcing the American and South Korean forces back toward the so-called "38th-parallel"--a defensive line that would later come to define the official border of North Korea and South Korea. By the time the fighting was over, in 1953, over three million soldiers and civilians had been killed.

(Fig 11.5) **American warships** off the coast of China during Chinese Civil War	(Fig 11.6) **American tanks** in South Korea during the Korean War.

Key Vocabulary

Containment: Also known as the **Truman Doctrine**--the United States' policy of intervening militarily and economically in order to prevent communism from spreading.

Chinese Civil War: 1946-1949, war between the Communist Party of China and the nationalist Kuominting. The communists won control over mainland China while the nationalists retreated to the island of Taiwan.

Korean War: 1950-1953, After the communist north invaded the nationalist south, the United States intervened sending 300,000 soldiers to the Korean peninsula. After the Chinese intervened on the communist side, the war ended in a stalemate along the 38th parallel.

Meanwhile, what had been happening back in Europe? As communist and anti-communist armies were fighting each other in Asia, the superpowers supporting either side were locked in a state of tension and confrontation on old, familiar battegrounds. In 1948, Soviet armies, eager to isolate the United States from their outpost in Western Berlin, imposed a military blockade of the city, allowing no supplies, including food and medicine, to be shipped in. The west responded with the **Berlin Airlift**, a series of flights over Berlin from which supplies were dropped by parachute. The following year, deciding that regional cooperation was needed to check Soviet hostility, the United States and the countries of western Europed formed the **North Atlantic Treaty Organization (NATO)**, a mutual defense agreement in which member countries agreed to defend one another in the event of a Soviet attack. NATO, an example of **collective security**, saw the establishment of networks of military cooperation among member countries, the sharing of intelligence, the establishment of joint military bases, and the positioning of weaponry, including nuclear missiles, strategically across borders. The Soviet Union responded to NATO with collective security agreements of its own. Though the Soviet Union and its satellite states had been allied since the end of World War II--an alliance which the Soviet Union largely controlled through an institution that came to be known as **Cominform**--in 1955 it would tighten its alliance through the **Warsaw Pact Agreement**. The agreement, signed by the Soviet Union and seven of its satellite states, pledged military cooperation and mutual defense in the event of western aggression and entailed military cooperation parallel to that of NATO.

(Fig 11.7) NATO and Warsaw Pact Countries

The tension between the west and the Soviet Union was not limited to the military. Early in the Cold War, the United States realized that the economic and cultural dimensions of the competition with communism would prove just as important. As part of the containment strategy, therefore, the United States instituted **the Marshall Plan**, a program of direct economic aid to countries in western Europe. The program had three goals: first to help its allies rebuild after the devastation of World War II, secondly to prevent the "harsh peace" conditions which had led to revanchement in Germany after World War I, and, most importantly, to create economic prosperity so that the people in western Europe would not be tempted by communist ideologies. From 1948-1951, the Marshall plan provided billions of dollars in economic support to Britain, France, Italy, Wesetern Germany, Turkey, and Greece.

Finally, on the cultural side, the United States enacted a series of domestic policies designed to limit the appeal of the communist ideology. Due to government subsidies to artists, writers, and entertainers, the theme of "anti-communism" became prevalent in much of American film, literature, and art. Other measures proved somewhat more restrictive. During the period of time known as **the second red scare**, the United States aggressively investigated individuals suspected of being sympathetic to communism. The **House on Un-American Activities**, conspired to prevent certain actors and screenwriters from working in Hollywood, and in 1950, Senator Joseph McCarthey led a series of anti-communist investigations of actors, lawyers, congressmen, and members of the military in an attempt to reveal and prosecute "secret communists." So-called **McCarthyism** reflected a deep hostility, verging on paranoia, among the American people about the threat of communism.

Key Questions: What you need to know

• What were the economic measures of the Truman doctrine?
• What were the political measures?
• What were the military measures?

(Fig 11.8) Much of Europe was rebuilt with Marshall Plan funds

The Cuban Missile Crisis and Proxy Wars (1962-1969)

If there was ever a moment, in this period, when it seemed inevitable that the Cold War would turn "hot,"it happened in October of 1962. The United States, under the policy of containment, had steadily been giving military and economic aid to anti-communist forces around the world. At the same time, it had steadily been increasing the size of its own military and building more and more nuclear weapons. In 1961, President Kennedy had installed nuclear weapons and missile launchers in Turkey, capable of delivering a nuclear strike nearly anywhere in the Soviet Union. The Soviet Union, in response, had increased its aid to communist forces, particularly in South America. In 1959, the communist Fidel Castro, with Soviet help, seized power in Cuba, only 90 miles from the American coast. Two years later, the United States attempted a disastrous counter-revolution, arming and training Cuban exiles and launching a failed invasion in what became known as **The Bay of Pigs**.

The operation was a fiasco and embarrassment for the United States, and the Soviet Union saw the failure as an opportunity to put pressure on America by increasing the strength of communist forces nearby. Countering the US installation of missiles in Turkey, the Soviet Union, the following year, began to install nuclear weapons in newly communist Cuba. The operation, which was quickly uncovered by American spy planes, resulted in a moment of near panic on the part of the American military. The missiles, once operational, would have been able to strike nearly all major cities on the east coast. Many high-ranking generals in the United States favored an immediate bombing campaign against missile sites, an act to which the Soviet Union would have likely responded with a counter-attack, perhaps with nuclear weapons. Fortunately, President Kennedy opted for a more conservative strategy, placing a naval blockade around Cuba. For ten days, the world held its breath, as military action seemed imminent. At one point, two out of the three officers on a Soviet nuclear submarine, believing war had already begun, ordered the launch of Russian nuclear warheads. It was only the restraint of the third officer, **Vasily Arkhipov,** who prevented the launch, and, in so doing, perhaps saved the world from nuclear holocaust. In the end, cooler heads prevailed. Soviet premier Nikita Krushcev agreed to withdraw Russian missiles from Cuba and President Kennedy agreed (though the agreement was never announced publicly) to withdraw American missiles from Turkey.

Key Vocabulary

Bay of Pigs: Following the communist takeover of Cuba, the American CIA trained a small force of Cuban exiles to overthrow the Castro regime. The operation failed and was a major embarrassment to the United States.

Cuban Missile Crisis: Following the Soviet attempt to install nuclear missiles in Cuba, the United States instituted a naval blockade in a stand-off that very nearly led to war.

Following the near-war of the Cuban Missile Crisis, both the United States and the Soviet Union realized that tensions were leading to a high level of danger and that **deescalation** was needed. The first step was to attempt to increase diplomacy, so, in June of 1963, a special communication device, the **Washington-Moscow Hotline** was installed in both the White House and the Kremlin. The device used "teletype," a precursor to the fax machine, in order to link the two offices. In a time of crisis, President Kennedy could send a message directly to Premier Kruschev, and vice versa. The same year, in August, the United States and the Soviet Union signed the **Partial Test Ban Treaty**, an agreement to stop testing nuclear weapons above ground. Both of these efforts were intended to reduce the levels of tension between the superpowers and decrease the imminent threat of war.

Despite these attempts, the remainder of the 1960's did not see a significant reduction in either tension or violence. The United States, under the leadership of Kennedy, and, after his assassination in 1964, Lyndon Johnson, continued the policy of containment. In 1965, the United States intervened in civil wars in both the Thailand and the Dominican Republic, supporting anti-communist forces, and briefly occupying the latter country. However, the most historically significant intervention of the period was the **Vietnam War**. As early as 1959 the United States had sent South Vietnam "advisors" whose job it was to help the nationalist government resist the communist north. Over the early 1960's, as the communist "Vietcong," aiming to reunite the country, had intensified its guerilla campaign against the south, the United States had gradually increased the number of advisors and had supported the South Vietnamese military with airstrikes. Finally, in December 1965, after a particularly violent North Vietnamese offensive, the United States committed to a wholescale military intervention. 200,000 troops were deployed to South Vietnam, beginning a lengthy, bloody, and ultimately futile effort to protect the south from a communist takeover. The ten-year war would prove to be widely unpopular and would be remembered as one of the major failures of the containment strategy.

Meanwhile, the Soviet Union had gradually come to adopt a similar containment strategy. In 1968, the government of the satellite state Czechoslovakia, under the leadership of Alexander Dubcek, had begun to institute liberal reforms to the Soviet system. Dubcek's government instituted economic reforms, eased political censorship and strengthened diplomatic relations with western countries. His reforms, known as "**socialism with a human face,**" were perceived as a threat in the USSR which feared losing its "buffer" against the capitalist west. In response, Soviet Premier Breznev proclaimed, "When forces that are hostile to socialism try to turn the development of some socialist country towards capitalism, it becomes...a common problem and concern of all socialist countries." His remarks, which encapsulated the **Breznev Doctrine**, meant that the Soviet Union was willing to intervene in any socialist country that attempted reform. In August of 1968, Breznev sent 200,000 troops into Czechoslovakia and violently reintroduced stricter communist control. The event, known as the **Prague Spring**, harmed the Soviet Union's reputation abroad but made it clear to the international community that both the west and the east were more than willing to protect their spheres of influence by force.

(Fig 11.8) President Kennedy (far right) meeting with his generals during the Cuban Missile Crisis in 1963.

(Fig 11.9) The **Washington-Washington Hotline** was set up following the Cuban Missile Crisis in 1963.

Fig 11.10 Prague protesters during the 1968 "Prague Spring." The Soviet Union's military intervention defined the Brezhnev Doctrine, refusing popular sovereignty to USSR satellite states.

(Fig 11.11) American bombers over Vietnam during "Operation Linebacker" in 1972. The Vietnam war represented one of the biggest failures of the containment strategy.

1970-1980 Detente and Rapprochment

The election of **Richard Nixon** in 1968 saw a shift of American policy towards the Soviet Union. Though Nixon was an anti-communist, he entered office declaring that the "time for negotiation" had arrived. His presidency was marked by a gradual reduction in tensions, known as **detente.** In 1969, representatives of the United States and the Soviet Union met in Finland and began discussing what would be known as the first **Strategic Arms Limitation Treaty** (SALT I). The treaty aimed at limiting the number of nuclear weapons in the American and Soviet stockpiles. Both the United States and the Soviet Union would retain enough nuclear weapons to destroy each other in the event of war (the idea of **mutually assured destruction** had long been part of the military policies of both countries), but the treaty would prevent the necessity of endless military one-upmanship.

Nixon also hoped to improve relations with China. Here, his political strategy was perhaps a touch opportunistic. Relations between China and the Soviet Union had been growing contentious after a series of disagreements known as the **Sino-Soviet split**. In 1969, a border disagreement led to a brief skirmish between the two powers in which dozens of soldiers were killed. Seeing the tension as a chance to weaken and isolate the Soviet Union, Nixon made generous diplomatic overtures toward China. He visited the country in 1972, meeting Chairman Mao, touring Beijing, and setting up a series of ping-pong matches between the American and Chinese national teams. Though some American newspapers ridiculed Nixon's efforts at **"ping-pong diplomacy,"** the visit was largely successful and established a new friendly relationship, or **rapprochement**, between the two countries. Rapprochement was key in the economic liberalization that China would undergo, in the late 70's, under the leadership of **Deng Xiaoping** and laid the groundwork for increasing cooperation between American and Chinese business interests.

| **(Fig 11.12) During Rapprochement**, U.S. President Richard Nixon and Zhou Enlai address crowds in Beijing. | **(Fig 11.13)** Richard Nixon greeting Mao Zedong. The US would recognize the legitimacy of the PRC for the first time. |

Key Vocabulary

SALT I: The first 'Strategic Arms Limitation Treaty' signed by the United States and the Soviet Union in 1972.

Rapprochement: The United States' establishment of friendly relations with China, following a visit by Richard Nixon in 1972.

The Beginning of the End (1980-1990)

The period of detente continued through the presidency of Jimmy Carter in the late 1970's. In 1979, Carter and Breznev signed another Strategic Arms Limitation Treaty (SALT II)--agreeing to further reductions in military stockpiles. A change, however, occurred later in the year. After a revolution on the part of the Muslim "mujahideen" against the communist government of Afghanistan, the Soviet Union, following the same "Brezhenv Doctrine" that had led them to intervene in Czechsolovaika a decade earlier, invaded with almost half-a-million soldiers. The act of aggression unsettled the NATO countries which had hoped detente would lead to a more peaceful, less interventionist international order. During the same year, Iranian protesters stormed and occupied the American embassy in Tehran, taking 52 American diplomats hostage. Though the **Iranian Hostage Crisis** was not explicitly related to detente, the takeover led many Americans to fear that American foreign policy had grown too passive.

This fear led, in part, to the election of Ronald Reagan in 1980. A representative of the growing **neoliberal movement**, in American politics, Reagan promised a more vigorous and confrontational foreign policy. Detent, he argued, had allowed the Soviet Union to continue its aggression while the United States had retreated from global leadership. Reagan's administration increased the American military budget, rejecting the restraint of the SALT treaties. He coordinated military exercises with NATO allies, aided the Afghani mujahideen in the war with the Soviet Union, and invested in an expensive missile defense system which came to be known as **"Star Wars."** In his political rhetoric, Reagan was more hawkish than any president had been since Truman, labeling the Soviet Union an "evil empire" and vowing to defend the free world against any aggression. Though the policies were highly controversial, with many fearing that his reckless military expansion would lead to a disastrous war, Reagan believed that enlarging the American military would put pressure on the Soviet Union, which, eventually, would prove to be too much for the overextended empire.

Things in the Soviet Union, Reagan knew, were not altogether stable. The Soviet military intervention in Afghanistan had proved extraordinarily costly. The Soviet command economy, in which all production decisions were undertaken by the state, was growing more and more inefficient, limiting the Soviet Union's ability to achieve economic growth. Finally, in the years following the Prague Spring, there had been simmering discontent among the Soviet satellite states, with political leaders throughout Eastern Europe calling for more freedom.

When Michael Ghorbachev became the Soviet premier in 1985, he knew that changes had to be made. One of his first decisions was to begin formulating an exit strategy for the war in Afghanistan. Although it would take nearly half a decade for the Soviet Union to complete its withdrawal, Ghorbachev's desire to pull the Soviet military back marked the end to the Brezhnev Doctrine and the beginning of what would be known as the **Sinatra Doctrine** in which the Soviet Union began to accept the right of other communist states to administer their own internal affairs. This policy, in effect, sent a message to the satellite states: they were free to make reforms, and the Soviet Union, for its part, would not intervene as it had done in Czechoslovakia and Afghanistan. Poland was the first of the satellite states to break away. In April of 1989, facing an economic crisis, the government agreed to hold free parliamentary elections. A few months later, the first non-communist government in over 50 years took power. Hungary was next. Followed by East Germany, where the infamous "Berlin Wall" was demolished in November. Next came Romania. By the end of 1989, in what became known as **the Autumn of Nations**, 26 former socialist states had allowed democratic elections. In none of them did communist governments retain power.

Meanwhile, back in Moscow, Ghorbachev was putting into place unprecedented reforms: *glastnost,* or political openness; and *perestroika,* or economic restructuring. Though Ghorbachev did not intend for these reforms to end the rule of the communist party it was not long before they did just that. *Perestroika* allowed for market reforms in the command economy, and *glastnost* allowed for more open and democratic debate. In 1989, for the first time in the history of the Soviet Union, competitive democratic elections were held in the Republic of Russia. Two years later (following a brief period of political turbulence), the communist party agreed to relinquish its hold on power. The nationalist Boris Yeltsin was elected, defeating the communist candidate 57%-16%. In one of the first acts of his presidency, he signed the Strategic Arms Reduction Treaty (START I) with the United States, drastically limiting the number of nuclear weapons in the Russian stockpile. The election of Yeltsin, along with the adoption of START, according to most historians, marked the "official end" of the Cold War.

Questions for discussions:

• The US and the Soviet Union avoided direct war during the Cold War. Does that mean the institutions of the Liberal International Order (LIO) did what they were supposed to do? Or was the Cold War "bloody enough" without direct war? Was this period in history a success or a failure for institutionalism?

• How does the Cold War period compare to the Great Powers period?

(Fig 11.14) Soldiers in Afghanistan, The invasion of Afghanistan in 1978 was a significant factor in the collapse of the USSR.

(Fig 11.15) Mikhail Ghorbachev's reforms brought economic and political changes to the Soviet Union.

Fig 11.16 In West Berlin, **Ronald Reagan** tells Ghorbachev "tear down this wall." Regan adopted a significantly more confrontational policy than other American presidents to the USSR.

(Fig 11.17) Crowds gather on the **Berlin Wall** in 1989 to celebrate its demolition. The event is often considered the symbolic end of the Cold War.

Summing Up: Key Chapter Points

1) The Cold War began due to mutual distrust between the western powers and the Soviet Union, combined with Stalin's refusals to withdraw his armies as he had promised at Potsdam and Yalta.

2) Early in the Cold War, the United States decided on a policy of containment, which included military, economic, and political measures designed to prevent Soviet expansion.

3) Throughout the 1960's, both the United States and the Soviet Union aggressively protected their interests in a series of interventions and proxy wars.

4) Following the election of Richard Nixon a period of "detente" occurred during which tensions between the United States and the Soviet Union decreased.

5) During the presidency of Ronald Reagan, the United States increased its military budget in order to put pressure on the Soviet Union, which had been weakened by a costly intervention in Afghanistan.

6) This pressure, along with Ghorbachev's policies of *Glastnost* and *Perestroika*, eventually led to the collapse of the Soviet Union and the end of the Cold War.

CHAPTER 12: DECOLONIZATION

> **Overview**
>
> This chapter tells the complicated story of decolonization, focussing on the motives, consequences, and paradoxes of the period. In particular we examine
>
> - The different political actors and their interests (The United Kingdom, France, The Soviet Union, the colonial elites, the colonized peoples, western settlers, western populations, the United Nations)
> - The different challenges faced by decolonized states (nation-building, security, economic development)
> - The difficult choices that decolonized states have had to make as they integrate into the global community.

While the Cold War was raging in the latter half of the twentieth century, another important political process was underway which has shaped global politics of the world today: decolonization. As we covered in chapter 8, the vast majority of the world, by the beginning of the 20th century, was either under direct or indirect European control. European powers—most notably Great Britain—but increasingly the United States—dominated the politics and institutions of smaller nations everywhere. After World War II ended, from the years, roughly, 1955-1985, nearly all of these colonized nations became independent nation-states.

It is tempting to view decolonization as a story of the triumph of formerly oppressed peoples winning their independence from the Great Powers. Unfortunately, the story was more complicated than that. It engaged a number of political actors in relationships that were sometimes cooperative, sometimes confrontational, and sometimes a paradoxical combination of both. To start, we can identify the major groups, each with its own interests. There was:

The United Kingdom: For over one hundred years, the United Kingdom had dominated the largest empire in the world. After World War II, however, it became apparent its global hegemony was not sustainable. The human and economic costs of the Second World War, most significantly the wreckage left by German bombing, meant that the UK's priorities had to be on domestic rebuilding. They had neither the resources nor the energy nor the political motivation to continue to be "invested" in their empire. In addition, the UK faced pressure from **nationalist** groups in the colonies with political actors in one nation after another agitating for independence. In addition it faced strong pressure, both moral and economic, from its ally the United States, who, on one level, believed imperialism was inconsistent with the principles of the Liberal International Order, and, on another more nakedly self-interested level, wanted to extend its economic and political influence over lands which had long enjoyed exclusive trading partnerships with the UK.

France: Though Britain realized that it would have to let go of its empire eventually and was resigned to do so without (too much) of a fight, France, who had been humiliated in World War II, was more reluctant to give up its colonial holdings. After its occupation by Germany, nationalist politicians under the leadership of Charles de Gaul were motivated to fight for the continued status of France as a major global power. Between 1945 and 1980, France fought wars against pro-independence groups in Vietnam (1945-1954), Madagascar (1947-1948), Algeria (1954-1962), Tunisia (1961), Cameroon (1955-1964,), and Zhaire (1977, 1978). These wars, particularly in North Africa, were protracted, bloody, and futile. In all cases, France was forced to abandon its colonies. The consequences of these wars have proved traumatic both for the French and for the decolonized nations, and led to significant political and demographic challenges continuing into the 21st century.

The United States: When World War II ended, the United States was quick to implement the **Marshall Plan** in order to rebuild Europe and solidify the partnerships that would form the Liberal International Order. The plan marked the start of the US's robust engagement in global affairs, its eagerness to be a political, economic, and military leader. Though it had moral reasons for being in favor of decolonization (the Wilsonian ideal of national self-determination, for one), it had economic reasons as well. By breaking up the British hold on the colonies, it would be freer to do business with and exert its influence over colonial markets. In many places, American businesses and investors entered and began instituting a kind of "soft imperialism" or "market imperialism" in areas vacated by the British.

The Soviet Union: The Soviet Union, however, would be unwilling to let the United States take over in the developing world. In much of the former western colonies, the Soviet Union was quick to supply political, economic, and military aid to communist nationalist groups. The influence of the Soviet Union in the former colonies led to a **bipolar order**, a global split between western-allied nations and Soviet-allied nations. At times, this split was merely a matter of economic competition and political influence. At other times (as in decolonized Vietnam) it led to proxy wars. Many newly independent nation-states felt the need to choose sides between the United States and the Soviet Union, a decision which could be dangerous since choosing one partner often meant inciting the wrath of the other. Many new nations were understandably unwilling to make such a choice and joined the **non-aligned movement** (NAM), a group of countries that did not want to side with either of the major powers.

The Colonial Elites: Among the wealthiest and most influential inhabitants of the colonies were those who had the most paradoxical relationship to the west. In many respects, the colonial elites were the most westernized of their people. In most cases, they had been educated in Europe, spoke European languages, and had thrived within the European system. They had risen within the imperial powers to become lawyers or journalists or entrepreneurs. In many cases, however, these elites proved to be the most energetic leaders of post-war nationalist movements. Perhaps the most obvious example is **Mahatma Ghandi**. Fluent in English and educated at law school in London, Ghandi nonetheless, quickly became one of the fiercest advocates for Indian independence. The reasons for nationalism among the colonial elites are multifaceted: partly having to do with a nativist patriotism and partly having to do with feelings of resentment toward *European* elites (i.e., the sense that a well-educated lawyer from Bombay would always come in second to a well-educated white lawyer from London). Finally, it would be naive to assume that a desire for power did not underlie their ambition, the realization that, with the Europeans gone, the new countries would be "theirs" to rule.

Colonial Populations: During the age of imperialism, colonized peoples tended to be lumped into one mass: the marginalized "natives" who needed to be bettered through western patronage. During the early period of decolonization, this sense of homogeneity continued (and was often encouraged by colonial elites) as the narrative was framed in populist terms of the "imperial occupier" and "the nationalist resistance." However, after decolonization, it quickly became clear that colonial populations were just as complex, contradictory, and historically messy as populations anywhere else. In many of the newly independent nation-states rival factions, divided along religious, racial, or tribal lines fought fiercely for power. European efforts to prevent this problem by partitioning the new nation-states along identitarian lines (in India/ Pakistan, for example, or Israel/ Palestine) often made matters worse. Nationalist groups, who believed such partitions took place against their consent, waged campaigns, often violent, to "fix" the borders that Europeans had drawn.

In this respect, it is hardly surprising that no small numbers of colonial inhabitants, particularly the small but not negligible middle classes, decided that they preferred the relative political stability and economic opportunity of the west to the new nation-states which they had inherited. The period of decolonization saw the beginning of increasing immigration to the west as many liberated colonials became either economic or war refugees. The expansion of commercial airfare, along with other technological improvements in the years following the war, made such immigration quicker and cheaper than it ever had before. Many of these new immigrants would fill low-wage jobs in the west leading to class divisions in western nations becoming increasingly intertwined with questions of race or ethnicity.

Western Populations: Western populations during the period of decolonization, in general, can be divided into two groups: **settlers** who had lived in the colonies (sometimes for generations) and often enjoyed economic or political privilege in the imperial system, and those who lived at home in Europe, seemingly unaffected by the goings-on across the world. Among those who lived in the colonies, many simply chose to return to Europe as the colonies gained their independence. The so-called **pied-noirs** who migrated from Algeria and Tunisia back to France following the French wars of decolonization are perhaps the most noteworthy example, but there are countless others. Among the Europeans who chose to stay, some integrated themselves into the new nation-states, using their talents and experience to help the new regimes. Others, fearing marginalization or persecution from the newly enfranchised majorities, "closed ranks," sealing themselves off in gated communities, hiring private security, or forming militias. Still others (most notably in Zimbabwe/Rhodesia and in South Africa, (both of which had gained a degree of de facto independence prior to World War II) attempted to hold onto power. These powerful Europeans formed minority governments often, as in the Apartheid system in South Africa, marginalizing the majorities along racial lines.

As for the westerners at home, although one might think that remained unaffected by decolonization, this was far from true. As immigration increased, from colonies and former colonies to the west, many westerners felt threatened by an influx of people with whom they felt they had little in common. At the same time that immigrants were increasingly coming in, many working class manufacturing jobs were beginning to go out. Improved technology and logistics in the post-war world, increasing investment in decolonized nation-states would lead, particularly in the 1970's and 1980's, to the globalization of manufacturing. Factories which had once been a fixture in Europe and the United States relocated to China and India as businesses, attracted by cheap labor and exploiting more efficient supply chains, moved production abroad. This combination of increased immigration and outsourced labor, led to increased resentment among working-class westerners who blamed immigrants for "stealing" jobs, taking over their neighborhoods, changing their culture, and increasing the crime rates. Again, this reaction was framed not only in nationalist but often in racialist language. As a result, the period of decolonization saw an increase in **nativist** and **ethno-nationalist** movements in the west, a resistance among white Europeans to demographic changes.

The United Nations: Last but not least, the newly established United Nations played a role in welcoming the new countries into the community of nations. As more became independent, the General Assembly of the United Nations grew proportionally. Although most had small economies and insignificant "hard power," they were often able to join together to drive the conversation at the UN. In 1960, the UN's **Declaration on the Granting of Independence to Colonial Countries and Peoples** declared that "the subjection of peoples to alien subjection.... constitutes a denial of fundamental human rights...and is an impediment to world peace." It further affirmed the "right to self-determination...freely pursue their economic, social, and cultural development." The declaration was taken to be an attempt to legitimize decolonization, and much of its language indeed paved the way for the liberation of Africa in the 1960's. Four years later, the UN created the United Nations Conference on Trade and Development (UNCTAD) which attempted to modify the Bretton Woods economic system in order to create a more favorable system for decolonized countries. In particular the UNCTAD attempted to allow decolonized countries the right to more easily nationalize their economies, taking control of their factories and farms from the major corporations which, at the time, were still largely dominated by Europeans.

(Fig 12.1) As more refugees came to Europe on cheap commercial air flights, there was a nativist backlash against them. British politician Enoch Powell famously declared that the influx of non-white immigration would lead to **rivers of blood** in England.

(Fig 12.2) Though Great Britain gave up its colonies without a fight, France engaged in a series of brutal wars. This propaganda poster, outside of an Algierian barbershop says, *The Algerian Revolution: A people at war against a barbaric colonizer.*

Key Questions: What you need to know:

• Why would not think of decolonization as a simple story of oppressed peoples "winning" their independence?
• Consider the political actors above: who are the allies? Who are the adversaries? Can you tell? What do these complex entanglements tell us about decolonization in general?

Challenges and Paradoxes

Decolonization, it is sometimes easy to forget, did not happen in the same way everywhere. Some nations—for example, the relatively small countries in the West Indies which had, even before independence a great deal of autonomy—transitioned with minimal turbulence. Others, such as the oil-nations in the Arabic Gulf, endured a period of growing pains, before eventually achieving rapid economic and political prosperity by taking advantage of natural resources and trade partnerships. Still others descended into a period of instability from which they have yet to fully recover. Yet, though decolonization did not happen the same way everywhere, almost all decolonized countries have faced, in one form or another, roughly the same set of challenges: security, nation-&-state building, questions of identity, conflicts with settled populations, and economic development.

Violence and Security: In reflecting on the security challenges of decolonized nations, we may remember our quote from Charles Tilly from Chapter 2: "War made the state, and the state made war." Not only were most of the new states formed as a consequence of warfare (primarily the fallout of World War II), but, for many of them, it would prove impossible to establish an independent state without first experiencing civil war and other forms of protracted political violence. In general, there were three sources of violence for decolonized states. First, there were the old imperial powers unwilling to give up their empires.

Figure 12.3 Portuguese soldiers in Angola during the Portuguese Colonial War (1961). Though the Portuguese military was better equipped, the Angolans would eventually achieve independence. Unfortunately, civil war broke out soon after.	**Figure 12.4** *Force Publique* soldiers during the **Congo Crisis** (1960). The Belgian occupation of the Congo was long and bloody and has led to significant postcolonial resentment among those who remember the excesses of the Belgian military.	**Figure 12.5** British soldiers crossing a stream during the Mau Mau Uprising (1952-1960). Though Britian was mostly willing to give up its colonies, it fought a number of guerilla wars and skirmishes in the 1960's and 1970's.

We have already mentioned France, and its wars in Northern Africa (Tunisia, Algeria, Morocco, Madagascar, Cameroon and Zhaire) as well as Vietnam. There was also the **Portuguese Colonial War** in which Mozambique, Angola, and Guinea Bissau rose up against and succeeded in winning their independence from Portugal. There was the **Mau Mau Uprising** in Kenya against the British, and the **Congo Crisis** in which various Congolese fought against the Belgian *force publique*. In all of these cases, the conflict was often framed in terms of "the rightful people" against the "foreign occupier," and the goal, for the nationalist militias was often *not* to outright defeat the Europeans on the battlefield but simply to wear them out, score political points, and make them realize that maintaining their colonies would be more trouble than it was worth.

A second (and often more severe) source of violence would prove to be the ethnic, religious, or tribal interests of the decolonized states. Culturally differentiated groups, often with diametrically opposed viewpoints, often immediately began fighting to fill the power vacuum the Europeans had left. Perhaps the most well-known example of this is the series of wars fought in India following the British withdrawal and the **Partition of India** in which Muslim and Hindu populations were given independent states. Between 1947 and 1971, no fewer than five wars (and several smaller skirmishes) occurred in India as Hindu and Muslim populations battled over borders and the rights to control the newly formed institutions. There are many other examples, in the period of decolonization, of wars fought for roughly the same reasons. After Nigeria gained its independence from Britain in 1960, for example, the new country split into five ethnically distinct regions. In 1967, a conflict broke out between (primarily) the Igbo people and Yoruba people, partially over control of the oil-rich south. As many as two-million civilians were killed during the three year conflict. In Rwanda, immediately after the Belgians left in 1959, long-standing conflict between the Hutu majority and the Tutsi minority erupted into violence. The civil war, which lasted two years, is frequently identified as a major causal factor in the notorious **Rwandan Genocide** in 1994. Again, the appearance of such conflicts during the period of decolonization should not be surprising. Tempting as it is to homogenize the colonized peoples as "the oppressed," the fact is that, in all decolonized nations, as in all nations everywhere in the world, age-old political tensions and rivalries had formed domestic faultlines which, in the absence of strong institutions, easily gave way to violence.

A final source of postcolonial violence was the global political turbulence which was caused by the Cold War. As new and relatively undeveloped countries, the decolonized states often had little choice but to turn to "the developed world" for economic, security, and technological assistance. The problem was that the developed world was locked in a dangerous military stand-off. Going to the United States or its allies for help meant, more or less, becoming a target of the Soviet Union. Going to the Soviet Union meant becoming a target of the United States. This put new nations in a difficult position. Some, such as those in the Arabic gulf, were able to use the situation to their advantage, inviting Americans to set up military bases in their countries. Though this meant a loss of sovereignty, it allowed for relative security and economic development. For others, the attempt to pick sides backfired. In 1946, Afghanistan adopted pro-Western policies under the leadership of Mahmoud Kahn. In response, the Soviet Union gave financial and military support to the communist Democratic Party of Afghanistan. In 1978, a bloody civil war broke out with the Soviet Union intervening on behalf of the communists. The United States, in turn, gave heavy military support to the anti-Soviet **Mujahideen**. During the nearly 10-year conflict, over 2,000,000 Afghanis were killed and domestic institutions were left in shambles. The modern chaos in Afghanistan, in no small part, can be attributed to the devastation inflicted on the country during the Cold War.

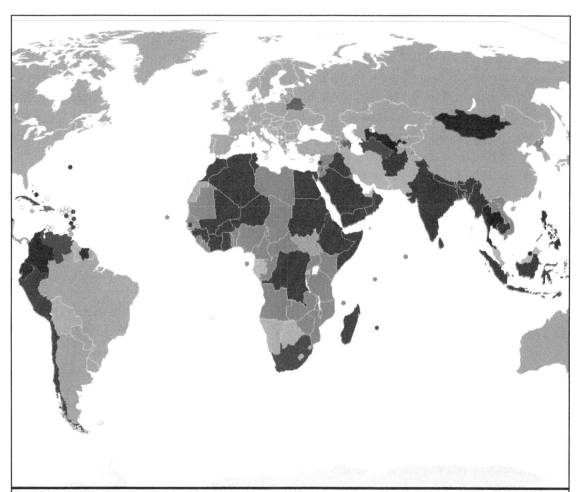

In an effort to avoid "choosing sides" between the United States and the Soviet Union, many countries, particularly in Africa, joined the **Non-Aligned Movement.** Many of them, unfortunately, got dragged into the Cold War anyway.

Date joined:
1961■1963 ■1970■1973■1976 ■1979■1983■1989 ■1993□1994–1995■1998–2000□

State-Building, National Identity, & Settled Populations: Though violence and security were often the primary threats for new nations, there were, even in times of peace, other issues that proved just as challenging. After gaining independence, new states had quite a bit of work to do in getting their new institutions to function properly. Well-funded schools, well-organized militaries, effective administration systems to oversee the economy, reliable bureaucracies for regulating currency, a fair and effective legal system, a responsible police force: all of these things, for decades, had been handled by the imperial powers. New nations often found that they lacked sufficient expertise to manage their institutions. They had too few college graduates, too few universities, and too few trained professionals to meet the needs of a modern state. Unfortunately, that meant relying on European experts, which, in the eyes of many, simply continued the asymmetries of power which had been established during the imperial period. It often proved difficult, in this regard, for the new nations to authentically differentiate themselves from their colonial past. European languages, European religions, European patterns of thought, and European social assumptions prevailed, particularly among the urban elite of the new states. What was the point of gaining independence if it only meant a perpetuation, through different political actors, of the European model?

A related problem was what to do with the (in many cases) substantial "settled populations" of Europeans. Many Europeans, after all, had lived in the colonial outposts for hundreds of years, had established families, social connections, businesses, and identities. Should these settlers still be regarded as outsiders? Complicating matters was the fact that many European whites had accumulated wealth and influence in the colonies, leading to no small amount of racial resentment between them and the majority populations. If white elites dominated positions of power in decolonized countries, isn't it arguable that the countries hadn't been decolonized at all?

Two historically instructive examples of the conflicts between settled populations and native populations are the rather different stories of South Africa and Zimbabwe. In both countries, a white minority, both before and after independence, controlled the majority of the institutions of power. South Africa, which gained nominal independence from Great Britain in 1910 and more complete independence in 1931 established a parliamentary government dominated by whites. In 1913, they passed the "Natives Land Act" making it increasingly difficult for non-whites to own land, and, from 1948-1994, operated the country under the notorious **Apartheid** system in which non-white South Africans were excluded from government positions, public accommodations, and business. These nakedly racist policies allowed South Africa's small, white minority to hold onto power without the consensus of the black majority.

After a long campaign marked by both internal armed resistance and external pressure **Nelson Mandela** and the African National Congress took power in 1994, marking the end of Apartheid and the beginning of democratic "majority rule" in South Africa. The question became, upon Mandela's election, what would happen to the white elites who had held power for so long? At the time, whites were roughly 10% of the population, yet controlled well over 80% of the country's wealth. Would they be allowed to simply keep their privileged positions? Or would property and prestige be redistributed to more adequately reflect the ethnic makeup of the country? Many of the white settlers didn't want to wait around and find out. In the year after the ANC took power, as many as a quarter million fled the country. Not only did this mean a loss of revenue for South Africa but also a loss of expertise as doctors, lawyers, teachers, and entrepreneurs relocated. Mandela quickly realized that—unjust as it may have appeared to many—it was in the best interest of South Africa to attempt to keep the white minority happy. He therefore adopted a policy of "reconciliation" with the intent of facilitating cooperation between the blacks and whites. He believed that, though such policies might be frustrating to the black majority in the short term, they would, over time, lead to significantly more harmonious social development.

Just to the north, in Zimbabwe, the story played out in almost the opposite manner. In 1965, the white minority in what was then called **Rhodesia** declared Independence from the British Empire. Great Britain (in a historical irony of the imperial power taking the side of the colonized majority *against* Europeans!) immediately imposed sanctions arguing that "independence without majority rule" would be unjust. During a 15-year period of independence, in a period marked by the **Bush War,** the white-dominated government held onto power at the barrel of a gun, using forced relocations, internment camps, and widespread military offensives to keep black nationalists out of power. By 1979, however, the Rhodesian government was on the brink of collapse. Opposed by the international community and the black majority both (and with the African Liberation movement at its height), they had no choice but, under British supervision, to hold free and fair elections. **Robert Mugabe** won a wide victory, marking the beginning of majority rule in what was then renamed Zimbabwe.

Mugabe was faced with the choice that Mandela would be faced with. What to do with the white minority that owned a vast majority of Zimbabwe's wealth? While Mandela would opt for reconciliation, Mugabe opted for a more confrontational policy. He seized the property of many of the richest whites by force (particularly that of farmers) and redistributed it to his allies. The result was economic catastrophe. The European population fled the country, taking their wealth and expertise with them. The recipients of the redistributed property lacked experience, and connections to make good use of it. Within a few years, Zimbabwe's economy had collapsed into famine and hyperinflation from which it has not yet fully recovered.

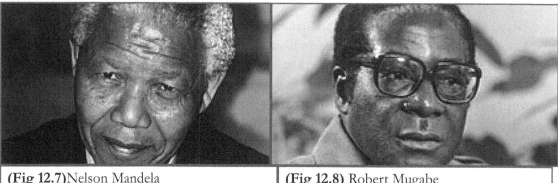

| **(Fig 12.7)** Nelson Mandela | **(Fig 12.8)** Robert Mugabe |

Economic Development: This brings us to our final challenge for decolonized countries: achieving stable economic growth. In the years following decolonization, few states had any significant independent economic infrastructure. Currencies, banks, tax systems, regulatory agencies: all of the institutions that allow for an economy to run smoothly had been managed by European powers. Though many former colonies had fairly abundant raw materials, they had yet to develop the means to capitalize on their wealth. In general, decolonized states went one of two routes. Some continued to maintain close connections to their imperial "parent country," allowing foreign companies and administrators (often for a hefty share of the profits) to run domestic businesses. Many have argued that such business ties continued the exploitation of the colonial period and kept newly decolonized states in a position of subservience and dependency. Others have argued that such arrangements were necessary to ensure stability while gradually building up domestic infrastructure. In most cases, states who retained close ties to their imperial occupier also created regional partnerships with other nearby developing countries. For example the **Economic Community of West African States** or the **Gulf Cooperation Council** established mutually supportive partnerships promoting trade and development.

Other decolonized nations followed a plan somewhat closer to the "Soviet model" of development. With high tax rates, centralized economies, and significant public power, these more socialist approaches attempted to build domestic economic infrastructure from the top down. While the justification of these more centralized policies is debatable, the economic consensus is that, in most cases, they tended to do more harm than good. During the **neoliberal revolution** (see chapter 22) of the 1980's and 1990's, the majority of formerly socialist states significantly liberalized, lowering tax rates, and increasing private power. During this time period, many followed the so-called **Washington Consensus**, a neoliberal recipe for development that the United States promoted in the developing world. The results were mixed. Some countries, like India, which liberalized in 1991, experienced rapid economic development: attracting foreign investment and boosting GDP. Others, like Brazil, Chile, and Mexico, experienced less robust results. For many political scientists, the Washington Consensus remains a controversial topic, with some arguing that it provides the best model for economic development with others maintaining that it results in nothing more than increased inequality.

Conclusion

In sum, the age of decolonization has been complex and paradoxical. It has involved a number of political actors across the world, from the old imperial powers of Great Britain and France to the newer hegemons of the United States and the Soviet Union. It has entangled colonized peoples in strange relationships, sometimes confrontational, sometimes cooperative as they struggled for self determination and control of their own institutions. It has led to challenges of establishing security, building national identity, and ensuring economic development. Though some of these challenges have been resolved as many formerly colonized states have risen from poverty and dependency to positions of power and prestige, for others, growing pains have continued well into the twenty-first century. In both cases, institutions, both global and domestic, have adapted to meet the needs of a changing world. Due to decolonization, the planet is no longer the domain of a few great European powers (see chapter 9) "managing" their dependencies, but a crowded, complex, and increasingly interconnected community of nations.

Colonizer	Decolonized Country
United Kingdom	Jordan (1946) New Zealand, India, Pakistan (1947), Myanmar, Sri Lanka, Israel, Palestine* (1948), Eritrea, Libya, (1951), Egypt, Sudan (1956), Ghana, Malaysia, (1957), Cyprus, Nigeria, Somalia (1960), Tanzania, Sierra Leone, Kuwait, Cameroon, South Africa, (1961), Uganda, Jamaica, Trinidad and Tobago (1962), Kenya, Zanzibar (1963), Zambia, Malawi, Malta (1964), Rhodesia, The Gambia, Maldives (1965) Barbados, Guyana, Botswana, Lesotho (1966), South Yemen (1967), Mauritius, Swaziland (1968), Oman (1970), Fiji, Tonga, United Arab Emirates, Bahrain, Qatar (1971), The Bahamas (1973), Grenada (1974), Seychelles (1976), Dominica, Soliman Islands, Tuvalu (1978)
France	Syria (1946), Cambodia, Laos (1953), Vietnam (1954), Tunisia, Morocco (1956), Guinea (1958), Ivory Coast, Benin, Mauritania, Niger, Burkina Faso, Mali, Senegal, Chad, Central African Republic, Republic of the Congo, Gabon, Cameroon, Togo, Madagascar, (1960), Algeria (1962), Comoros (1975), Djibouti (1977), Kiribati, St. Vincent and the Grenadines, St. Lucia, Zimbabwe, Vanuatu (1980), Belize, Antigua and Barbuda (1981), Brunei (1984)
Belgium	Democratic Republic of the Congo (1960), Rwanda, Burundi (1962)
Portugal	Guinea-Bissau (1973), Angola, Mozambique, Cape Verde, Sao Tome and Principe, East Timor (1975)
Spain	Equatorial Guinea (1968), Sahrawi Arab Democratic Republic (1976)
United States	Philippines (1946)
Netherlands	Suriname (1975)

Summing Up: Key Chapter Points:

1) The narrative of decolonization is complex.
2) It cannot be told without analyzing many competing political actors: Great Britain, the United States, France, the Soviet Union, colonial elites, the colonial majority, settled Europeans, western populations, and the United Nations.
3) Decolonized nations have faced a number of serious challenges.
4) Security challenges have sometimes been due to an aggressive former colonizer

and sometimes due to civil unrest.

5) "Reconciling" with settled Europeans has been a significant issue as the stories of South Africa and Zimbabwe illustrate.

6) Economic development, nation-building, and questions of identity have likewise led to significant "growing pains" for decolonized states.

CHAPTER 13: THE END OF HISTORY?

Overview

This chapter discusses the major developments in global politics since the end of the Cold War and the challenges faced by the Liberal International Order (LIO) in the twenty-first century. We examine:

- Fukayama's thesis of the **End of History**
- Bill Clinton's early **multilateral** policies
- The shift to **unilateralism** following the 9/11 attacks
- The continued unrest among countries outside the LIO
- Challenges faced by China, Russia, and the Middle East

The chapter concludes with a brief discussion of the **BRICS** countries and examines the possibility of a future **multipolar order** with Brazil, Russia, India, China, and South Africa each as the leaders of spheres of influence.

By the time the Cold War had come to a close, the institutions created at the end of World War II were nearly 50 years old. While the Versailles Treaty had barely lasted twenty years, the liberal international order had made it to the half-century mark. Was this a testament to the success of Churchill and Roosevelt? The wisdom of the Atlantic Charter? The foresight of Bretton Woods? Did the fact that the Cold War had ended without major war between the two global superpowers mean that these institutions had done what they were supposed to do? Or was the peaceful conclusion of the Cold War simply an accident? And how "peaceful" had the Cold War really been? Though the United States and the Soviet Union had avoided *direct* war, tens of millions of people had been killed in the proxy wars between the two powers. Two million dead in Vietnam. Three million dead in Afghanistan. Three million in Korea. Looking back on the Cold War, what does the legacy of continued international violence say about the idealism of Woodrow Wilson and his dream of global cooperation? Was the problem the liberal international order or was the problem the fact that the Soviet Union had never joined it? Or, to put all of these questions more simply, what next?

In 1992, the philosopher **Francis Fukayama** famously proposed that the answer was **"the end of history."** By this, he did not mean that the world would suddenly end. He meant that one definition of history was the record of international conflict. What defined "history" were the sharp differences between nations through which international orders had changed and developed. During the period of the Cold War, this struggle had reached a climax through the opposition between the West and the Soviet Union. The **bipolar order,** in which two superpowers were locked in ideological and economic competition, had dominated the entire world for half a century. Now, Fukayama argued, with the disappearance of the Soviet Union, that tension had been resolved. Nothing, in his view, would keep the United States and the West from achieving total global supremacy. The liberal international order would encompass the globe, and Western liberal democracy would become, as he put it, "universalized as the final form of human government." In other words, the dream of Wilson, after a long interval of struggle and resistance, would be perfected in a worldwide system of democracy, institutional norms, and integration.

Fig 13.1 Francis Fukayama	**Fig 13.2**

In the first few years after the Cold War, it seemed as if Fukayama was right. Democracy had spread through eastern Europe, leading to popularly elected governments in nearly all of the former Soviet Union. Though China was still communist, its economy had been liberalizing since Nixon's visit in 1978, and, it seemed only a matter of time before its political system, under the pressure of protestors such as those who occupied **Tiananmen Square** in 1989, would follow suit. Finally, America itself seemed eager to assume its position of leadership at the head of the global order. During the presidency of Bill Clinton (1992-2000), the United States pursued a policy of **multilateralism**: seeking the consent of the international community before taking global action and agreeing to follow the rules of the international institutions which it had helped establish. Throughout the 1990's, the United States entered into many international agreements and strengthened international institutions. Most notably it led an **expansion of NATO,** adding the

Czech Republic, Hungary, and Poland. Though there was no longer any Warsaw Pact for NATO to be "against," the expansion of the alliance seemed to indicate what Fukayama had prophesied: a gradual increase in cooperation and integration. In 1992, twelve European states--including the United Kingdom, Spain, Portugal, France, Italy, Germany (the largest and most powerful countries in western Europe) signed the **Maastricht Treaty,** the official "start" of the **European Union.** The agreement paved the way for open borders, collective security, a single currency, and economic interdependence. The divisions between European countries which, for centuries, had broken Europe into competitive rivals were blurred, if not eliminated. The political and economic power of the European states became shared and distributed in EU institutions.

To many, this idea of the new global order was appealing. Ideas of peace, democracy, and cooperation, after all, are inspiring. In addition, the liberal international order offered all nations, even small ones, a chance an opportunity to engage with the great powers of the world. Last but not least, there appeared to be a measure of safety in the idea of institutional rules. If a superpower like the United States would agree to follow the same rules as everyone else, there was less chance of it using its strength and influence to push smaller countries around.

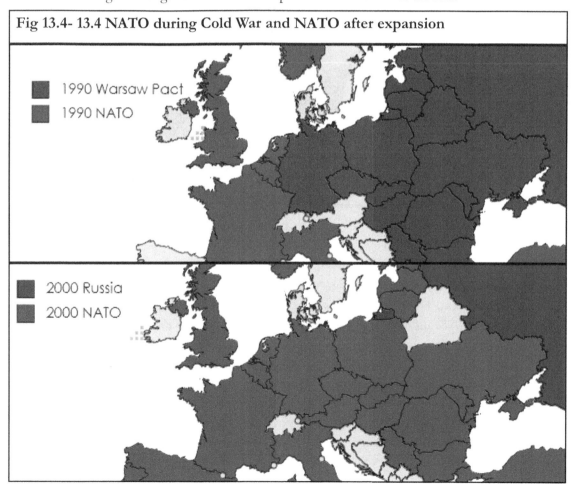

Fig 13.4- 13.4 NATO during Cold War and NATO after expansion

1990 Warsaw Pact
1990 NATO

2000 Russia
2000 NATO

Cracks in the facade: Russia, China, and the Middle East

Peace, cooperation, democracy, global harmony: what could go wrong? The first problems with Fukayama's vision occurred where any historian might have guessed they would: Russia. Though other states of the Soviet Union had managed to transition from communist economies to free-market economies relatively smoothly and, in some cases, with economic expansion, Russia had had a much harder time. The dissolution of the Soviet Union happened when Russia's economy was already strained and the sudden upheaval of the Autumn of Nations (chapter 6) put additional pressure on an already burdened system. In 1996, the Russian military launched a costly and bloody campaign in the southeastern province of **Chechnya** in order to retake it from the ethnic Chechans who had declared independence in 1991 and who (according to Russia) were oppressing the Russian-speaking population there. Though the Russians had vast superiority in men and weaponry, they were unable to win a quick victory. The campaign was a disaster and pushed the Russian economy to the brink of collapse. Two years later, in 1998, Russia defaulted on its debts in what became known as the **Russian Financial Crisis**. With the Russian currency failing, banks collapsing, and basic goods in short supply, President Yeltsin was forced to resign and Vladamir Putin took his place. Like many Russian leaders before him, Putin put the blame for Russia's economic woes on western (namely, American) hostility, pointing to the expansion of NATO as an American-led effort to surround and isolate the Russians on all sides. Under Putin, the economy of Russia stabilized, but at the cost of the democratic freedoms which were only just beginning to take hold. Under Putin's leadership, Russia became governed by a class of **oligarchs** who repressed political freedom and undid many liberal reforms. In addition, Russia, as it had during the Cold War, continued to define itself in fierce opposition to the United States and the West, seeking confrontation rather than cooperation on a number of international issues.

Key Vocabulary

Multilateralism: political action only with the consent of others--the American policy during the presidency of Bill Clinton

Maastrict Treaty: The 1992 agreement formally establishing the European Union.

Question for Discussion

In what ways might the establishment of the European Union be regarded as "Post-Westphalian?" Think about what the Peace of Westphalia (chapter 2) established. How is the EU in conflict with this idea?

Russia's Problems after the Cold War

(Fig 13.6) Economic: The Russian Financial Crisis, following the War in Chechynya, led to the resignation of Boris Yeltsin

(Fig 13.6) Political: Vladamir Putin, blaming the West for Russia's difficulties, rolls back liberal reforms.

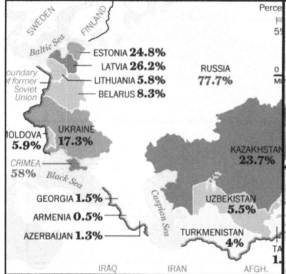

Fig 13.7 Regional: After the break-up of the Soviet Union, many non-Russians find themselves living as foreigners in non-Russian countries. (Map shows percentage of Russian speakers).

(Fig 13.8) Military: Russia would invade Chechnya in 1999 and 2009, Georgia in 2008 and in Ukraine in 2014. All of these wars brought Russia's military might into question.

Next door to Russia, the People's Republic of China proved to be another disproof of Fukayama's prophecy. Though China had liberalized its economy in 1978, transitioning, under the leadership of Deng Xioaping, from a command economy to a market one, its politics remained under the leadership of the Communist Party. In the late 1980's there had been a sporadic democratic movement in China, with protestors hoping to institute the sort of liberal reforms which had taken place in the former Soviet States. Yet the Communist Party of China was unwilling to follow their example. Instead, it tightened its control in a campaign which culminated in the 1989 **Tiananmen Square Incident**. The Chinese military dispersed protestors, imposing martial law on much of Beijing. In the following years, the Chinese Communist Party promoted ideas of "**democratic skepticism**," casting doubt on the supposed utility and benevolence of western-style democracies. Such democracies, they argued, were chaotic and unstable, leading to polarization, inequality, and inefficiency. The message was clear: though economic reforms in China had been successful, political reforms would not follow. The country would remain under the Communist Party and, therefore, would be at least partly on the outside of the LIO.

China's unwillingness to liberalize led to paradoxical consequences. On the one hand, as its economy boomed, it established important trading partnerships with the United States and the European Union. Cultural exchange followed economic cooperation, and China grew, in some ways, closer than ever before to the West. On the other hand, the Chinese and western political systems proved to be a source of tension—not only in the United Nations where the Chinese presence on the security council frequently proved oppositional—but also in southeast Asia. Japan and South Korea, who had long since joined the liberal international order, were suspicious of China's growing power. Smaller countries also feared the possibility of being swallowed up by their enormous neighbor. In 2008, ten small countries—including Singapore, the Philippines, Vietnam, Malaysia, and Thailand—signed the **"ASEAN Charter"** in an effort to form an EU-style alliance. Though the decision was motivated, in part, by economic considerations, it was also an effort to counterbalance China. Southeast Asia, therefore, has remained, in many ways, a complex "multipolar order:" with China on one side and Japan, South Korea on the other, and ASEAN somewhere in between.

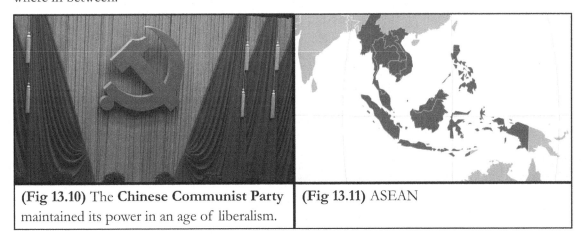

| (Fig 13.10) The **Chinese Communist Party** maintained its power in an age of liberalism. | (Fig 13.11) ASEAN |

Yet another obstacle to Fukayama's vision has been the continual turmoil in the Middle East. With few exceptions, the countries of the Middle East were "created" by the European powers after World War I and World War II. The famous **Sykes-Picot Agreement**, in 1916, divided the territory formerly controlled by the Ottoman Empire into British, French, and Italian zones of administration. Though some states (such as Egypt) were nominally independent, in reality, the entirety of the Middle East was under European rule. When World War II ended, the European powers gradually withdrew from the Middle East but left behind a land that was politically fragmented. Though all of the countries in the Middle East (with the exception of Iran) spoke Arabic and all shared a common religion in Islam, the Middle East was nonetheless broken, sometimes along tribal lines, into competing spheres of influence. Some wanted to unite all of the Middle East into one Pan-Arabic state, unified by Islam, and those who wanted to establish a secular, western-style political order. As a result, the new states quickly became dominated by autocratic governments who used the military to ensure political control. Not infrequently, the region has erupted into violence, as in the North **Yemen Civil War** (1962-1970) or the **Iran-Iraq War** (1980-1988).

Following the 9/11 attacks and the War on Terror (see following section), there has been increased violence and instability throughout the region. In the early 2010's, a series of popular uprisings, known as the **Arab Spring**, took place across many Middle Eastern countries. The motivations for these uprisings were various, with some groups wanting to overthrow the government in order to institute democratic reforms and others simply seeking to replace one authoritarian system with another. In some of the Arab Spring countries, the protests were successful in achieving beneficial reforms. In others, they had no effect, and, in still others, they escalated into full-scale civil war. Most notably among these latter cases were Libya, which became increasingly bloody and chaotic following a failed NATO intervention, and Syria, which continues to be unstable. The **Syrian Civil War** has led to at least 400,000 deaths, 3 million refugees, and the emergence of the terrorist group The Islamic State which launched an invasion of Iraq in 2014.

A related consequence of the wars in the Middle East has been the contention, in many other countries across the world, that the problem is religion: that Islam itself is prone to violence. This belief, known as **Islamophobia**, has led to nationalist policies restricting the peaceful exercise of religion. For example, in his Presidential campaign, Donald Trump advocated for (and in the early days of his presidency attempted to implement) a "Muslim Ban" preventing the travel to the United States of individuals from Muslim majority countries. Many countries in Europe (most notably France) have instituted bans on burkas and other traditional forms of Islamic clothing. Hindu nationalist parties in India have launched widespread attacks on Muslim communities in Kashmir and Assam, suspending civil rights and arresting Muslims without cause. Next door, in Burma, the Burmese military has carried out mass killings against the Rohingya Muslims of the country. Finally, in China's Xinjiang region, the government detains nearly one million Uighurs in "education camps." In all of these cases (which, of course, vary widely in severity) the governments claim that their actions are necessary to "fight terrorism."

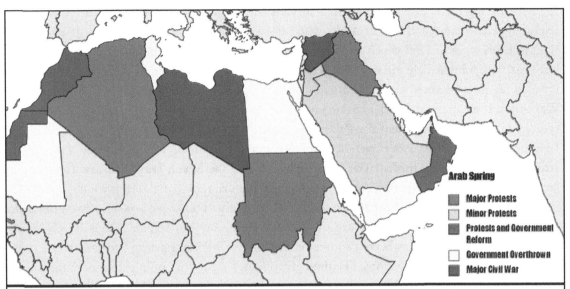

(Fig 13.11) The Arab Spring swept almost the entire Arab-speaking world in the early 2010's leading, in some cases, to major protests and the overthrow of the government.

(Fig 13.12)

Anti-Muslim protest in the Czech Republic. **Islamaphobia** has been increasing in the west since the outbreak of the **Arab Spring** and the **War on Terror**. The refugee crisis, as a result of the Syrian Civil War, sent many Syrians and others into Western Europe to seek aslyum, leading to a nativist backlash. Islamaphobia has also an intractable issue in Indian politics, with the rise of Hindu nationalism, and in Chinese politics with the government's crackdown on the Uighur population in the northern region of Xinjiang.

Israel-Palestine

One of the most intractable conflicts in the Middle East has been the continual tension in Israel and Palestine. Created by the United Nations mandate in 1948, Israel was meant to be a homeland for Jews, some of whom had long lived in the area but a majority of whom had arrived as refugees, fleeing European antisemitism. The arrival of large numbers of European Jews into the region angered many of the local Arabs who believed, not unreasonably, that the Jews had little right to possession of land which had been under Muslim rule since the days of the Persian Empire. In 1948, immediately after the United Nations mandate, a coalition of seven Arab nations invaded the newly created state and attempted to retake it. Their defeat in the first **Arab-Israeli War** not only established Israel as a (largely unwelcome) nation-state in the Middle East but also created a source of resentment for Palestinian Arabs who had been displaced from their homes. In 1967, fearing that the Arab states were planning another attack, Israel launched a preemptive strike against Egypt and Jordan. The attack, which began the **Seven Day War**, saw Israel occupy large parts of the two countries. Though Israel would return much of the land which it had taken, it continued to occupy the **West Bank** and the **Gaza Strip**. The areas, now known as **occupied Palestine**, have gained some measure of political autonomy but remain under Israeli military control. The occupation has been a source of outrage for Middle Eastern Muslims and a source of discomfort for western nations, like the United States, who, for complex political and cultural reasons, have long supported Israel. Again, the continual tensions in the Middle East are an obstacle to the expansion and the legitimacy of the liberal international order.

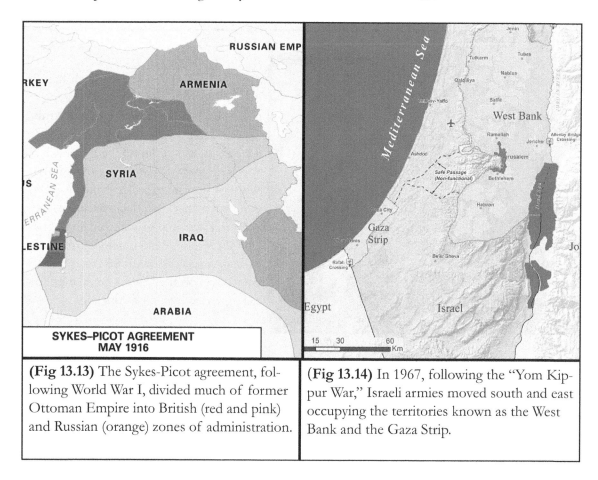

(Fig 13.13) The Sykes-Picot agreement, following World War I, divided much of former Ottoman Empire into British (red and pink) and Russian (orange) zones of administration.

(Fig 13.14) In 1967, following the "Yom Kippur War," Israeli armies moved south and east occupying the territories known as the West Bank and the Gaza Strip.

164

9/11 and the Unilateral LIO

On September 11, 2001, terrorists from **Al Qaeda** hijacked four American planes and flew them into civilian targets. The most deadly crash occurred in New York City where two planes struck the World Trade Towers, knocking them to the ground and killing nearly 3000 people. Among the most traumatic events in the 21st century, the **9/11 attacks** would lead to a sharp change in American political consciousness and foreign policy. The attacks led Americans to ask a number of troubling questions. Why had this happened? Wasn't America the global leader, a friend of democracy, peaceful and prestigious? For what reason had it become the target of such violence? The answers to those questions are complex, and are still the subject of much debate. At the time, however, it was natural to sidestep complexity and frame the events in the familiar terms of good and evil. President George W. Bush, in language that echoed the rhetoric of the Cold War, blamed the attacks on "**the Axis of Evil**," Iran, Iraq, North Korea, as well as terrorist organizations and states which supported them. The world was divided, according to Bush, into free, democratic, and tolerant societies; and those that were oppressive and hateful. It was the job of the United States and its allies to spread democratic ideals and eliminate havens for terrorism. The Bush government was willing to use military force to do so. In October of 2001, one month after the terrorist attacks, the United States began its invasion of Afghanistan, arguing that the **Taliban** government had sheltered Al Qaeda and other terrorists. Less than two years later, the United States invaded Iraq, which it had accused of manufacturing "weapons of mass destruction." These two wars, and related military interventions connected with them, began the American **War on Terror,** a series of operations targeting "state sponsors of terror" and individuals affiliated with terrorist groups.

Two key features on the War on Terror stand out in connection with the liberal international order. The first is that it was a war with a paradoxical relationship with the official "state." When the United States invaded Afghanistan, its quarrel was not *explicitly* with the Afghanistan government itself (the Taliban) but with the terrorist groups which were operating in Afghanistan, groups which had bases and leaders in multiple countries. Nonetheless, America believed that by overthrowing the government of Afghanistan, and installing a democratic system, it would prevent terrorist groups from flourishing there. The state of Afghanistan, in other words, was only a *secondary* enemy in the war. Furthermore, during the War on Terror, the United States frequently used airstrikes and drone-attacks to target individual terrorists within states with which the United States was not at war: for example, Pakistan or Yemen. Such targeted assassinations, undertaken unilaterally, could be regarded as violations of the sovereignty of non-enemy states—a violation which, of course, contradicts the central principles of the LIO.

The second key feature of the War on Terror is the paradoxical nature of America's relationship with the larger international community. Though the invasion of Afghanistan was undertaken with the support of the United Nations, America invaded Iraq without such permission. Iraq, for one thing, had not been explicitly connected to the 9/11 attacks and, for another, the evidence that it was stockpiling weapons of mass destruction was inconclusive. Prior to the invasion it was clear that the UN wanted America to pursue diplomatic methods of reconciliation further. It seemed, however, that America was willing to act, in defiance of the liberal institutions which it had itself created for the sake of its own security and self interest.

Could this claim be taken further? Is it possible to make the argument that the invasion of Iraq was really an act of outright *contempt* for the liberal international order, an effort to undermine its legitimacy? It's hard to say. The Bush administration believed (so it seemed) that the war would be quick and humane, that they would install a western-style government, and finally, that Iraq, shortly thereafter, would join the LIO. The war, in other words, so it can be argued at least, was fought to spread democracy and to strengthen its international institutions. The goal was to advance, through temporarily violent means, liberal values.

In any event, both the war in Afghanistan and the war in Iraq were highly problematic. In both countries, the United States faced a fierce insurgency and were unable to "nation build" successfully. The entrenchment of terrorist groups such as Al Qaeda and others which have arisen in the aftermath of the invasion (such as the Islamic State) have proven that America's military might alone, though formidable, is not wholly omnipotent. Finally, it remains a question as to how much the wars harmed international cooperation, weakening institutions designed to prevent such wars in the first place. At the very least, they seem to have cast doubt upon America's claim to be the moral leader of the LIO. Last but not least, the perceived failures of the wars have led to an increased call, among much of the American population, for a return to isolationism. President Trump's promise, in 2016, to put "America First" was, in many ways, a reaction against sixteen years of foreign conflict. It can be argued that America's difficulties in the wars in Iraq and Afghanistan have led to an American "retreat" from global involvement.

America: Enemy of the LIO?

During the wars in Iraq and Afghanistan the United States engaged in military actions which (at least it can be argued) violated the international norms which the United States itself had helped establish and institutionalize.

American Action	Possible Violation
Unilateral Invasion of Iraq	UN principle that wars cannot be undertaken without UN permission.
Targeted Assassinations in non-enemy states	UN principle of respect for territorial sovereignty.
Guantanamo Bay Prison	UN principles regarding due process, Territorial sovereignty of Cuba.
Advanced Interrogation Techniques	"Geneva conventions" prohibiting torture of prisoners of war.

President	Guiding Principle	Major Decisions
	Multilateralism -Expansion of NATO -Diplomatic involvement in -EU, World Bank, IMF -Investment in LIO institutions	-UN supported military intervention in Kosovo. -Kyoto Protocol on climate change -North Atlantic Free Trade Agreement
	Shift to unilateralism -Invaded Iraq without UN consent. -Idea of "spreading democracy" *perhaps* in harmony with LIO principles.	-Wars in Iraq & Afghanistan (Global War on Terror). -Withdrawal from Kyoto protocol -Rejection of the International Criminal Court.
	Mix of multilateralism and unilaterlaism -In favor of withdrawal from Iraq, but never did so. -Continued assassinations of suspected terrorists	-Troop surge in Afghanistan -Raid of Pakistan to kill Osama bin Laden -Transpacific Partnership
	Fully Unilateral -"America First" -Opposed to international institutions that restrict America's sovereignty.	-Protectionist tariffs -Restrictions of immigration -Withdrawal from many UN agreements

---

Key Questions: What you need to know

- What are the two "paradoxical" factors of America's War on Terror?
- What accounts for America's shift toward "unilateralism" after 9/11?
- Can it be argued that America itself is the "enemy" of the LIO?
- What explains Trump's "America First" agenda?

BRICS: Redrawing the Circle?

America's retreat from the LIO raises an important question: if the United States withdraws from its leadership position, what will happen to the institutions which it helped to create? Will the United Nations collapse and disband like the League of Nations before it? Will the other countries maintain the LIO, despite American apathy? Will the LIO break apart into multiple international orders, each with a different "center of gravity"? Certain political theorists believe the latter process has already begun. They point to the rise and influence of Brazil, Russia, India, China, and South Africa (the so-called "BRICS" countries) and argue that the world is entering a period of political **multipolarity** in which each of these nations will be dominant in "mini" international orders with separate spheres of influence and separate agendas. For example, Brazil will be the economic and political leader of a South American international order; Russia in an Eastern European international order, India of a Central Asian' international order, China of a Eastern Asian international order, and South Africa of an African international order. They point to the large population of these countries, their ability to control trade and leverage political influence over their neighbors as evidence that, collectively, they may have the power to replace America as the heart of the global system.

Other political theorists aren't so sure. Though it is true, they say, that the BRICS countries have influence in their regions of the world, it is questionable whether they have enough power to decisively reshape the world. None of the BRICS countries (with the exception of Russia and China) have significant military forces. Of the five countries, only China has an economy large enough to have a global impact. Furthermore, though America seems to have stepped back a bit from the position of leadership which it established during the Cold War, it is hardly clear that the United States is "in decline." It maintains, by far, the largest military and strongest economy in the world, controls numerous foreign military bases, oversees multiple international agreements, and, though it has offered resistance to the LIO in recent years, its presence is significant in nearly every meaningful international institution.

The question, therefore, of what will happen to the LIO is an open one. Time will tell. One thing is clear however. Fukayama's prophecy about the "end of history" and the inevitable unification of the world after the Cold War has been proven dead wrong. Disagreement, international tension, and polarization are alive and well. History, it seems, has never been younger.

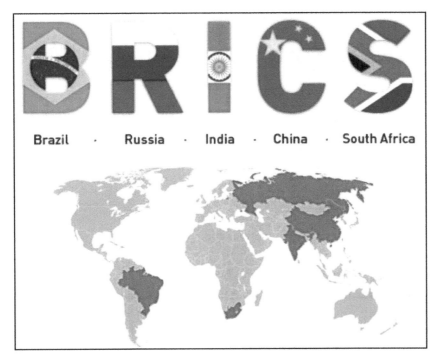

(Fig 13.15)

Summing up: Key Chapter Points

1) After the Cold War ended, Francis Fukayama predicted that "western liberal democracy" would spread all over the world and the liberal international order would become the final, universalized world system.

2) Problems with the LIO, however, arose in the immediate aftermath of the Cold War, as evinced in Russia, China, and the Middle East.

3) America's foreign policy abruptly changed following the 9/11 attacks. The presidency of George W. Bush marked a shift toward unilateralism.

4) It seems as though America has continued to retreat from the LIO, casting doubt upon the legitimacy of its institutions.

5) Some theorize that the BRICS countries may come to define a future "multipolar" world with Brazil, Russia, India, China, and South Africa each dominating individual spheres of influence.

PART II: THEORIES OF GLOBAL POLITICS

In the previous seven chapters, we have described "what has happened" in global politics over the past several hundred years. The next section of this book describes how we might understand those events by presenting different political theories. For our purposes, we will think of a theory as an **intellectual perspective** which allows us to explain social phenomena. A theory categorizes the objects of our perception through the application of

1) **specific terminology** which identifies the "types" of things which the theory will focus on
2) **causal relationships** which identifies how these types interact
3) **limiting frameworks** which decide what objects are appropriate to apply the theory to and what objects are not.

Throughout the history of political thought, there have been countless theories, each with variations and sub-variations. Some of these theories have been **meliorative**: they have concerned themselves with ways society might be improved to become more just or humane. Other theories are **descriptive**. They do not pretend to offer any solutions but simply attempt to depict political relations as they actually exist in the world. Meliorative and descriptive theories are not mutually exclusive. Any theory which offers a prescription for improving society must first give some sort of a descriptive account of what society is actually like in the first place. Furthermore, any description of society would be inadequate if it did not point out, even if only implicitly, the problems and injustices that exist within it.

A thorough account of all the theories of global politics would be a textbook in its own right. For the purpose of this introduction, we will limit our discussion to Realism, Liberalism, Marxism, Social Constructivism, Feminism, and Post-Colonialism. For each of these theories, we will describe first the basic theme, explain the relevant terminology, and, finally, conclude with a few common criticisms of the theory.

CHAPTER 14: REALISM

Overview

Our first theory chapter explains the basic principles and historical development of **realism**. We focus on

- The basic vocabulary of realism: **survival, statism, self-help, anarchy,** and **reason d'etat**
- Discuss the birth of realism in the 5th Century B.C. **Melian dialogue.**
- Discuss two important realist thinkers: Nicolli Machiavelli and Thomas Hobbes
- Explain why realism became more popular in the 20th century, during the Cold War, and discuss recent contributions to the theory.

---

416 B.C. The inhabitants of the island of Melos, known as Melians, found themselves surrounded by a large army from Athens. At the time, the Athenians were at war with their southern neighbors, the Spartans. Though the Melians were officially neutral in the conflict, the Atheninans wanted to control all of the islands off of its southern coast and so sent a fleet of forty ships and an army of over 3000 men to the island's shores. The Athenians gave the Melians a choice: submit to Athens and pay a large quantity of money as tribute or else have their men slaughtered and their women enslaved. In his *History of the Peloponessian War*, the Greek historian **Thucydides** records the negotiation between the ambassador of the Athenians and that of the Melians.

Athenians : We will use no fine phrases...Justice depends on the equality of power to compel. [We are not equals]. The strong do what they can and the weak accept what they must.

Melians : In our view, you should not destroy a principle that is to the general good of all men — namely, that in the case of conflict there should be such a thing as fair play and just dealing.

Athenians : No, as far as just dealing is concerned, those who preserve their independence do so because they are strong...If we fail to attack others, it is because we are afraid. By conquering you we shall increase not only the size but the security of our empire. We rule the sea and you are islanders...It is therefore particularly important that you should not escape.

Melians : It is difficult for us to oppose your power and fortune...Nevertheless we trust that the gods will give us fortune as good as yours, because we are standing for what is right against what is wrong.

Athenians: We think we have as much right to the gods' favor as you have…. Our opinion of the gods and our knowledge of men lead us to conclude that it is a general and necessary law of nature to rule whatever one can.

(Fig 14.1) The islands of **Melos** were officially neutral in the Peloponnesian Wars (431-404 BCE). Nonetheless, they got caught between two powerful neighbors in Athens and Sparta.	**(Fig 14.2)** Greek warrior, 7th century BCE vase.

The **Melian Dialogue** is often taken to be the first example of the political philosophy called **realism.** To begin with an oversimplification, realism is the philosophy that **might makes right.** Power, and little else, is what matters in politics. The dialogue above illustrates many of the themes in realist thought which have not changed much in the 2000 years since it was written:

1) **Statism**: The Athenians and the Melians encounter one another as two independent **states** (city-states, technically). Politics, according to realism, begins with the state, and individual states exist with one another in a *competitive arena* where the pursuit of power is of primary importance. Realist philosophers call this pursuit of power, this desire to be stronger than other states, the **raison d'etat**: French for "the purpose of the state."

2) **Survival**: Why is power so important? As the dialogue makes clear, the world is rather dangerous. The Melians, despite their neutrality, were attacked by a much larger force, threatening their survival. Though the Athenians negotiate from a position of strength, they explain to the Melians that their desire to conquer the island is motivated by concern for "the size and security of our empire." In a world where war is a constant threat, the surest way to ensure survival is by a politics of **self-help**, by accumulating strength for one's own state to gain a competitive advantage over others. As the Athenians put it, "Those who preserve their independence do so because they are strong."

3) **Anarchy**: Throughout the dialogue, the Melians appeal to higher principles of fairness and justice. In the last section, they claim that the gods will protect them because "we are standing for what is right against what is wrong." Yet the Athenians' reply amounts to a laugh. What gods? What justice? Justice is only possible between equals. The Athenians appeal to what is known as **anarchy**: the absence of a higher power or authority that enforces right and wrong between political actors. No "cosmic police," no "global government," no "benevolent god," in the realist view, will interfere with human affairs in the event of a violation of justice. Nothing prevents a strong state from imposing its will on a weaker one, and nothing prevents violations of justice except for strength.

As it happened, the Melians chose to resist the Athenian armies. After a brief siege, the Athenians carried out their threat, killed the men on the island and enslaved all of the women. However, in what may have been poetic justice, the Athenians, before long, suffered the same fate. Five years later, the Peloponnesian War came to an end with the defeat of Athens. Sparta liberated the island of Melos from its Athenian occupiers and allowed the survivors of the massacre to return home.

Key Questions: What you need to know

- What is meant by "statism?" Why are states important to realists?
- How do states ensure their survival?
- What is "anarchy" and what are its consequences?
- What is the "raison d'etat?"

The Fox and the Lion: Machiavelli

In the years after Thucydides *History,* realism (not yet called "realism") was an unpopular position in political thought. The traditions of philosophy of the ancient world, the middle ages, and the Renaissance stressed the moral dimension of public life. For philosophers like Cicero (106-43 BCE), for example, politics meant establishing social consent through just and fair rules. For Christian thinkers of medieval Europe, politics meant creating a world of virtue by rewarding what was right and punishing what was wrong, helping citizens to pursue the "the greatest good." Justice and virtue were regarded as the foundations of political action.

In 1532, however, the Italian diplomat Niccolo Machiavelli challenged the assumptions of such "virtuous" politics. In *The Prince* which Machiavelli described as a kind of handbook for rulers, he advanced a theory of government based on power, manipulation, and fear. It could be argued that the story of Machiavelli's own life explains his dark outlook. An aristocrat in the Italian republic of Florence, Machiavelli was an advisor of the ruling family and the captain of a citizen's army. When his army was defeated by the Spanish in 1512, he was captured, accused of conspiracy, tortured and thrown into prison. Though he was eventually released, the experience left him convinced that right and wrong often have no meaning in politics. What is "right" is simply whatever seizes power and keeps it.

Figure 14.3 Niccolo Machiavelli: 1469-1527

Figure 14.4 Painting of the destruction of Florence.

When he began to write *The Prince,* he discovered that this viewpoint helped him answer a puzzling question. How is it, he wanted to know, that **principalities** (his word for a state governed by a prince) hold so much power against the will of the people? Many of the states in Europe at the time ruled territory that had been conquered from others. In most cases neither the old rulers nor the people who had been conquered were enthusiastic about the arrangement. Furthermore, as a scholar of ancient history, Machiavelli also knew that the Roman Empire had been established through the conquest of warlike rivals. How then was it possible for a state to survive and maintain its power despite the fact that it was surrounded by enemies?

Machiavelli had three rather dark answers to this question: power, cruelty, and manipulation. The first point, power, is the simplest. Survival, for rulers, depends first and foremost on military might. No prince, no matter how charming, popular, or intelligent lasts long, in the dangerous world of politics, without the backing men and guns. "I judge those princes self-sufficient," he wrote, "who are able to gather together a suitable army and fight a good battle against whoever should attack them." Defensive structures such walls and fortifications, in his analysis, were as necessary as offensive capabilities. He gave the example of the cities of Germany which, at his time, "would fear no other power as they are fortified in such a manner that everyone thinks their capture would be a tedious and difficult affair. They all have sufficient moats and walls, and they have adequate artillery....A prince who has a strong city...cannot be attacked, and, even if he were attacked, the enemy would have to depart in shame."

On the offensive side of things, military power had to be deployed, Machiavelli argued, boldly and mercilessly. It was necessary for a ruler to seem cruel in order to eliminate his enemies or frighten his rivals. If potential enemies were allowed to live, they would pose dangers to the government which, over time, could potentially lead to greater and more continuous violence than would have occurred if they had simply been killed at once. "A conquerer," as he put it, "should weigh all the harmful things he must do and do them all at once so as not to have to repeat them every day....Anyone who does otherwise, either out of timidity or because of poor advice, is always obliged to keep his knife in his hand." Though such use of violence may seem cold-hearted, the world, Machiavelli thought, was dangerous by nature. "From the twenty-six Roman emperors from Cesar to Maximinuns," he pointed out, "sixteen were assassinated and only ten died a natural death." Violence is simply the way politics works.

Well used are those cruelties...that are carried out at a single stroke, done out of necessity to protect oneself and are not continued but instead are converted into the greatest possible benefits for the subjects."

-Niccolo Machiavelli

Question for Discussion

Why did Machiavelli think that violence was necessary? Can you think of any examples, from modern history, of political leaders using violence in a way that Machiavelli would have approved of?

Last but not least, Machiavelli thought that power and cruelty had to be joined to a certain level of sophisticated calculation. A ruler could not always be honest but would have to use tactical lies to his advantage. "The princes who have accomplished great deeds," he wrote, "are those who have known to manipulate the minds of men by shrewdness." In a well known parable, Machiavelli uses the example of **the fox and the lion** in order to illustrate the way in which strength had to be joined to political cleverness. "The lion cannot defend himself from traps, and the fox cannot protect itself from wolves. It is necessary, therefore, for a prince to be a fox in order to recognize the traps and to be a lion in order to frighten the wolves." This "foxiness" also meant knowing when to be tricky. Just as Machiavelli justifies cruelty by pointing out the frequency of violence in the political world, so too he justifies lying by noting the fact that everyone, in politics, lies. "Since men are a contemptible lot and will not keep their promises to you, you likewise need not keep yours to them." To use a motto which would become popular after Machiavelli's day, **the ends justify the means.** Whatever tricks rulers use to hold on to power will be justified and considered "right" as long as their power is maintained.

"It is far safer to be feared than loved...Let a prince therefore act to conquer and to maintain the state; his methods will always be judged honorable."

-Niccolo Machiavelli

Key Questions: What you need to know

- What three things did Machiavelli argue were necessary for a king to maintain his power?
- Think about the key vocabulary from the previous section: statism, survival, self-help, anarchy, raison d'etat. How could we apply these words to Machiavelli's thought?

| (Fig 14.5) "A fox to watch for traps, a lion to frighten the wolves." | (Fig 14.6) "Well used are those cruelties..." |

Nasty, brutish and short: Thomas Hobbes

Machiavelli's chief concern was with *how* rulers could maintain power in a dangerous world. One hundred years later, the English philosopher Thomas Hobbes concerned himself with a related question: *why* was the world so dangerous in the first place? Like Machiavelli, Hobbes had had a number of traumatic political experiences. During the English Civil War (1642-1651), he was accused of sympathy for King Charles I (who had been beheaded as a tyrant) and was forced to flee for his life. When he returned to England, he found favor with the military dictator, Oliver Cromwell, who believed that Hobbes's political philosophy justified the absolute authority of any ruler: whether king or general.

While Machiavelli came to his conclusions based on observation: the cycles of violence which had plagued history, Hobbes's starting point was a theoretical concept. Imagine, Hobbes says, human beings as they might exist without any form of government, in a system of pure freedom and equality which he termed **the state of nature**. In such a state (quite similar to **anarchy,** as defined above), there would be no authority to exact punishment for a crime. Each person would be forced to defend himself against potential attack from all sides. Before long, the state of nature would lead, in his famous phrase, **to a war of all against all**. Hobbes enumerates six reasons why he believed this to be so:

1) In a world of scarce resources, individuals are always in competition with each other.
2) In addition to being in competition for resources, individuals compete with one another for prestige, honor, and fame.
3) Pride and dissatisfaction often lead individuals to find fault with one another and to disrupt systems of order and peace.
4) Individuals have a tendency to lie to one another for their own advantage.
5) Many individuals tend to be unhappy even when things are going well.
6) Humans do not *naturally* agree but only agree when there is the threat of a penalty.

Given these reasons Hobbes came to believe that the state of nature would be a lonely and fearful place where human life would be **"nasty, solitary, brutish, and short."**

The need for safety and self-preservation, Hobbes argues, leads people to agree to give up their freedom and be governed by an absolute authority. He calls this agreement the **social contract** (an important concept in political thought) and refers to the absolute authority as **the Leviathan.** Leviathan, a term found in the Bible for a great sea monster, was, for Hobbes, the enormous power of the state—its ability to control individuals and keep them in "a state of awe" or fear. It did not matter, for Hobbes, whether the Leviathan happened to be embodied in a democratically elected government or an absolute monarch. It also made no difference whether the citizens had set up their own institutions or whether the institutions had been imposed by a conquering army. What mattered was the ability of the Leviathan to enforce the social contract, which meant, in the simplest terms, to punish crime, enforce obedience, and thereby prevent the state of war of all against all.

| (Fig 14.7) or Hobbes, it didn't matter who the government was. It just mattered that it had the capacity to keep the people in "a state of awe." | (Fig 14.8) **The Leviathan** was a sea-monster from the Bible. Hobbes used it as his metaphor for the great power of the state. |

Key Questions: What you need to know

- What did Hobbes mean by "state of nature?"
- What was wrong with the state of nature?
- What is the purpose of a social contract, according to Hobbes?
- What did Hobbes think the purpose of government was?
- What is the importance of "anarchy" in Hobbes' view?

Twentieth Century Applications

The political traditions of Thucydides, Machiavelli, and Hobbes became more popular in the middle of the twentieth century, during which time the term "realism" was first coined to describe them. The reason for its popularity was because it seemed to explain, with striking accuracy, the continual wars which had wreaked such havoc upon Europe for hundreds of years. After World

War I, the Great Powers (see Chapter 4) had come together to attempt to create an institutional order to prevent violence. This optimistic time, which later came to be called the period of **interwar idealism**, failed miserably, and, as World War II led into the Cold War, with the fierce rivalry between the United States and the Soviet Union poised, it seemed, to erupt into a nuclear holocaust, political theorists turned back to Machiavelli and Hobbes in order to understand why violence seemed so ineradicable.

One influential 20th century realist was **John Herz**. In his book *Political Realism and Political Idealism*, he coined the term **security dilemma** to describe the reason why politics always seems to be on the edge of violence. Namely, the actions which states take to protect themselves, by increasing their security, have unintended consequences. One state, in order to protect its borders, for example, may build ten tanks. A neighboring state, viewing the tanks as a threat, may build twenty in response. The first state, seeing itself potentially outgunned, builds an aircraft carrier. The other state builds two aircraft carriers. Before long, an **arms race** begins, as the attempt to prevent war by increasing security creates the continued conditions for war. The idea of the security dilemma is Hobbsian in that it regards competition for **relative power** as the source of potential instability and violence in the international system. When Herz wrote *Political Realism and Idealism*, the United States and the Soviet Union were in the midst of a dangerous arms race, with each power attempting to build more nuclear weapons than the other. The idea of the security dilemma seemed to explain why this was occurring and also why the process would be unlikely to simply end on its own.

Twenty years later, **Kenneth Waltz** added another chapter to the story of realism by examining the way power, over time, tends towards a precarious balance. In *Theory of International Politics*, Waltz put forward an idea which he called **defensive realism**, the notion that states, in seeking "safety first" tend to produce international orders in which large powers become locked in symmetrical rivalries. Say a small country, for example, happens to share a border with a large and powerful one. What should it do to ensure its safety? According to Waltz, the small country has three choices. It can decide to ally with the small country, a tactic known as **bandwagoning**, in order to seek its protection. It can try to increase its own power in order to compete with the large country, which Waltz called **internal balancing**. Or it can join with other smaller countries in an alliance against the large one, which Waltz called **external balancing**. Over time, these actions create a **balance of power** in which rival sides are more or less evenly matched. The balance of power acts as a deterrent to war because states of equal strength are unlikely to attack one another. Nonetheless, according to Waltz, balances can often shift leading to an outbreak of violence.

Key Questions: What you need to know

- Why did realism become more popular in the twentieth century?
- What did John Herz mean by "the security dilemma?"
- What did Kenneth Walz mean by "balance of power?" How was it achieved?

| **(Fig 14.9)** Realism became a dominant theory in political science in the 20th century due to its explanations of the failure of institutions and the constant outbreak of war. | **(Fig 14.10)** Internal balancing, external balancing, bandwagoning: realism seemed to explain the cold war international system. |

Twentieth Century Realists	Key Ideas
Hans Morgenthau *Politics Among Nations*, 1948	Realism can be described in terms of "six principles," all based, roughly, on the pursuit of power. Power politics can be reconciled with human nature, morality, and law.
John Herz *Political Realism and Political Idealism*, 1951	The term "security dilemma" describes the way that states, pursuing their own security, paradoxically continue to create the conditions of war.
Kenneth Waltz *Theory of International Politics*, 1979	Balances of power form spontaneously as states seek "safety first." Bandwagoning, internal balancing, and external balancing are three actions states can take when faced by a larger and more powerful rival.
John Mearsheimer *Tragedy of Great Power Politics, 2001*	The condition of anarchy causes states to be in a position where they are never quite certain how safe they are. This uncertainty leads to constant build-ups of power.

Criticisms

Realism, since the days of Machiavelli and Hobbes, has been long subject to criticism. On the technical level, theorists often consider the realist idea of political organization too simple. For example, while the state is important in world politics, does it follow that the state is the only key political actor and that there is nothing between one state and another besides total anarchy? What about international organizations? Trade partnerships? Religious groups? Basic norms? Some critics argue that realism does not do a good job in accounting for these non-state actors and forces. Furthermore, while few would deny the importance of power in global politics, it does not seem obvious that *all* political decisions are motivated by power and security. Social relationships are complex, and human motivation cannot be reduced to a single variable.

However, the most common criticism of realism is that it is too pessimistic a view. Though war has been a frequent political phenomenon, it is not true that any given country is *always* at war. There've been, throughout history, periods of peace and cooperation, and it does seem, in many parts of the world, that progress has been made—even if unevenly. For example, in the twentieth century Europe was devastated by two wars, and yet, the European Union is, in many ways, a model of peaceful cooperation, sharing open borders, a single currency, and collective institutions. It is unthinkable that France and Germany would go to war again. Or that Japan would attack Pearl Harbor. Or that Italy would invade Ethiopia. Realism has a hard time explaining such apparent progress.

Last but not least, one of the most penetrating criticisms of realism is that it leaves no place for common-sense morality. It seems clear, for example, that modern liberal democracies are "better" in a moral sense than genocidal dictatorships. Yet, if the raison d'etat is simply the accumulation of power and security, how is it possible to critique regimes like Nazi Germany or Imperial Japan? There is nothing "wrong" with tyranny and murder, in the Machiavellian sense, if those actions happen to further the intersts of the state. If power is what justifies political action, then how is it possible to say that a regime which accomplishes its goals peacefully is "more just" than one which does so through mass killing? Though recent realist thinkers have attempted to reconcile moral intuitions and power politics, the issue of moral justification remains a significant issue for the theory.

Perhaps the best counterargument that realists can make against these criticisms is the evidence of global affairs themselves. More than 100 million people were killed globally in wars during the twentieth century, and though, so far, "only" a million or so have been killed in the twenty-first, the era could hardly be described as "peaceful." The United States, taken to be the model of liberal enlightenment and democracy, has been at war in Afghanistan for nearly twenty years and frequently engages in bombings and assassinations as part of the War on Terror. Only ten years have passed since the genocide in Rwanda and a genocide is currently underway in Myanmar. It's up to history, a realist would say, to show that peace and progress will prevail. And history doesn't seem likely to demonstrate that any time soon.

(Fig 14.10 and 14.11) Adolf Hitler and Nelson Mandella: should we really admit that "power" is the only thing we should judge political leaders for? Is there no difference between the politics of Hitler and of Mandella?

Realism At A Glance

General Theme	Competition for power and security in a dangerous world
Starting Point	The state existing in a world of anarchy where there is no higher power ensuring justice and fair play
Human Nature	Fearful, greedy, competative, violent
International System	Anarchic. States cannot trust each other. Self help is neccessary.
Purpose of Government	Raison d'etat. Maximize relative power to survive.

Summing Up: Key Chapter Points

1) Realism is one of the oldest political theories, dating back to the "Melian dialog" of Thucydides' *On the Peloponnesian Wars.*

2) Key concepts in realism include "Statism, Survival, Self-Help, and Anarchy."

3) Machiavelli, one of the great classical realists, argued that rulers stay in power through military might, cruelty, and manipulation.

4) Hobbes argued that the "state of nature" (given anarchy) inevitably leads to violence, to protect against which individuals form a social contract to live under the authority of an absolute state.

5) Realism has grown more popular in the twentieth century due to World War I, World War II, and the Cold War, with contemporary realist thinkers introducing "the security dilemma" and "the balance of power."

6) Criticisms of realism focus on its overly simplistic world picture and its inability to explain moral intuitions.

CHAPTER 15: LIBERALISM

In this chapter we introduce the tradition of **liberalism** focusing on four main historical developments:

- The emphasis on **human rights** following the British Civil War
- The French tradition and its more secular aims
- The **utilitarian** contribution by John Stuart Mill and others
- The move towards **institutionalism** in the 20th century

As we tell the story, we introduce key thinkers of the movement, spending time on John Locke, Jean Jacques Rousseau, John Stuart Mill, Immanuel Kant, and Jeremy Benthem.

In 1646, the British pamphlet-writer Richard Overton was locked in prison in London. During the **English Civil War** (1642-1651), he had helped form a group known as **The Levellers**, a political faction in favor of religious freedom and democratic rule. The Levellers were primarily opposed to King Charles I who thought that kings ruled by "Divine Right," (see ch 2). In addition to opposing the king, The Levellers also fought against many of the rebel groups too. They claimed that these so-called reformers simply wanted king-like power for themselves. Needless to say, The Levellers often found themselves with few political friends. From his prison cell, Overton wrote a pamphlet with the provocative title, *An Arrow Against All Tyrants* which began:

> To every individual in nature is given an **individual property** [right] by nature not to be invaded or usurped by any. For every one, as he is himself, so he has a **self-propriety**, [self-ownership] else could he not *be* himself; and of this no second may presume to deprive any of without manifest violation to the very principles of nature... No man has power over my **rights and liberties**, and I over no man's.... For by natural birth all men are equally and alike born to like propriety, liberty and freedom; and as we are delivered of God by the hand of nature into this world, every one with a natural, innate freedom and propriety...never to be obliterated.

Overton's belief in human "propriety, liberty, and freedom" came from his religion. A Christian reformer, Overton emphasized a theological principle known as **imago dei**. This is the idea that humans are created "in the image of God," and thus have innate rights. One important right is what Overton called "self-propriety," the idea that you are your own property. Even if you own nothing else in the world, you at the very least own yourself. No one else can experience your thoughts and feelings. No one else can take away your ability to "choose" what to do with them.

Though Overton and the Levellers would eventually be defeated, their ideas, in the aftermath of the civil war, would help form the foundation in European politics for **liberalism** (from the word "liberty"), a political tradition emphasizing individual rights, free choice, and equality.

AN **A R R O W** AGAINST ALL TYRANTS And Tyrany, ſhot from the Priſon of New-gate into the Prerogative Bowels of the Arbitrary Houſe of Lords. and all other Uſurpers and Tyrants *Whatſoever.* wherein the originall riſe, extent, and end of Magi- ſteriall power, the naturall and Nationall rights, freedomes and pro- perties of Mankind are diſcovered, and undeniably maintained; the late oppreſſions and incroachments of the Lords over the Commons legally (by the fundamentall Lawes and Statutes of this Realme, as alſo by a memorable Extract out of the Records of the *Tower* of *London*) condemned; The late Presbyterian Ordinance (invented and contrived by the Diviners, and by the motion of Mr. *Bacon* and Mr. *Tate* read in the Houſe of Commons) examined, refuted, and exploaded, as moſt inhumaine, tyranicall and Barbarous. By *RICHARD OVERTON*

(Fig 15.1) The period between **1642 and 1688** was marked by political turmoil in England. (See timeline below). Opposition to the rule of King Charles I led to some of the earliest "liberal" writing in Europe. Unlike later liberalism, these early liberal theorists based their opposition to arbitrary rule on religious grounds: arguing that equality and freedom were "God-given" rights. This represents, in many respects, an important reversal of the Divine Right of Kings (see chapter 2) tradition. It is the ordinary person, not the king, that has a divine right.

Reimagining the Social Contract: Locke

In the years following the Civil War, British thinkers found themselves wrestling with basic political questions. What was the source of the government's authority? What form of government was most effective? Why was government necessary in the first place? Though these questions were old ones, the political turmoil made them all the more urgent. England had gone from a monarchy, to a military dictatorship, and then, in 1660, to a monarchy again (see chart above). Was a system of kings and queens really best? Or were Levellers like Overton right? In the last chapter, we discussed **Thomas Hobbes** and his *Leviathan* (1651) which argued that it didn't matter much what form of government was instituted. What mattered was that its power was absolute—that it could inspire "fear and awe" and thus maintain social order.

Other political thinkers in the late 17th century resisted Hobbes' conclusions. One of the most significant of these was **John Locke**. Regarded as the greatest liberal philosopher of his age, Locke was the son of a lawyer who had fought on the side of the anti-royalist forces during the Civil War. Following in his father's footsteps, Locke became closely associated with the **Whigs**, a political party in England which, at the time, favored government through Parliament and advocated for more civil freedoms. Locke's views got him into trouble with the government of Charles II, and he was forced to flee England. However, after the **Glorious Revolution** (see table), he returned to England and began publishing philosophical works. In *Treaties on Govermnet* (1689) he argued for the right of the people to rebel against oppressive leaders.

British Liberalism in the 17th century

(Fig 15.2) King Charles I (1625-1649) was a firm believer in the **Divine Right of Kings**. His attempt to rule without the cooperation of parliament led to the **English Civil War** (1642-1651). Charles I is defeated and executed.

(Fig 15.3) During the **English Civil War**, many British political thinkers questioned the need for a king in the first place and advocated for greater levels of democracy, equality, and religious toleration.

(Fig 15.4) The Puritan general **Oliver Cromwell** and his forces won the war, leading to what was essentially a military dictatorship, known as **the interregnum**, from 1649-1660.

(Fig 15.5) Due to the failures of Cromwell's government, the monarchy is restored. **Charles II** reigns from 1660-1685. Though he is more tolerant than his father, there are fears about excessive royal power and Charles II support for Catholicism.

(Fig 15.6) After Charles II dies, the **Glorious Revolution** (1688) brings William and Mary to the throne but requires them to respect consent of parliament, elections, and free speech. These rules form the first English **Bill of Rights** (1689).

(Fig 15.7) The more restrained monarchy, ruling by constitution rather than divine right, reflected liberal political theory. John Locke's **Of Government** argued that rulers only rule by the consent of the people.

Locke's arguments, like Hobbes' before him, were based on the **state of nature**, the imagined "original position" of mankind prior to laws and government. While Hobbes had argued the state of nature would be a "nasty" place full of anarchy and war, Locke emphasized its positive elements. Like the Levellers, Locke believed human beings were made in the image of God and, as such, were innately free and equal. Their freedom, Locke argued, was obvious in the experience of self-ownership: the awareness that we control our bodies and can do what we want. Self-ownership does not mean that, without government, we would all use our freedom for selfish ends. Locke believed that humans in the state of nature would still be governed by **natural law**, a basic sense of right and wrong. **Reason**, the ability to evaluate actions and choose rightly, would guide humans toward lawful choices. He thought, for instance, that people would not *naturally* choose to harm one another, that they would not want to lose their freedom by putting themselves in a condition of slavery, and that they would understand that things like stealing were wrong.

(Fig 15.8)

"This freedom from absolute power is so necessary to, and closely joined with a man's preservation, that he cannot part with it but by what forfeits and his preservation and life together. For a man not having the power of his own life, cannot by compact, or his own consent, enslave himself to any one."

--John Locke

This does not mean, however, that everything would be perfect. Disputes would arise, particularly over property. Individuals would violate natural law, and, when they did so, in the absence of higher authority, each individual would be forced to be the "executor" of the law by defending his or her own rights. If you attempted to steal my food, for example, I would have no choice but to be my own police force. In order to create a more effective system of enforcing the law, individuals entered into societies, creating governments. The purpose of these governments was to serve as an **umpire** between individuals, an objective judge in the case of disagreements. Doing so became society's means of protecting the "**life, liberty, and property**" of its members. Importantly, Locke thought that governments could only be formed by **free consent**. Individuals voluntarily gave the government permission to rule. Locke thought that individuals had a duty to rebel against the government if it exercised arbitrary power or violated individual rights.

Key Questions: What you need to know

- What did Locke think about the "state of nature?"
- Why was it not as bad as Hobbes imagined it would be?
- Why was government needed?
- Why did individuals have the right to rebel against government?

The Noble Savage: Rousseau

The British monarchy went through its period of crisis in the mid 17th century. 100 years later, it was France's turn. Though France had long been one of the most powerful countries in Europe, the reign of King **Louis XV** (1710-1774) would bring the nation to the brink of collapse. Costly wars, political corruption, and reckless spending led to widespread hardship and dissatisfaction with the French political class. Eventually, during the reign of **Louis XVI**, (1754-1793), these resentments would erupt in **The French Revolution** (1789) which would overthrow the monarchy and lead to the beginnings of representative government.

Long before the revolution began, French political thinkers had been asking some of the same questions that the British had the century before. What form of government is most legitimate? Why does the king get to be the king? Where does authority come from? Though the English answers to these questions were often informed by religious belief, one crucial difference of the French liberals is that they tended to be more **secular.** The 18th century marked the period of **the enlightenment** (ch 3) in which the power of the churches, across Europe, began to decline and the power of "rational" bureaucracies began to increase. Liberal philosophers during this period, therefore, tended to base their political positions more on "common sense" or "objective reason" than religious tradition.

One of the most influential of these French liberals was **Jean Jacques Rousseau** (1712-1788). He had read Locke's treatise and would take his ideas farther. He was particularly interested in the "state of nature." While Hobbes had regarded the state of nature as a miserable place and Locke had thought it relatively good yet imperfect, Rousseau was a complete idealist about the original conditions of humanity. For Rousseau, the state of nature was a paradise. The physical demands of hunting and building shelters made people strong and vigorous. The motives of what he called **amour de soi** (self-interest) and **pitié** (compassion) enabled individuals to live at peace with one another. Most importantly, the absence of hierarchy guaranteed that there could be no embedded inequality. Inequality, after all, does not come, usually, from strength or intellect. Rather it comes from "official positions" in social institutions: the idea of a king, lord, beaurocrat, or boss. The development of civil institutions, therefore, was a destructive event, introducing these sorts of social distinctions, and, along with them, the selfish principle of what Rousseaux called **amour propre** (love of prestige).

French Liberalism in the 18th century

(Fig 15.8) In the 18th century, France was in severe financial trouble due to costly wars such as the **Seven Years War** (1756-1763), and the poorest of the French were facing conditions of dire poverty and hunger.

(Fig 15.10) Many French intellectuals blamed France's hardships on the reckless policies of **Louis XV** and the corrupt French aristocratic class. They believed the *ancien regime* only cared about their own privledges.

(Fig 15.11) They also felt that religious authorities had too much power, and were getting rich at the expense of the public. They wanted ro reduced the power and influence of the Catholic church and its clergy.

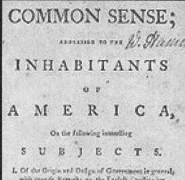

(Fig 15.12) French philosophers like **Jean Jacques Rousseau** (1712-1778) had long argued in favor of liberal reforms. According to Rousseau, institutions are only fair when they reflect the "general will."

(Fig 15.13) Many of these ideas spread to America. Thomas Paine, for example, argued that democratic government was simply a matter of "common sense" (1775). The American Revolution broke out the following year.
.

(Fig 15.14) The principles of liberty, equality, and fraternity defined the ideology of the French Revolution (1789), which attempted to bring these reforms (popular sovereignty, democratic government) to France.

According to Rousseau, The fight for property and honor, which defined advanced civilization, corrupted the natural goodness of primitive people. This belief in the **noble savage**, the pure and uncorrupted person who lived prior to modern institutions, represented an inversion of traditional political thinking. "Progress and development" instead of making life better, had made it worse. The best form of government, according to Rousseau, would be one which returned to the individual as much freedom as possible, and protected private rights from the burdensome and oppressive "chains" of civilization

"I should be glad to have it explained to me what kind of misery a free being, whose heart is at ease and whose body is in health, can possibly suffer. I would like to know which is more likely to become insupportable: the life of society or of nature. We hardly see anyone around us except people who complain of their existence and many deprive themselves of it....I would like to know if anyone has heard of a savage, who took it into his head, when he was free, to complain of life and to kill himself."

-Jean Jacques Rousseau

Key Vocab

Amour de soi: Self Humanity's desire to pursue its safety and happiness.

Pitié: Compassion. Ensured that humans, in the state of nature, would not inflict suffering.

Amour propre: Love of prestige. Source of competition and unhappiness.

Question for Discussion

In what ways do our own institutions sometimes create unhappiness?

How would you describe Rousseau's "amour propre" today?

At first blush, a government which returns humanity to a state of "savagery" seems like a contradiction. How is a government which does not impose rules and order a government at all? Rousseau's solution (like Locke's) was embodied in the idea of consent. Each individual in the community must freely agree to live in accordance with laws which are formed to reflect "**the general will**" or common good. According to Rousseau:

> "Civil association is the most voluntary act in the world; every man being born free and master of himself, no one can, under any pretext whatsoever, subjugate him without his consent... If, then, at the time of the social pact, there are found some opponents of it, their opposition...prevents them from being included in it. They are foreigners among citizens. When the State is instituted, consent is in residence. To live in a territory is to submit oneself to sovereignty."

In other words, consent to the laws of society must be freely chosen. In mature states, citizens imply that they have chosen to submit to society by simply living there. Though Rousseau was to give little practical advice as to how such a society of freedom was to be achieved, he recommended that it involve "assemblies" in which all the citizens would gather, periodically, to determine the general will and express their agreement to follow the social contract. When the French people, just before the revolution, formed the democratically-elected **National Assembly** (1788), they were putting Rousseau's ideas into practice.

The "useful" liberal: Mill

One last important theorist of individual liberty deserves to be mentioned: John Stuart Mill (1806-1873). Writing fifty years after Rousseau, Mill would come to similar conclusions about the importance of human freedom. He would arrive at these conclusions, however, through different logic. Unlike Locke and Rousseau, Mill was writing at a time when the power of kings and queens in Europe (where they existed) was highly limited. Democracy was much more widespread. European governments ruled more by constitution than by royal whim. The right to vote, though limited to property-owning men, was expanding. Industry was growing, and, as it did, states were increasingly governing by **rational bureaucracies**. Mill's concern, given this environment, was less with the idea of "legitimacy" and more with that of **utility**. What form of government was the most *useful*? One of the founding fathers of the philosophical movement known as **utilitarianism**, Mill's concern was with understanding the principles which would maximize human happiness.

 In his quest for such happiness, he began where the other liberal philosophers had begun: with the state of nature. Oddly, Mill's view of the state of nature was the opposite of Locke's and Rousseau's and more closely akin to Hobbes's. Nature, for Mill, was a violent and dangerous place, a place of suffering, ruled by impersonal laws, where no god or overarching intelligence existed to offer to humans comfort or support. Comparing natural violence to political violence, he wrote:

The waves of the sea...seize and appropriate the wealth of the rich and poor...with the same accompaniments of stripping, wounding, and killing as their human antitypes. Everything which the worst men commit either against life or property is perpetrated on a larger scale by natural agents.....Anarchy and the Reign of Terror are overmatched in injustice, ruin, and death by a hurricane and a pestilence.

| **(Fig 15.15)** John Stuart Mill | **(Fig 15.16)** Chaos, by G Frederick Watts |

To a certain degree, both Hobbes and Mill saw, in government, "safety" from the anarchy of the natural world. Yet, unlike Hobbes, who believed that "the civil power" had to be stern and strict in order to protect its subjects, Mill believed that government had to allow as much human freedom as possible. His reason is simple: doing so produces the greatest happiness for the greatest number of people. Not only are individuals themselves happier when left alone to pursue their own tastes, ideas, and choices, but society as a whole tends to be better off. By allowing freedom, society generates a kind of "healthy competition" in which the best ideas and choices, over time, win out. According to Mill, there was only one circumstance in which a society should interfere with human freedom: what he termed the **harm principle**. If an individual's action caused *direct* harm to another, then society ought to restrict it. Otherwise human freedom must be respected. Crucially, Mill believed that it was not only law and government which must be prevented from impinging upon freedom, but also society in general. What Mill called **the tyranny of the majority** and **the tyranny of social opinion** could be as great a danger as governments, since, as he put it, those hidden forms of oppression "are more difficult to escape and penetrate more deeply into the details of life." In short, Mill advocated for a highly tolerant society in which even taboo behaviors, such as alcohol, drug-use, gambling, and sexual deviance, would be permitted.

Liberalism in the 19th century

(Fig 15.16) After the American and French revolutions, the idea of popular sovereignty sweeps Europe. Most European states, by now, feature democratic reforms, constitutions, and limited monarchies.

(Fig 15.17) That said, In most countries, the right to participate in government (through voting and serving as representatives) is restricted to a relatively small class of wealthy men.

(Fig 15.18) At the same time, however, the industrial revolution is increasing the size and complexity of the labor force. As wealth becomes more broadly distributed, the middle class begins to grow.

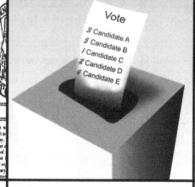

(Fig 15.19) More widespread education, enabled by better printing technology and other factors, enables the new middle class to be aware of political events and to seek reforms, particularly labor and wage related reforms.

(Fig 15.20) Along with improved labor rights, many western countries expand access to voting by the mid 19th century. Non-property owning men can vote in Britain and America for the first time.

(Fig 15.21) As women enter the workforce, they slowly gain political rights as well. The suffrage movement would begin in the mid-19th century though women would not receive the ballot until after World War I.

Thinker	State of Nature	Social Contract
Hobbes	Anarchy: the war of all against all. Life is nasty, solitary, brutish, and short.	The "Leviathan" keeps individuals in a state of "fear and awe" thus guaranteeing social order.
Locke	Individuals are free, equal, and guided by reason. Reason helps reveal the "natural law," defined by self-preservation and respect for the property of others.	Individuals voluntarily join civil societies in order to ensure the protection of their "life, liberty, and property." The government serves as an "umpire" to settle disputes. Individuals have the duty to rebel against the government if it exercises arbitrary power.
Rousseau	Fundamentally good. Individuals are guided by self-love and compassion, and, as such, live free, happy, and vigorous lives. Entering into civil institutions corrupts humans by introducing envy and competition.	Citizens consent unanimously to be governed by "the general will." Consent to the social contract is implicit in the decision to live in a country and can be explicit in democratic "assemblies" in which citizens affirm their support for the society.
Mill	Violent and anarchic. Governed by indifferent natural laws. Nonetheless the natural pursuit of happiness and utility leads to the creation of civil societies which, in turn, establish social justice and safeguard freedom.	Rejected the idea of a contract. Societies evolved toward liberal democracies through the pursuit of utility.

Liberal International Relations: Bentham, Kant and Beyond

Locke, Rousseau, and Mill were primarily concerned with *domestic* government: what was the legitimacy, scope, and justification for authority within a society. But what about international politics? What does liberalism have to say about that? One possibility is to simply expand liberal thinking to international situations. For example, the liberal emphasis on individual rights finds its counterpart in the idea of national independence and sovereignty. Limited government has its equivalent in the idea of non-interference. Equality of citizens can be magnified to describe a fundamental equality of all nations.

Domestic Principle	International Application
• Individual Rights	• National independence and sovereignty
• Limited Government	• Non-interference
• Individual Equality	• Equality of Nations
• Right to Property	• Right to Free Trade
• Social Contract	• International Institutions

Liberal philosophers, however, have also addressed the problems of international relations more directly. In doing so, they have emphasized the ways in which liberal principles direct nations to cooperate and establish consent-based rules to ensure peaceful international orders.

One of the first thinkers to apply liberal principles to the international realm was **Jeremy Bentham**. The tutor of John Stuart Mill, Bentham was also a utilitarian, believing that social progress consisted in the pursuit of happiness and of achieving "the greatest good for the greatest number of people." Applied to international politics this meant the greatest good for the greatest number of *nations*. How was this to be achieved? Benthem thought that the answer lay in law or "jurisprudence." Laws which produced global "utility," Bentham thought, would involve cooperative agreements, lower tariffs, smaller armies, and an end to colonization. In order to negotiate these laws, Bentham recommended a kind of social contract among nations--a kind of "international congress" at which representatives and diplomats could meet to agree upon laws. Enforcing these laws once they had been established, according to Bentham, required an international court. The court would disseminate its judgements around the world through diplomats, and, if necessary, would enforce them through an army which would be made up of the soldiers of member nations. These ideas should sound familiar. The 20th century **Liberal International Order** (see ch 10) with the United Nations, the International Court of Justice and the Security Council derived many of its principles from the thinking of Bentham and his followers. For 20th century liberals, the creation of these international institutions creates global trust through the establishment of rules and norms. Thus, nations realize an underlying **harmony of interests**, the understanding that what is good for nations *together* is good for them *individually*.

Perpetual Peace

A contemporary of Benthem's, **Immanuel Kant** made the connection between domestic and international liberalism even more explicit. For Kant, the story of international affairs was a story of progress, albeit of a slow and painful sort. Kant, after all, had read Hobbes and Machiavelli. He knew that war and violence had been frequent throughout history. He believed, however, that as governments became more liberal that bloodshed would eventually decrease. According to Kant, one crucial cause of war was authoritarian government. Kings and absolute rulers risked very little in going to war (nothing more than money and prestige) since the common citizens did all of the fighting. A representative government, a government in which consent of the people was a necessary condition of political authority, therefore, would be more peaceful because the people, who would have to risk their lives in a war, would never choose to go to war except in extreme circumstances. As he phrased it:

> Each state must be organized internally in such a way that the head of state, for whom the war actually costs nothing (for he wages it at the expense of others) must no longer have the deciding vote on whether war is to be declared or not, for the people who pay for it must decide...The people will not readily place itself in danger...out of a mere desire for aggrandisement....And thus posterity...will be able to make perpetual progress towards a morally superior state.

This idea, known as the **democratic peace theory,** has become popular in twentieth century liberal theory. Democratic states, it is argued, do not go to war as frequently as authoritarian states, and, if they do, they almost never go to war with one another.

"The stag hunt" is a thought experiment about cooperation, trust, and the difference between relative and absolute gains. Jean Jacques Rousseau first told the story of the stag hunt in his essay "Discourse on the origin of Inequality." Imagine, he says, a group of hunters out to catch a deer. In order to succeed, all must stay vigilantly at their posts. Suddenly, one of the hunters notices a rabbit. He has a choice to make. He could abandon his post and chase the rabbit or he could remain where he is and help catch the deer. If he waits for the deer he will have more food *overall* (an absolute gain). However, if he chases the rabbit, and allows the deer to escape, he will have less food overall, but more food than they do (a relative gain). Now, suppose *all* of the hunters happen to see a rabbit at the same time. Their choices will depend, firstly, on whether they value absolute or relative gains, and, secondly, on how much they trust their fellow hunters. Realists (see previous chapter) would argue that the hunters *must* abandon their posts and chase the rabbits. Liberals however, emphasizing the importance of the social contract, would argue that the hunters ought to stay put and go for the deer. Doing so allows them to realize that they share an interest in common and that what's good for all of them together is good for each of them individually. The question becomes, then, how can they trust one another enough to cooperate? One answer is that social rules, institutions and norms build patterns of repetitive behavior which, over time, generate trust. Over many separate stag hunts and many chances to observe one another's behavior, the hunters will come to trust each other more and more.

Representative government, however, was only the first step of Kant's vision for a **"perpetual peace."** Like Benthem, he agreed that international discourse and cooperation were necessary in ensuring cooperation. He therefore proposed **"a federation of free states"** which would establish mutually beneficial laws. Finally, he believed that human rights had to be extended worldwide. He proposed a "spirit of cosmopolitanism" in which "universal hospitality" would ensure a basic respect for all. As in the case of Benthem, these ideas would be instrumental in the formation of the twentieth century Liberal International Order.

Key Question: What you need to know

• What is the "harmony of interests" and how is it illustrated by the "stag hunt?"

• What are the three condition's for Kant's "Perpetual Peace?"

The turn towards Institutionalism

Benthem's and Kant's ideas contain the seeds of an important development of liberal thought—particularly in the 20th and 21st centuries. For earlier liberals, like Locke and Rousseau, it was enough if the government kept its distance and respected life, liberty, and property. The relatively optimistic view of the state of nature informed the belief that, with limited government, human flourishing would ensue. However, as governments gradually liberalized and the perennial problems of war, inequality, and exploitation remained, later liberal philosophers came to the conclusion that freedom and equality would not simply take care of themselves. Rather, they had to be "established" through civil institutions. Sharing a view of nature that is more or less Hobbesian, modern liberals, such as John Rawls, argue that the state and associated civil institutions must take a more active role in ensuring social stability, economic fairness, and the rule of law.

The turn towards **"institutionalism"** is reflected in the development of the Liberal International Order between the end of World War I and the end of World War II (ch 5). "Idealists" like Woodrow Wilson were closer to classical liberals in their belief that, if the basic rights like national self-determination were respected, international peace would prevail. However, the Great Depression, the rise of fascism, and World War II seemed to refute this idea. The other architects of the post-World War II Liberal International Order had a much more pessimistic attitude about "laissez faire" policies. The stronger institutions of Bretton Woods and the United Nations reflect a belief that order-making organizations are necessary to overcome conditions of international anarchy. Indeed, 21st century liberals have often come to the conclusion that even quite *pervasive* institutions are necessary for the maintenance of economic stability, political trust, and human rights. The balance between such Hobbsian interventionism and the desire for individual liberty represents a crucial tension in modern liberalism.

Liberal Institutionalism in the 20th Century

(Fig 15.22) After World War I, the victorious powers came to believe that the international system couldn't be "left alone." Institutions were necessary in order to create conditions for peace and prosperity.

(Fig 15.23) Guided by liberals like Kant and Jeremy Benthem, Woodrow Wilson helped found the League of Nations in order to help create trust and improve diplomacy

(Fig 15.24) Though well-intentioned, the first attempt to create a Liberal International Order failed. The weakness of its institutions was soon apparent and World War II soon followed.

(Fig 15.25) After World War II ended, the allies created stronger institutions with the League of Nations, designed to ensure global peace, and the Bretton Woods system, designed to create economic stability.

(Fig 15.26) A key component of the Postwar Liberal International Order is the Keynesian idea that states must actively intervene to ensure economic stability. "Freedom" isn't enough.

(Fig 15.27) In much contemporary liberalism, the idea prevails that "equality" and "human rights" are not *natural* conditions but must be institutionally established.

Key Questions: What you need to know

- How can liberal principles be applied to international relations?

- According to modern liberals, why are institutions so important?

Criticisms

Liberalism, both domestic and international, has been subject to criticisms from all directions. Perhaps the most common criticism has been that theory is "too individualistic." The idea of human rights takes as its starting point the free and equal individual. Attractive as that idea may sound, individuals do not exist "on their own." They are born into societies, whose language, customs, norms, and ideas are imposed as children grow into adults. The society *precedes* the individual. Therefore, the idea of autonomous and independent individuals, freely agreeing to social contracts, is problematic.

A related criticism has to do with the "selfishness" of liberal theory. Early liberals, such as Locke and Rousseau represented an elite, property-owning class. Their emphasis on personal property, so it has been argued, only reflected the interests of an aristocratic few. What about the millions of poor who did not own any significant property? What about women who were, in many cases, legally prohibited from property ownership? What about slaves and servants who would have been, in many "liberal republics" regarded as non-persons? Socialist and feminist critics argue that liberalism does not address these issues adequately because its emphasis on the individual fails to take into account economic inequality and class oppression.

A final criticism has to do with the historical record of so-called liberal governments. While Kant argued that democratic states were far less likely to go to war, history does not seem to agree. Free and democratic countries, such as the United States, have been involved in nearly *all* the major wars of the twentieth century. They have committed war-crimes abroad and, in many cases, atrocities at home. Perhaps these liberal states are hypocrites, failing to live up to their own ideals. Or perhaps liberal principles themselves are not as peaceful and progressive as they at first appear.

Despite these criticisms, liberalism remains one of the most dominant theories in international politics. There are 75 liberal democracies in the world. Nearly all of the great powers (the United States, Canada, Europe, Japan, and South Korea, for example) are liberal. It is difficult, furthermore, to see what plausible alternatives exist to liberalism. The goal of "making the world a better place" only seems sensible when emphasizing the *people* that the world will be better for. Ideas of personal happiness, freedom, and fulfillment can never be far from any discussion of political justice.

Liberalism At A Glance

General Theme	Human rights, limited government, cooperation
Starting Point	The intrinsic value of human beings, free choice, and consent
Human Nature	Reasonable
International System	States can achieve a harmonious international order through co-operation, institutions, trust, and the application of democratic principles.
Purpose of Government	Protection of individual rights, liberty, and property.

Summing Up: Key Chapter Points

1) An important starting point for liberalism was the "Leveller" movement during the British Civil War.

2) The Christian idea that humans are made in the "image of God" was crucial to early conceptions of human rights.

3) John Locke emphasized the fundamental freedom and equality of all in the "state of nature" and argued that the government ought to be limited to the protection of "life, liberty and property."

4) Jean Jacques Rousseau believed that humans were naturally good and corrupted by institutions. The best government was one that maximized freedom and exercised authority only through direct consent to "the general will."

5) Utilitarians like John Stuart Mill regarded freedom as fundamentally "useful" in maximizing happiness.

6) Domestic liberal principles can be applied to international relations.

7) Benthem believed a liberal international order would create laws and norms through diplomatic discussion, an international court, and, if need be, an army drawn from all nations.

8) Kant believed that democratic states would be more peaceful, and proposed a "confederacy of free nations" linked by cosmopolitan principles of universal hospitality.

9) Criticisms of liberalism generally center on the idea that liberalism is too individualistic, elitist, and hypocritical.

CHAPTER 16: MARXISM

> ### Overview
>
> This chapter introduces the basic vocabulary of Marxist theory and explains its implications for global politics. In particular, we introduce
>
> - The **labor theory of value**
> - The idea of "class conflict" between the bourgeoisie and proletariat
> - The exploitative nature of capitalism with an emphasis on **alienation** and **commodification**
>
> We'll explain Marx's ideas of the development of history, examining **historical materialism** and giving an account of how later thinkers have developed these ideas to address the globalized world.

Labor Theory of Value

Let's start with two basic questions. What makes something yours? And, once something *is* yours, what makes it valuable? The questions seem too simple, and your answer to them probably has something to do with *money*. Something is yours because you paid for it. Something is valuable because it costs a lot of money. Those answers, obvious as they appear, do not answer the questions at all, but simply rephrase them. What makes money yours? Why is money valuable in the first place?

In 1690, **John Locke** (whom we have just discussed in our chapter on liberalism) gave another answer to the question: **work**. Something is yours because you work for it. And, the harder you have to work, the more valuable it becomes. Locke illustrated this idea, called the **labor theory of value**, with a famous example. Consider an apple tree in the wilderness. The apple tree does not belong to anyone but exists in what he called "**the commons,**" free and open to all. What do you do to make the apple yours? A small amount of work: you climb the tree, reach up, and grab it. You might do a bit *more* work—for example, you might core the apple, plant the seeds, and grow an orchard. But, in any case, your work is what "annexes" (takes) the apple from the commons and makes it your personal property. Locke thought that the right to property was an extension of the right to bodily freedom and self-preservation. If you're free to move your hand (and any animal is) then you're also free to grab an apple with it and free to eat the apple to stay alive.

There were, according to Locke, only two conditions to the right to property: first, you couldn't steal someone else's property; and, secondly, you couldn't destroy the commons: for example, by cutting down the apple tree or picking all the apples and allowing them to go to waste. Doing that, Locke said, would be violating the right of others to make use of the commons and would be an act of war against all society. Other than that, Locke said, someone could take as many apples as he or she could reasonably use. In 1690, he believed the world was big enough, that the commons was abundant enough, that there would be more than enough apples for everyone. It is important to note here that Locke's argument reflects the liberal idea (see previous chapter) of the right to individual freedom and **agency.**

(Fig 16.1) John Locke believed **the commons**: the idea that there was enough land which was free and open for anyone to use and develop. In the 17th century, when Locke wrote, there was a great deal of public land throughout Europe.	**(Fig 16.2)** The British Enclosure Act (1783) erected walls on many large estates, effectively eliminating "the commons" in England. With all land privately owned, there was an increase in the prosecution of the poor who hunted and foraged on the property of the landowners.

Key Vocab

Labor Theory of Value: The idea, derived from John Locket, that the value and ownership of something is a reflection of work. Karly Marx would later define the value of a commodity in terms of the amount of "socially necessary labor time" to produce it.

The commons: Locke's ideal of an "unclaimed" state of nature in which resources were free for the taking.

Bourgeoisie and Proletariat

120 years later, a young journalist named **Karl Marx** was reporting on a peculiar problem in Germany. Courts were prosecuting, at high rates, men and women for the crime of gathering fallen wood from the estates of wealthy landowners. In the 1830's, in the states of Prussia and the Rhineland, almost 90% of all criminal cases (hard to believe) concerned the "theft" of fallen wood. Why was this such a problem? As industry had developed in Germany, demand for lumber had increased. The landowners used fallen wood, not only for their own purposes but also to sell for a profit. While in the 18th century people had been allowed to gather wood freely, now, as wood became scarcer and more profitable, they were forced to buy it. To Marx, these prosecutions were outrageous. If "the common mass of propertyless people," as he put it, could not so much as pick up a stick off the ground without facing a criminal charge, then they seemed to be completely helpless in the world. If Locke had been alive, it is likely that he too would have regarded such a situation as morally troubling. Echoing the spirit of Locke, Marx wrote, "If every violation of property...is theft, would not private property itself be theft? Through my private property do I not exclude someone else from this property?"

(Fig 16.3) *The Poacher*, by Frederic Rouge (1908) depicts a man "stealing" from the large estate of a landowner. Prosecutions for the theft of wood outraged a young Karl Marx who believed that the wealthy owning all of the property "excluded" everyone else from acquiring any property of their own. This idea resembles the Lockean idea of property as legitimate only given a commons which was big enough for everyone.

Indeed, in Marx's time (as in ours), this situation was not only true in the case of wood but for any commodity. Apples, clothing, housing, tools, medicine—all of the things necessary for the sustenance of life—cost money. No "commons," in Locke's sense, existed. Nothing was "there for the taking." Everything was already owned by someone else—either a wealthy corporation or wealthy individual. Marx referred to this state of affairs as **the private ownership of the means of production**. "Means of production," meant the land or equipment necessary for the creation of essential products. The factories, farms, and machines were largely owned by a class of wealthy elites called **the bourgeoisie**. Everyone else, the ordinary people, who Marx referred to as **the proletariat**, were required to sell their labor to the bourgeoisie to make a living. In the case of the wood-gathers, the wealthy estate owners represented the bourgeoisie and the "thieves" represented the proletariat. For Marx, the relationship between the bourgeoisie and the proletariat was an immoral one, indicative of deep economic inequality.

Key Vocabulary

Means of production: the factories, farms, tools, and raw materials necessary to produce the commodities needed for life.

Bourgeoisie: The small fraction of wealthy elites who own the means of production.

Proletariat: The "working class" that sells its labor to the bourgeoisie for a wage.

Capitalism and Exploitation

Over time, Marx worked his economic preoccupations over the relationship between the bourgeoisie and proletariat into a unified theory. In philosophical and economic writings such as *The Communist Manifesto* (1848) and *Das Kapital* (1867), he concluded that **post industrial capitalism**, the economic system in Europe following the industrial revolution, was based on exploitation and conflict. How so? Part of it could be deduced from simple observation. Cities had expanded in post-industrial Europe. The population had grown. Men, women, and (in many cases) children worked in cramped factories making consumer goods for very low wages. While the bourgeoisie had prospered, the majority of people had very little for themselves, toiling away in dangerous conditions, poorly housed, fed, and dressed.

Yet there was more to the economic story than simple wealth inequality. Furthermore, the fact that the rich were getting richer and the poor poorer was not caused by any cold-hearted greed on the part of the bourgeoisie. Rather, Marx thought, exploitation, inequality, and poverty were *necessary* for the functioning of capitalism. The situation was, to use a term later Marxists would adopt, "**systemic**." To understand how this is so, consider the consequences of basic capitalist principles such as profit, supply, and demand. In order for any product to be made, under capitalism, it is necessary that the price exceed the cost. If it costs ten dollars to manufacture a pair of shoes, for example, the shoes cannot be sold, say, for nine. They have to be sold for at least eleven or twelve. The process of making a product, therefore, generates **surplus value** or "profit." If this profit were returned to the proletariat (through higher wages), then the cost of production would increase and the price would increase in turn. Therefore, the surplus value, under capitalism, must be kept by the bourgeoisie. Marx called this **the law of capitalist accumulation**. Put simply, it means that the bourgeoisie must keep the value that the workers create.

Another source of exploitation, Marx thought, was related to the basic function of supply and demand in the labor market. Any society, by necessity, will have *some* level of unemployment.

There will always be more potential workers than jobs. The existence of the unemployed, whom Marx referred to as **the surplus army of the proletariat,** will keep wages low for the simple reason that the supply of workers will always exceed the demand for work. There may be charitable bosses who choose to pay high wages, but this, in the capitalist system, will be the exception rather than the rule. In a competitive market, a boss who pays low wages will be able to produce goods more efficiently and outcompete one who pays high wages. Because of surplus unemployment, he'll always be able to find workers willing to accept less and less. For this reason, the earnings of the proletariat will always tend toward the minimum necessary for survival.

(Fig 16.5) The **surplus army of the proletariat**: there will always be more jobless people, according to Marx, than available jobs. Thus, wages will always be low under capitalism. (Pictured: an impoverished family, 1931).	**(Fig 16.6) Industrialization** in Europe led to an increase in factory workers working in dangerous conditions for low wages. It seemed obvious to Marx that these workers were being exploited by wealthy bosses.

Alienation and Commodification

This exploitation not only affected the wages of the workers but had negative psychological effects as well. It is only natural, Marx thought, to feel a certain connection between identity and work, between who you are and what you happen to be doing. In our own culture the common question, when meeting a new person, "what do you do?" reflects the close relationship between self and job. Ordinary human wishes, however, are wide-ranging and various. In the morning, you might feel like hunting, and, in the afternoon, fishing, and, in the evening, to use Marx's example, writing criticism. Moreover, if you do any of those things, you expect, ordinarily, to enjoy the fruits of your labor. The pleasure of hunting an animal or catching a fish or writing a bit of criticism is that you get to keep what you've worked for. However, in a capitalist society, there is rarely this connection between work and satisfaction. "Each worker," Marx wrote, "has a particular, exclusive sphere of activity, which is forced upon him and from which he cannot escape. He is a hunter, a fisherman, a herdsman, or a critical critic, and must remain so if he does not want to lose his means of livelihood." Put simply, workers do not do what they want to do but what the job demands. The ordinary connection between work and reward, creating and creation is lost in capitalism. This is so firstly, because, in an industrial society, due to the **"division of labor,"** most workers only make *part* of a product; and, secondly, because, as soon as the product is made it is **commodified**: appropriated by the bourgeoisie and exchanged for money. Marx called this lost connection between the worker and the product **alienation** and believed that the life of most workers was marked by frustration and boredom. While workers were at work, they felt deprived of their individuality, transformed into an impersonal process, mere **"cogs in a machine."** A worker, as he put it, "does not feel not feel content but unhappy, does not freely develop his physical and mental energy but mortifies his body and ruins his mind. The worker only feels himself outside his work, and in his work feels alienated."

Key Vocabulary

Commodification: The process in which a thing is turned into a "product" to be exchanged for money.

Alienation: The dissatisfaction of workers due to the fact that they are forced into an "exclusive sphere of activity" and that the things they make do not belong to them.

Dialectical Materialism

Another crucial element of Marx's theory was his account of history. This stemmed from a basic question, seemingly unrelated to economics: what comes first: ideas or things? Mind or matter? Marx thought this was one of the most crucial questions in philosophy, and his answer was the latter. Before anything else, people must produce what they need to survive. The material conditions of the world, what Marx called the **base,** are primary. Once the material conditions of society are established, once people have created the patterns of life which enable them to feed and clothe themselves, then mental life—culture, philosophy, religion, art, politics—what Marx called the **superstructure**—appears as a consequence. For Marx, this relationship—base first, superstructure second—undergirded historical development. Marx's colleague Engels referred to this theory as "materialist dialectics." Later Marxists swapped the order of the words and called it "**dialectical materialism.**" The "dialectical" part means that history develops in a back-and-forth (a dialect) between matter and mind, and the "materialism" part means that the matter comes first.

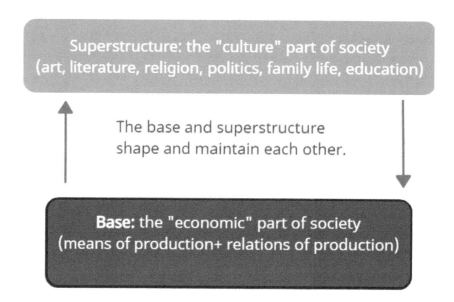

Dialectical materialism makes Marxism a **holistic theory.** It is not only about the economy and social relations but about everything else too: history, politics, religion, culture. How can this be so? Because, if, as Marx thought, everything starts with material conditions, then everything can be reduced to the simplest terms. A society begins creating an economic base: a farm, for example. Over time, economic activity creates culture as a reflection of the base. The culture "maintains and conditions" the economic activity. As the base of a society changes, the superstructure changes along with it. As farm life transitions to factory life, the culture develops. This theory allowed Marx to critique nearly every aspect of the European world. Religion, for example, which he famously termed **the opium of the people**, reflected an economy which demanded that workers serve powerful elites. An omnipotent God demanding obedience from men and women stuck Marx as a reflection of a powerful boss requiring service from dependent workers. Novels and works of art depicting an exaltant hero, triumphing over lesser characters, mirrored an economy in which powerful men believed they had earned the reverence of their social inferiors. If these examples seem too lofty and far-reaching, consider the culture in our own day. It seems obvious that many of the cultural choices that people make—the clothes they wear, the music they listen to, the television shows they watch—arise from powerful economic interests: the Walmarts, and the Apples, and the Warner Brothers of the world.

The relationship between the base and the superstructure, Marx argued, was not permanently stable. **Class struggle** within a society had led to crises throughout history and would continue to do so. "The history of all hitherto existing society," he wrote at the start of **The Communist Manifesto**, "is the history of class struggle." The tension between the bourgeoisie and the proletariat was only the most recent manifestation. Before the industrial revolution, there had been the nobility and the commoners, and, before that, the lords and the serfs. The opposition between these groups had preceded, time and time again, "a revolutionary reconstitution of society at large:" in short, a new base and a new superstructure. Marx believed that various instabilities within the capitalist system (overproduction, economic competition, widespread poverty) would eventually lead to the proletariat rising up and overthrowing the bourgeoisie, seizing the means of production, and emancipating the oppressed workers. In doing so, they would first create **a socialist government**, where a large government centralized the means of production and redistributed its value to society at large and then, later, a **communist society**, where all wealth and production would be communally owned. This egalitarian utopia would not be very different from Locke's original conception of "the commons." In a prophecy which now seems rather naive, he thought the communist society would be the final stage in human social development, ending class struggle once and for all, and, along with it, the series of revolutions that had characterized epoch after epoch of human history.

Key Vocabulary

Class Struggle: The dominant "dialectical" force in history which led, over time, to revolutions in which a new economic base gave rise to a new superstructure and, with it, "entirely different social relations."

Communistic Society: The final form of historical development, according to Marx, in which the means of production would be communally owned.

(Fig 16.8) Balfour Kers' 1906 *From the Depths*

Questions for discussion

• What did Marx mean when he said that "the history of all hitherto existing society is a history of class struggle? What other revolutions might he have had in mind?

• How does Marx's idea of "class struggle" relate to his broader paradigm of the base and the superstructure?

International Politics

What does any of this have to do with international relations? Marx himself wrote surprisingly little about global politics, directing most of his intellectual energy toward the analysis of national (primarily British) capitalism. However, later Marxist thinkers, beginning in the early twentieth century, began to extend Marx's thought to the worldwide economy. Two of the earliest applications of Marxist theory to international relations were **Rosa Luxemberg's** *The Accumulation of Capital* and **Vladamir Lenin's** *Imperlialism: The Highest State of Capitalim*. These books argued that capitalism, needing cheaper labor (i.e., an even *larger* surplus army of the proletariat) and new markets in which to sell the goods it produced, inevitably led to global expansion (see Ch. 7). In the process of this expansion, Lenin argued, wealthy nations, which he termed **the core,** came to exploit poorer ones which he termed **the periphery**, forming a global model along the lines of Marx's bourgeoisie- proletariat relationship.

    In the later twentieth century, **Immanuel Wallerstein** developed this idea into he termed **world-systems theory:** a model of understanding global relationships in terms of the unequal exchange of labor, materials, and manufactured goods. To Lenin's basic framework of the core and the periphery, Wallerstein added the "semi-periphery," a group of nations with a medium level of development, which correspond to a kind of "middle-class" between the wealthy core and the impoverished periphery. The semi-periphery, according to Wallerstien, prevented global revolution in two ways: first, by providing poorer nations a model to emulate and, second, by breaking the working class up along nationalist lines. If the working class in core nations "blamed" the working class in periphery or semi-periphery nations for stealing jobs, then they would see the class enemy not, as Marx thought, as the bourgeoisie but as "foreign" workers. Wallerstien's world-systems theory remains an influential critical tool in articulating how the international relations can be understood in Marxist terms.

Questions for discussion

Marx divided all society into "bourgoisie" and "proletariat," yet says little about the middle class. What would Marx have thought about the middle class? Whose side were they on? What would he have thought about instances of "social mobility" where someone starts out poor and works his or her way up to the top?

Marx famously opposed social welfare schemes (labor laws, social security, unemployment insurance) calling them "a disguised form of alms." Why do you think he did so? Why, from a Marxist perspective, might social welfare be a bad thing?

World Systems Model of Exploitation

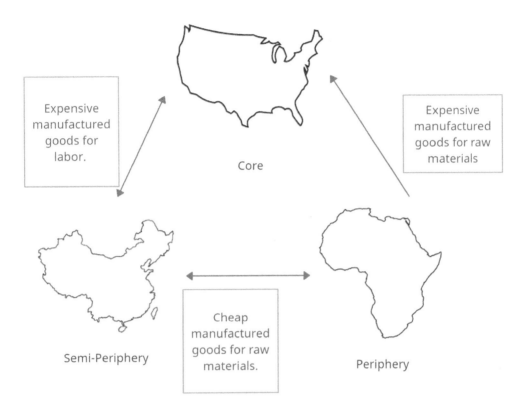

20th Century Marxists

Thinker	Innovation on Marxist Theory
Rosa Luxembourg (1871-1919)	Capitalism will always expand into foreign markets. Imperialism and colonialism are necessary consequences of the capitalist system.
Vladamir Lenin (1870-1924)	The world is divided into the developed "core" and the undeveloped "periphery."
Antonio Gramsci (1891-1937)	The bourgeoisie creates "cultural hegemony" by creating a dominant culture which the majority of society accept.
Paul Baran (1926-2011)	Key figure in the "Dependency School." Argued that the highly developed core both exploits nations in the periphery but also prevents their development.
Immanuel Wallerstein (1930-2019)	Added the "semi-periphery" to Lenin's core-periphery model. Argued that the semi-periphery stabilized the capitalist system by dividing the workers and preventing revolution.

Criticisms and legacy

There have been many criticisms of Marxist theory, both at the philosophical and pragmatic levels. Philosophically, critics have questioned many of Marx's fundamental assumptions. For example, many economists have regarded the "labor theory of value" as simplistic and inaccurate. Labor seems to be only one factor among many in how value is created in an economy. Water in the middle of the desert, for example, is significantly more valuable than water in a wetland, though it may have been no more difficult for the workers to build the pipes. A Boeing 747 is more valuable than an biplane, even though the biplane probably took longer to make and its pilot, in all likelihood, has to work harder to fly it. Other critics find fault with Marx's "fixed classes" of bourgeoisie and proletariat. It is possible, and in many cases not infrequent, for an individual to begin at a low-wage job, save money, enter the middle class, and, over time, become quite rich. Even assuming social classes are more or less fixed, does it follow that social relations "dominated" by class conflict as Marx thought? Friendships, romantic partnerships, parent-child relationships, peer groups, hobby groups, religious communities: all of these interconnect, forming an interwoven complexity of social life. To insist that "class" is the force which underlies and controls everything else is perhaps too simple. Finally, even in the context of wage labor, is the relationship between boss and worker necessarily as immoral as Marx thought? The underlying exchange between worker and a boss, after all, is one which is freely chosen by both. The boss thinks it is in his best interest to hire the worker, and the worker, often, thinks it is in his best interest to go to work. Marx perhaps failed to realize that free consent can often lead to unequal conditions, yet conditions which are not necessarily exploitative. To take an example from the libertarian philosopher Robert Nozick, suppose everyone in a society earned the same wage, and, once a year, everyone decided to pay twenty-five cents to watch a great basketball star play. With an additional twenty-five cents per person added to his salary, the basketball star would be far wealthier than anyone else. Yet such wealth inequality, based on free exchange, could hardly be described as unjust.

The most devastating critiques however, have been those based on the observations of what has happened in Marxist countries. During the twentieth century (see ch. 6), the Soviet Union, China, and many other nations adopted communist governments and attempted to put Marx's theories into practice. Beginning with the **Russian Revolution** in 1917, nearly fifty nations adopted communism and promised to emancipate the workers from conditions of capitalist oppression. With few exceptions, however, these experiments were failures, leading to poor economic growth, violations of human rights, dictatorial governments, and, in several cases, mass killings. The Marxist leaders of the twentieth century: Joseph Stalin, Pol Pot, Fidel Castro, Kim Il Sung are often remembered as tyrants, victimizing their own people for political gain. Promising liberation, such leaders, at best, can be said to have replaced an oppressive bourgeoisie with an even more oppressive state.

Figs (16.9-11) Stalin, Pol Pot, and Kim Il Sung. The most devestating critique of Marxism has been the cruelty and inefficiency of Marxist governments.

Despite these philosophical and historical criticisms, Marxism remains a highly influential theory in global politics, international relations, and the humanities. In every university in the United States, there are economists, political scientists, literary critics, and artists who identify as Marxists and who keep Marxism alive and well in the intellectual community. It cannot be denied that few theories, in the history of philosophy, have combined such a comprehensive picture of how the world works with such a rousing vision of how to make it a better place. Few theories have so evocatively tapped into the widespread human intuition that it is, at best, boring, and, at worst, dehumanizing, to have to work an unfulfilling job for less money than you want. It is for these reasons that, whatever its shortcomings may be, Marxism will remain an essential part of the "marketplace of ideas" for years to come.

Summing up: Key Chapter Points

1) Marxism builds on Locke's "labor theory of value," the idea that labor is what ultimately underlies property and value.

2) In a world in which "the means of production" are owned by a tiny minority of elites, the bourgeoisie, scarcity forces the majority of people into the unhappy circumstances of selling their labor for a barely adequate wage.

3) The exploitation of the proletariat by the bourgeoisie is not a result of personal greed but the normal functioning of the capitalist system.

4) Marxism is a holistic theory, applying not only to the economy but to every aspect of society and culture.

5) Marx's "dialectical materialism" analyzes historical development in economic terms, showing how the material base of a society conditions the superstructure.

6) Class conflict leads to revolutions in which a new base gives rise to a new superstructure.

7) Though Marx himself wrote little about international relations, later Marxist theorists, such as Luxembourg, Lenin, and Wallenstein applied his theories to global politics.

8) Criticisms of Marxism rest both on inaccuracies in Marx's central assumptions as well as the failures of communist governments.

9) Despite these criticisms, Marxism remains a potent force in political theory.

CHAPTER 17: FEMINISM

Overview

This chapter introduces the history, theory, and praxis of feminist politics. We examine

- **Protofeminism** as a consequence of the enlightenment emphasis on autonomy
- The **labor movement** and 19th century female participation in the workforce
- The impact of World War I on **suffrage movements**

Toward the end of the chapter we explain the different directions modern feminism has taken. In particular:

- **Empirical feminism**: examining differences in living standards between men and women
- **Institutional feminism**: examining how feminists attempt to reform institutions to make them more equitable
- **Cultural feminism**: examining how feminists analyze language, pop culture, literature and film in order to expose and critique the **social construction of gender**

In 1972, the American poet Adrian Rich wrote a poem called "Diving into the Wreck" which has since become a key text in the feminist movement. Her poem describes a scuba diver exploring an underwater ruin and ends with the lines

> You are
> By cowardice or courage
> The one who finds our way
> Back to this scene
> Carrying a knife, a camera
> A book of myths
> In which
> Our names do not appear.

Rich intended the final lines as a metaphor about what it is like to look at history from the perspective of a woman. In the historical "book of myths," the names of women are nowhere to be found. Where are they? History is all about men. Male generals who led their nations to victories in war. Male kings and presidents and statesmen. Male artists and writers and scientists and historians. Why do women seem so *invisible*? This is the foundational question for **feminism**. As a political theory, it aims to draw attention to the historical invisibility, marginalization, and oppression of women. As a form of **advocacy**, it is dedicated to fighting against it.

> **Key Vocabulary**
>
> **Feminism:** Both a political theory and a form of advocacy, feminism draws attention to the historical oppression of women and leads political actors to fight against it.

Early Foundations

Notions of the basic equality of the sexes, the intellectual aptitude of women, and the injustice of oppression, are often taken to be modern ideas. But, in fact, they are present in many of the oldest texts of the ancient world. Plato's *Republic* (375 BC) for example, written at a time when the inferiority of women was taken for granted, argues that, in an ideal society, women would be allowed the same opportunities as men:

> "The guardians of our state are to be watch-dogs, as we have already said. Now dogs are not divided into his and hers. We do not take the male dogs to hunt and leave the female dogs at home to take care of the puppies. They have the same duties. The only difference is that the one sex is physically stronger. But if women are to have the same duties as men, they must have the same education. They must be taught music and gymnastics, and the art of war.... Women are the same in kind as men, and have the same talents... in medicine or gymnastics or war...And if their natures are the same, the conclusion is that their education must also be the same. There is nothing unnatural or impossible in a woman learning music and gymnastics. The education which we give them will be the very best."

Many other ancient texts—philosophical treatises, religious books, and ancient poems contain strains of thought which might be called **protofeminist**, expressive of themes and concerns which would be expanded on in later feminist thinking.

Despite the presence of these elements in ancient texts, a continuous and coherent feminist tradition (at least in Europe) appears only the 1500's. The **invention of the printing press** during the early Renaissance led to a sharp increase in literacy and education, the result being that women, particularly those of the upper classes, had many more opportunities to read and write and be generally educated. No small number of these distinguished themselves in literature, scholarship, and the arts. In Italy, **Sofonisba Anguissola** became one of the best painters of her generation, producing portraits and genre pieces which continue to be exhibited in museums throughout Europe. In France, **Louise Labé** made herself famous as one of the best poets in France. In fact, her *Complete Works* contains a strongly-worded preface in which she urges women to take advantage of opportunities in education:

> By myself, I cannot fulfill the sincere wish I have for our sex, to see it surpass or equal men not only in physical beauty, but in knowledge and virtue. I urge noble ladies to raise their minds...and to dedicate themselves to making the world understand that if we are not made to be leaders, we should not be disrespected as partners....Beyond the fame our sex will receive, we will benefit the public good, since men will put more effort and study into valuable disciplines in order to avoid the shame of seeing themselves surpassed by women, over whom they have always claimed to be superior in almost everything.

In England, there was Arabella Stuart. An aristocrat judged to be a threat to the royal family, Stuart lived under a form of house arrest. Yet she mastered French, Italian, Latin, Greek, and Hebrew and is the author of some of the most intriguing and learned letters in the Renaissance period. Last, but by no means least, several countries in Europe, in the 16th century, had been ruled by (highly effective) female monarchs. While the reasons these queens ascended the throne is complex and often had more to do with the interests of the ruling families and empowered nobles than any cultural progressivism, women like Queen Elizabeth I of England, Isabel I of Spain and Jean d'Arbet of Narvarre prove that it was it was at least possible, during the Renaissance, for women to attain the highest positions of power and influence.

These women, of course, represent an aristocratic few. Opportunities for such fame and prestige were far beyond the grasp of ordinary women in the 1500's and 1600's. Their achievements, nonetheless, are essential in laying the foundation for later feminist thought. In particular, they gave to the feminist cause two valuable things. First they supplied to art and literature **the feminine perspective**. In a culture dominated by men, they expressed what it was like to be a woman living in their time and place. Secondly, they proved women, if given the opportunity, could achieve great things. In so doing, they set an example for later ambitious women to follow.

Question for Discussion

Why does the feminist tradition emphasize artists and writers? What does this say about the connection between politics and the arts?

Does the achievement of women like Sofonisba Anguissola, Louise Labe, and Arabella Stuart provide evidence that sexism "wasn't as bad" hundreds of years ago then we often assume? Why or why not?

Rise of Women in Early Modern Europe

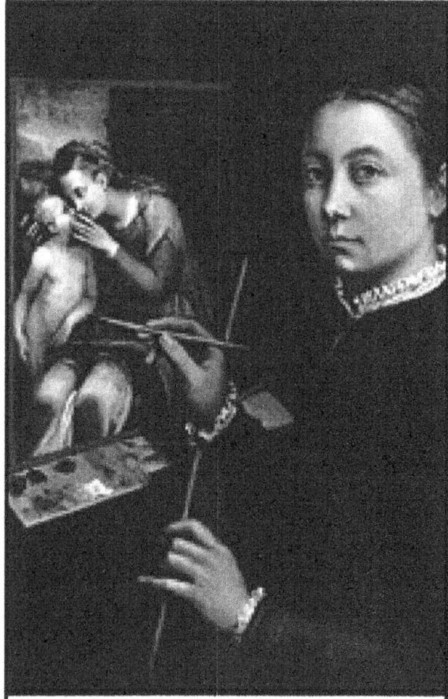

Figure 17.1
Sofonisba Anguissola
Italian painter

Figure 17.2
Louise Labé
French Poet

Figure 17.3
Arbella Stuart
English scholar

Figure 17.4
Jean d'Albret
Queen of Navarre

Figure 17.5
Isabel I
Queen of Spain

Figure 17.6
Elizabeth I
Queen of England

Liberalism and the case for rational equality

The feminist tradition grew stronger in the late 17th and early 18th centuries following the **liberal movement** in politics and philosophy (chapter 16). Just as liberal philosophers demanded freedom from **arbitrary power** and insisted on the rights of all individuals to think for themselves, early feminists of this period demanded **liberation** from the power of a male dominated world. At the time, the majority of women had no independence from their husbands and their fathers. They held little political power, little property, did not work outside of the home, and were, in effect, passed from one "guardianship" to another. Liberal feminists grounded their idea of female independence in the idea of **rationality**. It may be true, they argued, that men in general are physically stronger than women, but the core of human identity is not strength but reason: the capacity to perceive, analyze, and decide. Like other liberal philosophers, they invoked Christian ideas of "the soul" in order to argue that the spiritual self was more important than the "**gendered**" body. For example, **Mary Astell**, often referred to as the "the first English feminist" wrote in "A Serious Proposal to the Ladies:"

> Since God has given Women as well as Men intelligent Souls, why should they be forbidden to improve them? Since he has not denied us the faculty of Thinking, why should we not...employ our thoughts on Himself...Being the Soul was created for the contemplation of Truth as well as for the fruition of Good, is it not as cruel and unjust to exclude women from the knowledge of the one as the enjoyment of the other?

Atsell argued for the equal education of men and women, claiming, in particular, that teaching women "rationalist" philosophy would allow them to become more virtuous, enlightened, and independent.

Question for discussion

What is the connection between early feminism and the liberal tradition (ch 16)? In what ways might the ideas of liberalism still be useful to feminists? Do you think feminists *must* be liberals or is there room for feminism in other approaches to politics?

By far, however, the most impressive work of feminism from the liberal period is **Mary Wollstonecraft's** *Vindication of the Rights of Women.* Not only does *The Vindication* assert women's autonomy but also argues the revolutionary point of the view that the subjection of women is bad for society as a whole, harming even the men who hold positions of power. Beginning with Atsell's view that women were endowed with reason, and, as such, equal to men in intellectual and moral capacity, Wollstonecraft went on to argue that a society which prohibits "a certain degree of independence" to rational and moral humans cannot be a free and prosperous one. The subjugation of women not only denies the world the benefit of teachers, physicians, merchants, and artists but also perpetuates ideas of oppression that poison the whole of society. Wollstonecraft's primary goal was the same as Atsell's: to advocate for more opportunities in education for women. Yet, she went beyond Atsell in insisting that women be granted the opportunities to enter civil professions, writing:

> "Women might certainly study the art of healing, and be physicians as well as nurses... They might, also study politics, and settle their benevolence on the broadest basis...Business of various kinds, they might likewise pursue, if they were educated in a more orderly manner...Is not that government then very defective, and very unmindful of the happiness of one half of its members, that does not provide for honest, independent women, by encouraging them to fill respectable stations? But in order to render their private virtue a public benefit, they must have a civil existence in the state, married or single; else we shall continually see some worthy woman, whose sensibility has been rendered painfully acute by undeserved contempt, droop like "the lily broken down by a plough share."

Wollstonecraft's argument was forceful, and educational opportunities for women increased following the publication of her book. Still, it would not be until 1848, more than fifty years after her death, that **Queen's College in London** would become the first university in the world to grant women the chance to earn that same academic degrees that men did.

Question for discussion

Is it possible to separate education from professional life? What seems more important to feminism: the right of women to develop their "inner lives" through learning or the right of women to advance their "outer lives" by entering professions?

First Wave Feminism

By the middle of the 19th century, the idea that women could be the intellectual peers of men and, therefore, had a right to be educated was gaining broader social acceptance. The idea of women holding political power was another matter entirely. Though several states in Europe had had female monarchs, the vast majority of women had no real influence over state affairs. Women could not vote, be elected to parliaments, serve as representatives, or, in many cases, hold property independently of their husbands. The argument for denying women these rights was based on the idea of **separate domains**. The government, it was argued, makes decisions about two things: military affairs and industrial ones. Since women do not participate in either of these, it is inappropriate for them to exercise power over things they have no experience in. Women ought to leave the political sphere to the men who engage in these activities. Meanwhile, in the private sphere, women should be free to pursue self-improvement through art, education, and religion. Such a separation of the public and private domains seemed, at the time, to be a reasonable trade-off. Women were denied political influence, but they were also spared the rigors, say, of serving as a soldier or working in a coal mine. Furthermore, it should be noted that, at the time, few *men* had much political power either. In both Europe and the United States, there were significant property requirements to both vote and hold office, meaning that many men were just as politically helpless as women.

This thinking, however, began to change during the **Industrial Revolution** (chapter 8). Factories required large numbers of workers, and factory machines often required little physical strength to operate. Women (and unfortunately children) were cheaper to hire than men, the result being that women throughout Europe and the United States (particularly immigrant women) began entering the workforce as wage laborers. Political and economic rights followed, but only gradually. Advocacy during this period generally focused on improving working conditions in factories, increasing wages, and permitting a reasonable work-day. Pursuing these goals, female labor activists cooperated with men in the rising **labor movement**. For example, in the middle of the 19th century, the majority of workers involved in the manufacture of matches were women. These so-called "matchstick girls" worked long hours in conditions that exposed them to dangerous chemicals, such as white phosphorus, which caused rotting of the bones. Throughout the 19th century, the matchstick girls went on multiple strikes and organized a number of large public demonstrations. In 1871, thousands of matchstick girls marched to the British parliament in order to present a petition demanding a repeal of taxes on matches which would have reduced their wages. Ten years later, the political activist **Annie Besant** wrote an influential article comparing the working conditions of the matchstick girls to "white slavery" and organizing a boycott of products manufactured in dangerous factories. Over time, feminist labor advocacy, through marches, strikes, and protests gradually won political reforms.

Key Vocabulary

Labor Movement: A series of political strikes and protests in the 19th century aimed at increasing wages, reducing work-hours, and ensuring safe conditions in factories. Women were instrumental in many of these protests.

(Fig 17.7) Matchstick girls, England 1880

Economic power was a major step forward in the feminist movement. The right to political representation, however, would take longer. Starting in the 19th century, activists for **women's suffrage**, such as **Lucretia Mott** and **Elizabeth Cady Stanton** had argued that all women, in addition to all men, be granted the right to vote. In 1848, Mott and Stanton organized the **Seneca Falls Conference**, the first conference in the world explicitly dedicated to the problem of women's rights. Throughout the 19th centuries suffrage movements sprang up all over Europe and the United States, often allying with other liberal causes—such as labor reform and rights for racial minorities. It would not be, however, until the end of World War I that women's suffrage would become a reality. During the war, a large percentage of the male population was drafted into the army, leaving factories, particularly munitions factories, in desperate need for workers. Women entered the labor force in even larger numbers, earning more money than ever before, and, with it, increasing their political influence. By 1921, all of the major western powers had granted women the right to vote and the right to hold office.

1821: Widows and other single women permitted to own property in several US states.

1840: Married women permitted to own property independently of their husbands in several US states.

1848: Queen's College in England becomes first university in the world. to offer degrees to women

1860: Women permitted legal custody of their children in several US states.

1886: Women permitted to seek divorce unilaterally in case of "cruelty" in several US states.

1920: Right to vote made legal in US, Britain, Germany and many other western countries.

(Fig 17.8)

Second Wave and Third Wave Feminism: Beyond Suffrage

With the passage of the economic and political reform laws in the 1920's, women had acquired a degree of **formal equality.** They could own vote, own property, serve on juries, receive university education, and enter professions: rights which had previously been legally denied to them. Nonetheless, women still had a long way to go. Though they were equal to men "in law," it did not follow that they were equal "in fact." Throughout the twenty and twenty-first century, feminists have taken three different approaches to the remaining problems of women's rights.

First, there have been **empirical feminists** who have studied the facts and figures of inequality. These feminists have pointed out, for example, that women earn significantly less than men for doing the same jobs (about 24% less in the United States). They have demonstrated that women are less likely than men to hold advanced degrees, to be doctors, lawyers, professors, and heads of state. They have shown that women are more likely to do unpaid labor than men, more likely to lack comprehensive health insurance, and more likely to be victims of certain types of violence. Making these facts known, say empirical feminists, is the first step in advocacy. A problem cannot be solved unless it is fully understood. Such feminists have exposed and publicized problems affecting women by publicizing the cold, hard facts of **the gender gap.**

Key Vocabulary

The gender gap: empirical data showing the ways women are politically and economically unequal to men.

Institutional feminists have a slightly different focus. They have directed their attention to the social and economic institutions which underlie such inequalities. The laws and customs that prevented feminists from voting, owning property, and obtaining a divorce, such feminists have pointed out, represent only one type of institution: legal institutions. There are also family institutions, corporate institutions, academic institutions, and religious institutions. Reforming these institutions is more complex, because the sexism present in them is often hidden, implicit, or informal. For example, a workplace that offers no family leave or health insurance does not *explicitly* discriminate against women but it nonetheless makes it much more difficult for women to advance their careers there. A gymnasium with nothing but heavy weights may have no "official policy" of keeping women out, but many women will likely find themselves excluded by the fact that they do not feel comfortable there . A university which spends millions of dollars on its football team but only a few thousand on its volleyball team may have no intent to be sexist but its extracurricular expenditures have the effect of favoring men over women. Institutional feminists expose such hidden forms of inequality in order to fight for fairer institutional practices. For example, in recent years, feminists in the United States have successfully advocated for **Title VIII** and **Title IX** laws, stipulations which require all schools which receive government funding to have equal opportunities for male and female athletics, and, in addition, to have rigorous policies to prevent sexual harassment. Nearly all large corporations in the United States, due to feminist advocacy, offer maternity leave and the majority of businesses attempt to portray themselves as inclusive and sensitive to the experiences of female customers. (Whether they really *are,* of course, is a matter of debate).

Last but not least, **constructivist feminists** examine the basic elements of culture, such as language, art, music, and film in order to reveal the ways in which unconscious assumptions reflect male power. For example, it is common, in English, to refer to a poor player in a football or baseball game as someone who "throws like a girl." Though the expression is usually not intended to be sexist, it nonetheless indicates basic prejudices: namely, that men are strong and skillful while women are weak and clumsy. Constructivist feminists refer to these hidden assumptions as part of what is called the **social construction of gender**. It is true, such feminists say, that basic biological differences exist between men and women. But such differences do not explain the way that men and women are perceived or the way expectations and perceptions are woven into language. Such ideas of "gender" (as distinct from sex) are culturally learned. In western societies, these patterns tend to portray masculinity as dominant, strong, and reasonable; and femininity as inferior, weak, and irrational. Constructivist feminists attempt to reveal these connotations in order to reverse them. Because these assumptions are often hidden in various cultural forms, feminists are particularly interested in literature, film, music, and pop-culture, and many of the leading feminists in this domain are writers, musicians, and critics.

Key Questions: What you need to know

• What are the differences between empirical, institutional, and cultural methods of feminist critique?

• Are these methods mutually exclusive? If not, how do they relate to each other?

Feminist Advocacy in Academia, Government, and the Arts

  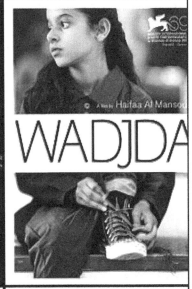

Figure 17.9

The American feminist **Gloria Steinem** founded *Ms. Magazine*, the first magazine devoted to feminist social critique. Due in part to Steinem's advocacy, there are currently hundreds of feminist journals and nearly all large universities have a Department of Women's Studies.

Figure 17.9

In 1948, women were allowed to serve in the United States military. Since then, feminists have advocated for greater roles and protections for female soldiers. Making organizations of power more inclusive is a central goal to institutional feminists.

Figure 17.11

Female Saudi Arabian film maker **Haifa Al- Mansour** produced the first movie in the history of Saudi Arabian cinema. A story of a young girl in the city of Riyahd, *Wadjda* has been an important film in depicting womanhood in the Gulf Arabic world.

Questions for discussion:

• Unlike other political philosophies, feminism, particularly cultural feminism, pays close attention to movies, pop-culture, music, and literature. Why do you suppose this is? In what ways are these forms of expression political?

• Can institutions be "gendered?" What might this mean? Give an example of a gendered institution?

Feminism and International Relations

With the globalization of world politics, many of the concerns of feminism have shifted from the domestic to the international level. Questions such as "in what ways are women global actors" and "what effects does international relations have on women" have become increasingly relevant in feminst theory. The historical root of these questions, at least in the twentieth century, it could be argued, traces to the foundation of the **Women's International League of Peace and Freedom.** Formed during World War I, the WILPF originally organized in order to fight for an end to World War I. During the interwar period, it petitioned the League of Nations to undertake an investigation of international women's issues, the first internationally-sponsored study of its kind. The WILPF remains active in the United Nations and, along with other international feminist groups, helps make sure that UN resolutions include measures to protect women, particularly women exposed to conflict.

Indeed, the role of women as political actors in promoting peace has a long international history, and has been increasingly important in the past decades. For example, in 1977 women in Afghanistan formed the **Revolutionary Association of the Women of Afghanistan**. Their initial purpose was to open schools and orphanages in parts of Afghanistan which had been devastated by the invasion of the Soviet Union. During the period of Taliban rule, the RAWA were important in publicizing the human rights abuses of the government. In 2001, when the United States invaded Afghanistan, the RAWA's advocacy turned truly global in scope. They wrote to the UN opposing the invasion, formally petitioned the United States and testified before the German parliament in an effort to convince Germany to leave the military coalition. The RAWA demonstrates the capacity for feminist organizations to be decisive in international diplomacy.

Another significant issue in feminist global politics relates to the clash of cultures. Does "women's rights" mean the same thing to a woman in Switzerland as to a woman in Pakistan? Whose definition of "womanhood" is correct, and how does this dilemma effect international institutions? Such questions have grown more urgent in recent years due to the debate, in many European countries, over the permissability of Muslim head-scarves in public. To certain law-makers in France, for example, the veils and burqas traditionally worn by Muslim women in the Middle East are a symbol of sexual oppression. They point to the poor human rights records in Muslim countries and argue that garments which reflect male domination have no place in European society. This, however, is not the way many Muslim women feel. To many of them, the hijab and the burqa are part of their essential identities. To them, the western idea of womanhood—with its emphasis on commercialized sexual glamor—is what seems oppressive. They point out that wealthy western women have too long dominated the discussion of what it means to be a feminist and that other perspectives are needed.

(Fig 17.12) Women in France protest government bands on certain Muslim head-coverings	(Fig 17.13) A Gathering of the Women of Liberia, Mass Action for Peace, a group which was largely successful in helping to end the Second Liberian Civil War

Criticisms

Criticisms of feminism, from men and women alike, have been widespread throughout the theory's history. These criticisms tend to fall into two main categories: criticisms that allege that feminism is bad for women, and criticisms that allege that feminism is bad for politics more broadly. On the bad-for-women side, certain critics point out that much of feminism is centered on the acquisition of power. Such power tends to be highly individualized and confined to those (men and women both) in the highest reaches of the cultural elite. Few women throughout history, it is true, have been doctors, lawyers, professors, and politicians. But, in terms of gross numbers, few men have either. The vast majority of men (like the even vaster majority of women) have been historically excluded from power and have had to earn a modest and not terribly dignified living in the menial professions which define the bulk of any country's labor force. To insist that women have been "denied power," then, is firstly to provide a distorted understanding of the way power is distributed in society and, secondly, to impose upon women a "standard of achievement" which is often degrading. Women are expected to enter the competitive "ratrace" and to measure their worth in terms of their educational and career attainments. In doing so, the argument runs, women are forced to become "like men." Thus, liberated women share in all of the misery of manhood.

Criticisms which argue that feminism is bad for society as a whole tend to focus on the notion that feminism is an "oppositional" philosophy. It often suggests that men are "the oppressors" or "the enemy" and that the political goal is to take power away from the men who have it. This mindset prevents society from being envisioned as a cooperative whole: one in which individual men and individual women care for one another and work together for the common good. It is also pointed out that the competitive nature of feminism obscures political problems by directing attention to the wrong things. For example, the politburo of the Soviet Union had no female members. Neither did the highest offices of the Nazi party. Would it have been good for women to have served on them? The obvious answer seems to be no. Likewise, major corporations have few female CEO's, but why should it be desirable for women to be CEO's of major corporations? Is it "good" to be a CEO? Would simply changing the gender of the CEO's make corporations any better? Assuming nothing else changed, it does not seem that simply changing the gender of one individual or another in positions of power would lead to a more just world. The more important question, critics argue, is what power is being used *for*, not who happens to hold it.

Feminists, of course, have numerous responses to these criticisms, but perhaps the simplest is to point out that simply "having the conversation" is, by itself, a feminist act. This chapter began by quoting the Adrian Rich line about "the book of myths/ in which [women's] names do not appear." The debate over feminism, of necessity, pays attention to women and to women's voices. That attention itself, it might be argued, is the first step to making sure that women's names *do* appear in the books which future generations will read.

Feminism at a glance

Gernal Theme	The fight against the oppression of women
Starting Point	Women have been subjugated to men throughout history and denied political, economic, and social power.
Human Nature	Socially constructed--particularly with regard to assumptions about men and women.
International System	Gendered, dominated by men.
Purpose of Government	To create a more equal world in which women are included in positions of power and leadership.

Summing up: Key Chapter Points

1) Though protofeminist ideas are present in ancient texts, a continuous feminist tradition appears in Europe roughly around the time the printing press was invented.
2) Early success by women in art and literature proved that women could be as talented as men if given the opportunity.
3) Early feminists in the 18th century built upon the liberal tradition in demanding freedom from arbitrary power on the grounds of reason and autonomy.
4) The industrial revolution and World War I helped women to gain political and economic rights as they entered the labor force in larger numbers.
5) More recent feminist thinkers have focused on empirical, institutional, and constructivist elements of society.
6) As society has globalized women have proven key actors in international politics.

CHAPTER 18: SOCIAL CONSTRUCTIVISM

Overview

This chapter introduces the vocabulary, concepts, and political implications of social constructivism, analyzing

- The idea of **holism** and how it applies to politics
- The relationship between **agents** and **structures**
- The types of structures that inform our day to day lives: discourse, identities, social facts, and norms
- The relevance of social constructivism in the politics of advocacy

---

Parts and wholes

Let's start with a thought experiment. Take a look at your hand. How many parts can you divide it into? The big palm with all of its lines—the fingers and the thumb, and the bones inside of them: knuckles, nails, muscles, tendons, nerves. You can think about each part in turn, give it a name, and understand its function. At the same time, it's obvious that you can't understand these parts without understanding the entire hand, just as you can't understand the hand without the body. The body, the complete "togetherness" of its form and functions, is the explanation of the parts.

This idea, called **holism**, has a long philosophical history. It is the notion that **the whole is greater than the sum of its parts**, or, more academically phrased, that individual units cannot be understood in the absence of overarching structures. The metaphor of the body, as an illustration of this idea, is common in politics. For example, it is a common cliche to refer to a nation or a society as a "political body" made up of many different social roles (teachers, laborers, politicians, engineers, artists). All American money is inscribed with the Latin motto *e pluribus unum*: "out of many, one."

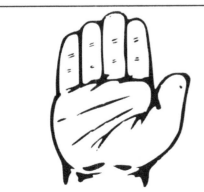

Holism: the idea that structures are the explanation of individual units and that individual units cannot be understood in the absence of structures.

Social constructivism: the idea that politics is best understood as the relationship between decision-makers (agents) and social conditions (structures).

This simple idea is a useful place to start a discussion of a much more complex one, **social constructivism,** one of the most popular theories in politics today. As the name implies, social constructivism looks at the broader wholes or "structures" which make up society. The starting point of this theory is that there is a "back and forth" between these structures and various decision-makers, or **agents**. Structures precede and help to form agents, and yet agents, through their decisions, help to shape and change these structures. An unpoetic sentence which appears again and again in the literature of social constructivism is "structures construct agents" and then, later on, "agents construct structures." To use a simple example of this relationship, consider what it's like playing a game. The rules of the game provide the structure to the gameplay. They come *before* the individual players decide to play. However, during a game, the players might come up with a slight variation or an improvisation or a new rule. Over time, over the course of many games and many players, these variations might entirely change the game into a new one which, then, will be left for new players to, in turn, to play and modify.

But how does this apply to politics? What are the political structures that shape political actors? How do agents shape structures, and why does it matter? This chapter will provide a brief overview of the vocabulary and issues of social constructivism in politics.

Discourse and Identity

One of the most subtle yet pervasive structures underlying political behavior is **language** itself. We do not invent the words and ideas we use to refer to reality. Each of us are born into a world which is noisy with meanings. We inherit from our culture an enormous vocabulary, thick with suggestions, pressures, assumptions, nuances, and biases. These meanings, and not simply our own natures, are often the source of the motivations behind our actions. In analyzing how this happens, post-structuralist thinkers often owe a debt to the **poststructuralist** philosophers of the 1960's, particularly to the work of **Michel Foucault** and **Jacques Derrida**. One of Derrida's major insights is that words in language often do not exist in a state of neutrality but rather as part of "hierarchy of differences." As we talk to one another, as we engage in **social discourse**, certain terms are unconsciously validated and others are just as unconsciously delegitimized. To take the example from the previous chapter, a lousy baseball player might be accused of "throwing like a girl." Though the expression is generally considered to be a fairly *mild* insult (as insults go), it reveals the hierarchical patterns in our thinking. It is a common assumption (and has been so for many years) that femininity is associated with gentleness, weakness, emotionality, dependency, and subservience; and masculinity with boldness, strength, reason, independence and leadership. For the most part, we do not "discover" these meanings through our own experience. Rather they precede us. They form the "semantic environment" that we are born into and which we unconsciously internalize by virtue of participating in society. The example of masculinity and femininity is part of what is called the **social construction of gender**, the way discourse itself forms our assumptions about what it means to be male or female.

(Fig 18.2) Michel Foucault (1926-1984) argued that the very structure of institutions exerts unconscious power over agents. A major figure in poststructuralist philosophy, his work continues to influence political thought today.

(Fig 18.3) Jacques Derrida (1930-2004) understood language to operate within a hierarchy of differences. A controversial and often obscure thinker, his work has likewise proved foundational to much contemporary political thought.

Gender, of course, is hardly the only identity to be socially constructed. Consider religious identity. What does it mean to be a Christian or a Muslim or a Jew or a Hindu or a Budhist? To a certain degree, it depends who you ask. Each religion has a set of "predicates" (descriptions) which help define what it means to be a believer. Often these predicates serve as a barrier between "self" and "other," between the "in-group" and the "out-group." Furthermore, these predicates can be highly **relative**, indexed to the speaker and his or her assumptions. If, for example, a Jewish person says the word "Jew," he is referring to one of his own, and the world likely conveys connotations of "warmth" or "piety." But if a non-Jew says the word "Jew," he may be referring to something alien and other, perhaps even a "heathen" or an "infidel."

Such dichotomies can apply to political identities and ideological propositions as well. For example, in the United States, political activists who are in favor of legalized abortion use the term "pro-choice" to describe their position and refer to their oponents as "anti-choice." They will often refer to legalized abortion as "reproductive rights." Notice the way the language itself motivates political action on its own. Their ideological counterparts, of course, do the same thing. Activists who oppose legalized abortion refer to themselves as "pro-life" and to their adversaries as "anti-life." Once again, the implications of the words themselves are doing ideological heavy lifting. Or consider the difference between referring to members of an armed political group as "terrorists" or "freedom-fighters." Or between calling the results of an interstate conflict "genocide" vs "tribal warfare."

The point, in all of this, is not deciding what words are "correct" or what descriptions are "true." The point is simply that these meanings *precede our* own consciousness and agency. They are one of the structures that we are summoned into, and they tend to shape the norms of political action before we have a chance to subject them to rational **critique**.

Social Facts

Related to discourse is the idea of the world being composed of **social facts**. If we look at the world around us, we encounter certain "hard" facts that seem to be in no way dependent on our mental states or linguistic practices. For example, we live in a world of cats and dogs and mountains and rivers and flowers and stars. These things seem to be out there on their own, and their existence does not rely on human **consensus**. However, we also live in a world of time and money and train schedules and songs and holidays. These things, social facts, do depend on consensus. They are a reflection of cultural agreement, formed over time, and reinforced with each new generation. At times, it can be hard to tell the difference between a hard fact and a social fact. For example, that fire radiates heat seems to be an unmistakable hard fact about the world. But that it burns at, say, 2500 degrees Fahrenheit or 1400 degrees Centigrade is a social fact, since the units of measurement that we use are socially constructed. The insect that is perhaps crawling around your classroom at this very moment seems to be a hard fact. But that we call it a "spider" in English and classify it, in Latin, as belonging to the order of *araneae* is a social fact. It isn't that hard facts exist "over here" and social facts exist "over there." Hard facts and social facts are inextricably knotted together in the human experience of the world, woven so tightly into one another that it is sometimes hard to tell them apart.

What does this have to do with politics? Well, consider some of the big political ideas we've learned about so far. Think about the ideas of "sovereignty" or "rights" or "terrorism" or "law" or "justice" or "legitimacy." None of these things is "out there" in the world. Rather, they are understood as a kind of linguistic contract. They depend on people categorizing the world in a certain way, accepting certain "scripts" and "presuppositions." The way that we understand politics—and even the international system—is therefore highly contingent on the way we "talk about it." This ought to cause us to think twice about our theoretical assumptions about how politics operates. In our chapter on realism, for example, we learned that realists think of the international systems as **anarchic**, a kind of empty space, without overarching rules, where self-interested political actors compete for resources. But, if the social constructivists are right, true anarchy is never really possible: at least not among people. The social facts that we inherit, and the ideas that they implicitly program us with, create ubiquitous structures even in the absence of formal institutionalized rules.

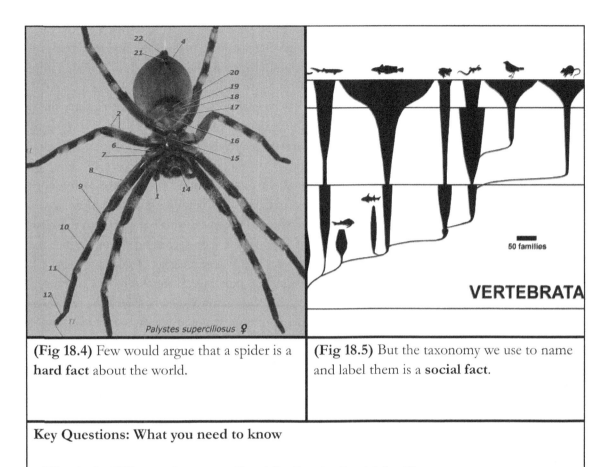

(Fig 18.4) Few would argue that a spider is a **hard fact** about the world.

(Fig 18.5) But the taxonomy we use to name and label them is a **social fact**.

Key Questions: What you need to know

• What is the difference between a "hard fact" and a "social fact?"
• Why is it sometimes hard to tell them apart?

Norms

Facts, of course, are not passive things. Social facts and hard facts give rise to behaviors. We learned back in chapter one that behaviors do not occur randomly but according to standards of what is normal and acceptable, called **norms**. Social constructivists regard the idea of norms as central to the understanding of politics. Norms, they argue, form part of an essential political and social cycle which is foundational to the organization and operation of society. A norm gives rise to a pattern of behavior, called a **practice**. Practices, in turn, often reinforce social facts, fitting into our idea of how the world works. These social facts inform our vocabulary, the names that we use to label and categorize the world, and this vocabulary, finally, institutionalizes the norm. Let's take a concrete example. Monogamous marriage is a fairly standard norm for much of the world. The norm of marriages gives rise to practices of marriage (weddings, cohabitation, co-parenting, etc). These practices define social facts: what it means, for example, to be a husband or a wife. These social facts require a vocabulary and this vocabulary institutionalizes the norm: for example, in marriage contracts which a husband and wife sign before a wedding, or in laws defining inheritance or terms of divorce.

Understanding how norms motivate behavior plays a key role in understanding the international system. It was once thought, for example, that political actors behaved according to a **logic of consequences**. A state, for example, decided to declare a war or to pursue diplomacy because it desired or feared certain logical outcomes. Social constructivists, however, argue that more often than not consequences are only part of the picture. Just as often, states will follow a **logic of appropriateness**, behaving the way they do because of certain underlying ideas of what is normal and acceptable in the international system.. For example, China's response to the **Hong Kong Protests** may be viewed as an instance of a powerful state regarding norms, rather than consequences, as the key determinant of its behavior. On a simple analysis of consequences, China, with its superior security forces, might be justified in going into Hong Kong and keeping the peace by brute force. It is reasonable to conclude that the reason China has declined to exercise such an aggressive option is that the international community would regard it as a violation of norms. The desire to follow the "legitimate" course of action is a key motivating factor in China's response.

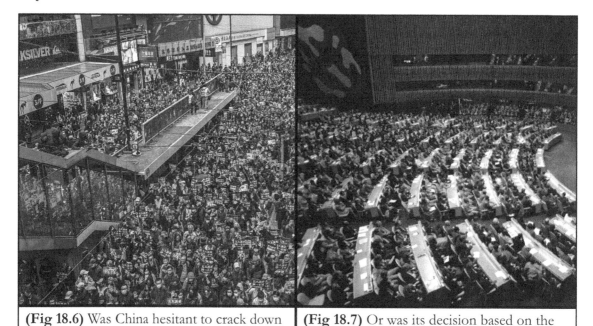

(Fig 18.6) Was China hesitant to crack down on the Hong Kong protests because it feared "consequences," such as economic sanctions, retaliation, infrastructure damage, or some other political harm?	(Fig 18.7) Or was its decision based on the fact that it didn't want to violate norms of international legitimacy? Under this view the socially constructed "logic of appropriateness" is the crucial determiner of political action.

Broader Applications

In addition to helping us understand why political actors behave the way they do, social constructivism has broader applications, related to activism and reform. Reform-minded philosophies such as feminism and postcolonialism owe a debt to poststructuralism. Poststructuralist ideas are not only important in understanding the assumptions of both theories (i.e., the social construction of gender or the social construction of race) but they are also essential in helping guide their praxis. To take the example of "throwing like a girl:" many modern feminists would argue that such language ought to be actively discouraged in polite conversation. They would also argue that certain gender-specific expressions such as "policeman," "actress," "stewardess" and "fireman" should also be avoided and replaced with "gender-inclusive" language. Though the point seems to be a small one, social constructivists take language seriously. As political structures are determined, in no small part, by names and labels, it is possible, the argument goes, to bring a more just world into being simply by talking about it. It is for this reason that social constructivists often direct their attention to cultural productions which are not usually considered political. Art, music, literature, television, and pop-culture are all considered to reflect important social forces in social constructivist theory, since all help create the discourse that underlie political structures.

One prominent example of this in recent memory is the revolution which has taken place in many western countries respecting LGBT rights. It was not terribly long ago, in both Europe and the United States, when same-sex couples were regarded as either "perverse" or mentally ill or otherwise subversive. A change in thinking did not occur through either force or fiat. The LGBT community, in most cases, did not take up weapons and march to the government and demand rights. The government didn't simply issue a command. Neither was it necessarily settled through rational debate. Rather, reform seemed to take place, in the west, through subtle changes in naming and labels. Certain "homophoic" slurs came to be regarded as impolite and offense. More inclusive language was gradually adopted. In film, books, television, and media, LGBT characters and celebrities became increasingly visible. Labels shifted, and, with those labels, norms. By 2016, gay marriage was legal and same-sex relationships widely regarded as socially acceptable across North America, western Europe, and even much of South America. This story does much to reveal how socialization can change norms, and norms can change institutions.

Another example—one with perhaps not so favorable a conclusion—relates to the refugee and migration crises which have gripped both Europe and the United States with particular intensity since the outbreak of the Syrian Civil War in 2015. Consider the possible labels which those fleeing their homes across international borders might be assigned. Besides "refugees," they might be called "migrants" or "asylum seekers" or "displaced persons" or even "illegal immigrants." Why does the label matter? Because international law stipulates that "refugees" (particularly war refugees) be granted certain protections. Many European states, as the refugee crisis worsened into 2017, began denying those fleeing into their countries refugee status. The United States, likewise, has also been reluctant to refer to those crossing its southern border as refugees. Instead, they are labelled either "illegal immigrants" or "undocumented aliens" or "undocumented border-crossers." Again, the point, to social constructivists, is that the language itself underlies the norm, and the norm shapes the institution.

| (Fig 18.8) Pro-LGBT demonstration | (Fig 18.9) Security patrols the US-Mexico border. |

Key Questions: What you Need to Know

• How does social constructivism inform the politics of advocacy?
• What is the relationship between norms and institutions?
• How can changing "language" bring about reform?

Question for Discussion

Realists state that the international system is governed by "anarchy," no higher authority between state and state. Would a social constructivist agree? Why or why not?

Criticisms

Though social constructivism has become one of the most popular theories in contemporary politics, it has been subject to multiple criticisms from more traditional thinkers. Perhaps the most common criticism is that it is too "relativistic" failing to account for objective facts about the world. Though, earlier on, we distinguished between "hard facts" and social facts (and pointed out that they can often be entangled), critics often argue that social constructivists attempt to reduce *everything* to social structures, and, in so doing, miss important truths about the world. A related criticism is that social constructivism offers only a vague and incomplete explanation for power politics, warfare, and social chaos. Though it may be true that norms, labels, and discourse underlie much of human behavior, it is also true that pure brute force is often the simplest explanation for political behavior. The German armies invaded southern Russia because they wanted their oil fields. The invasion failed because it was too cold and their tanks weren't good enough. These straightforward facts about behavior don't seem to require any more elaborate of an explanation.

Lastly, a strong criticism states that social constructivism can be both belittling and dehumanizing. As an intellectual perspective, the argument goes, social constructivism tends to reduce agents to mere "effects," passive products of their social environments. Though social constructivism claims to take agency seriously, it often fails to give a satisfying account of how human beings can exercise free choice and make decisions. This view of humanity, it has often been pointed out, can be said to mask an arrogant "hegemonic" outlook. Social constructivist philosophers claim to be able to analyze the structures of other cultural groups (traditional Muslims, say) and to thereby "reduce" Islamic paradigms to relative social forces. But this whole process of "analysis," if social constructivists are to be taken seriously, is already situated in structures of its own: the western, academic, post-enlightenment secularism. Post structuralists, the criticism runs, often claim to be the one "non-blind man" confidently claiming to be capable of seeing the whole elephant.

Despite these criticisms, it seems clear that social constructivism (and sociological theories in general) are here to stay. Not only do they offer a persuasive lens of analysis for critiquing political processes, but they also are highly compatible with other theoretical approaches. It is possible to be a social constructivist and a Marxist, a social constructivst and a liberal, a post-structuralist and a feminist. Unlike many theories, social constructivism is not an either-or but a broad approach that allows for no small amount of flexibility. Finally, social constructivism, it seems clear, could only ever be refuted by "talking about it." And talking about theory, i.e., engaging in discourse, puts us right into the core of what social constructivism is all about.

Social Constructivism at a glance

General Theme	Politics is a function of broader social structures.
Starting Point	Discourse, identities, norms, and social facts.
Human Nature	No definite nature, emerges from structures
International System	Not anarchic. Interplay of norms.
Purpose of Government	To institutionalize socially constructed norms

Summing Up: Key Chapter Points

1) One helpful way to start with social constructivism is to understand the idea of "holism," that the whole structure of something often explains the behavior of its parts.

2) Social constructivism regards individual agents as shaped by the broader structures that they're born into. Agents, in turn, can modify these structures.

3) Perhaps the most important structure to social constructivists is language itself. The hierarchy of meanings that we inherit in our day-to-day language often shapes our identities, ideas and practices.

4) Names and labels also help to shape "social facts." Social facts are formed by common consensus.

5) Social facts often underlie norms, which, in turn, structure political institutions.

6) Social constructivism has broader applications in political advocacy: for example in the issues of LGBT rights and the refugee crisis.

CHAPTER 19: POST-COLONIALISM

> **Overview**
>
> In this chapter we explain the history and concepts of postcolonialism. In particular we discuss
>
> - Early **anticolonial writing**
> - The political, cultural, and institutional character of the international order shaped by European dominance
> - The complex and ambivalent attitudes of Euoropeans about colonialism.
>
> We conclude the chapter by outlining different forms of postcolonial theory of post-colonial theory, focusing on *empirical, cultural, racial, and institutional* modes of analysis.

In 1542, the Spanish priest Bartolome de las Casas sat down and began to write the history of "Hispaniola," the island Christopher Columbus had landed on 50 years before, claiming the New World on behalf of Europe. Casas had been among the earliest explorers of Hispaniola, one of many Spaniards who hoped to get rich from the gold mines that they believed existed in the interior of the islands. Though Casas had once thought of Spain's colonies with feelings of pride and hope, by 1542, he looked back on his experiences with disgust:

> This was the first land...to be destroyed and depopulated by the Christians, and here they began to enslave women and children, taking them away to abuse them, eating the food they provided with their hard work. The Spaniards were not happy with what the Indians gave them of their own free will, which was always too little to satisfy their enormous hunger, for a Christian eats and consumes in one day an amount of food that would suffice to feed three houses of Indians in one month. And they committed other acts of force and violence and oppression....For they took infants from their mothers breasts, snatching them by the legs and throwing them headfirst against the crags or snatched them by the arms and threw them into the rivers, roaring with laughter and saying, as the babies fell into the water, "Boil there you children of the devil!" Others they killed with the sword alongside their mothers. They made some low gallows where they hanged victims whose feet almost touched the ground, and there they set burning wood and their feet and thus burned them alive.

When Casas's history was published in Spain, it generated significant outrage. The Spanish had allowed themselves to believe that their presence in the New World was beneficial to the "Indians." Yet Casas's narrative, along with others that appeared around the same time, argued that the Spaniards had "destroyed and depopulated" the land in the name of salvation.

Colonialism and Anticolonialism

(Fig 19.1) Christopher Columbus (1451-1506) discovered the island of "Hispaniola" (Haiti/ Domincan Republic) in 1492.

(Fig 19.2) Early depictions of the interactions between the Spanish and the natives depicted trade and hospitality.

Fig 19.3 The priest **Bartolome De Las Casas** (1474-1566) was among the explorers of Hispaniola.

(Fig 19.4) Following the publication of his *Brief Relation*, many questioned the motives of colonialism. This Dutch woodcut depicts the brutality of the Spanish settlers.

Casas history is generally regarded to be the first example of **anti-colonial** writing in European history. Though anti-colonialism is complex (and includes diverse forms of expression as music, poetry, fiction, visual arts, and journalism), in general there are three important themes which unify the tradition.

1) An emphasis on **cruelty and violence**. Note the way Casas's almost too-vivid descriptions are intended to assault the emotions, to shock the reader into sympathy with the indigenous people.

2) An emphasis on **economic exploitation**. Casas's line that "a Christian eats and consumes in one day an amount of food that would suffice to feed three houses of Indians in one month" is intended to show the greed of the colonists, the way they (economically as well as literally) consume the products of others' labor.

3) An emphasis on **cultural displacement**. Casas's frequent use of "Christian" carried associations which would not have been lost on his Spanish readers. The "superiority" of the Christian culture which the Spanish intended to spread to Hispaniola is ironically refuted through the depictions of their un-Christian violence.

From the years 1492 until the end of **decolonization** in the 1960's, the debate between anti-colonialists like Casas and apologists for the colonial system was an important part of European culture. As the west industrialized and expanded (see ch 8), it increased its political, economic, and cultural domination over the world until, by the early 20th century, nearly 85% of the globe was either under the rule of western powers. Casas was among the first (but by no means the last) to point out that this European domination often entailed a good deal of dehumanization and inequality. In what follows, we will take a look at the circumstances of that inequality and outline its implications for political theory today.

Key Questions: What you need to know

- What is "anti-colonialism?"
- What three features do anti-colonial writings tend to share?

Questions for Discussion

- **In what ways might anti-colonialism remind you of feminism?**

- **If colonists had always treated the indigenous inhabitants kindly, would colonialism and imperialism be morally justified?**

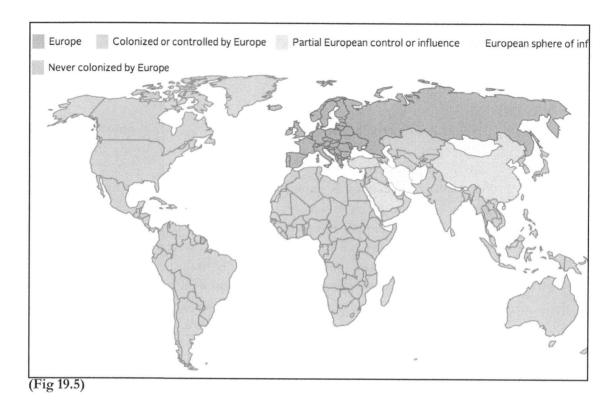

Europe | **Colonized or controlled by Europe** | **Partial European control or influence** | **European sphere of inf**

Never colonized by Europe

(Fig 19.5)

Conquest, Displacement, Assimilation: The Americas

Bartolome de las Casas history soon became part of a chorus of voices calling for at least some oversight and reform. The so-called **Laws of Burgos** (1512) had already been put into place in which Spanish settlers were forbidden from abusing the native populations. The laws read in part:

> We order and command that no person or persons shall dare to beat any Indians with sticks, or whip him, or call him dog, or address him by any name other than his proper name alone; and if an Indian should deserve to be punished for something he has done, the said person having him in charge shall bring him to the visitor for punishment, on pain that the person who violates this article shall pay, for every time he beats or whips an Indian or Indians, five pesos gold; and if he should call an Indian dog, or address him by any name other than his own, one peso in gold.

In 1537, Pope Paul III outlawed all enslavements of the native populations, and, in 1550, Emperor Charles V published *The Laws of the New Indies* which allowed the native inhabitants of the Americas protections as "legal subjects" of the Holy Roman Empire.

Though such laws were well-intentioned, they were impossible to enforce. Furthermore, the specific crimes that the laws prohibited provide fairly good evidence that those were precisely

240

the practices which colonists were frequently engaging in. Finally, the idea of "legal protections," however good the motives may have been, were themselves an act of conquest, making the indigenous inhabitants of the Americas "subjects" of Europe without their consent.

In any event, (as detailed in Chapter 6) throughout the 16th and 17th centuries, Spanish and Portuguese colonists went through South America, eventually gaining control of virtually all the land between the Atlantic and the Pacific oceans. To the north, British and French colonists followed suit, establishing settlements of their own along the coasts of the North American continent and in the West Indies. The maps below show the extent of European control over the Americas by the end of the 17th century.

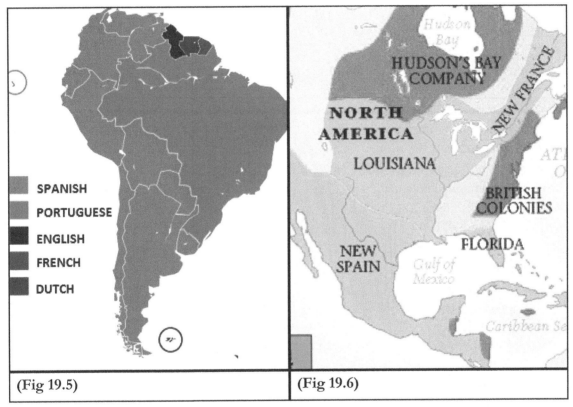

| (Fig 19.5) | (Fig 19.6) |

The European domination of the Americas can be understood in terms of long-lasting cultural, political, and economic displacement. Culturally, the traditions of the indigenous peoples died away as European language, religion, and norms became dominant. When Columbus landed on Hispaniola, there were well over 500 languages spoken in South America. Of these, only 350 remain, 110 of which are classified as endangered. With the loss of language came the loss of music, poetry, story-telling, and history. Indigenous religions suffered the same fate. One of the justifications that Europeans used for conquering the Americas was the fact that the natives could be converted to Christianity. Though some indigenous inhabitants converted of their own free will, many were forced to convert through intimidation and violence. Indigenous religion, with small exceptions, has all but disappeared from the continent.

The political and economic story is similar. As the Europeans established control, they brought with them their institutions. The centralized state, a money-based economy, and the system of fixed territory replaced native forms of social organization. Though Europeans have often told themselves the story that their institutions were "better" or "more advanced" this presupposes Europe to be the **standard of civilization** to which all other cultures ought to rise. Many of the civilizations of the Americas, even when viewed through the European lens, were remarkably sophisticated. The Aztec and Inca empires had large cities with impressive forms of architecture. The more nomadic tribes of North America, though without sedentary cities, nonetheless had long-established traditions of identity. The destruction of these things represents, few would argue, a loss to humanity as a whole.

Independence, Sovereignty, yet Continued Marginalization

In the late 18th and early 19th centuries, the European colonies of the Americas achieved their independence and became sovereign states (Chapter 7). It would, however, be obviously wrong to say that this represents the natives "taking their land back" from their European conquerors. By the time that north and south American colonies began to achieve their independence, European institutions had long dominated the continent. The leaders of the revolutions all spoke European languages (English, Spanish, French), all practiced European religions (Catholic and Protestant Christianity), and all had internalized European norms. Though many indidgenous people had achieved a certain degree of political and economic power, the most successful were those who had assimilated European ways. Therefore, it is most accurate to regard the North and South American revolutions *not* as a colonized people fighting off a colonizer, but, rather, as something more akin to a civil war: one group of Europeans breaking off from another group of Europeans. Within the newly independent states of the Americas, furthermore, the indigenous inhabitants continued to experience the same marginalization that they had while under direct European rule. In 1830, for example, the United States passed the **Indian Removal Act** (chapter 8), forcing all Native Americans in the southeast to relocate to Indian Reservations in the west. The so-called **Trail of Tears** saw the forced relocations of over 100,000 people and led to the deaths of perhaps as many as 10,000 many through malnutrition and disease. In the **conquest of the desert** in 1870, the Argentinian military cleared almost all indigenous peoples from the territory of Pategonia, killing 1000 and displacing 15000. In Brazil, the government, well into the 20th century, pursued policies of forced relocation, leading to the extinction of over 80 indigenous tribes and the endangerment of many others.

Key Questions: What you need to know

What impacts did colonization have on the indigenous inhabitants?

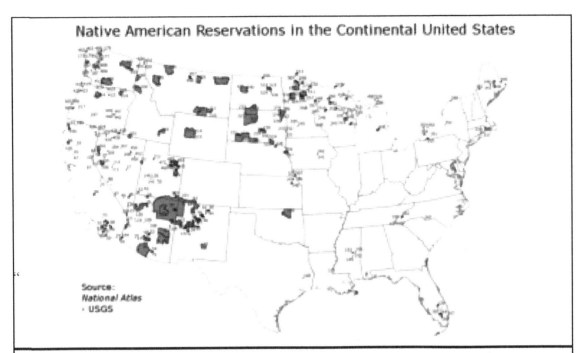

(Fig 19.7) Following various "Indian Removal Acts" in the 19th century, the indigenous peoples of the United States were moved to a number of "reservations" in the west. Though these reservations are nominally independent, they remain politically and economically marginalized.

The First Black Republic:" Haiti

A *possible* noteworthy "exception" to this story of European domination of the New World occurred with the independence of Haiti in 1804. Originally settled by the Spanish in 1492 and gradually taken over by the French in the early 17th century, Haiti had grown to be a prosperous colony, growing sugar, coffee, cocoa, and other crops. In order to support the agricultural economy, the French used a large number of African slaves which were forced to live according to the system known as **code noir** (the black code). By the middle of the 18th century, the number of black slaves was nearly 500,000 while the number of European colonists was perhaps 40,000 at the most. In the years following the French Revolution, when France was engulfed in political chaos, the Hatian slaves, led by **Toussaint Louverture**, rose up, and, after a struggle of nearly a dozen years, achieved their independence in 1804. In so doing they founded what soon became known as "the first black republic." The Hatian Revolution then was unique among the revolutions of the Americas in that it featured a subjugated "under-class" rising up against a European power. Nevertheless, even in Haiti, the earliest leaders were those who spoke French, practiced Catholicism, and had acquired a good deal of wealth through systems of European trade. Furthermore, the African slaves themselves, it bears pointing out, were not the indegenous inhabitants of Haiti. The original "Taino" natives of the island have been almost completely displaced. Therefore, colonial identities, therefore, even in "non-white" states like Haiti have obtained an almost complete supremacy in the New World. Where vestiges of indgenous identity exist, they have been relegated to the margins of society.

(Fig 19.9) Born into slavery in Haiti, Toussiant Louverture gained his freedom as a young adult and gradually gained significant wealth and property. After leading the slave revolt against France, Louveture became known as the "Father of Haiti."

(Fig 19.10) In 1675, the French King Charles V published *le code noir* (the black code)a series of laws governing black slaves in French colonies. The laws made Catholicism mandatory and restricted the rights of freed blacks.

Key Questions: What you need to know

• Why was the establishment of independent states in North and South America not an example of the colonized "getting their land back?"

• In what ways was the Hatian revolution a possible exception to this?

European Hegemony

We have already learned, in chapters 8 and 12, the story of the **age of empires**. In the 19th century, the European powers divided Africa between them, with Britain taking largest share and conquering, along the way, India, Australia, Hong Kong, and New Zealand. The period of European imperialism is, of course, highly controversial. On the one hand, Europeans invested heavily in infrastructure, building roads and railway systems, many of which are still in use today. They dug canals and expanded the use of arable land. Living standards increased with the expansion of western medicine, and new universities in major cities allowed colonized peoples to receive a western-style education, which enabled them to enter a growing "middle class." In many colonies, the indigenous became European subjects, protected by the law, and given the same rights (in theory) as any other citizen of the empire. Due to the rise of liberal thinking in the 20th century, European governments had at least a nominal concern for the human rights and dignity of the populations which they considered themselves as engaged in "bettering."

On the other hand, it would be naive to think that European rule was unambiguously "good"—at least not for the majority of the colonized people. While the economies developed, the benefits of that development flowed back to Europe. European monopolies on both raw materials and consumer goods made it so that Europeans (both settlers and at home) owned a disproportionate amount of wealth in the colonized states. Finally, European rule entailed cultural domination in which those who adopted European identities," (e.g., speaking European languages and receiving a western education) were most likely to succeed.

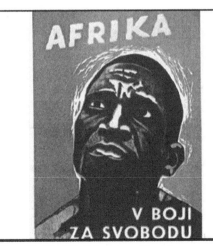	
(Fig 19.11) Well-known Dutch poster from the period of African decolonization which reads "Africa: its fight for freedom."	**(Fig 19.12)** Article from the *Hindustan Times* announcing Indian independence in 1947. The English-language paper appealed primarily to India's well-educated middle-class and upper-class.

Theoretical Considerations

So "where do we go from here?" What's next? What does "post-colonialism" as a theory have to say about the different stories of colonialism? While the answers to these questions are diverse, in general we can divide postcolonial responses to global politics into four categories: empirical, cultural, racial, and institutional. Like feminism and Marxism, postcolonialism, in each of these categories, is often concerned with both "theory" and "praxis." That is, it is concerned not just with "how the facts should be understood" but with "how the world can be made a better place."

Empirical approaches: Of the three approaches, empirical postcolonialism is the most direct. It reports on "the facts" of the postcolonial experience, often in order to point out continued imbalances between the west and the non-west. For example:

- Pointing out the number of languages which have died out due to the dominance of the European languages
- Compiling accurate casualty numbers of those who have been killed in colonial wars
- Showing the economic imbalances between western and non-western peoples in countries whose economic institutions have been shaped by colonialism
- Compiling demographic data on migration and immigration to and from colonial empires

All of these are empirical approaches in that they attempt to determine, through clear-cut facts, the consequences of European dominance. They also, in many cases, have measurable goals for post-colonial progress: for example, increasing the representation of indigenous peoples in the labor force, lifting wages, or increasing the number of native speakers of an endangered language.

Cultural approaches: Cultural approaches to postcolonialism are often more subtle. They're concerned not simply with "what happened" but with "how it looks." Cultural approaches are interested in, for example

- How "Eurocentrism" (or, the European perspective) is evident in discourse. For example the fact that "expat" is used for a European living abroad while "immigrant" is used for a non-European in Europe.
- How non-European cultures are regarded as "other," "exotic," or "subaltern."
- How cultural norms are shaped to favor the idea of European superiority. (For example, in the cultural dominance of European film, music, art, and literature).
- How the idea of being non-European is an "organizing principle" dividing what is considered the cultural "center" from the "periphery."

All of these examples are fundamentally *cultural,* concerning the more abstract and often invisible social and mental structures which colonialism has left us with. Cultural approaches often go ouside of politics into disciplines which more often are considered part of the humanities: e.g., art, pop-culture, literary criticism, and musicology.

Racial approaches: Related to cultural approaches are those which examine the legacy of post-colonialism in terms of race. These approaches often dovetail with **critical race theory**, a mode of analysis which examines the way ideas of race structure our encounters with the world. For example:

- The way the dominance of whites (white supremacy) has shaped most cultural systems (systemic racism).
- The way non-whites have been marginalized both culturally and economically.
- The way whites utilize unearned advantages (white privilege) to maintain their cultural dominance.

Institutional approaches: Last but not least institutional approaches attempt to critique and reform the various political institutions which bear the legacy of colonialism. For example:

- Changing university curriculum to include more non-European narratives.
- Creating societies to protect and teach endangered languages.
- Passing legislation to protect uncontacted indigenous communities.
- Advocating for financial reparations to historically wronged peoples.

These approaches tend to be forms of advocacy, efforts to shape the dominant institutions in order to help colonized peoples.

Criticisms

Perhaps the most common criticism of postcolonialism is that it is nothing more than a form of "grievance politics." It is certainly true that European colonists inflicted physical, psychological, and cultural harm upon those they colonized. Then again, every civilization in the world exists in the aftermath, somewhere in history, of warfare, destitution, and oppression. Though it is important to know these stories, fixating on grievances seems to be an ineffective way to spur social progress. A related criticism is that post-colonialism is too reductive. It puts "Europeans" in one category and "the oppressed" in another category, ignoring the fact that not all Europeans are the same and not all of the colonized were the same. An illiterate farmer somewhere in the provinces of Europe probably was just as marginalized as many in the colonies (perhaps more so), yet post-colonialism, so the criticism runs, simply reduces all identities to nation or race and neglects to account for any nuance. Lastly, some level a similar criticism at postcolonialism that is often levelled at feminism: that it is "oppositional" philosophy. It suggests that Europeans are "the oppressors" or "the enemy" and that the political goal is to take power away from them and give it to others. This "zero-sum game" mindset prevents society from being envisioned as a cooperative whole: one in which Europeans and non-Europeans might work together in mutual interest.

Post-colonial thinkers, of course, have a number of responses to these criticisms, but perhaps the most common and effective is simply to point out that simply "debating" the merits of postcolonial theory is progress in and of itself. If non-Europeans, for much of western history, have been hidden from sight and kept on the sidelines of mainstream political discourse, the act of talking about post-colonial theory, even to criticize it, is one way of nudging them a bit closer to the center.

Postcolonialism at a glance

General Theme	Marginalization of non-European peoples.
Starting Point	History of European domination.
Human Nature	Socially constructed. Particularly by "Eurocentric" norms and expectations.
International System	Dominated by European interests and institutions.
Purpose of Government	To empower non-European peoples and cultures.

Summing up: Key Chapter Points

1) The long tradition of post-colonialism began with the "anticolonial" writing of th 16th century, emphasizing cruely, exploitation, and displacement.

2) The period of colonialism and imperialism saw economic, cultural, and institutional displacment of non-Europeans.

3) The Revolution in Haiti is significant as the first example of marginialized people attaining statehood.

4) Modern postcolonialism is divided into empirical, cultural, racial, and institutional approaches.

Part III Issues in Global Politics

In some respects, "everything" is an issue in global politics. There is seemingly no end to political questions: some earth-shattering, some mundane. In our final section of the book, we limit ourselves to the most common categories and structures of the political process. We begin with war, paying special attention to the "paradoxical" factors of warfare, the oddity that, though war is a destructive force, it can also be a source of meaning, progress, and interdependence. We next move to nationalism, distinguishing the multiple types of nationalism that exist in today's world and discussing the historical conditions which have made nationalism possible. In our following section, on international political economy, we distinguish the way public power and private power integrate with one another in shaping trade, production, and finance. From these oppositional and occasionally destructive issues, we move, in the second half of the section, to more "constructive processes." Our chapter on democracy examines the historical critiques and justifications for democratic decision making processes. In our lessons on religion and law, we examine two "cultural universals" and discuss the way they have shaped and changed in historical development. Finally, we end by looking at the idea of social justice more broadly, discussing what justice means and different perspectives on making the world a better place.

CHAPTER 20: WAR

Overview

This chapter explains the prevalence of war in politics and provides a starting framework for talking about war. We address

- The ubiquity of war in history
- The paradox of war as both a destructive and constructive force
- The relationship between war and politics
- **Clausewitz's trinity** of passion, chance, and reason
- **Just War Theory**

We conclude with a discussion of whether the world will become more peaceful as institutions develop or whether warfare will remain an intractable part of the global condition.

"I sing of wars and of a man" begins Vergil's *Aeneid*, epic of the Roman Empire. In 20 BC, when he wrote it, there'd been plenty of wars to sing about. The *Pax Romana* had endured 22 wars in the century prior, an average of one every 3.5 years. Such history has not been unique to ancient Rome. The world has been at war for most of recorded history (92% of it to be exact). As you read these words, there are, in all probability, at least 30 wars going on somewhere on the globe. Each day, an average of 1100 people worldwide die in an armed conflict. Taking the broad view, it is easy to agree with former American president Barack Obama who said, in a speech accepting the Nobel Prize for Peace:

> War, in one form or another, **appeared with the first man**. At the dawn of history, its morality was not questioned; it was simply a fact, like drought or disease - the manner in which tribes and then civilizations sought power and settled their differences.

Few would deny that this is tragic. Yet, paradoxically, it also seems to be, as the journalist Christopher Hedges has phrased it, "a force that gives us meaning." National symbols—art, literature, films, monuments—often have an intense focus on the romance and heroism of war. Wars are not simply historical events, but, as we mentioned in chapter one, part of the vocabulary of our culture. They ground our knowledge and experience of citizenship and help to color our national consciousness. Why? What is it about war that makes it such a persistent and powerful force? Why do wars occur and what political function do they serve? Finally, as the world develops and becomes more integrated, will war become less frequent? Or, as Obama said, will war be with us forever, "simply a fact" from the first man up until the last man?

(**Fig 20.1-20.3**) War has provided a focus for filmmakers all over the world. *War Witch* concerns child soldiers in the Congolese Civil War. The Kurdish language *Turtles Can Fly* depicts life in Iraq preceding the US invasion in 2001. *Bashu, The Little Stranger* is one of many Iranian films in the so-called "sacred defense" genre about the 1980-1988 Iran-Iraq war. These examples demonstrate the paradoxical power of war. Although tragic, war's intensity has made it a potent source of cultural expression.

Defining War

In order to answer these questions, we need to start with a workable definition of war. It seems clear, at the very minimum, that war involves violence. Yet two men having a fight outside of a bar or a group of children scuffling in a schoolyard obviously does not constitute a war. In war, the violence must be large-scale and politically organized. How large is large-scale? The question is often relative. The smallest war to be called a "war" was the 1896 British invasion of Zanzibar. Over in about 40 minutes, it consisted, mainly, in British warships blowing up the Sultan's harem. Compare this to World War II which lasted for six years and involved some 70 million soldiers. When a war is big enough to be called a war depends, to some degree, on a number of seemingly arbitrary factors.

The second part of our definition, "political organization" is, in a way, clearer. Wars are fought between political actors, with political objectives. Despite the way it often seems, wars do not happen for no reason. There are always political aims: sometimes small, such as the capture of a particular strip of land; sometimes large, such as the establishment of a new state. In Chapter one, we mentioned Carl von Clausewitz's famous quote "war is a continuation of politics by other means." The political process has the potential to lead to war, and, when it does, the violence that ensues often only stops through political negotiation (a surrender, say). This reveals an important element of politics itself: namely its capacity both to *incite* and to *control* violence. To take a contemporary example, the Egyptian government, since 2016, has been threatening Ethiopia with military action unless it agrees to stop construction of a dam on the Nile river which, Egypt says, will endanger its water supply. Egypt, in other words, is utilizing violence (or the threat of violence) to achieve a specific political goal. Ethiopia, for the time being, has agreed to delay the filling of its dam, thereby using political diplomacy in order to prevent violence.

(**Fig 20.4**) An Egyptian Military vehicle: Egypt has threatened military action against Ethiopia if Ethiopia continues construction of a dam along the Nile River. The political process has the potential to
• incite violence
• control violence.

One final characteristic of warfare deserves to be mentioned. It is easy to forget that war, fundamentally, is a kind of *relationship*. We may think of war as "division" or "polarization," and, in many ways, it is. Strange as it may sound, however, war brings political actors together and forges long-lasting bonds. Not only has America maintained military bases in Japan, for example, since the end of the Second World War, but it has also invested significant economic resources in developing and modernizing the country. Likewise, in Europe, the regional integration of England, France, and Germany can be understood, in part, as a consequence of World War II. War, for all of its bloodshed, entangles political actors in relationships of interdependence which often last long after the guns fall silent.

Key Questions: What you need to know?

- What is the definition of war?
- What is the relationship between war and politics?
- In what ways is war a "relationship?"

Types of War

We typically think of war as happening "between countries," so called **interstate wars**, in which one nation-state battles another. We might also think of **civil wars**: wars that happen between rival factions *within* a state, often in order to gain control of the government or establish political independence. These two categories, however, are not mutually exclusive. Often inter-state wars *lead* to civil wars (as, for example, when the partition of Korea following World War II led to the Korean war a few years later). Or, the other way around, civil wars may attract foreign intervention, leading to interstate wars (for example, when the United States invaded Vietnam to support the South Vietnamese government in a civil war between it and the north). Such intervention can alter the trajectory of wars in surprising ways. For instance, when Japan invaded China at the beginning of World War II, the two Chinese factions in the midst of fighting a civil war (the Kuomintang and the Communists) *joined sides* in order to fight against the Japanese. When the Islamic State of Iraq and the Levant (ISIS) began an uprising in Kurdish controlled parts of Iraq, two rival Kurdish militias (the Peghmegra and the PKK), though long enemies, forged an alliance to regain control of Kurdish land. Finally, both interstate and civil wars can involve diverse political actors in ways not explicitly linked to the fighting. A state, for example, may provide financial or humanitarian aid to civilians in a neighboring country during a war. Or it may accept refugees fleeing a war, as was the case in Europe following the Syrian Civil War in 2014. These examples illustrate the difficulty of neatly classifying war and the ways in which war's complications can spread far beyond the battlefield.

Key Vocabulary

Interstate war: A war that occurs between two separate nation-states.

Civil war: A war that occurs within a single nation state.

Total War: A war which mobilizes all resources of the state, the loss of which would mean the state ceases to exist.

Limited War: A war fought for a lesser goal than the survival of the state.

Some have argued that the early 21st century has seen the development of a new type of "globalized" war. After the September 11th terrorist attacks, the United States commenced the **War on Terror**—a series of military actions against Islamic terrorist groups in the Middle East. Though the War on Terror included two interstate wars (The War in Afghanistan, 2001; and the War in Iraq, 2003), much of the United States' military activity has been directed against *individuals* affiliated with terrorist groups and has not been focused on states themselves. The United States military, for example, has conducted drone strikes and assassinations of suspected terrorists in states with which the United States claims to have a friendly relationship (such as Pakistan). Likewise, America's opponent in the War on Terror does not identify with any specific state or make any particular territorial claim. What binds the various terrorist groups together is **ideology**, a group of ideas and ideals, more specifically, a extreme form of fundamentalist Islamic ideology which regards the West as at war with Islam. Many political thinkers have argued that the non-traditional nature of the war on terror demands an intellectual revision of what is meant by war, perhaps a **global approach** that explains the effect which ideological globalization has had on the causes for and effects of warfare.

Key Questions: What you need to know

- What are the different types of war?
- Why are these types not mutually exclusive?
- What makes the "War on Terror" distinct?

Elements of War

Besides violence, what characterizes war? What political elements make it up? One of the oldest and most famous answers to this question is from the beginning of **Sun Tzu's** *Art of War* A Chinese general of the Zhou Kingdom, in the 5th century B.C., "Master Sun" divided war into five key elements: "the moral law, heaven, earth, the commander, and discipline:"

> **The Moral Law** causes the people to be in complete accord with their ruler, so that they will follow him regardless of their lives, undismayed by any danger. **Heaven** signifies night and day, cold and heat, times and seasons. **Earth** comprises distances, great and small; danger and security; open ground and narrow passes; the chances of life and death. **The Commander** stands for the virtues of wisdom, sincerity, benevolence, courage and strictness. By method and **discipline** are to be understood the marshaling of the army in its proper subdivisions, the graduations of rank among the officers, the maintenance of roads by which supplies may reach the army, and the control of military expenditure.

Sun Tzu's characterization has been influential to theorists of war, and in 1832, Karl Von Clausewitz refined these five elements into just three. His so-called **trinity of war** characterized warfare as an interplay between **passion, chance,** and **reason**. Passion is what motivates and rallies both soldiers and civilians to engage in the war effort in the first place. Soldiers in the field, obviously, have to have emotional drive in order to do the dangerous and often dehumanizing work of fighting. Love for their fellow soldiers (*espirit de corps*) as well as hatred for the enemy, according to Clausewitz, serve as necessary conditions for any military campaign. Yet civilians at home, more often than not, also experience passion. This can take the form of political willingness to support the war effort. Governments of belligerent states often play an important role, often through political propaganda, characterizing the soldiers as brave, patriotic, and dutiful and characterizing the enemy as evil, dangerous, or subhuman. Often the language of nationalism (see following chapter) is utilized to incite passion in the civilian population, for example, by encouraging national solidarity or fomenting anger at enemy countries.

(Fig 20.5-20.7) World War II Propaganda Posters: Note how the poster in the center depicts the Japanese invader. According to Clausewitz, fomenting hatred of "the enemy" is as necessary as inspiring patriotism among civilians and solidarity among soldiers.

The second element in Clausewitz's trinity, chance, reflects the fact that anything can happen in a battle. As he puts it: '

> [War] is therefore everywhere brought into contact with chance, and thus incidents take place upon which it was impossible to calculate.... As an instance of one such chance: the weather. Here the fog prevents the enemy from being discovered in time, a battery from firing at the right moment, a report from reaching the General; there the rain prevents a battalion from arriving at the right time, because instead of for three it had to march perhaps eight hours; the cavalry from charging effectively because it is stuck fast in heavy ground.

According to Clausewitz, chance primarily affects soldiers in the field, who, amid the "fog of war" are required to test their instincts and training against the unpredictable events.

Lastly, **reason** represents the "intellectual" or "calculated" aspects of warfare. These may be short term **tactics**, i.e., specific manoeuvres that soldiers make in order to gain a specific advantage on the field. Or they may be long term **strategies**: i.e., decisive goals, such as the capture of a city or the implementation of a blockade in order to strangle the economy of the enemy state.

Reason, for Clausewitz, was primarily associated with the military's leadership: both the embedded commanders and the governing politicians who gave them orders.

Clausewitz's Trinity at a glance

What	*Who*	*Ex:*
Passion	Soldiers in the field who have to summon the emotions to put their lives at risk and to kill the enemy, as well as civilians at home who the government motivates to support the war by encouraging patriotism and/or xenophobia.	Patriotism, *esprit de corps*, hatred of the enemy, fear, loyalty.
Chance	Soldiers in the midst of a battle who have to test their instincts and training against unexpected obstacles.	Weather, failure of equipment, errors in communication.
Reason	Commanders and leaders who devise short term tactics as well as long term strategies.	Manoeuvres, acts of deception, spying, political objectives.

The three elements of Clausewitz's trinity do not operate in isolation. Rather, in each military engagement, all three factors play an interrelated role. For example, in the Battle of Agincourt, the English King Henry and his commanders first devised the strategy (reason) of luring the French cavalry forward into a muddy valley in order to attack them with their archers. In order for this strategy to be effective, however, it had to have rained enough to flood the valley (chance). Finally, in order to rally his soldiers, Henry, according to the historical accounts, made a rousing speech prior to the battle (passion) inspiring his men by evoking the fame they would achieve if they won.

Key Questions: What you need to know?

- According to Sun Tzu, what are the different elements of war?
- What is Clausewitz's "trinity" and how do the three parts relate to each other?

War and Historical Development

We tend to think of war as a *destructive* force, one that ruins lives, wrecks cities, and sets humankind wretchedly back. Paradoxically, however, war has often served a *constructive* purpose, for example, by shifting international orders or bringing about the development of new technologies. One of the most famous examples of this concerns the political changes which occurred following the development of the **stirrup** in Europe the 8th century A.D. (We here note that the stirrup had long before this been used in China and the Middle East). A stirrup, as an equestrian knows, is a pair of rings designed for inserting the feet into while mounting or dismounting the horse. It gives a rider better balance and control of the horse, and, in the days when horses were used in battle, allowed cavalry soldiers more efficient use of thrusting and shooting weapons. Prior to the invention of the stirrup, it was difficult to coordinate an effective cavalry charge, and military strategists, therefore, relied mostly on massed infantry: the Greek phalanx, the Roman legion, the Anglo Saxon shield wall. It takes relatively little skill to fight with a spear and a shield, and infantry lines, with sufficient discipline and in sufficient numbers, could usually overcome a few mounted soldiers. However, with the development of the stirrup, the cavalry charge became a devastating battlefield tactic. Rows of well-mounted, armored soldiers, could stampede into lines of infantry, sending even well-disciplined soldiers into a disorderly retreat. In the **Battle of Tours** (732 AD), Charles Martell used cavalry, equipped with the stirrup, to drive Arabic invaders out of France. In doing so, he founded the **Carolingian Empire**, one the largest and most influential empires in medieval Europe.

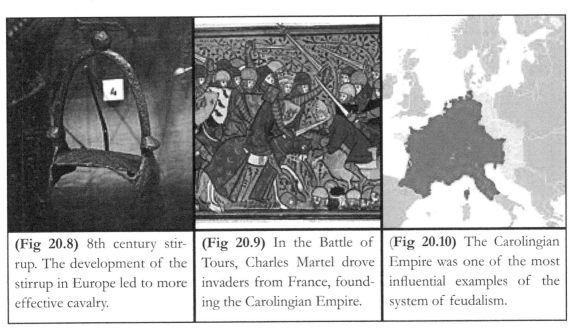

| (Fig 20.8) 8th century stirrup. The development of the stirrup in Europe led to more effective cavalry. | (Fig 20.9) In the Battle of Tours, Charles Martel drove invaders from France, founding the Carolingian Empire. | (Fig 20.10) The Carolingian Empire was one of the most influential examples of the system of feudalism. |

One difficulty with cavalry, however, that horses require significant land for pasturage. In addition, a mounted army requires training and equipment. The Carolingian Empire, therefore, developed an important political system, **feudalism**, in order to meet these challenges. The king would grant land to a local "lord" to rule as he saw fit. In exchange, the lord promised to provide horses and soldiers to the king in the event of war. The ordinary citizens, living under the lord, were granted small plots of land to farm on their own, under the condition that they likewise would go to war if and when their lord needed them. Feudalism, in other words, was a largely decentralized political system, one which made use of overlapping and interconnected political hierarchies. Over time, this led to the further fragmentation of Europe (see chapter 2) into multiple centers of power. A sharper division of Europeans into defined classes would emerge: titled lords, land-owning aristocrats, landless peasantry These hierarchies would continue to shape European political structures long after the end of the feudal period.

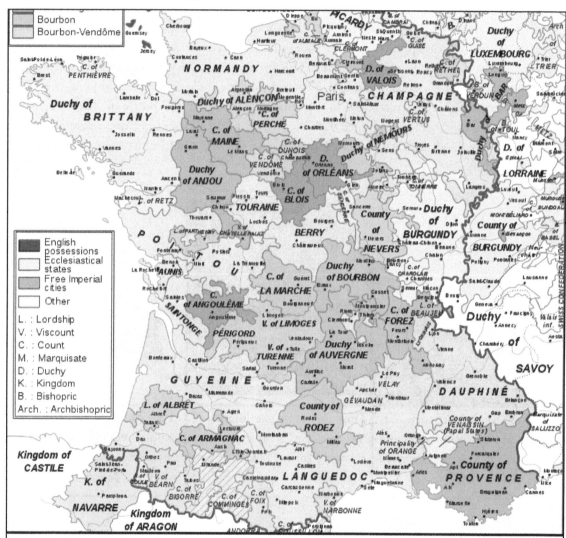

(Fig 20.11) Map of France ~1480 showing different Feudal territories. The Decentralization of power was one consequence of the heavy reliance on cavalry following the adoption of the stirrup in the west.

What's the "big idea" of this example? The story of the stirrup reveals the fact that military conflict is often a catalyst for great social change. Not only can war *directly* change international orders (through conquest or regime change) but also *indirectly* through the development of new technologies or forms of organization. Some political scientists take this idea a bit farther, arguing that the majority of significant cultural developments have occurred in just this manner. Just as the stirrup led to the establishment of feudalism, so too the later development of gunpowder led to the end of feudalism and the creation of highly centralized European nation-states. Later on the development of the combustion engine, necessary for tanks and warplanes, led to a more interconnected world, increased travel, and larger supply chains. The development of nuclear technology, motivated for the purpose of building nuclear weapons, revolutionized the way societies used electricity. This idea, known as **technological determinism**, posits that technology, which is often developed for the purpose of battle, drives political development.

Technological determinism: Inventions of war lead to political change

Invention	Consequences	Political Change
Stirrup	Need for land and specialized training	Feudalism
Gunpowder	Massed infantry capable of defeating cavalry	End of feudalism, centralized nation-states
Steam Engine	Battleship technology allows European countries to project power around the world.	Imperialism
Combustion Engine	Tanks, warplanes, longer supply chains	Globalized war, and, subsequently, globalization.
Nuclear Power	Atomic weapons, mutually assured destruction.	Cold War, Liberal International Order, NATO

> **Key Question: What you need to know:**
>
> How does war directly and indirectly produce political change?

Is War Justified?

Asking whether or not war is justified often seems like speaking about fire-safety after your house has already burned down. Historically war seems to "just happen" whether it's justified or not. Nonetheless throughout history philosophers have wondered whether or not war is ever the right thing and, if so, under what circumstances. **Just War Theory** (or "Just War Tradition") began with early Catholic philosophers in the days following the fall of the Roman Empire. Their aim was to use the influence of the church to both limit the occurrence of war (by defining only narrow situations in which it might be permissible) and to protect civilian populations in the event of its outbreak. Their ideas of a just war involved two specific categories of justification: **jus ad bellum** (or, a just *cause* to go to war) and **jus in bello** (or, just actions within war). Over time, other philosophers have deliberated over and refined these categories so that, currently, JWT comprises nine accepted principles.

Jus ad bellum:.

1) **Just Cause**: War is only permissible in self-defense or in defense of an innocent third party who has been attacked.

2) **Legitimate authority**: War can only be waged by those who have legal authority to declare war. In effect, this means sovereign states.

3) **Just Intention**: War must be waged with the intent to right a specific injustice (principle 1) and not for the purpose of glory, expansion, or wealth.

4) **Reasonable hope of success**: Wars should only be waged if there is a good chance that it will bring about the desired outcome.

5) **Proportionality**: The good which the war is meant to achieve must outweigh the evil which will occur during the war.

6) **Last resort**: War should only be fought after all forms of diplomacy have failed to bring about a peaceful solution.

Jus in bello:

1) **Minimalism**: Warring states must use the least amount of force necessary to achieve their goals.

2) **Discrimination**: States must discriminate between combatants and non-combatants and must only use violence against combatants.

3) **Due Consideration**: States be aware that war will bring "unintended effects" to civilian populations. States must do everything they can to avoid or minimize these.

It is debatable whether these nine conditions are realistic (i.e., whether it is even *possible* to have a war in which all nine conditions are met). It is also unclear whether any war in history has ever *come close* to meeting even a handful of these conditions, and most political philosophers argue that none has. For example, the second condition of *jus in bello* requires states to distinguish between soldiers and civilians. Any modern war, which relies heavily on aerial bombing, cannot possibly do so, making it impossible for any modern war (so the argument runs) to be justified.

Whether the conditions are reasonable or not, they have long been codified, in some form, in **international law**. The United Nations Charter, for example, emphasizes both *jus ad bellum* and *just in bello* permitting war only in self-defense and requiring that non-combatants and prisoners of war be protected. Again, historical practice, time and again, has often violated these laws.

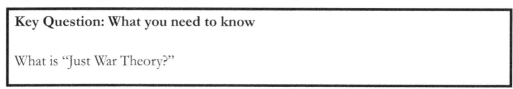

Key Question: What you need to know

What is "Just War Theory?"

War in Christian and Islamic Traditions

(Fig 20.12) St. Peter's Cathedral, Rome. Christian nations have waged many wars and have used religion to justify their violence (The Wars of Religion, the Crusades), yet in general, Christian philosophy has had a long tradition of pacifism. Just War Theory has its origin in two medieval Christian philosophers: Augustine of Hippo and Thomas Aquinas. Despite the many acts of violence which have been perpetrated by Christian nations, the official position of the Catholic Church permits war only as a last resort, in defense of the innocent.

(Fig 20.13) Dome of the Rock, Jerusalem. Perhaps no word is more misunderstood and polarizing than jihad (Arabic for "struggle). Certain terrorist groups have used the term as justification for violence against civilian targets and have interpreted it as requiring Muslims to spread Islam through war. The majority of Islamic scholars, however, understand jihad as mandating war only in self-defense. Others argue that the primary meaning of the word describes a spiritual struggle--the "inner war" in which the believer must fight against temptation and immorality.

Will War Always Be With Us?

One of Clausewitz's insights was that war, as an idea, has no "logical" end. Nothing "inside" a war requires that it stop. If my army shoots at your army and yours shoots back at mine, then the only conclusion is the absolute destruction of one of us. Clausewitz called this **ideal war**, war as it would exist without political interference and with an unlimited supply of men and ammunition. Such a war would, in theory, go on forever. In reality, such a war is impossible. Eventually, one side runs out of resources or loses the will to fight. But Clausewitz's notion of ideal war is connected to an important realization: war does not end through events that happen "in" war but events that happen "outside" war: a negotiated surrender or a treaty or a cease-fire. In other words, it is the politics, in some form, that brings war to an end.

Liberal philosophers (chapter 9) take this idea a step farther. If politics is what ends war, then, surely, constructing the right political framework, having the right institutions in place, can keep war from getting started in the first place. Liberals argue that economic interdependence, regional integration, and the spread of democracy can eventually create enough trust among nations to bring about **perpetual peace**. Such an idea underlies the Liberal International Order (chapter 16), the architecture of institutions and rules designed to solve potential conflicts diplomatically. Certain liberals point out that, since the establishment of the Liberal International Order, the world has gotten less violent, with conflict deaths, as a percentage of the global population, being lower than they have been at any other point in history. As democracy, enlightenment, and economic development continue to spread across the world, wars will become less and less frequent and will eventually disappear entirely.

Realists (chapter 15) however aren't so optimistic. While it is true, they say, that combat deaths as a percentage of population have declined in recent years, this is, in all likelihood, simply a matter of improved medical treatments and refinements in the technology of war rather than any decrease in hostilities. Furthermore, *total* combat deaths have increased since the establishment of the LIO. Secondly, whatever the benefits of a democratic system of government may be, it does not seem plausible that democracy, by itself, will eliminate war. The twentieth and twenty-first centuries are full of war instigated by democratic regimes, with the "War on Terror" being a prominent recent example. Finally, institutions may be a good idea, but the selfishness of human nature and the anarchy of the international system, will always make violence more likely than not.

The realism vs liberalism debate is one, of course, in which we should hope the liberals are right. Every sane person should hope for and try to construct a future in which, as it says on the outside the UN building, "the nations do not learn war any more." Time will tell whether that dream is achievable. But, given the current level of global violence and humanity's long history of warfare, it is likely that, if there is a future without war, none of us will be around to see it.

Summing Up: Key Chapter Points

1) War is defined as large-scale violence between political actors.
2) Wars goals are political in nature. War entangles political actors in a relationship.
3) Wars may be civil, interstate, total, limited, or some combination thereof.
4) Sun Tzu defined war as made up of five elements: the moral law, heaven, earth, the commander, and discipline. For Clausewitz, war was a trinity of passion, chance, and reason.
5) War can be a constructive force, leading to new technologies and forms of political organization.
6) Just War Theory attempts to describe the circumstances in which war is permitted. *Jus in bellum* contains six principles, *jus ad bello* contains three.
7) Liberals argue that institutions, democracy, and progress will eventually bring war to an end, while realists argue that the international system will always be plagued with violence.

CHAPTER 21: NATIONALISM

Overview

This chapter explains the development and types of nationalism. We analyze

- Whether nationalism is ancient or modern (i.e., the difference between the **primordial** and **modern** viewpoints)
- The different types of nationalism (**state-supporting, state-opposing, civic, ethnic, popular, elite**)
- The importance of national symbolism (**ethno-symbolism**)
- The way states use nationalism to accomplish **national interests**

We end the chapter with a discussion of stateless nations and ask whether nationalism is a force for good or a force for evil.

Why is a country a country?

In the northern hemisphere, there is a landmass of about 2.5 million square kilometers. The one-hundred fifty million people who live there share the same language, the same history, and, with a few exceptions, the same religion. They hold in common music, literature, art, food staples, and styles of dress. If I asked you how many countries the people here live in, you would certainly be justified in saying just one. Isn't a group of people, culturally similar, occupying the same land, speaking the same language, and sharing the same history the definition of a country? The answer, however, is twelve: Bahrain, Iraq, Jordan, Kuwait, Lebanon, Oman, Qatar, Saudi Arabia, Syria, the United Arab Emirates and Yemen. All of these countries speak Arabic (in a similar dialect). All are Islamic, and, particularly, Sunni Islamic. All share roughly the same past and cultural traditions. Yet, they are divided into a dozen separate countries.

A few hundred miles away, there is a landmass roughly the same size. This one is home to nearly 10 times as many people. The people who live here speak twenty-two different languages. The population is divided into six mainstream religions. Cuisine, dress, music, and art vary wildly among the inhabitants. How many countries do the people here live in? You'd be justified in guessing many. However, the answer is just one: India.

These examples underscore how problematic the idea of a "country" is, the complex connection between "people" and "power" and the practical and theoretical issues that are at stake in the analysis.

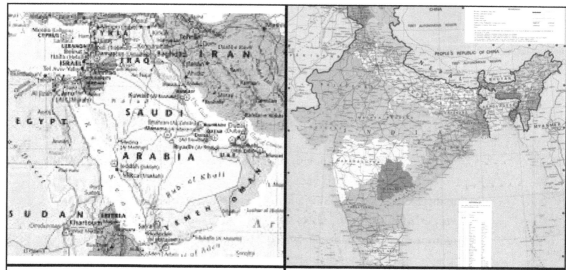

(Fig 21.1) The case of the Arabic Peninsula: During the 19th century, the Arabic Peninsula was governed by the Ottoman Empire. The Ottomans, however, were often incapable of asserting their authority in Arabic provinces leading to significant decentralization. Tribes, military alliances, and warlords gained significant regional control. After the British defeated the Ottoman Empire, these tribes consolidated their control, negotiating independence from the British and forming separate states.

(Fig 21.2) The case of India: When Great Britain solidified its control over the Indian subcontinent in 1858, it placed the various ethnic communities under the control of one political system: the British Empire. During the movement for Indian independence, in the 20th century, opposition to British rule, "anti-colonialism" unified these diverse ethnic groups against the "invading European occupier." Thus both imperialism and anti-imperialism served a role in uniting India.

Nation and State

At the beginning of chapter 1, we said that the word "country" is vague, and that political scientists prefer the more precise term **nation-state**. This clarifies that a country is composed of two separate elements: the "nation," or people bound together by a common sense of identity, and the "state," or the formal institutions of power which solidify their relationship. One intuitive assumption is that every nation ought to have its own state—that the people in the nation should control the government, military, and public institutions in the territory which it occupies. History, however, is not so tidy and rational. Frequently the same territory is claimed by multiple national groups. National groups may disagree about the make-up of the state. Or, national groups may find themselves swept up in historical forces beyond their control, as when they find themselves conquered by a large empire.

Nation (people)	State (institutions of power)
Language Religion Culture Territory Relationships	Legal System Beurocracies Legislative Assemblies Military Written Contracts

Later, in chapter 9, we defined the term **nationalism** to mean a sense of political loyalty, centering on membership in a nation. We clarified that nationalism can be "state supporting"—in which the existing state is regarded as a good thing, to be fought for, strengthened, or purified; or "state opposing," in which it is a bad thing, to be fought against, reformed, or separated from. This is certainly a good place to start our discussion. But this simple framework leads to many things we might be curious about. For example, how did we get this idea of a nation? Is membership in a nation determined by "objective" factors (such as land, language, or religion) or is it a kind of "imagined" community, a big fiction? What is the point of nationalism? Is it good or evil? Finally, will nationalism always be with us or, as society becomes increasingly globalized and integrated, is it on its way out? We will consider each question in turn.

Real or Imagined?

It might be tempting to think of a nation as an ancient fact about the world. As long as we have had history, we have had societies. These societies have lived in a general territory, speaking a language, sharing traditions. History books tell us about the "Greeks" and the "Romans" and the "Chinese" and the "Egyptians." Weren't these ancient civilizations nations? The view that "the nation" is an ancient and fundamental form of human organization is known as **primordialism**. The philosopher George Wilhelm Herder coined the term **volksgeist** (literally "spirit of the people") to describe this national essence, which, as it moved through history, might change in this or that detail but had certain eternal qualities that would exist as long as the people did. For Herder, a permanent energy defined and bound the "folk" throughout history. Throughout the 19th century, many philosophers, particularly in Germany, used this term to describe certain fixed characteristics that preceded the state and undergirded its politics. For Herder, the volksgeist was connected with the permanence of language. For other thinkers, it was related to race or lineage or some other form of heritage.

This idea has a certain appeal. And many politicians have used it in order to rally patriotic or romantic sentiment for a national cause. Nonetheless, many more recent political scientists have argued that it has little historical justification. It is true, of course, that societies have long histories and that many social bonds (language, kinship, religion) are ancient indeed. But were ancient societies "nations" as we now define the term? Think about what it means to be a member of a nation today. If you are born in, say, France, you are "French" simply by virtue of your birth. Without doing anything, you become a citizen, with basic rights, such as protection under the law, and, eventually, when you become an adult, the ability to participate in civic processes. Instantaneously, you share something equally with all other members of the nation. You understand that your nation is distinct and "yours." You're not Canadian or Japanese or Swiss. You "belong" to France, and France belongs to you.

Now imagine being born 1000 years ago in the same place. France, at that time, was ruled by a royal family (the house of Capet, to be exact). Say you were born in a small village somewhere away from the capital. You might have some knowledge of the king and maybe of the kings of other peoples, but it's not certain that you would have felt that you had much in common with your monarch or the aristocrats of the ruling class. You would not have expected to participate in the affairs of the state. Your relationships to politics would have been formed with either the local landlord or the local church. In all probability, you would have not felt a sense of solidarity with a villager whom you had never met, 200 miles away, on the other side of France. The king's army could have marched into your town and forced you to pay taxes or to join them on an expedition. But you would have been a subject, ruled by the powerful nobility, not a citizen participating in the construction of a common identity. If you had been born in a wealthy family, the story would be much the same, except the other way around. It is improbable you would have felt a sense of belonging with the commoners that lived in the vague wilderness on the other side of your castle. Your primary relationships would have been with your family and the families you were allied with. You were a member of "the House of Capet" rather than "France."

Most political scientists, therefore, regard the idea of "the nation," as we mean the term today, as a more recent development. The term **modernism** refers to the theory that social changes over the past two hundred years have created it. Before these changes took place, the various empires, kingdoms, cities, and tribes, however powerful they may have been, were not nations. Modernist theories about "what changes" were important are complex. Nevertheless, modernists, in general, identify four important factors.

1) **Technologies of communication**: With the invention of the "printing press" in the fifteenth century, it became possible to communicate words and images more widely. Knowledge became more standardized, and education became more widespread. In the late nineteenth and twentieth centuries, newspapers, the radio, and television accelerated this process, solidifying a common frame of reference. This shared "lifeworld" gave the majority of the population an overlapping understanding of their **imagined community**.

2) **Industrialization**: Prior to the industrial revolution, most trade occurred in "microeconomies"--encompassing, perhaps, a few communities relatively nearby. After the industrial revolution, large territories became interconnected through increasingly complex trade routes. (See "shrinking

of the planet" in chapter 8). The social benefits and burdens of economic activity became more wide-reaching, leading to a corresponding expansion of the idea of the nation.

3) **Popular Sovereignty**: After the American and French revolutions in the late 18th century, the idea of popular sovereignty (see chapter8) spread through Europe, and then, through imperialism and globalization, through the rest of the world. Individuals are co-owners of the country, political participants with rights and duties. This is evoked in the idea of common citizenship, which, in turn, establishes the nation which each member is an equal representative of.

4) **Warfare and Conscription**: After the establishment of popular sovereignty, many nations in Europe instituted policies of "mass conscription" in which all adult males in the country were required to provide military service. Such experiences not only created a national "fighting spirit" but also helped translate the idea of the nation into "us vs. them" terms.

Questions for discussion

• Think about the things that define your "membership" in your nation. What objects, rituals, or conditions are essential to your political identity? Do of these seem "primordial" to you or do they all seem to depend on certain modern conditions?

• Is it possible that the meaning of "the nation" has changed over time? Might there have been one kind of nation 500 years ago and another kind today? In other words, is it possible that primordialism and modernism might *both* be true?

Key Vocabulary

Nation: A community bound together, over time, by a common culture, sense of identity and, often, territory.

State: The institutions of power that formalize membership in a community.

Primordialism: The view, popular in the 19th century, that "the nation" is ancient and fundamental and that each nation has its eternal qualities.

Modernism: The view that the idea of "the nation" is dependent on economic, technological, and political changes which have occured over the past 200 years.

Possible Timeline of Development of the Nation in the West

Figure 21.3
Peace of Westphalia establishes principle of **territorial sovereignty**

Figure 21.4
French Revolution establishes **popular sovereignty**, leading to a shared sense of citizenship.

Figure 21.5
Mass **conscription** leads to a national "fighting spirit" and an "us vs them" mentality.

Figure 21.6
Industrial Revolution strengthens national infrastructure, leading to a broadening of economic relations.

Figure 21.7
Increased efficiency of the state allows for greater taxation and **bureaucratic** organization.

Figure 21.8
Mass communication contributes to a shared "imagined community" among even distant members.

Types of Nationalism

Figure 21.9
State Supporting Nationalism: The state is regarded as good, to be strengthened and fought for.

Figure 21.10
State Opposing Nationalism: The state is regarded as bad, to be reformed, fought against, or separated from.

Figure 21.11
Civic Nationalism: Membership in a nation is defined by participationg in civic society.

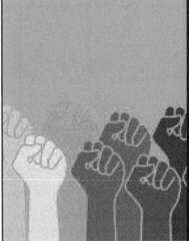

Figure 21.12
Ethnic Nationalism: Membership in a nation is determined by race or ethnicity.

Figure 21.13
Elite Nationalism: Powerful leaders in a country use the language of "the nation" to achieve political goals.

Figure 21.14
Popular Nationalism: The "common people" rather than the elites define the character of the nation.

National Self Determination

Whether the nation is regarded as "primordial" or "modern" or something else, nationalism has been a potent force in the history of politics: sometimes for good, sometimes for evil. Perhaps the most obvious use of nationalism has been the creation and solidification of independent nation-states. The idea of **national self-determination** (Chapter 11-12) has, in one form or another, been responsible for every country on earth. NSD, in the twentieth century, became firmly established after World War I when the victorious powers blamed the war, in the words of Woodrow Wilson, on "disregard of the rights of small nations." It was believed that, by giving every national group the right to its own state, the sorts of political traumas which resulted from "oppressed minorities" opposing "dominant empires" would be avoided. Treaties which established NSD led, in the 1920's, to the creation of dozens of new countries around the world. Similar movements for NSD occurred after World War II, during the period of decolonization in the 1960's, and, finally, immediately after the collapse of the Cold War. It should be noted here that the term "national self-determination," though helpful, is slightly misleading. Though it is safe to say that the nations which have become independent in the twentieth century have all "wanted" to be independent, it is not this wanting itself which has freed them. What has determined that has not been the "self" of the nation but, rather, the totality of the international community which regards them as independent. A willing international order is necessary (at least it seems) in order to create and legitimize nation-states in the eyes of the world.

Question for Discussion

National self-determination is obviously necessary for the creation of new countries, but is it all that is necessary? What role does the international order play? How would you describe the relationship between the international order and the individual nations that make it up?

National Interests

Within a country itself, nationalism is often put to the use of concrete objectives: economic development, scientific advancement, or other "national interests." For example, during the 1960's, the United States funded the National Aeronautics and Space Administration in order to explore the possibility of space travel. The state did not undertake this venture for the sake of pure, scientific curiosity. Rather, they framed it in natonalist terms, as a fight for American technical superiority over the Soviet Union, which had been developing its own space program. The iconic image of the American flag planted on the moon has served, for many years after, as part of a nationalist myth of pioneerism and ambition. Similarly, in the 1960's, when China was attempting to industrialize, the various "five-year plans" were not described as simply "economic" programs but rather great national campaigns. Patriotic posters covered the walls of the cities and national slogans appeared everywhere. As these cases make clear, the spirit of nationalism can be used to inspire technological or economic progress.

(Fig 21.15) An American postage stamp featuring NASA astronauts planting the flag on the moon.	(Fig 21.16) A Chinese poster from the 1950s. Industrialization was seen as a "national cause."

National Symbolism

In addition to these global and domestic functions, nationalism has cultural purposes as well. Ideas of the nation often stir the hearts of citizens, inspiring powerful emotions of patriotism and loyalty. Art, literature, music, and myths reinforce these feelings. In every country, there is a national anthem and a national flag. There are national poet laureates and state-sponsored artists who create statues, murals, and paintings. In school, children are often asked to memorize certain songs or pieces of literature or political speeches. There are customs, ceremonies, and rituals. There are refined formal vocabularies, sonorous words, and meaningful gestures. Political scientists refer to such cultural expressions as ethno-symbolism and argue that this allows the idea of the nation to penetrate beneath politics into the very core of human identity. This is one of the reasons why people are often willing to devote themselves to their nations: to kill or die in wars, for example, to dedicate their lives to a national cause or movement. Nationalism connects individual identity to the myth of a power greater than the self, and, in doing so, provides purpose and meaning like few other ideologies.

Ethno-Symbolism

(Fig 21.17) Emanuel Luetze's famous painting of George Washington crossing the Delaware features oarsmen hard at work clearing ice from the river. Note the giant flag and the towering Washington.

(Fig 21.18) The American flag is unfurled before the singing of the National Anthem at an American football game. The use of the anthem at sporting events has a long history but became more prominent during World War II.

(Fig 21.19) Robert Frost reads "The Gift Outright" at the inauguration of John F. Kennedy. The lines "the land was ours before we were the land's" encapsulates the nationalist myth of a primordial homeland.

(Fig 21.20) The words e pluribus unum, "out of many, one" are featured on the back of American money, expressing the "civic nationalist" idea of diversity within unity.

(Fig 21.21) American schoolchildren, with their hands on their hearts, recite "The Pledge of Allegiance." Each day children attending American public schools are required to say "the pledge."

(Fig 21.22) African American Civil War Memorial. Since the "civil rights" movements in the 1960's, a deliberate effort has been made to include racial and ethnic minorities in American national art.

Good or evil?

Not all uses of nationalism are benign. Even a casual glance at history reveals that nationalist language and imagery have often accompanied war, genocide, slavery, and oppression. A nation, after all, is fundamentally exclusive. It cannot help but divide the society into members that "belong" and ones that "don't belong." More than once over the course of history, the state has attempted to kill the ones it regards as outsiders. In Nazi Germany, after all, to take an extreme example, the government attempted to create an ideal German race by killing, imprisoning, or expelling all people it believed were undesirable. From the perspective of the Nazis, the genocide which it conducted was an act of national self-preservation, to strengthen and protect the authenticity of the German people. More recently, in 1994, the efforts of the majority Hutus to eliminate from Rwanda the minority Tutsis relied on a similar nationalist idea of the "true people" defending themselves from the "invasive outsiders." The Islamic State in Iraq and Syria have followed a similar script. Seeking to create a "pan-Islamic" state for Sunni Muslims, they have killed or driven out of their territory all Shia Muslims as well as Jews, Christians, Yazidis, and others regarded as infidels. This religious nationalism is, with the shift of a few vocabulary words, identical to the Nazi variety. With few exceptions, every genocide and ethnic cleansing in history has been carried out with nationalist justification.

Nationalism: A Force for Evil?

Genocide	*Nationalist Justification*
Holocaust: (1939-1944) German Nazi Party kills over six million Jews and other racial and religious minorities.	Purify Germany of "subhumans" in order to create a ethno-state for the "Aryan" race.
Armenian Genocide (1915-1922) Turkish government kills and deports 1.8 million Armenians in western Turkey.	To eliminate the minority Christian Armenians from Turkey in order to solidify Turkey as Muslim and ethnically homogenous.
Cambodian Genocide: (1975-1979)The communist Khmer Rouge kill over 2 million Cambodians.	To create an "agricultural utopia" based on the ideal purity of the Khmer people.
Rwandan Genocide: (1994) The majority Hutu tribe kill over a million of the minority Tsutsis following the assassination of the Rwandan president.	To purge Rwanda of the minority Tutsis, who were regarded as having a monopoly on power and influence.
Circassian Genocide: (1864-1867) The Russian empire kills and deports 1.5 million Circassian people from the Northern Caucus regions.	To eliminate the Circassians from their homeland to prevent threats to the Russian empire and enable Russian settlement.

Does this mean that nationalism is inherently evil? Certain cosmopolitan or universalist thinkers have argued that nationalism, by definition, leads to a kind of chauvinism in which outsiders are belittled, dehumanized, or oppressed. National divisions, they say, place humans into an unjust "hierarchy of value," providing ripe conditions for atrocities. However, does it follow, just because nationalism can be put to evil uses, that nationalism itself is evil? To take a common example, electricity can be used to detonate a bomb (in fact, all bombs are detonated with electricity), yet it can also be used to power a hospital. Is electricity itself evil? Perhaps it is better to say that nationalism, like electricity, is a powerful force, and, as such, can be put to good uses as well as evil ones.

Nationalism in a globalized world

One final question about nationalism remains: will it always be with us? It is tempting to answer no. As the world becomes more connected, more culturally-similar, indeed, more "Western," it is reasonable to conclude that, over time, national borders will become obsolete, that political authority will be transferred into global or "transnational" institutions, and that the idea of the independent nation will be a thing of the past. Some argue that if such a global unity were ever achieved it would likely be tragic. It is difficult to see how political integration would occur without a loss of the irreplaceable languages, cultures, and identities which render humanity distinct. Globalism has already led to significant homogenization, and, with it, the unfortunate erosion of indigenous identities and practices. Over five hundred languages have disappeared over the last two-hundred years as the ethnic groups that spoke them have been absorbed by dominant cultures. Of the more than 6000 languages which are currently spoken, well over a third are in danger of dying out. The same can be said of other forms of cultural identity: such as religion, art, festivals, and music. Since nationalism is a force which, among other things, acts to preserve national-identity, the loss of nationalism, it would seem, would likely further threaten human diversity.

Others, however, disagree with such a bleak assessment. The political theorist Iris Marion Young, for example, coined the term **differentiated solidarity** to describe how cultural diversity could continue to exist within a globalized world. The loss of nationalism, according to the idea of differentiated solidarity, would be the loss of political not cultural difference. The political institutions which separate and nations and make them hostile to one another, could be integrated while respecting cultural diversity. Indeed, it is possible that nationalism itself has been more harmful to distinct cultures than nationalists care to admit. The loss of language and cultural identity, for example, has often been a consequence of some nationalist groups seeking to impose their own identity, through force or coercion, on others. Without such domination, the argument goes, cultural distinctiveness will be free to flourish. The European Union, for example, has been able to maintain the individual languages, cultures, and identities of its member nations while integrating, for the most part, many of its political institutions.

Still others argue that the debate is moot, because nationalism shows no signs of going away. Indeed, as the world becomes more globalized, many nationalist movements have risen up as a reaction to their perceived loss of sovereignty. The 2016 election, in the United States, of Donald Trump, who campaigned on a pro-sovereignty "America first" platform accompanied the rise of nationalist leaders in many of the largest countries throughout the world. India, Brazil, Hungary, Poland, and the Philippines are all governed by explicitly nationalist leaders. Outside of the Liberal International Order, nationalism is as strong as ever. Chinese nationalism, Russian nationalism, Arabic nationalism: the list goes on and on. And this is hardly surprising. Given how crucial the nation has been in forging both collective and personal identity, it seems unlikely that it will disappear without a fight. And given how bloody fights over nationalism have been in the past, it's probably a fight that we'd be better off not having.

Stateless Nations

Not all "nations" have their own "state." The following table includes four large national groups who each have advocated for their own independent state through both violent and non-violent means.

People	Violent Independence Movements	Non-Violent Independence Movements
Tamils: 75 Million Hindu. Population concentrated in India, Sri Lanka, and Malaysia.	The so-called "Tamil Tigers" carried out a series of public attacks in the 1970's and 1980's.	The Transnational Government of Tamil aims at independence through non-violent political advocacy.
Kurds: 45 million Muslim. Population concentrated in Turkey, Iraq, Iran, and Syria	Kurdish militias control significant (though unrecognized) land in Iraq, Iran, Turkey, and Syria.	The Kurdistan Regional Government hopes to negotiate for an independent Kurdistan.
Uyghers: 12 million Muslim. Population concentrated in Xinjiang region of northern China.	The "Turkistan Islamic Party" has carried out attacks in mainland China and against embassies. In response, the Chinese government has placed parts of Xinjiang province under de-facto military occupation	The World Uyghur Conference hopes to bring global awareness to the Chinese government's mistreatment of Uyghers with the eventual goal of achieving national self-determination in Xinjiang.
Palestinians: 2 million Muslim. Population concentrated in West Bank and Gaza strip, occupied by Israel	The "Islamic Resistance Movement" or Hamas has carried out an armed struggle against the state of Israel for many years. It hopes for a "one-state solution" in which an Arabic, Muslim state replaces Israel.	The Palistinian National Liberation Movement, or Fatah, since 1988 has dedicated itself to non-violently advocating for Palistinian statehood.

Summary: Key Chapter Points

1) Though it seems logical that every "nation" should get to have one state, this idea has been historically problematic.

2) What makes a country is difficult to answer. The same territory can be claimed by different nations, and the same nation can disagree about what "the state" should be.

3) Primordialists argue that the nation precedes the state, that nationalism has existed as long as human societies have.

4) Modernists argue that the idea of the nation is a recent development: a result of popular sovereignty, technologies of communication, industrialization, or conscription.

5) Certain attributes of the nation are "real" (such as language and territory) while others are "subjective" (such as the idea of a "common identity").

6) There are many varieties of nationalism: civic, ethnic; state supporting, state opposing; elite, popular.

7) Nationalism can be used for many different purposes: the creation of states (national self-determination) the pursuit of "national interests" and the bonding of people through national symbolism.

8) It is debatable whether nationalism is a force for good in the world or a force for evil.

9) Some argue that, as the world becomes more globalized, nationalism will be a thing of the past, while others argue that nationalism will survive (and perhaps even grow stronger) through globalization.

10) Nationalism is important in the many "independence movements" of stateless people around the world.

CHAPTER 22: INTERNATIONAL POLITICAL ECONOMY

Overview

This chapter analyzes the way economic power and political power are interconnected. Specifically we discuss

- Public power vs private power
- The importance of currency
- The distinction between the gold standard and fiat currency

We conclude with a discussion of the turn towards **neoliberalism** at the end of the 20th century and evaluate whether or not the less regulated global economy is a good thing or a bad thing.

What if I told you there is a country in the world with no army, no capital city, and only 150,000 citizens. Yet, despite its small size, it has embassies in 240 cities around the world and controls a GDP of 260 billion dollars per year, larger than that of Greece, Portugal, Poland, and the Ukraine. Would you believe me? What country would you think I'm referring to?

The "country" is Apple, Inc: the technology corporation based in Silicon Valley. By "citizens," I mean employees, and by "embassies" I mean locations. Apple, of course, not a "country" in any traditional sense, but a **transnational corporation** (TNC). Still it is richer and, in many ways, more powerful than many nation-states. Apple, moreover, is hardly the biggest TNC in the world. The table below lists a half-dozen even larger corporations and their revenue in comparison to well-known countries.

Company	*Revenue*	*Comparable to*
Walmart (Retail, American)	524 billion USD	Sweden (530 billion)
Sinopec (Energy, Chinese)	407 billion USD	Austria (430 billion)
Volkswagon (Automotive, German)	283 billion USD	Pakistan (284 billion)
Amazon (Retail, American)	280 billion USD	Finland (264 billion)
Toyota (Automotive, Japanese)	260 billion USD	Colombia (248 billion)

We tend to think of companies as organizations that operate "inside" countries, encompassed by the "larger" state that regulates them. Yet a chart like this may make us think twice about that assumption. Might it be possible to think of things the other way around, imagining countries as political units that operate inside an economic order created by the broader acts of production and trade which sustain the lives of the people within it? Can we imagine states as (at least in part) conditioned by the powerful economic actors which produce the goods and services that are required for power? This question is one of the starting points for the field of study known as **international political economy**, a discipline which seeks to understand the complex relationship between politics and the global economy.

Key Question: What you need to know

What is one criticism of the standard assumption that companies operate "inside" of countries?

Public Power vs. Private Power

A good place to start our discussion of International Political Economy (IPE, hereafter) is with the familiar (and perhaps false!) distinction between "**public economic power**" and "**private economic power.**" In the simplest terms, public power describes economic actions that governments can take. Governments can levy taxes, pass regulatory laws, or spend money on projects. Sometimes public power has the effect of helping certain businesses. For example, a government may give special "tax benefits" to promote "eco-friendly" products. Or it may decide to purchase military equipment from a large aviation company. Other times, governments may "hurt" certain businesses. For example, it may ban products which emit too much pollution or impose tariffs on products from a rival country.

Activity	*Helps*	*Hurts*
Tax	• May encourage certain types of economic activity. • May limit inflation	• May drive industries away from host country. • May limit employment
Regulations	• May lead to a fairer market • May eliminate corruption and fraud	•May slow economic growth • May lead to a "race to the bottom"
Spending	• May boost overall employment and total economic growth	• May lead to waste and inefficiency.

Private power, on the other hand, describes economic actions that private citizens or businesses may take. These generally encompass three interrelated domains: **trade**, or the exchange of goods;

production, or the creation of new goods; and **finance**, or investment. These three domains are not separate but are interrelated and often cyclical. For example, when consumers buy a product, computers, say, (trade), this, in turn, creates demand and influences the type and quantity of computers that are made (production). The increased sales of these computers then likely attract investors in the companies that make them (finance). Because of these relationships, trade, production, and finance are often referred to as the **trinity of IPE**.

Key Questions: What you need to know

- What is the difference between public power and private power?
- What is the "trinity of IPE?"
- How do trade, production, and finance relate to one another?

It is often assumed that public power is always greater than private power. Governments, after all, can issue currency, make laws, and command armies to enforce them. However, as the table at the beginning of this chapter makes clear, corporations can often command more financial resources than governments can, a fact that gives them significant negotiating power. For instance, a corporation might threaten to shut down a factory in a host country unless the government enacts certain policies. Or a corporation might heavily donate to a particular political candidate in order to **lobby** for certain pro-business legislation.

Furthermore, private corporations do not *necessarily* lack hard power. Independent security firms have often engaged in military operations. Though most corporations have neither the means nor the desire to threaten nation-states, their role, historically, could not be described as peaceful. Perhaps the most well-known example of this is the extensive military activity of the **British East India Company** during the 19th century in India (chapter 7). Initially the East India Company only had a few hundred soldiers, more or less as "security guards." As their operations grew and they encountered different forms or resistance from the Indian population, the company expanded its security force, often recruiting from the local population, until it had, at its peak, nearly 100,000 armed soldiers. In 1857, this force put down an Indian rebellion against it, effectively putting the entire subcontinent under occupation. Though it seems unlikely that a private corporation would do such a thing today, the example shows that private corporations *can* protect their interest through force. This is yet another reason we should therefore be reluctant to conclude that public power is always stronger than private power.

Question for discussion

How would you describe the relationship between public power and private power? Which is "greater?"

(Fig 22.1) British East India Company Ships in Bombay Harbor. In 1857, the BEIC effectively "ruled" all of India.

Making the Rules: Regulation and Currency

Regulation: The relationship between public power and private power often appears in the idea of "rules." What is the overall system which guides economic activity? Again, you might think that governments are the first ones to set the rules which companies are obliged to follow. Historically, however, that has not always been the case. Economic activity, more often than not, appears organically, as, to borrow Marx's metaphor (chapter 10), a kind of **base** to society. Government rules have often come later, shaping or modifying this base in order to guide or improve the underlying economic activity. For example, in 1908, when Henry Ford produced the "Model-T," the first affordable car, there were no speed-limits, stoplights, traffic rules, or driver's licenses—no requirements for airbags, brakes, safety-glass, or eco-friendly engines. The economic activity came first; the system of regulations came second.

	Economic Activity	Later Regulations
	**(Fig 22.2)** The invention of the steam-engine (1768) created new markets in manufacture and transportation. It also created new forms of labor and complicated the relationships between far off micro-economies.	• Railroad safety laws • Standardized equipment for different railroads • Workplace safety laws • Factory labor laws • Standardized routes and schedules • Standardized licenses for railroad engineers
	**(Fig 22.3)** The development of the first affordable automobile (1908) created one of the most profitable industries of the twentieth century, significantly changing the relationship between the city and suburbs.	• Speed limits • Drivers licenses • Insurance requirements • Emissions standards • Vehicle inspection laws • Drinking and driving laws • Registration requirements • Vehicle safety feature requirements
	**(Fig 22.4)** The so-called "digital revolution" of our day has created numerous new fields of economic activity in marketing, logistics, data-analytics, and information-processing.	• Privacy & anti-hacking laws The digital revolution is still new enough that regulation remains minimal. It is unclear how the state will respond to the growing digital marketplace.

Currency: Another way of understanding the relationship between the government and the economy is by thinking about **currency**. After all, perhaps no domain illustrates the close connection between public power and private power than the use of "official" money guaranteed and regulated by the government. In order to understand the issues related to the use and function of currency, it is necessary, first, to go back in time and take a brief historical detour through the development of currencies.

You are likely aware that all currency can be reduced to the ancient practice of **bartering**: an apple for a hunting arrow; a hunting arrow for a measure of rice. And so on. Any object that

281

you own has, in addition to its **use value** (i.e., whatever you use it for) a certain **exchange value**. It can be traded, even if only theoretically, for other items or services.

Over time, currency developed in order to make the process of exchange easier. Instead of trading your apples for hunting arrows and your hunting arrows for rice, you can trade your apples for money, and then use the money to buy whatever else you want. This simplifies bartering by transforming objects of exchange into a single common denominator.

One issue with currency, however, is that it often, by itself, has no particular **use value**. A dollar bill cannot be eaten, planted, milked, or lived in. It only becomes valuable when embedded in a broader social system in which all members contract to use it as a form of exchange. This is where the government comes in. A government can back up a currency by standardizing it, requiring that it be used, producing or regulating it. One of the earliest and most primary functions of government, indeed, was to do just this. The oldest minted coins, stamped with an image of the king or emperor, say, in effect, "This is valuable. This is what we'll use. The government guarantees that this is worth something." On the back of all U.S. dollars is printed: *"This note is legal tender for all debts, public and private."* This is simply the government's way of ensuring value by connecting currency to the **fiat** (authorization) of the state.

Key Questions: What you need to know

- What is the difference between "use value" and "exchange value?"
- Why does government play an important role in making currency legitimate?

| **(Fig 22.5) Russian Woodcut** of traders bartering their goods. In bartering there is a close connection between **"exchange value"** and **"use value."** Objects which are traded are ones which have a definite "use." | **(Fig 22.6) Ancient Coin**: Inscribed with the image of the Persian King Darius I, this silver coin was in circulation around 500 BCE. Coins (like paper money) have no immediate "use value," so they must derive their **"exchange valu**e" from widespread social consent. This consent is often ensured by government fiat. |

Currency produced by and assured by the government is, of course, only as legitimate as the government is. What happens when a government is corrupt, untrustworthy, or incompetetant? Among other things, the currency becomes dubious. Historical instances of this are numerous. The oldest known example occurred in the 4th century C.E. when the Western Roman Empire attempted to enlarge its military despite lacking the funds to pay the extra soldiers. To "solve" this problem, the Roman government minted additional coins, diluting the gold and silver with metals like bronze and copper. The result was **hyperinflation,** an extreme devaluing of and subsequent loss of trust in the currency. Hyperinflation has occurred time and again in history from Ancient Rome to Yuan China to Weimar Germany to present-day Venezuela. Occurring when governments attempt to increase spending by increasing the supply of money, hyperinflation reflects a lack of trust in the state.

Currency	Cause of Hyperinflation
	**(Fig 22.7)** Roman denarius. In the 4th century C.E., the Roman government began diluting the silver denarius with bronze and copper. After a period of instability, the denarius became worthless and passed out of circulation.
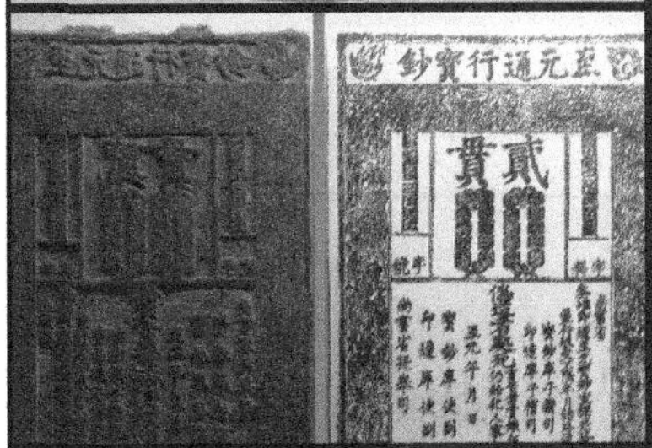	**(Fig 22.8)** A 2 "guan" note from the 13th century C.E. Yuan China. Although an early form of guan was linked, at a fixed rate, to silk, by the 14th century overproduction of the note led to hyperinflation and the failure of the currency.
	**(Fig 22.9)** A five-million mark coin from Germany in 1923. Attempting to repay its WWI debts by printing more and more money, the Weimar Republic caused one of the worst economic crises in the 20th century, leading to the political chaos which eventually culminated in the Nazis' rise to power.
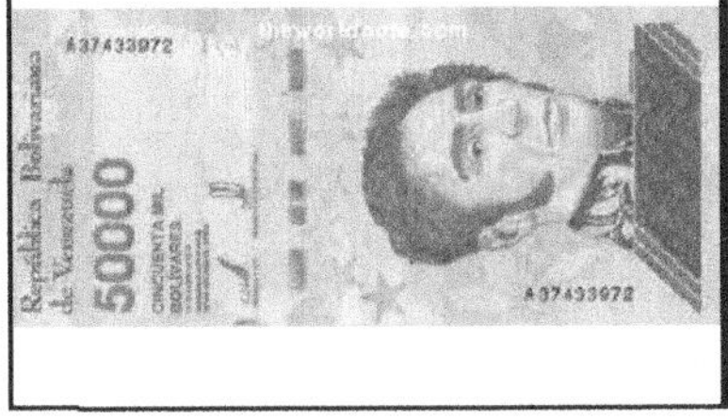	**(Fig 22.10)** A fifty-thousand Bolivar note from Venezuela. Hyperinflation in Venezuela, symptomatic of the current economic crisis, has led to widespread use of the U.S. dollar as an alternative currency.

Gold Standard

One way for a government to create trust in its currency is by connecting it, at a **fixed rate**, to *another* highly trusted currency, like the U.S. dollar or the Euro, or to a commodity, like gold or silver. For many years, in the west, the **gold standard** was the way governments made their currency creditable. Into the early 20th century, in the United States, each paper dollar could be traded, at a fixed rate, for a certain weight of gold or silver held in the government's treasury. The advantages of a fixed-rate currency are twofold. First, it creates trust: there is no worry about devaluation or hyperinflation. Secondly, it makes international trade easier, provided the countries who are trading with one another both use a similarly linked currency.

A gold standard, however, also has a disadvantage: it limits the supply of money. As an economy develops, the number of goods and products increases: more cars, phones, refrigerators, etc. One would expect a corresponding growth in the supply of money to purchase these new products. Given, however, a limited quantity of gold, the growth of money cannot match the pace of the economy. This results in irregularities in prices which often disincentivize the production of certain goods. A second problem occurs in the event of a social trauma such as a war, a natural disaster, or a depression. The government cannot rapidly increase the money supply to stimulate the economy in response to the crisis, making the crisis longer-lasting and more severe.

Key Question: What you need to know

• What are the advantages and disadvantages of a fixed-rate currency?

On and off the Gold Standard

Due to these problems, the majority of the governments in the west chose to abandon the gold standard in the early twentieth century. World War I was looming, and military expenses proved greater than the limited supply of gold could purchase. Britain, France, Germany, and the United States all decoupled their currency from gold, becoming **free-floating**. Although, in the short term, this allowed for an increase in spending, paying for the war and funding economic expansion into the 1920's, in the long term, it led to steep inflation. In the years following World War I, the cost of goods more than doubled in all of the countries which had abandoned the gold standard. In response to this inflation, the gold standard returned. Prices stabilized, but once again, the limited money supply left governments powerless to adequately respond to shocks. When the Great Depression struck in the 1930's, the major western economies left gold for a second time. Then, they went back on it after World War II. Then they abandoned it again, for a third time, in the 1970's. The history of currency in the 20th century, in other words, can be described as a somewhat chaotic swing on and off of the gold standard. The table below summarizes the changes and the reasons for them.

On and Off the Gold Standard

(1800-1914) Most western economies have either a gold-standard or a "bimetallic standard" (silver and gold). Precious metals had been used as currencies since the days of the Roman Empire.	(1914-1927) The outbreak of World War I forces nearly all major western economies to abandon the gold standard in order to fund the increased costs of the war. Steep inflation results.	(1927-1931) In an effort to control inflation, western economies return to the gold standard. Prices stabilize but there is a period of deflation, and governments, once again, have difficulty funding public expenses.

(1931-1945) The outbreak of the Great Depression, followed by World War II, leads western economies to abandon the gold standard again.	(1945-1973) The period of **embedded liberalism**, all major currencies become linked to the U.S. dollar, which, in turn, becomes linked to gold in an attempt to facilitate free trade.	(1973-present) President Nixon takes the US off of the gold standard in order to stimulate the economy. The other major economies followed, and, today no economy uses the gold standard.

As the previous page shows, the major world economies abandoned the gold standard, the final time, in the 1970's. There are currently no governments who issue a currency linked to gold. The major currencies (the American dollar, the British pound, the Euro) are all free-floating. In each of these countries, the government decides how much money to print. These decisions are regulated by economic institutions within each country, such as the Federal Reserve Board in the United States. These institutions aim to control the currency-supply in such a way as to limit inflation, on the one hand, and to ensure economic growth on the other. Proponents of the current free-floaing system argue that it provides both stability and flexibility: that since major governments such as that of the United States are trusted all over the world, there is no longer any need to link currency to an external commodity. Opponents of the system argue that, although these governments "seem" stable, there is no guarantee that they will continue to be so. The last hundred years, after all, has seen major shocks: wars, depressions, political crises of all sorts. Simply hoping that the major governments of the world will continue to be reliable "underwriters" of currency shows a naive disregard for the course of history. In the twenty-first century, many skeptics of the free-floating system have turned to so-called **cryptocurrencies**, such as Bitcoin, electronic currencies which use a computer code, known as "blockchain" to prevent forgery. Like gold and silver, cryptocurrencies are decentralized and limited. Some argue that, as technology continues to develop, cryptocurrencies will offer individuals suspicious of the free-floating system, an alternative form of money.

Key Questions: What you need to know

- What accounts for the fact that the major western economies abandoned and resumed the gold standard so many times over the course of the 20th century?
- Why are some people suspicious of free-floating currency?

Embedded Liberalism to Neoliberalism

In chapter five, we introduced **embedded liberalism**, the period of time immediately following World War II. The major world powers, desperate to prevent another large-scale conflict, decided the global economic order had to accomplish two goals: first, the facilitation of free-trade to create trust among different nations; and, second, the attainment of "full employment" to ensure domestic stability. At the Bretton Woods Conference, in 1944, all of the major world economies created a system of institutions designed to achieve both goals: the fixed exchange rates to help free trade, the International Bank of Reconstruction and Development (IBRD) in order to grow global economies, and the International Monetary Fund in order to regulate and stabilize the global economy. From 1945-1975, the system worked well, and most of the economies which had adopted the Bretton Woods system grew steadily.

By the mid-1970's, however, all was not well with Bretton Woods. Nixon's decision to abandon the gold standard, a key component of the agreement, was, perhaps, the first major blow. Secondly, high oil prices throughout the 1970's damaged the economies of many nations in the west, leading to a period of what is known as **stagflation**, high inflation with minimal economic growth. Finally, a consensus had emerged that governments in the west had too much power: taxes were too high, regulations were too burdensome, and spending, particularly on the **welfare state**, had grown wasteful. The result of these problems is what is known as the **neoliberal revolution**, a series of reforms, particularly in the United States and Great Britain, which (to refer to our earlier distinction) decreased public power and increased private power. Under President Ronald Reagan in the United States and Prime Minister Margaret Thatcher in the UK, taxes, regulations, and spending all decreased. More freedom was given to private individuals and corporations. The theory that by decreasing government interference in the economy, businesses would produce more goods, which would lead to greater prosperity for everyone, was known as **supply-side economics**.

(Fig 22.11-12) Ronald Reagan and Margaret Thatcher: Key figures in the "neoliberal revolution"

Key Vocabulary

Neoliberalism: The reforms in the 1980's which reduced taxes and regulations in order to stimulate the economy.

Supply-side economics: The belief that taxing and regulating producers hampers the production of goods, and that minimizing such interference leads to a maximum of production.

The results of neoliberalism, in the years following the reforms, have been contested. On the one hand, economic growth has increased steeply since the 1980's. The GDP's of both developed and developing economies have increased. Large corporations (as we mentioned at the opening of this chapter) have grown exponentially. Standards of living, according to various measurements, have gone up, particularly in the west and in southeast Asia. Critics, however, have pointed out that this development has been unequally distributed. While, in the years following the neoliberal revolution, the rich have gotten *much* richer, the (far more numerous) poor have not become proportionally better off. Inequality has increased across the world, with the top 10% of individuals currently owning more than 85% of the global wealth. Finally, critics of neoliberalism point out that the lack of regulation has led to numerous social and environmental problems. Large corporations have roamed the world, moving to countries where the cost of labor is low and environmental standards are loose, creating products at the expense of underpaid workers and polluting the environment at will. Critics claim that it is necessary to reign in neoliberalism, by, once again, increasing public power: raising taxes, increasing regulations, and breaking up monopolistic corporations.

Proponents of neoliberalism argue that these criticisms are naive. While it is true that inequality has increased over the past decades, this is not *necessarily* a bad thing. If everyone in a room has 1 dollar, and, then, suddenly, a benevolent benefactor gives one person 100 dollars and doubles everyone else's money, then everyone in the room is better off. Wealth inequality has increased dramatically (after all one person now has 50x more than everyone else!) but so has total wealth. Everyone in the room has twice as much as they had before. Furthermore, say defenders of neoliberalism, it's not clear *what* increasing taxes and increasing regulations is supposed to achieve. Highly taxed and regulated corporations would almost certainly produce fewer products and lay-off workers, off-setting whatever economic benefit the government is able to obtain by increasing spending on the welfare state. Currently the debate between the "pro-neoliberal" side and the "anti-neoliberal" side is a major point of contention in western politics.

Is inequality a bad thing? The Wilt Chamberlain Argument In 1974, the libertarian philosopher **Robert Nozick** provided a novel argument against the idea that inequality is always "bad." Imagine a society with a perfectly appropriate distribution of wealth. Then imagine a great basketball player, Wilt Chamberlain, (Fig 22.13) who all the citizens love and give 25 cents to see play. Before long, Wilt would have more money than anyone else. Yet is there anything wrong with this situation? Everyone voluntarily paid to watch him play (and paid a very modest amount). The question, according to Nozick, is whether or not that inequality is the result of *voluntary* decisions or *involuntary* ones. Nozick claims that, in capitalism, the major sources of wealth inequality are voluntary exchanges of goods and services in which both parties believe they benefit.

Whose Consensus?

The debate between neoliberals and their opponents brings us to our last question: what system is best to ensure economic flourishing? What is the appropriate balance between public power and private power? What are the best trade, production, and financing practices? During the Cold War (chapter 11), the United States and the Soviet Union came to opposite conclusions with each superpower attempting to impose their system on the developing world. Countries in the Soviet Union's sphere of influence were forced to adopt a **planned economy** with the government in complete control of all production and finance. In communist countries, in other words, public power was dominant. Countries in the United States' sphere of influence, conversely, maintained capitalist economies with private power having the upper hand. Since the collapse of the Soviet Union and the rise of neoliberalism, it appears that the capitalist side has won. Currently, the United States, along with many other countries in the west, recommend an economic recipe known as the **Washington Consensus:** low taxes, low regulations, low spending, free trade, and private property rights. Often making the adoption of the Washington Consensus a condition for economic aid, the United States argues that the sooner developing nations adopt neoliberal principles, the faster they'll achieve economic growth.

The Washington Consensus has been a target of sharp criticism, and many economies (China's most notably) have achieved strong growth without it. Critics argue that it favors the wealthy, increases inequality, and prevents the government from protecting its citizens. However, perhaps the biggest problem with the Washington Consensus is the idea that an economic program can be imposed from above. As we mentioned in the beginning of this chapter, in the domain of the economy, the government does not "come first." Economic activity is *basic*, reflecting the decisions, individual and communal, in the production and allocation of goods. Regulation is what happens only after the organic process of making, buying, and selling has gotten underway. It would be more accurate, therefore, to call the Washington Consensus, the Washington *description*--a story of "what has happened" in certain economies. The neoliberal policies of our present day are not original plans which started *ex nihilo* but rather reactions and responses to long sequences of prior conditions and considerations. They are *effects* as much as causes. Neoliberalism maybe reflects a new chapter in the economic story of the west, but that story, like many stories in politics, is one whose writers and readers have only a very limited idea of what comes next.

Key Questions: What you need to know

- What is neoliberalism?
- What are some of the chief criticisms of neoliberalism?
- What is the Washington Consensus?
- Why might inequality not always be a bad thing?

Summing Up: Key Chapter Points:

1) International political economy is the study of the relationship between economic and political power.

2) We often think that governments are "more powerful" than companies, but large corporations, both now and in the past, often dwarf many nation-states.

3) Public power means everything governments can do. Private power means everything individuals and private companies can do. Public power and private power affect each other in "cyclical" relationships.

4) One important role of public power is in the regulation of currency.

5) Throughout much of history, major world governments used a "fixed rate" currency linked to gold.

6) In the twentieth century, major global economies went on and off the gold standard in response to various political crises.

7) After World War II, the Liberal International Order created an economic system known as "embedded liberalism" designed to ensure both free trade and full employment.

8) Following the "stagflation" of the 1970's, major economies lowered taxes and deregulated leading to the "neoliberal revolution."

9) Critics of neoliberalism argue that it increases inequality, harms the environment and creates other social problems.

10) Defenders of neoliberalism argue that it is the best "recipe" for economic growth.

CHAPTER 23: DEMOCRACY

Overview

This chapter provides an overview of democracy with an emphasis on

- The definition of democracy as a "decision making process"
- The different types of democracy
- Classical and modern criticisms of democracy

We then offer the classical responses to these criticisms focusing on the ideas of account-ability and legitimacy. The chapter concludes with a discussion of whether the world will become more or less democratic as a result of globalization.

If you ask an American (or anyone from the west) what they think is best about their political system, they will likely answer you in one word: "democracy." They may not be entirely happy with their government. They may be bothered by certain political leaders or certain policies. They may think that one (or both!) political parties are misguided. But, in general, they will agree that democracy is a good thing. Citizens expressing their opinions, voting on their leaders, protesting against injustice, advocating for reforms—in short, freely and actively participating in the political process—this, they will argue, is the foundation of any legitimate government. Recent surveys have shown that close to 90% of Americans believe that a democratic political system is a good way of governing a country, and 77% believe such a system is preferable to any kind of goverment.

You may be surprised to learn that democracy has not always enjoyed such a good reputation. As far back as Plato's *Republic* (375 BCE), political philosophers have argued that democracy can be highly problematic, causing chaos, inefficiency, and corruption. In recent years, political thinkers from one-party states, such as the People's Republic of China, have revived many of these ancient arguments, claiming that western-style democracies are, at best, overrated and, at worst, dangerous. In this chapter we will explore this age old debate about the usefulness and desirability of democracy. After defining democracy, we will present the standard criticisms of democratic governments. We will respond to these criticisms, offering the general theories which underlie western-style democracies. Finally, we will conclude with a discussion of the future of democracy in a globalized world.

What is Democracy?

Though people often assume that democracy is a form of government, it is, in its broadest sense, a decision-making process. If you and your friends are trying to decide what movie to see and you take a vote, this is a democratic decision. If, on the other hand, you flip a coin or roll a dice or just go to the movie that your loudest friend insists on, this is not democratic but arbitrary. For the time being, we will define a decision as democratic if those who are affected by it are able to participate in making it. Of course not every decision affects everyone in the same way, and not all forms of participation are equal, but, at the very minimum, this is what is necessary for a democratic process.

Voting on what movie to see is an example of **direct democracy**. In direct democracy, popular election settles all decisions. If a country were governed by direct democracy, all of the inhabitants would come together and vote on every issue of social organization. Every time, for example, the government wanted to make a law or set a tax rate or build a road or form an agency, the matter would be settled, then and there, by direct referendum. In a way, there would be no government at all. The government would be identical with the totality of the people.

In the modern world, this is not practical (and probably would not be desirable even if it were). All democratic countries today employ a form of **indirect democracy** or **representative democracy**, in which citizens vote not for policies but for representatives. These representatives, in turn, make the policy decisions of the state. In the United States, for example, the President and members of Congress are representatives. The people, in electing their representatives, *indirectly* influence government actions.

In addition to these two different *methods* of democracy, there are two different theories by which the *purpose* of democracy can be understood. In the example of the movie, what matters is simply the decision itself. If five people vote for *Batman* and two people vote for *Dirty Dancing*, *Batman* wins, and that's all there is to it. It doesn't matter how the voters feel or what the merits of the respective movies are. The purpose of the vote is simply a kind of "contest" used to figure out the will of the voters. The term for this understanding of democracy is **aggregate democracy**. Democracy, in the aggregate sense, is simply a tool for calculating the preferences of the majority. One problem with aggregate democracy is that it seems to give a very one-sided and limited picture of political forces. Does the majority vote the way it votes for no reason? Does it simply want to win? Or is the purpose of a vote more complicated? In the example of the movie, it is likely that you and your friends would have had a conversation—perhaps a long conversation—before taking the vote. In your conversation you would have discussed many things: the actors, the genre, the showtimes, the reviews. According to the model of **deliberative democracy**, this conversation, rather than the decision itself, is the purpose of the democratic process. What matters is not the vote but the ongoing debate, the exchange of ideas and perspectives, through which democratic actors engage with one another. This engagement, even when it does not arrive at agreement, allows for the rational deliberation through which the terms, arguments, and perspectives of the various participants become known. In other words, democracy helps to construct the **public sphere**, the shared world which communally binds individuals to one another. In the deliberative understanding of democracy, the process never ends" The purpose is the ongoing constructive conversation, in which the different decisions that get made are only resting points along the journey that has no ultimate destination. This is why, according to a deliberative understanding of democracy, **free speech** is so essential to the democratic process. Without a free exchange of thoughts and ideas, the process of deliberation, the constructive discourse by which the community engages with its members, is impossible.

Key Vocabulary

Direct Democracy: A democratic system in which voters vote on every single policy decision.

Indirect Democracy: A democratic system in which voters vote for representatives.

Aggregate Democracy: A model of democracy in which what matters is discerning the will of the majority.

Deliberative Democracy: A model of democracy in which what matters is the rational conversation among democratic actors.

Public Sphere: The mutually acknowledged "reality" of terms, arguments, and perspectives through which democratic conversation is made possible.

The Ship of Fools: Ancient and Modern Criticisms

Believe it or not, the earliest political philosophers didn't have many good things to say about democracy. They thought it was divisive, chaotic, and ineffective. In one of the most famous passages of *The Republic,* Plato compares democracy to a "ship of fools."

> "Imagine a ship with a captain who is a little deaf and near-sighted. The sailors are arguing with one another about the steering. Everyone thinks that he has a right to steer, though he has never learned the art of navigation. They swarm around the captain, begging him to let them steer. If at any time they do not succeed, but others are chosen over them, they kill them or throw them overboard. Then, having first chained up the captain's senses with drink or some narcotic drug, they rebel and take possession of the ship. They plunder the cargo and the stores, eating and drinking and proceed on their voyage. Whoever is their spokesman and cleverly aids them in their plot, they call "Good sailor! Pilot! Able seaman!" They never consider that the true pilot must pay attention to the year and seasons and sky and stars and winds."

| (Fig 23.2) Albrecht Durher: Ship of Fools | (Fig 23.3) Plato compared democratic politicians to lion-tamers. |

Plato's language is poetic, but his point is straightforward. In democratic societies, what matters isn't expertise but the ability to win influence. In a later passage of *The Republic* he compares the majority to an enormous lion, and the politician to a lion-tamer. A successful politician isn't one who necessarily knows about law or tax rates or military strategy or the public good. A successful politician is simply one who can get the lion of the public to roar in the right way. The leaders in a democratic society, Plato argues, will not necessarily have any other talent besides telling the majority what it wants to hear.

Thomas Hobbes (whom we have already discussed in our chapter on Realism) had a slightly different criticism of democratic government. In *The Leviathan* (1651), he points out that the problem with democracy is constant political division. While, in a monarchy, Hobbes argues, the king is, by definition, unified in his decision-making, in a democracy, rival factions and quarreling politicians cause disorder in the political body. Because passion is a stronger motivating force than reason, Hobbes believed that democracy would quickly descend into unrest in which powerful and wealthy manipulators would incite anger and outrage in order to seize power. Democratic assemblies, Hobbes concludes, "in all great dangers and troubles, have need of *Custodes Libertatis*; that is of Dictators, or Protectors of their Authority."

In recent years, there has been a revival of interest in these ancient arguments. This has been due, in no small part, to the power and influence of "undemocratic" states like the People's Republic of China. In 2014, Daniel Bell, a political scientist in China wrote *The China Model,* a defense of China's one-party system. First, Bell points out, (in an argument that echoes Plato) in the west, election to public office depends on a candidate's ability to woo the majority. The most successful politicians are con-men who excel at nothing other than flattery, big promises, and fear-mongering. Campaigning rouses up the worst passions, and emotional impulses win out over careful deliberation. As this process occurs, the wealthy and powerful are able to manipulate public choice in order to serve their own interests. While political parties are engaged in endless back-and-forth, one party inevitably sabotages another, making it impossible to govern. Meritocratic governments, like China's, on the other hand, view the ruling of a nation in the same way that a corporate board views the running of a business. Leaders are selected and promoted through careful internal review and elevated to positions of power based on talent. A Chinese politician, by the time he reaches the top, has demonstrated, over many years, high achievements in state admin-istration, beginning at the village-level, proceeding to the city level, the province level, and lastly the national level. These officials are not elected, but their legitimacy derives from their skill in overseeing public affairs. Finally, Bell claims that since membership and advancement in the party is open to all citizens, the system is broadly inclusive, allowing all Chinese a chance to participate. Meritocratic oversight ensures that the only best and brightest rise to the highest positions of na-tional power.

Daniel Bell's *The China Model* argues that the Chinese system of "meritocracy" is an effective alternative to western-style democ-racy. Many of the criticisms that Bell makes of western democracy are hundreds of years old, having antecedents in Plato and Hobbes. I.e., that democracy is "chaotic," that politi-cians care more about flattering the prejudices of the masses than mastering the nuances of statecraft, that democratic societies lack focus, and that a careful meritocracy, with multiple levels of accountability, ultimately provides a more stable gauruntee of political order over time.

Accountability, Inclusion, and Legitimacy: The Advantages of Democracy

At first blush, the criticisms of democracy seem convincing. Wouldn't we all be better off under a government of talented, wise, and benevolent rule-makers? Yet, there are powerful arguments in favor of democracy too, arguments which have shaped the development of many of the largest democracies today. These arguments tend to focus on three key advantages of democratic societ-ies: accountability, inclusion, and legitimacy.

Accountability: Accountability, in the simplest terms, is about who the boss is. In a monarchy, for example, government officials are accountable to the king or queen. Say you are a tax collector in a country governed by a royal family. Who do you want to please? Who pays your salary? Who might promote you to a higher position in government? Obviously, the king. Doing your job well means making the king happy, and if you take a little extra tax at the expense of the people, then, as long as it serves the interest of the monarchy, it isn't likely to hurt your career. But say you're a tax collector in a democratic society. Who pays your salary then? Who controls your fate as a public servant? The elected official. If the tax rate is too high or the official is incompetant or the people, for any other reason, don't like the job that he's doing, then he'll simply be voted out at the next election. The official who wants to keep his job will have to find a way to please the people one way or another. In democratic societies, the government is accountable to the people, and the people have the power to change ineffective governments.

This is why, according to pro-democracy thinkers, democratic governments can become highly effective even though (as Plato and Hobbes pointed out) both the politicians and the electorate can be corrupt, selfish, and immoral. **Alexis DeToqueville**, one of the greatest 19th century political thinkers on the theory of democracy, put it this way:

> The men who are entrusted with public affairs in democracies, are frequently inferior, both in capacity and of morality, to those whom aristocratic institutions would raise to power. But their interest is identified and confounded with that of the majority of their fellow citizens. They may frequently be faithless and mistaken, but they will never systematically adopt a line of conduct opposed to the will of the majority, and it is impossible that they should give a dangerous or an exclusive authority to the government. Under aristocratic governments public men are swayed by the interest of their order, which, if it is sometimes confounded with the interests of the majority, is very frequently distinct from them.

In other words, no matter how "inferior" democratically-elected officials might be, their own self-interests are necessarily connected to the interests of the people who elect them. No matter how intelligent and talented officials in non-democratic states might be, their self-interests are connected to those of the ruling class. For this reason, as DeToqueville says, "in aristocratic governments, public men may frequently do injuries they do not intend, and, in democratic governments, they produce advantages they never thought of."

Alexis DeToqueville (fig 23.4) was one of the greatest theorists in the 19th century. In his book *On Democracy*, he discusses the idea of "accountability." In a democracy, government officials, no matter how incompetant, will have to serve the majority of the people, since their livelihood depends on it.

Inclusion: A second advantage of democracy has to do with inclusion. The more perspectives that are available to a community, the more accurate the public information is likely to be. Suppose you are a government official in charge of making a map of your territory. Your map will obviously be more accurate if it takes into account the observations of as many people as possible: not only the wealthy elites living in the cities, but the farmers in the countryside and the miners up in the mountains. A more accurate map, in turn, means a more efficient system of roads, a more effective utilization of natural resources: in short, a more complete representation and administration of your country.

The inclusion of multiple perspectives has a cultural advantage as well. When more people contribute to the public conversation, there will be a greater chance for innovation than when perspectives are limited. In a "noisy" public space, where everyone is free to speak their mind, there will no doubt be many unhelpful opinions. But there will also be more clever and creative ones. Through a robust discourse, a "competition of ideas" (see John Stuart Mill in ch 16) will take place through which the best will eventually win out. A community with free speech, free assembly, and free press allows for as many people as possible to engage in the public conversation. In doing so, it maximizes the potential for novel and beneficial input.

(Fig 23.4) David Wilkie: Chelsea Pensioners reading the Waterloo Dispatch. A "noisy" public sphere including as many voices as possible is a theoretical advantage to democracies.

Peace and Legitimacy

Last but not least, democratic societies, (so it is argued) are more peaceful and stable than non-democratic ones. Why? History teaches us that there are two main sources of political violence: insurrection and international war. What happens in non-democratic societies when a majority is unhappy with the government? They either endure their unhappiness, or, if they become desperate enough, they launch an armed rebellion. Other than hoping that their leaders change their minds, there is no other way to bring about reform. What about in democratic societies? The people may protest, complain, and denounce the government (a process which may be a healthy form of catharsis) but, in general, they have little incentive to launch a civil war. It's easier, safer, and probably more effective to simply wait for the next cycle of elections and vote the leaders whom they don't like out of office.

The case of international war is similar. We have already discussed the idea of **democratic peace theory** in our chapter on liberalism. Non-democratic societies, according to this theory, are more prone to war than democratic ones, because, in the case of any war, the ordinary citizens are the ones who do all of the fighting. People who have to risk their lives in a war will only vote for one in extreme circumstances. Therefore, democratic decision making acts as a kind of check on the aggression of governments.

Both of these examples essentially reduce to one idea: legitimacy. In democratic societies, with few exceptions, the citizens tend to feel that the government has the right to rule. The people voted for it. The people can vote against it. The state is simply a reflection of the collective will of the people. Engaging in the sort of the violence that would harm the state is, at least in theory, politically contradictory as it would be in direct opposition to the expressed interests of the people themselves.

Checks and Balances: The Limits of Democracy

Does this mean that the criticisms of democracy mentioned in the first part of this chapter are unfounded? Not entirely. Political theorists in most democratic countries have long recognized the problematic aspects of democracy that Plato and Hobbes pointed out. Most large democracies contain certain "undemocratic" limitations on the democratic process in order to protect against some of the more dangerous aspects of majority rule.

For example, the authors of the **Federalist Papers** (1788), a series of essays written to explain the basis of early American democracy, feared that excitable mobs might recklessly vote for dangerous leaders. What, after all, would stop a bigoted majority from voting to oppress a religious or ethnic minority? To guard against such possibilities, the American constitution needed to have ample **checks and balances**: limits on the power of majorities as well as **separations of powers** so that different branches of government could keep an eye on one another. A famous passage from the Federalist Papers reads:

> A dependence on the people is, no doubt, the primary control on the government; but experience has taught mankind the necessity of auxiliary [additional] precautions. The policy of supplying, by opposite and rival interests, the defect of better motives, might be traced through the whole system of human affairs, private as well as public. We see it particularly

displayed in all the subordinate distributions of power, where the constant aim is to divide and arrange the several offices in such a manner as that each may be a check on the other that the private interest of every individual may be a sentinel over the public rights.

In other words, separate branches of government would prevent power from becoming too concentrated in any one group. "Rival interests" would tame one another, limiting each other's power. In practice, such a **separation of powers** took the form of separately elected and differently constituted government bodies. In the United States today, the President, the House, and the Senate are all separately elected and, more often than not, in control of different parties. The Supreme Court, with the power to overturn laws deemed unconstitutional, is not elected at all but rather appointed by the President. The deliberate gridlock and inefficiency created by the separation of powers, though often regarded to be a flaw in the system, is an intentional feature designed to serve as a firebreak against "the tyranny of the majority."

Historically, a second limit on democracy has been limiting the vote to certain groups on the basis of **competency**. No current democracy, for example, allows children to vote, and many of them do not allow convicted criminals to vote either. Many are surprised to learn that, at the founding of the United States, only about 20% of the adult population, at most, was eligible to vote. Voting was limited to white men who owned a certain amount of property. The property-requirements were not eliminated, in each of the states, until 1828. African Americans did not gain the right to vote until after the Civil War in 1868. Women could not vote until 1921, and people aged 18-21 could not vote until 1965. "Literacy tests" and "poll-taxes" designed, in general, to restrict access of African Americans and the poor were not abolished until 1966. Other modern democracies likewise tended to begin with very restrictive measures and only enfranchised their populations *gradually*.

The point is that, while there is a tendency in the west to view democracy as a "natural" state of affairs, this hardly reflects history. Though a few democracies existed in the ancient world (the Greek and Roman Republics being obvious examples), in general, democracies have been few and far between throughout history. The democracies of the present day were only established relatively recently in history, and, even then, in fits and starts, with numerous undemocratic conditions and limitations. .

(Figs 23.6-8) Alexander Hamilton, James Madison, and John Jay: authors of the *Federalist Papers.*

Global Democracy: Present and Future

In Chapter 7, we discussed **Francis Fukayama** who famously argued that the spread of western-style democracy would mark "the end of history," i.e., would cover the globe and become "universalized as the final form of human government." While it is true that the richest and most powerful countries in the world, at the moment, are democratic and many smaller countries (due partly to the legacy of colonialism) are democratic as well, there is only limited evidence that democracy will continue to spread. Perhaps the most obvious counter-example to Fukayama's vision has been the rise of the People's Republic of China. Though, since 1978, the economy of the PRC has liberalized, and though there is limited democracy at the local level, in general, all major state decisions are managed by the Communist Party. There is no separation of powers, and elections, when held, are largely rubber-stamping affairs. Nonetheless, China has developed, in the late twentieth and early twenty-first centuries, into a highly effective and economically advanced global power, one which provides a high standard of living for many of its citizens. Among many Chinese intellectuals an attitude of democratic skepticism persists: "Why *should* China change its system of government? The country is stable and growing. The communist party seems to be managing things well. The United States, furthermore, seems politically shaky. What would China gain through a revolution?"

(**Fig 23.9-10**) From the age of Mao Tse Tung to that of Xi Jinping, the Chinese Communist Party has maintained one-party rule over the Chinese mainland.

China is only one example among many. The countries of the Arabic Gulf (Saudi Arabia, Oman, Qatar, the UAE, Kuwait), are all governed by traditional monarchies. Russia, after a brief attempt at democracy in the 1990's, has gone back to single-party leadership. In all of these cases, economic development and (relative) political stability have given legitimacy to the regimes and made near-term democratization unlikely. Not without reason, the political leaders in these countries fear the upheaval which may accompany efforts at reform. It seems as though all of these countries will be undemocratic (or only marginally so) for the foreseeable future.

Another barrier to the spread of democracy can be seen in the imbalances of the global system itself. Earlier in this chapter we defined a decision as democratic if those who are affected by it have the opportunity to help to make it. The world of the twenty-first century, however, is thickly interconnected. A decision about tariff levels made in the European Union will affect the economy of Japan. A currency exchange rate set by a bank in Argentina will affect the market in Canada. Given the fact of territorial sovereignty (chapter 4), how is it possible for any global decision to be truly democratic? Should individuals, anywhere in the world, get to vote in elections in countries they don't live in? The suggestion seems ridiculous. Nonetheless, given interdependence, if the decisions made in these countries have global effects, then it seems that, by our earlier definition, they cannot be fully democratic since those who are affected by them have no immediate power to shape them. And this is simply limiting the conversation to countries. What about other global political actors? Large corporations. UN committees. The boards of directors for large universities. All of these actors make decisions every day which affect millions of people around the world. Yet, with few exceptions, those affected have limited power to make their voices heard.

It is for these reasons that, despite the prestige of democracy in many of the most powerful countries in the world, democracy as a global decision-making system is likely to remain limited. The prospect of democracy sweeping through the world, structuring all countries and all global institutions, is likely a fantasy. Nonetheless, the *idea* of democracy is unlikely to fade from global prominence either. As long as there are political decisions to be made, those who must reap the consequences of them will want to have a say in what they are and how they are decided. That much, at least, the world can agree to unanimously.

Summing Up: Key Chapter Points

1) Democracy can be defined as a "decision-making process" in which those who are affected by the decision have the opportunity to contribute to making it.

2) Democracy can be divided into "direct and indirect" forms. In a direct democracy, all citizens vote on every issue. In indirect democracy, they elect representatives.

3) Democracy can be theorized as "aggregate" or "deliberative." In an aggregate democracy, what matters is the "choice." In a deliberative democracy, what matters is the process of discussion and deliberating.

4) Ancient political thinkers such as Plato and Thomas Hobbes were highly critical of Democracy.

5) Modern democratic have revived many of these ancient criticisms.

6) Nonetheless democracy has a number of advantages having to do with accountability, inclusion, and legitimacy.

7) All western democracies have "limits" on simply majority-rule.

8) It seems unlikely that democracy will spread throughout the entire globe. China, the Arabic Gulf, and Russia have achieved economic development and stability without democracy.

CHAPTER 24: RELIGION

This chapter analyzes the role that religion plays in global politics. We address:

- The difficulty of defining religion
- The "cultural universal" of religion
- The growth of **secularism** beginning in the 17th century
- Four different models of secularism

We end with a discussion of whether religion will become more or less important in a highly connected, technologically advanced society.

There are two subjects (the saying goes) which are rude to discuss at the dinner table: politics and religion. The fact that these are no-go zones partly comes from common sense. People feel strongly about both of them, and, if they disagree, the disagreements are often ugly. Since ugly disagreements are best avoided, domestic diplomacy usually means sticking to safer topics. Sports, films, food, or the weather.

Of course, dinner isn't the *only* time when it's considered impolite to discuss religion. In general, we don't talk about religion at work (some companies may have policies restricting it), rarely mention it at school, and approach the topic only with caution even among our friends. Most days, you don't see much about religion in the news headlines or in movies or on television shows. It's possible to go an entire week, maybe an entire month, without encountering **religious discourse** in public. You'd surely be justified in believing, therefore, that religion is *rare*. But nothing could be further from the truth. In the United States, 72% of people profess to follow one religion or other (with Protestant Christianity and Catholic Christianity being the most dominant at 43% and 20% respectively). In the EU, though often taken to be more secular, the numbers are similar with 73% professing to adhere to a religion (44% Catholic, 11 % Orthodox, 10% Protestant). In the global south, the numbers are even higher. 91% of people in South America claim to be religious (with Catholicism being dominant). 93% of people in the African continent (Christianity and Islam) and 98% of people in the Middle East (Sunni and Shia Islam) are religious. Even in China, where the Communist Party maintains a stance of "state atheism" certain surveys have maintained high percentages of the population retain religious belief (such as in heaven, hell, and supernatural forces) and higher still engage in religious practices (such as prayer, incense-burning, and regularized devotions). Even taking low estimates, China has 250 million Buddhists as well as 50 million Christians and 20 million Muslims.

Religion	Demographics	Geopolitical issues
	• **Christianity** (Fig 24.1) 2.4 billion adherents. (~50% Catholic, 35% Protestant, 12% Orthodox. Decline in developed world offset by increase in developing world.	• Once the dominant institution in the west, has maintained a position of political importance despite secularism, & has become a large part of many non-western identities.
	• **Islam (Fig 24.2)** 1.8 billion adherents (~80% Sunni, 15% Shia). Heavily concentrated in Arabic Peninsula & Northern Africa. A growing minority (~5%) in the west and in China.	• Tensions between the Islamic world and the west (see **War on Terror**) have remained a problem. Sunni & Shia conflicts have been a faultline in the Middle East particularly between Iran and the Arabic Penninsula.
	• **Hinduism (Fig 24.3)**. 1.2 billion adherents (67% Vaishnavism, 26% Shaivism). Concentrated in India and Nepal with significant minority populaties in the West Indies and South America.	• Violent conflicts between India's Hindu majority and Muslim minority, particularly in Kashmir. Continual tensions with Muslim majority Pakistan.
	• **Buddhism (Fig 24.4)**~ 500 million adherents. Majority in Cambodia, Burma, Laos, Thailand and Sri Lanka. Large minority in China.	•History of conflict with Chinese Communist Party. The state of Tibet is largely Budhist. Conflict with Rohingya in Myanmar currently classed a genocide.
	•**Judaism (Fig 24.5)** Heavily concentrated in Israel (70% of population). Small but influential minority in United States (2%), Europe and various Middle Eastern countries.	• The Israel-Palestine conflict has been one of the most persistent and intractable problems in the Middle East.

Religion is what anthropologists call a **cultural universal.** Like other universals such as music, literature, marriage, and law, it appears in every society, often pervasively, and, as far as we can tell, has existed as an institution throughout human history. Why, then, is there this social phobia about discussing religion openly—at least in the west? What is the relationship between religion and politics? What accounts for the enormous power that religion has in the world? Finally, is religion an inspiration for social progress? Or is it a cause of division, hatred, and superstition? Answering these questions requires us to look at the complex relationships between many political actors and to examine how the function of religion intersects with that of other political institutions.

Defining religion

"Defining" religion is a difficult, if not impossible task. An intuitive definition might be something like, "belief in God(s), the supernatural, and the rituals through which they are encountered." This is not a bad place to start. Still, when compared to the actual practices of many of the world's religions, it becomes clear that this definition is not inclusive enough. Several of the world's largest religions, (Buddhism, Confucianism) do not include belief in gods. Many modernist interpretations of Christianity, Hinduism, and Islam the miraculous and supernatural as "metaphorical." Many people, within all religions, finally, claim to follow or practice their religion without any *systematic* adherence to rituals. It seems clear, then, that this basic description isn't quite broad enough to capture the varieties of religion that exist today.

The theologian Paul Tillich had a much looser definition. In his book *The Interpretation of History*, he defined religion as "the state of being grasped by an **ultimate concern...**which contains the answer to the question of the meaning of life." This is a more inclusive definition, and many have found it to be apt and memorable. Nevertheless, it seems clear that it is too imprecise to distinguish religion from other domains with which one might be "ultimately concerned." A tennis player may be ultimately concerned with tennis. It may be, for him or her, the absolute meaning of life. But we would not say, except as a kind of hyperbole, that tennis is a religion.

Many **sociologists** have attempted to find a midpoint between the narrowness of the common-sense definition and the broadness of Tillich's. Emile Durkheim, for example, defined it as "a unified system of beliefs and practices relative to sacred things...beliefs and practices which unite into one single moral community called a Church all those who adhere to them." This is better, but it is also a bit too circular. What, after all, are sacred things? If one definition of "sacred" is simply "religious" then the definition gets us nowhere. According to another sociologist Clifford Geertz, religion is "a system of symbols which acts to establish powerful, persuasive, and long-lasting moods and motivations...by formulating conceptions of a general order of existence." This is somewhat plausible, but, again, it doesn't seem to hit the nail on the head. What is a "system of symbols" supposed to mean? What is a "long-lasting mood?" Geertz's terminology, in an effort to be abstract enough to capture everything that religion might be is so abstract that it seems to have little meaning.

Philosopher	Definition of Religion
	**Immanuel Kant** (Fig 24.6) In this manner, through the concept of the highest good as the object and final end of pure practical reason, the moral law leads to religion. Religion is the recognition of all duties as divine commands...as essential laws of any free will as such.
	**Karl Marx** (Fig 24.7) Religious suffering is, at one and the same time, the expression of real suffering and a protest against real suffering. Religion is the sigh of the oppressed creature, the heart of a heartless world, and the soul of soulless conditions... It is the opium of the people.
	**James Frazier** (Fig 24.8) By religion, then, I understand a propitiation or conciliation of powers superior to man which are believed to direct and control the course of nature and of human life. Thus defined, religion consists of two elements, a theoretical and a practical, namely, a belief in powers higher than man and an attempt to propitiate or please them.
	**Clifford Geertz** (Fig 24.9) Religion is a system of symbols which acts to establish powerful, persuasive, and long-lasting moods and motivations... formulating conceptions of a general order of existence.
	**Huston Smith** (Fig 24.10) [All people] find themselves faced with three inescapable problems: how to win food and shelter from their natural environment (the problem nature poses), how to get along with one another (the social problem), and how to relate themselves to the total scheme of things (the religious problem).

Given the disagreement about (and the general imprecision of) definitions of religion, it is probably best to take a more skeptical approach. When asked to define "time," the theologian St. Augustine said "If you don't ask me, I know. If you ask me, I don't know." That seems like a reasonable attitude to take toward many concepts—time, religion, music, emotion-that seem, in a way, both too basic and too complex to sit neatly under a simple description. Instead of attempting to say what religion "is," it might be more helpful to say what it "often involves." To that end, we'd generally agree on

- A traditional and "separate" vocabulary
- A broader "community" or historical tradition
- A body of texts, stories, or literary works (written or oral)
- A set of "values" about what is good or bad
- A metaphysical theory about "how the world works"
- A body of "practices" such as songs, prayers, or rituals that reinforce personal commitment to the religion.

Again a religion need not contain all of these elements, and individual believers, within religions, may not ascribe to each of them, but, in general, these elements are often associated with religious practice.

Key Questions: What you need to know

- What are some different ways that scholars have tried to define religion?
- What does religion "often involve?"
- What does it mean that religion is a "cultural universal?

Religion: a "recent" concept

The effort to define religion—to put it into a separate category apart from "ordinary experience" is a relatively recent one. Though religion itself is ancient, the act of thinking "about religion" *per se* only came about rather gradually and was not well established until the 19th century. If you could travel back in time 1000 years ago and ask a European "what is your religion?" it is doubtful that he or she would have understood you. As we mentioned in Chapter 2, the Catholic Church, at the time, was the dominant institution in Europe. It was not only a religious institution, but it was a *social* institution. It was where the community gathered to talk and form friendships. It was a *legal* institution: the place where contracts were signed, births were recorded, marriages took place, and funerals were held. It was an *educational* institution: the foundation of university training. It was a *political* institution: the source of the legitimacy of the king's "divine right." Finally, it was an *international* institution: the cultural link that joined one kingdom to another. In short, religion, at the time, was so pervasive that it could not really be separated from the "non-religious." The old joke that it is impossible for a fish to define water applies to religion in the middle ages. It was so intertwined in political, cultural, and social life that it was to be, in some sense, invisible to the people at the time.

This is not to say that Europeans had no sense at all of difference when it came to their beliefs. In the early 7th century, the **prophet Muhammad,** inspired by a series of visions in the mountains around Mecca, brought his revolutionary message to the various tribes in the Arabic peninsula. Sometimes by persuasion, sometimes by conquest, he gradually converted many of the largest tribes to **Islam**. By the time of his death, almost all of present-day Arabia was Muslim. His successors—a series of rulers making up the **Rashidun Caliphate**—extended Islamic control into northern Africa. The next generation of Islamic leaders, in the **Umayyad Caliphate**, went even further, conquering most of the Iberian Peninsula and pushing up into southern France. Thus, the Christians in south of the former Western Roman Empire (see chapter 3) came into violent conflict, in the early middle ages, with the Muslim conquerers. Over hundreds of years, Christian and Muslim forces would fight back and forth in southern Europe, northern Africa and the Levent in a series of wars known as **The Crusades**. To the Christian forces, the Crusades were an attempt to try to reclaim the **holy lands** of the former Roman Empire. For the Muslims, the wars meant protecting and consolidating their new territory, thereby firmly establishing Islam as one of the major faiths in the ancient world.

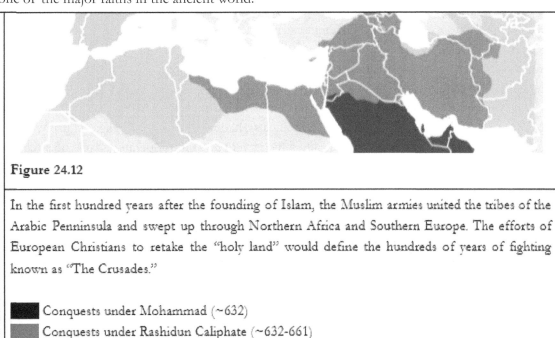

Figure 24.12

In the first hundred years after the founding of Islam, the Muslim armies united the tribes of the Arabic Penninsula and swept up through Northern Africa and Southern Europe. The efforts of European Christians to retake the "holy land" would define the hundreds of years of fighting known as "The Crusades."

▮ Conquests under Mohammad (~632)
▮ Conquests under Rashidun Caliphate (~632-661)
▯ Conquests under Umyyad Caliphate (661-750)

(Fig 24.13) **The Rashidun Caliphate** (632-661) consolidated the gains of Mohammad and took control of much of Persia and northern Africa.	(Fig 24.14) During the **Umayyad Caliphate** (661-750), Islamic conquest reached its high point, conquering Spain and parts of southern France.

Europeans, therefore, understood that there was a difference between Christianity and Islam. They also understood that Chrsitiantiy itself was prone to disagreements and in-fighting. In 1054, in an event known as **the great schism**, the Eastern Catholic Church (thereafter known as "Orthodox Church") broke away from the Western Catholic Church. The two branches of Christianity recognized different leaders, used different calendars, held different rituals, and professed slightly different theological beliefs. Though the schism was not nearly as traumatic for Europe as the Protestant Reformation 500 years later, it showed the vulnerability of church institutions to fragmentation and change.

Given the obvious presence in the ancient world, therefore, of these religious differences, how do we maintain that ancient people, nonetheless, had no concept of "religion" itself? Simply because there was no domain of ancient life which could be said to operate outside of a religious frame of reference. If you had asked a soldier in the Crusades what he was fighting for, he might have said "for God" or "for our church" or "for how God should be worshipped." Yet he would not have put "God, church, and worship" into a category separate from "ordinary public life." In order for that to happen, Europe would have to develop **secularism**, or the separation of the state (and other public institutions) from the sphere of religion.

Key Questions: What you need to know

- Why would ancient peoples not have understood what was meant by "religion?"
- What were early Christians and Muslims fighting about?

Key Vocabulary

Caliphates: The early Muslim states that expanded the influence of Islam and conquered much of the Middle East, Northern Africa and Europe. The Rashidun Caliphate (632-661) was followed by the Umyyad Caliphate (662-750)

Great Schism: The division of the Christian Church, in 1054, into the western Catholic and eastern Orthodox branches.

Secularism: the separation of the state and other public institutions from religion.

Religious War and the seeds of secularism

It is difficult to say when the principle of secularism began in western culture. There were probably always activities and practices that people regarded as having nothing *explicitly* to do with religion. One key moment in the European intellectual tradition, however, occurs, perhaps ironically, in the work of Martin Luther. In the early 16th century, Luther, and his early Protestant followers, had a problem. They were, at least in the beginning, a minority in heavily Catholic territories. How was it possible to get along in Europe when, from the Protestant perspective, the dominant institutions were wrong about God? Luther's solution was what he called the **doctrine of the two kingdoms**. Luther realized that for much of early church history, Christians had lived side-by-side (often harmoniously) with many non-Christians. The reason they were able to do so, Luther reasoned, was that there were many domains of life in which precise religious dogma played little role: buying and selling goods, honoring contracts, caring for children, and enforcing basic laws. All of these things, according to Luther, rested on moral universals and could be done without the need of the Bible or religious revelation. He referred to this non-religious realm of life as the **"secular kingdom"** and argued that it comprised the public things that made up "civil society." Religious life, Luther argued, made up the **spiritual kingdom**. The spiritual kingdom was more important than the secular kingdom in that it concerned "eternal truth" and "salvation" rather than mere temporary affairs. Yet, though it was greater, it was also, by its very nature, private. It concerned the relationship of an individual believer to God and, as such, could not be imposed by outside authorities.

Despite Luther's (theoretical) understanding of the difference between the secular and the sacred, European states in the 16th century and much of the 17th showed very little tolerance for different beliefs. We learned in chapter 4 about the **Wars of Religion** and how the years that followed the Protestant Reformation were marked by widespread violence perpetrated by Protestants and Catholics alike. From 1525 until 1648, one war followed another with Catholic and Protestant rulers fighting for control of Europe. In chapter 5, we learned that the **enlightenment** transformed institutions, making religion less central to life, particularly among the elite. During this time, to many scientists and philosophers of the enlightenment, "reason" and "experiment" seemed to do a better job of explaining certain aspects of the world than religious revelation did. If you were wondering about the weather, you could pray to God and ask for rain, or you could study the clouds, measure the air-pressure using a barometer, take note of the speed and direction of the winds and figure it out for yourself. The Bible didn't say anything about how to sail to the far-off lands of India or the Americas; but ship-builders, through observation and calculation, could construct enormous galleons and navigate across the globe using increasingly accurate compasses and maps. Priests and pastors might be able to pray for and comfort the sick, but university-trained doctors, with increasingly accurate knowledge of anatomy and pathology, could diagnose illnesses and prescribe treatment without any reference to the supernatural. To put it simply, science and reason seemed to make religion unnecessary: at least when it came to explaining the basic operations of the laws of nature. The world became, to borrow Max Weber's term, "**disenchanted**," imagined, by many people, in terms of material forces and impersonal laws rather than supernatural presences and divine wishes. As the French scientist Pierre-Simon Laplace put it, when questioned by Napoleon about the place of God in his model of the solar system: "I no longer have need of that hypothesis."

This is not to say, of course, that religion suddenly became obsolete in Europe. Many of the scientists that were instrumental in bringing about the enlightenment (such as Isaac Newton) were religious themselves. The majority of people in European countries continued to attend church, say prayers, read the Bible and observe religious holidays. After all, while science did an excellent job of explaining the physical and material properties of the world, it had far less to say about the more profound dimensions of human existence: life, death, love, hatred, ultimate values. All of those "mysterious" aspects of our humanity, matters of heart more than head, do not seem to reduce easily to scientific rules. They continued to draw post-enlightenment Europeans to religion as it continues to draw many to religion today. The enlightenment did not eliminate those important spiritual questions. What it *did* do, however, was to establish a separate domain of thought (and a large domain) in which traditional religious practices and traditional religious answers did not apply and were no longer seen as valid. That secular domain increased the number of institutions (and correspondingly the number of social activities) which could operate outside of religion. It created a kind of religion-free space in European culture, and many individuals, understandably enough, decided (as many continue to decide today) that that space was all the space that was needed.

Key Questions: What you need to know

- How did the enlightenment lead to "disenchantment" in European culture?
- What institutions changed during the enlightenment?

Farther Separation of Church and State: The Atlantic Revolutions

Toward the end of the 18th century, the fact that the vast majority of Europeans were Christian (whether Catholic or Protestant) does not mean that all Euorpeans were fond of their religious leaders and institutions. The tradition of the enlightenment, moreover, made it possible to do many things without religion. In many places in Europe, there was strong political opposition to church authorities, and perhaps nowhere was anti-religious sentiment as strong as in France. In the mid-18th century, the Catholic Church was the largest landowner in the country, with rights to over a tenth of all French land. The church imposed a ten percent tax (a tithe) on all French citizens, no matter their income level. Finally, the church closely cooperated with the royal family in order to oppress Protestants and other dissenters. To many in France, the Catholic Church had far too much power and used its power for selfish ends. During the **French Revolution** (Chapter 8), therefore, many decided the time had come to take power away from the church. Church lands were confiscated, monasteries were dissolved, and priests were required to swear an oath of allegiance to the new constitution. Some of the more radical revolutionaries took these reforms even farther, abolishing the Gregorian calendar (the calendar most of use today) and replacing it with a new more "rational" calendar. The so-called **French Republican Calendar** eliminated the religious symbolism which had been associated with the months of the year and replaced it with "democratic" and "scientific" language. Other revolutionaries argued for replacing the Christian religion altogether with the more "enlightened" religion of **deism** (which posited an impersonal God that did not interfere with human affairs) and replacing the Catholic Church with the so-called **Cult of the Supreme Being**. Though these reforms didn't catch on, they demonstrated the anti-religious fervor of many of the revolutionaries. In the years after the revolution, the French government was thoroughly **secularized**, and greater distance was placed between church and state. As Napoleonic reforms spread through Europe, other European governments became less religious as well.

(Fig 24.16) Some French Revolutionaries attempted to replace the Catholic Church with the "Cult of the Supreme Being."	**(Fig 24.17)** Drawing celebrating the establishment of the more secular "French Republican Calendar," which was purged of Catholic symbolism.

Meanwhile, across the Atlantic Ocean, the Americans were also wrestling with questions of religion and power. Though the American revolutionaries were not quite as bitterly anti-religious as the French were (partly due to the fact that the Anglican churches and Protestant churches in England and the United States were not perceived to be quite as oppressive), they were concerned about the place of religion in their new country. In the 18th century, **The Wars of Religion** still loomed in American consciousness, and many of the American founders came from families who had been driven to the New World by religious persecution. Furthermore, America had, compared to other western countries, a great deal of religious diversity. There were Catholic, Puritans, Quakers, Anglicans, Jews, and Deists. Prior to the Revolutionary War (and for some time after) the local governments of many of the colonies had enacted laws favoring the dominant religion: laws requiring taxes be paid to support the local church or requiring church attendance on Sunday. American leaders were afraid of what would happen if these policies were to be established in the national government. They had learned from European history and feared that their new democracy would be dominated by contentious religious competition in which one religion would pit itself against another religion in order to seize power and oppress its rivals. Therefore, the American founders, in the very first amendment to the U.S. constitution required the government to be neutral in religious matters. The first amendment states: "The government shall make no law respecting an establishment of religion or restricting the free exercise thereof." In other words, the government is not allowed either to favor one religion over another (to create an "established" or "official" church). Nor is it allowed to restrict people from practicing the religion of their choice. This policy keeping government out of religion is commonly referred to as **the separation of church and state**. Thomas Jefferson used the metaphor of "a wall of seperation" to define the idea that the affiars of government ought to be confined to secular matters. Though what counts as "secular" has been the focus of much debate, particularly in the American courts, by and large the American government has succeeded in maintaining a policy of religious neutrality.

(Fig 24.18) Engraving of the **first amendment** outside of Washington, D.C.

(Fig 24.19) 19th century cartoon showing American religious leaders attempting to break down the wall separating church and state. The sign reads "non-sectarian institution."

Church and State: Four Models

Both France and the United States effectively **secularized** in the early 19th century, putting a "wall of separation" between church and state. However, as both countries developed, into the 19th and 20th centuries, their versions of secularism proved to be very different. In France, due to the anti-religious sentiments that developed during the revolution, secularism became much stricter than in the United States. The French tradition known as **laïcité** effectively continues to discourage conspicuous expressions of religion in public. Politicians rarely (if ever) invoke religion. Schools, government buildings, and public hospitals are typically "religion-free." In 2004, France passed a law banning people from wearing religious symbols (such as Muslim head-scarves, large crosses, or stars of David) in schools and other public places. Though opponents of such rigorous laïcité argue that the laws are unduly oppressive and unfairly target France's Muslim minority, proponents say that religion belongs in private and that it is only by collectively acknowledging a "neutral" public space that France's religiously diverse population can ensure that individuals who disagree can live in harmony with each other.

In America, by contrast, secularism is much looser. American culture is often permissive of public expression of religion, provided it does not prevent others from expressing their own (contrary) views or exclude those with different beliefs from participation in society. It is not unusual, for example, to hear politicians and government officials speak openly about their faith. Until the mid 20th century, many public schools broadcast daily Bible-readings (though students were allowed to leave the classroom for them). Many public events, including those sponsored by the government, are preceded by "non-denominational" prayers. Finally, American money features the words "In God We Trust." Though, in recent years, many American secularists have protested the continued presence of religion in much of public life, the fact remains that the American model of secularism is much more inclusive of conspicuous religious practice.

(Fig 24.20) France bans "conspicuous religious symbols" in public places. Laïcité is a strict form of secularism.	**(Fig 24.21)** Pastor Rick Warren prays during Barack Obama's inauguration. American secularism tends to be more tolerant of open and public displays of religiosity.

The French and American models are two of the most common forms of secularism throughout the world, with most countries falling somewhere between the strictness of French laïcité and the openness of American expressivism. However, these two models are hardly the only ways that modern states engage with religion. Operating at the two extremes of state-enforced religion, on the one hand, and state-enforced atheism, on the other, are the Muslim countries of the Arabic Penninsula and the Communist (or quasi-communist) countries of the far east.

Though many Muslim countries (such as Turkey and Tunisia) have adopted western-style secularism, the Gulf Countries, such as Saudi Arabia, Iran, Oman, and Yemen are radically different. Religion is heavily promoted by the government. The state broadcasts daily "calls to prayer," forbids conversion to other religions, and governs according to the official Muslim law known as "**Sharia**. In many respects religion and government are as thoroughly integrated as they once were in Europe before the Reformation. Why the Middle East has not secularized to the degree the west has is, to some degree, a historical mystery. Some have argued that the Islamic countries along the Gulf have remained ethnically and culturally homogenous. Though there are divisions within Islam (such as between Sunni and Shia Muslims), for the most part Muslim communities have featured a much greater degree of uniformity than Christian ones. This lack of internal contention may have made it unnecessary for Muslim states to adopt secularism as a strategy for accommodating different points of view. Others have argued that Middle Eastern states have deliberately avoided secularism in an effort to avoid what many regard as the superficial and morally-empty culture of the west. What the west gains in religious tolerance, critics of secularism argue, it loses in social unity and cultural depth. In much of the Muslim world, therefore, there is a certain degree of skepticism about the value of the western model.

At the other end of the spectrum are the official "communist" countries of the world. Communism (as we learned in chapter 16) is highly suspicious of religion, regarding it as a source of social division and superstition. China (though home to many religious believers) uses the state to discourage religion and promote "Marxist atheism." All religious groups in China must register with the government, and the government has, from time to time, put policies in place aimed at making worship more difficult (such as confiscating church property, censoring sermons, or banning minors from attending services). Though the degree to which China "represses" religion is a matter of debate, it seems clear that the Chinese government, like many other communist governments, is suspicious of the free exercise of religion. Its discomfort is particularly acute when it comes to religious practices which it regards as "anti-state" or "separatist" in nature. In recent years, many reports have circulated in the west of Chinese crackdowns on Islam in Xinjiang and on Budhism in Tibet—crackdowns which seem to have as more to do with politically recalcitrant minority groups than with the content of the religious teachings themselves.

Key Question: What you need to know

What are four different approaches to the relationship between church and state?

(Fig 24.22) A "house church" in Beijing. Religious gatherings which are not registered with the government are technically illegal. The Chinese government has sometimes tolerated them and sometimes broken them up.	**(Fig 24.23)** King Abdulaziz Gate outside the Grand Mosque in Saudi Arabia. In Saudi Arabia, as in all of the Gulf countries, Islam is fully endorsed and encouraged by the government, and there is minimal "state secularism."

Kingdom Come: The future of Religion in Global Politics

The future of religion in global politics is, of course, anyone's guess. Some argue that, as society becomes more developed and people become more educated and wealthier, secularism will become more pervasive. Religion will gradually become less relevant as the social, psychological, and political functions which religion has provided become taken over by more "efficient" institutions. There are many who argue that such an outcome will be a good thing: pointing to the wars and social divisions religion has caused. Others, however, find such a prediction unconvincing. Though religious participation has been declining (though modestly) in western countries, it has been strong as ever in the global south. China, despite its official atheism, has seen sharp religious growth in recent years and will soon have, if trends continue, more Christians than the United States. Many argue that religion may see a revival rather than a decline in coming years. Though capitalism and the neoliberal model (chapter 22) have provided great wealth, they have also brought inequality, competition, and a sense of cultural despair. Many people, in the richest countries in the world, find that they work long hours, make lots of money, and yet, despite their advancement, see little fulfillment in their work. The loss of a sense of community and the absence of a feeling of higher purpose represents, many have argued, the downside of secular materialism. It is quite possible that many in the west will return to religion as a way to free themselves from a capitalist value system that many find empty.

We began this chapter pointing out the awkwardness and difficulty of talking about religion in public. Our explanation of the historical reasons behind such reluctance may be convincing or they may not be. But one thing is clear. Despite the silence there remains much to talk about.

Summing up: Key Chapter Points

1. Despite the absence of religion from much of western public life, religion remains an important part of politics all around the globe.
2. Religion is notoriously difficult to define. Rather than saying "what it is" we should probably content ourselves with describing "what it involves."
3. For much of western history "the church" was the dominant institution. Europeans would not have understood the idea of "religion" as separate from other domains of life.
4. The earliest seeds of secularism were planted following the Protestant reformation. After years of war, it became necessary for religiously diverse Protestants to learn how to co-exist.
5. The Enlightenment brought increasing secularism to Europe. The rise of science made certain religious explanations less plausible. Though Europeans stayed devoutly religious certain domains of life, for the first time, became "religion-free" spaces.
6. The power of the Catholic Church in France led to strong anti-religious backlash. After the French Revolution, the revolutionaries attempted to take power away from the church.
7. Due to their history of anti-clericalism, the French model of secularism is quite strict. Conspicuous religious expression is generally not welcome in public.
8. The United States also created a wall between church and state. The American model of secularism, however, is significantly more tolerant of open religiosity than the French model.
9. Communist governments and Islamic Republics of the Arabic Gulf have different models of church and state with the former actively discouraging religious activity and the latter strongly promoting it.
10. Some argue that, as the world continues to develop, religion will become less relevant. Others argue that people will turn to religion as an "alternative" to empty capitalist values

CHAPTER 25: LAW

Overview

This chapter defines and discusses the concept of law, emphasizing

- The ancient history of law
- That all law concerns, in one way or another, retributive justice, distributive justice, procedures, and hierarchies
- **Fuller's canon** (what makes a law a law)
- The difference between positivist law and natural law

The chapter concludes with the ways international and domestic law differ and the difficulty of enforcing and legitimizing law among separate nations.

4000 years ago, if you walked through the city of Babylon, you would have seen several huge slabs of limestone covered with intricate writing. If you'd stopped to read them, you would have seen, (after numerous lines praising the gods and the king) almost 300 laws, like these:

- If any one brings an accusation against a man, and the accused goes to the river and leaps into the river and sinks... his accuser shall take possession of his house. But if he escapes unhurt, the accuser will be put to death...
- If any one finds a runaway slave in the open country and brings them to their master, the master will pay him two shekels of silver....
- If any one owes a debt for a loan, and a storm destroys the grain, or the harvest fails...he does not need to give his creditor any grain. He washes his debt-tablet in water and pays no rent for the year.

These laws, from the so-called **Code of Hammurabi** are among the earliest laws that we have records of. Many would strike us as bizarre today. Jumping into a river may seem a rather ineffective (and dangerous!) way of establishing one's innocence (though trial by ordeal existed in most of the world well into the 15th century). Returning slaves to their masters for a bit of silver might also trouble us (though institutionalized slavery existed for even longer). Nonetheless, though the specifics of the laws reflect their ancient setting, the concepts ought to seem familiar. The Code of Hammurabi dealt with the same general categories of things that our laws tend to deal with today:

1) **retributive justice** punishments for crimes, procedures for judging criminals, and means of compensating victims

2) **distributive justice**: the rights of property, rules of debts and repayment, and procedures for trading and exchange.

3) **Procedural or ceremonial justice**: the steps to follow during legal or political processes, the ceremonial duties of rulers and citizens.

4) **Hierarchy and privilege**: social ranks, duties of rulers and ruled, the extent of rights.

On this last point, it could be argued that ancient codes such as the Code of Hammurabi contain more references to social hierarchy than our laws do (e.g., the reference to slaves), but, in fact, many of our own laws make many references to status and privilege. Language, for example, outlining the duties of political leaders or judges, are a modern way of expressing "who ranks where" and of allocating rights accordingly.

The Code of Hammurabi is only one example of an ancient system of laws. Every ancient society that we know of had something similar. During the period of the Roman Empire, there were the twelve tablets, a list of rules posted prominently around the cities. During Biblical times, there was the Mosaic Law, kept in the Jewish temple and read at public occasions. Ancient China had the Tang Code, and the Umayyad Caliphate employed Sharia, or Islamic Law, which is still in widespread use today. Though these systems of law varied according to their cultural contexts, they all focused, in general, on these four categories: retributive justice, distributive justice, procedural justice, and hierarchy. Furthermore, insofar as all of them, one way or another, concern processes of social organization (see chapter one), all of them are indisputably "political" documents.

Fuller's Canon

These are not the only ways that these ancient laws were similar to ours. In 1964, the legal philosopher Lon Fuller, formulated a list of eight "canon" or rules that virtually all laws, throughout history, have had in common. According to Fuller laws are:

- **General**: applying in multiple situations.
- **Public**: available for most people to see and are not kept secret.
- **Clear**: easy to interpret as possible.
- **Consistent**: not contradicting each other
- **Feasible**: possible to follow.
- **Constant**: not prone to sudden change
- **Prospective**: not declaring things illegal long after they've happened
- **Congruent**: enforced as they're written.

Ancient Laws

(Fig 25.1) Part of the Code of Hammurabi, (1750 BCE) one of the oldest list of laws known.

(Fig 25.2) The twelve tables (~450 BCE) were engraved on stone and erected around Ancient Rome.

Fig 25.3 An Islamic legal text from the Umayyad Caliphate. Sharia is still in use today. throughout the countries of the Arabic Penninsula.

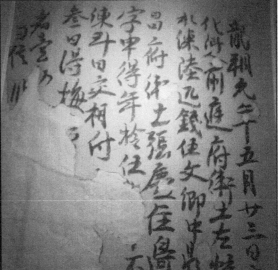

(Fig25.4) A Tang Chinese legal document (~700 CE) establishing the selling price of a slave.

Where do laws come from? Positivist vs Natural Law Traditions

What made the laws in the Hammurabi Code or any of the other legal documents laws in the first place? What about our own laws? Though the question at first may seem simple-minded, there are two complicated intellectual traditions built around this question. One intuitive answer is that laws reflect the authority of law-makers: whether those law-makers are gods, kings, or elected assemblies. For example, during the middle ages in Europe, when kings claimed to rule by divine right (chapter 2), law was understood as a simple outline of hierarchy. God made the law for the world. The king, appointed by God, made the law for the people. The law was a command from an empowered ruler, a "sovereign" to the people whose duty it was to obey it. As society liberalized in the 18th and 19th centuries, civilization moved away from the concept of a divinely appointed king and towards the concept of a "popularly-appointed" government. The source of laws, therefore, changed. Law-makers, in the age of popular sovereignty, have been those who rule with the consent of the people. The law is no longer the command of a god but the command of the majority.

This way of looking at law represents the so-called **positivist** tradition in legal thought. According to positivism, laws are simply the orders (what is "posited") from people authorized to give orders. They may be good, or they may be bad. But the quality of the law is irrelevant. What matters is what the sovereign posits. Although positivism explains, convincingly, how laws become laws, it leads to a question: why do we have the laws we do? Granted laws are commands, but why command one thing instead of another? Why forbid stealing instead of encouraging it? Is it simply the whim of the law-maker? The "accident" of culture?

The most obvious answer is that laws are made, in general, to discourage bad behavior and encourage good behavior. They are a reflection of basic morality. Morality (depending on your point of view) may come from God or from social custom or from careful deliberation. Whatever the source of morality is, however, the fact is that we all have a basic sense of what's right and wrong, a series of intuitions about the way people ought to behave. Laws are made to reflect these common moral intuitions. This connection between law and morality embodies the tradition of **natural law**. According to natural law, a law is legitimate if and when it aligns with the moral order. A law isn't a law because it is a command but because it's right.

The difference between the traditions of positivist law and natural law can be seen in a famous legal debate from the 1950's. The debate concerned a case in Nazi Germany, where a young woman, plotting to kill her husband, decided to report him to the Nazi authorities for criticizing Hitler. At the time, any criticism of the Nazi government was illegal and entailed severe penalties, including tortutre and death. The man was arrested and imprisoned. After the allies liberated Germany, the man was freed and, once he was out of jail, he promptly reported his wife to the police. The question is this: should his wife be arrested? According to positivist thinking, his wife may have done something profoundly immoral but she did not do anything illegal. Law is simply the command of an authority: whether right or wrong. The wife acted within the bounds set by the government at the time. It is not possible to punish her because to do so would be imposing

320

law "after the fact" (which violates the principle that law must be "prospective"). According to the natural law tradition, however, the wife ought to be arrested and prosecuted. According to natural law, what makes a law binding is its moral dimension. The moral judgement of any rational person, it would seem, would say that turning your husband into the fascist authorities for criticizing a dictator is evil. The law that forbade criticism of the Nazi government, therefore, violated natural morality and was illegitimate.

This debate, the so-called **Hart-Fuller debate** (named after Herbert Hart, and Lon Fuller, whom we discussed at the beginning of this chapter) has led to a great deal of legal criticism. Though most students who encounter the problem for the first time tend to side with the husband and argue that the wife should indeed be prosecuted, the case is more problematic than it seems. Questions like "what are our moral intuitions?" and "what makes moral intuitions a better guide than laws?" and "can our moral intuitions be trusted?" add to the complexity of the debate. Both positivists and natural law theorists have many advocates among philosophers of law today.

(Fig 25.5) **Hugo Grotius** (1538-1645) was a theorist of natural law. Though many natural law philosophers based their ideas on religion, Grotius believed that right and wrong could be discovered through human reason.

Figure 25.6 **John Austin** (1790-1859) was an important thinker in the tradition of positivism. Austin believed that law could be more or less defined as the command of an empowered "sovereign."

Key Questions: What you need to know

- What do laws have in common?
- What is a law according to positivism?
- What is a law according to the "natural law" tradition?
- How does the case of the wife in Nazi Germany illustrate the differences between the two traditions?

International Law

Thus far we have been imagining law inside of a state: so-called domestic law. What happens if we consider the state of affairs outside of a state: the realm of international or global law? To many, the idea of international law is highly problematic. Such critics point out the existence of global anarchy (chapter 8)—the lack of an effective "world police" to enforce laws. Law works inside of a state (the claim goes) because of a thick web of community. If I steal my neighbor's wallet, my neighbor knows where I live. He can tell the police, and the police will come to my door. They will likely tell my employer, and I'll probably lose my job. If I'm arrested, I'll be taken to the local courthouse, and I'll have a trial where I'll be judged by a jury made up largely of other members of my city. The deep and pervasive community bonds and the existence of widely accepted social hierarchies (police, judges, juries, lawyers) all help the law do its job. The law isn't anything I have to accept or agree to. I am embedded in the law simply by the fact that I am born into my community, participate in its institutions, internalize its norms, and make choices with reference to the many interlocking relationships that it sustains. The international domain isn't like this. While there are many global political actors, whose actions affect different states, these actors do not form a "natural" community. The international community is instead constructed, over time, through negotiations and interactions among representatives. These representatives, more often than not, do not live in the same country and do not have the same frame of reference. If one state breaks the international law (steals the "wallet" of another state), there is no "neighborhood" police that can come to the door of the thief (barring an act of war). Perhaps there could be a "trial," but, in that case, who would get to be the judge? Are all states fundamentally equal or is there a hierarchy? If states are equal, then how can one judge another? If there is a hierarchy, then doesn't it seem like international law is simply a system in which the wealthy and powerful countries impose their wills on everyone else? Finally, if law could solve disputes between states, then why hasn't global peace been achieved yet? History shows us one broken agreement after another: with states constantly violating one another's rights for the sake of power. The philosophy of realism (chapter 14) points to these facts and argues that international law, more often than not, is futile.

Proponents of international law generally admit that international law is different from domestic law and much more difficult to enforce. But this does not mean it is impossible. Liberals (chapter 15) argue that the solution to the problem of inter-state anarchy is institutions: the creation of agreements, rules, and norms to create trust and encourage regular patterns of behavior among states. Unlike in domestic law, however, these institutions, for the most part, do not already exist through thousands of years of history and socialization. Institutions have to be actively established and actively maintained through continuous diplomacy. In order for such institutions to work, in general, four conditions must be met:

• First, in order for institutions to be legitimate, they must be **consensual**. Each state which participates in the institution must actively and continuously agree to be bound by its rules. An obvious example of this is the European Union where member states continuously agree to be governed by common rules and can leave (e.g. Brexit) unilaterally.

• Second, effective international institutions cannot simply include one or two states. In order to work well, they must be broadly **multilateral**. As many states as possible must agree not only to the rules themselves but also to the procedures of negotiation. One reason, for example, why the United Nations has been (arguably) more effective than the League of Nations is because the U.N. has achieved a greater level of multilateralism. More states participate in the UN and recognize its authority.

• Third, international institutions must recognize what international law can do and what it can't do. It makes no sense, for example, for an international law to set the speed limit on highways inside of particular countries. International law must, in generally, confine itself to those **global domains** which multiple states have in common: laws of international commerce, for example, or rights of waterways, or rules for the legitimate use of force.

• Fourth international institutions must recognize that not everything in global politics is a state. While, traditionally, international institutions have considered states as the appropriate subject of laws, more recently there has come to be a recognition that **non-state actors** such as corporations, international organizations, and individual human beings often have as much of an effect (if not more an effect) on global affairs as people do.

Liberals argue that, if these conditions are met, there is no reason why institutions cannot be strengthened over time in order to create and enforce legitimate laws for the global community. This idea, of course, is by no means new. In the concluding table, you can see examples of key treaties intending to create legally binding institutions and agreements among multiple states.

Key Questions: What you need to know

- What is the difference between domestic and international law?
- What are some of the dinstinct problems of international law?
- What are international institutions supposed to do?
- What conditions must be met for international institutions to function effectively?
- What are some examples of efforts to create international legal agreements?
- What problems often arise in international agreements?

Agreement	*Stipulations*	*Problems*
Peace of Westphalia, 1648	• Principle of territorial sovereignty. • Recognition of independence of certain territories and rights of monarchs.	• Not quite multilateral enough. • Europe was at war again within a decade. • Many rulers refused to abide by terms.
Treaties of Utrecht, 1713	• Ended Wars of Spanish Succession. • Increased territorial sovereignty by establishing rights and borders.	• Did little to stabilize relationships between kingdoms. • Legal borders are only effective if states peacefully respect them.
Treaty of Versailles, 1911	• Ended World War I • First effort at "Liberal International Order." • Established rules and procedural norms.	• Lack of legitimacy. • The United States refused to join. •Japan and Italy simply withdrew.
Charter of United Nations, 1945	• Second effort at Liberal International Order. • Improved LON institutions. • Broad multilateralism.	• Too many states (most notably the United States) simply act unilaterally. • Weak enforcement, particularly in the realm of human rights.
Rome Statute, 2002	• Established the International Criminal Court (ICC). • Made an effort to hold "individuals" not just states accountable for war crimes.	• Lack of legitimacy. • The United States, among other countries, refuses to recognize the ICC's authority.

Summing up: Key Chapter Points

1) Like religion, law is a cultural universal and has existed for as long as people have had writing.
2) Though laws in different cultures and at different periods of time have differed widely in details, they are all similar in concerning retributive justice, distributive justice, procedural justice, and hierarchy.
3) Lon Fuller's "canon" provide eight characteristics all laws have in common. Laws,

according to Fuller, must be "general, public, clear, consistent, feasible, constant, prospective, and congruent."

4) The source and legitimacy of laws can be understood according to the "positivist tradition" (in which laws are simply what the ruler "posits") or the "natural law tradition (in which laws reflect moral truths.

5) The domain of international law creates a number of factors which make it distinct from (and in many cases more problematic than) domestic law. In particular, legitimacy is not a natural consequence of the community in international law and must be actively constructed through multilateralism, diplomacy, and institutions.

CHAPTER 26: GLOBAL SOCIAL JUSTICE

This chapter defines and explores the concept of global social justice. We focus on

- The definition of justice
- The difference in approaches between John Rawls and Robert Nozick on the question of political justice
- The differences between a "hands on" and a "hands off" approach in addressing social justice problems
- The application of these ideas to problems of poverty, environmental justice, and violence

In 400 B.C., the philosopher Socrates was outside of an Athenian court waiting for his trial to begin. On the steps, he met a young man, **Euthyphro**, who was about to prosecute his own father for a serious crime. Believing that the young man must be an expert in law to be taking such a bold course of action, Socrates asked him a question which has echoed down the ages. "Euthyphro," he asked, "What is justice?"

"Easy," said the young man. "Justice is doing what the gods command! It means obeying their laws!" Socrates was quiet a moment and then responded, "But why do the gods command what they command? Do they command it because it's just? Or do they command it for no reason?" The young man didn't know what to say. If he had said, "because it's just," then he wouldn't have answered Socrates's original question. What, after all, makes it just enough for the gods to command it? But if Euthyphro had said, "For no reason!" then he would have reduced justice to the arbitrary whim of the law-makers. There would be no intrinsic reason why one action would be just and another unjust.

The so-called **Euthyphro problem** has been a famous puzzle in philosophy, and remains, in many respects, a mystery down to this very day. What is justice? Why do "the gods" (or "the government" or "society") command what they do? In this final chapter, we'll look at some contemporary approaches to this problem and discuss their implications for global politics.

Figure 25.1 In the Euthyphro dialog, Socrates explores how difficult it is to define justice. If we say that justice means "following some rule" (whether a social norm or a command of the gods) then we seem to have a hard time of saying why the rule is a rule in the first place.

Rawls vs Nozick

More than 2000 years after Socrates, the political philosopher John Rawls had his own idea about justice, or political justice at least. In his book *Justice as Fairness* (1971) he proposes a thought experiment. Imagine, he says, you had the responsibility of creating a new society. You would be a member of the society but (here's the catch) you wouldn't know what social position you'd occupy. Maybe you'd be the king or a doctor or a lawyer or a professor. Maybe, on the other hand, you'd work in a factory or drive a forklift or pave roads. Maybe, you'd even be a beggar on the streets. The point is you don't know who you'd be. The question is this: how would you order this society? What sort of a community would you like to live in if you didn't know what community member you would be? Or, to put the question in even simpler terms, how would you cut a pie not knowing what piece you'd to get?

Rawls thought the answer was obvious. If you're cutting a pie, you'd want to make sure you got a big piece even if you happened to get the smallest. If you're organizing a society, you'd want to make sure that you could have a successful life even if you found yourself, relatively speaking, on the bottom. For Rawls, in other words, justice meant maximizing the minimum (or "**maximin**" as he called it). A just social arrangement is one, he argued, in which social benefits are distributed most favorably to the poorest of the poor.

Rawlsian Justice: Rawls asks us to imagine a so-called original position in which we, under the "veil of ignorance" do not know what position in an imaginary social hierarchy we would occupy. How, he asks, would we want society to be organized in such a case? Obviously, we would want to make sure that we'd have a fair enough life even if we happened to be at the very bottom of society.

Does this mean complete communistic equality? Not necessarily. Consider, for example, a community that wants to build a factory in order to create jobs. If the factory is built, the factory owner will be a lot richer than everyone else. However, the poorest members of the community will be better off too. If the factory is not built, everyone will be more "equal" but the poor will be poorer. Under Rawls's framework, the factory should be built—even at the cost of economic inequality—since a factory will raise the floor for the lowest members of society.

Justice as Fairness quickly became one of the foundational texts for twentieth and twenty-first century **social democracy**. As a part of the left wing of Western politics, social democrats advocate for a large state, the exercise of public power, and a robust welfare system. It's the business of the government, they argue, to make sure that everyone's life—especially the lives of the poor—go fairly well. To accomplish this, the state should make sure everyone has enough to eat, medical care, well-paying jobs and a good education and shouldn't hesitate to aggressively tax large businesseses or wealthy individuals if it can be established that such taxes would benefit the poorest members of society. In many respects, the modern welfare state, such as exists in Western Europe and (to a lesser degree) the United States, has been fashioned on Rawlsian principles.

Key Questions: What you need to know

- How does Rawls define justice?
- What is the relationship between Rawls's idea and the "welfare state" model of Western Europe?

As noble as such a vision sounds, Rawls's idea has had its detractors. In 1974, **Robert Nozick** provided a famous counter-argument against Rawls's paradigm for justice. Like Rawls, Nozick begins with a thought experiment. Imagine, he says, a society where everything is distributed exactly the way you would prefer. Maybe this means a communist utopia. Maybe it's a generous European welfare state. In any case, social benefits are spread around your society completely (in your opinion) fairly. Nozick then asks a simple question: "then what?" Suppose a great basketball player (Nozick gave the example of Wilt Chamberlain, though we would probably say Lebron James today) came along. He's so good that all of the citizens in your ideal society agree to give 25 cents per game to watch his team. Before long, Wilt Chamberlain has a lot more money than anybody else. The distribution isn't what it was before. Repeat the experiment with a great musician, a great entrepreneur, a great engineer. You would see, Nozick says, within a very short period of time, a rapid increase in "social inequality." But would this be unjust? How could it be? Everything was distributed ideally to start out with. All people did was to make voluntary decisions about how to spend their personal resources.

Nozick's point isn't that all inequality in a society is due to either voluntary decisions or talent. He recognized that, in any community, bad luck, systemic failures, and what is often called "the lottery of birth" play a rather large role in the question of who gets what. His point was simply that Rawlsian ideas of justice have a blind spot. They assume that when "things are divided fairly," society just stops. But in any society, people make decisions all the time, and those decisions, invariably, affect the broader distribution of benefits and burdens. The question of justice, Nozick says, isn't who winds up getting what but who decides what and how they decide. If inequality (or even poverty) is a result of people making voluntary choices, then it becomes difficult to say that there's anything necessarily unjust about it. Nozick's vision of justice, then, (which is often described as **libertarian**) is one that emphasizes not outcome but **procedure**. Free choice, consent, and minimal interference with individual decision-making are at the heart of Nozick's conception of a just social arrangement.

In *Anarchy, State, and Utopia,* Robert Nozick makes the point that justice isn't necessarily about who gets what but about how the decisions are made. For Rawls, social transactions must be voluntary to be just. Rawls is often taken to be the intellectual founder of modern economic libertarianism.

Rawls and Nozick, then, line up on opposite sides of the spectrum on the question of justice. In general, those who favor Rawls's vision advocate for a much stronger **hands on** approach with the government intervening in social affairs in order to attempt to actively engineer a more just society. Those who favor Nozick advocate for a more **hands off** approach where the state doesn't get involved in voluntary transactions. To put this another way, Rawls's supporters are proponents of an aggressive response to questions of social justice, while Nozick's tend to favor a "wise passiveness." Now that we have defined the two ideological poles, let's look at how these ideas might illuminate some of the more common social justice problems of our time.

Key Questions: What you need to know

- What is Nozick's critique of Rawls?
- How are Rawls's and Nozick's conceptions of justice different?

Poverty and Development

One of the most obvious social justice problems is global poverty. Though poverty has declined significantly over the past several decades, it remains a major problem in many countries of the world. Roughly ten percent of the world's population (close to 700 million people) are classified as living in extreme poverty, defined as living on less than $1.90 USD per day. Twenty percent of the world's population lack access to reliable health care, and a whopping 50% make ends meet on less than $5.50 USD per day. No one can deny that poverty contributes to a great deal of human suffering. The question is, of course, what can be done about it?

Hands on (Rawlsian) and hands off (Nozikian) political thinkers have completely different answers to this question. To hands in the on camp, the best solution is aggressive economic development. For some, this can mean **socialist** "planning" in which the state exercises public power to actively develop industries which the country lacks. To others, this development is best achieved through aid-based approaches in which food aid, medical care, or financing are actively given to the poorest communities—perhaps by NGO's, perhaps by UN relief agencies, or perhaps by the state itself. In any case, hands on thinkers believed that the end goal is a transformation of the economy, often by changing traditional agriculture or subsistence-based practices into "modern," industrial, "for profit" economies. They tend to measure progress in the traditional terms of GDP, average wage, access to resources, and labor force participation.

Hands off political thinkers are often skeptical of both these approaches and the data used to measure them. It is true, they say, that a great deal of the world's population survives on very little money. But should money be the only standard of development? Why should the American dollar be the yardstick the rest of the world is measured by? If a traditional, agrarian community is functional—able to meet their basic material, social, and cultural needs—is it necessarily in the best interest of that community to impose a capitalist system of individualism, careerism, and profit? A common example to illustrate this perspective might be the American Amish community. Though, by many standards, they are "poor" (at least compared to other Americans), lacking electricity, indoor plumbing, and most modern consumer goods, their communities provide social solidarity, spiritual connection, and, so it would seem, as good a chance for happiness as that found in the career and consumer oriented cities around them.

But even if economic development were the only solution, does it necessarily follow that the best way to achieve it is by aggressive intervention? Political scientists of the **neoliberal** school, for example, would argue that lower taxes, less state interference, and fewer regulations spurs economic growth and attracts investment. Others point out the unintentional damage that is done by well-meaning aid-programs. For example, a relief agency that provides free food to a hungry community may achieve a short-term reduction in overall hunger, but, in some cases the free food may have the effect of undercutting local farmers and putting merchants out of business. The resulting economic instability, the argument goes, destroys the benefit provided by the aid.

(Fig 25.2) Palettes of food delivered by UNICEF as humanitarian aid. UN relief has been important to many food insecure nations, yet there is debate as to whether such efforts do more harm than good.	(Fig 25.3) An uncontacted group of indigenous people in Brazil. Though "poor" by standards of monetization, their community is nonetheless functional and self-reliant.

Warfare and Violence

A more dramatic and often more devastating form of social injustice is the warfare and systematic violence that has plagued many societies for years. As we discussed earlier (in chapter 20) warfare has been endemic to the human race, and there are, in all likelihood, as many as 30 wars in progress at this very moment. As with poverty, hands on thinkers and hands off thinkers have widely divergent views on how to bring about peace.

For hands on thinkers, the solution is often twofold: **humanitarian intervention** to stop the violence and robust **institution-building** to keep the peace. There is simply no reason, they argue, why widespread killing should be allowed to continue in war-torn countries when the United Nations has more than enough resources to prevent it. These thinkers argue that the international community has a **responsibility to protect** (RtoP) the lives of innocent civilians from crimes against humanity. Such intervention, they say, does not necessarily need to be (and perhaps should not be!) led by the West. In many instances in the twentieth century, humanitarian interventions have been led by non-western states (such as India in east Pakistan, Vietnam in Cambodia). Cooperative intervention, the argument goes, is necessary to stop the violence in cases when military action is the only realistic means of protecting civilians. Once military operations have ended, furthermore, there must be continuous and active efforts to build the institutions necessary to preserve peace. Internationally supervised elections, guided state-building, foreign aid, and (perhaps) UN occupation may all be necessary to establish the political structures to prevent future violence. In short, states who violate international law by engaging in warfare that harms civilians, should be treated like criminals who violate any other law: they should be subject to restriction and reform.

Hands off thinkers argue that such interventions, however well-meaning, are likely to do more harm than good. In the first place, the UN charter does not authorize military force without the full consent of the security council. Given that the security council (for various complicated political reasons) rarely is able to fully agree to authorize uses of force, many inventions (such as the United States war in Iraq) have technically violated international law. Even if the security council does happen to authorize the use of force in an intervention, such authorization is hardly a guarantee that it would be successful. Historically, many interventions have been counter-productive, resulting in civilian deaths, refugee crises, and long-term political instability. A commonly cited example is the 2011 intervention in Libya. Following a security council authorization, NATO, led by the United States intervened in an effort to stop the **Libyan Civil War**. Though a temporary cease-fire was achieved, ultimately the NATO efforts led to disaster. Widespread sectarian killings and institutional collapse followed in the wake of the intervention with American President Barack Obama eventually calling it the "worst mistake" of his presidency. The point of the non-interventionists is simple: violence can't be "fixed" by escalating the violence. As ugly and painful as it may be, it's often in the best interest of all involved to let belligerent states "fight it out" and solve their own problems.

Intervention	Purpose	Impact
Operation Provide Comfort/ Desert Storm (Iraq, 1991)	Protect Kuwait from Iraqi aggression and prevent attacks on Kurdish refugees.	Mixed. Although the intervention succeeded in pushing Iraqi troops out of Kuwai, the lack of an effective long-term solution eventually culminated in the U.S. invasion of Iraq in 2003.
Unified Task Force (Somalia, 1992)	To deliver food and other humanitarian aid to civilians in Somalia affected by ongoing civil war.	Mixed. The operation succeeded in delivering aid to civilian populations, but violence and instability in Somalia continued for many years after the intervention, and the state is still considered extremely fragile.
Operation Uphold Democracy (Haiti, 1994)	To remove the military government that overthrew elected president Jean Bertrand d'Aristide and restore democratic institutions.	Mostly successful. The military government agreed to step down and Aristide was returned to power. Nonetheless, Arisitde was overthrown a second time in a 2004 coup d'etat.
UNAMIR (Rwanda, 1994)	To end the Rwandan Civil War and negotiate peace between the Hutu government and the Tutsi militias.	Failure. The UN troops lacked the firepower to effectively keep the peace. Negotiations collapsed and the Rwandan genocide unfolded, leading to the deaths of close to a millon civilians.
UNTAET (East Timor, 1999)	To end crimes against humanity and civilian displacement due to ongoing conflict between Indonesia and East Timor.	Largely successful. The UN administered East Timor for over a year. In 2001, East Timor had its first presidential election and has maintained sovereignty free on Indonesian occupation since then.
NATO bombing of Yugoslavia (1999)	To stop the ethnic cleansing of Albanians and deliver humanitarian aid to those affected by violence in Kosovo.	Mixed. NATO forces were victorious and brought peace to Kosovo, but the mission has been criticized for lacking UN security council authorization and leading to significant civilian casualties from use of aerial bombings.
British intervention in Sierra Leone War (2000)	End Sierra Leone Civil War and deliver humanitarian aid to displaced civilians.	Successful. Gradually, Sierra Leone has become to recover from the civilian and economic damage of the war.
Coalition intervention in Libya (2011	End the Libyan Civil War and protect endangered civilian groups.	Failure. Continual violence and political instability in the region. Libya is now widely regarded as a failed state

---

Questions for Discussion

• What is the difference between hands on and hands off thinkers when it comes to warfare and violence? Which position seems more reasonable to you?

•Research one example when the international community intervened to try to put an end to violence and one example where they chose not to do so? In your opinion did the international community make the right decision in these cases?

Environmental Justice and Climate Change

A final issue of justice which has received increased attention lately has to do with global efforts to limit pollution and stop climate change. With a few contrarian exceptions, there is now widespread scientific and political consensus that anthropogenic climate change has been occurring for some time and that continued climate change poses a threat to the flourishing of life on earth. There is also broad agreement that sustainable development—that is, economic growth which does not harm the environment or add to the carbon footprint—is necessary. The question, once again, is how such sustainable development is to be achieved.

Hands on political thinkers believe solutions must be pursued at both the state and the international level. At the state level, it is imperative for governments, particularly in the developed world, to actively intervene in their economies to ensure that regulations are both instituted and followed. Laws limiting emissions and mandating eco-friendly industrial processes are essential, the argument goes, for the first-world to lead by example. At the international level, meanwhile, consensus must be built to achieve effective global environmental governance. Developed and developing countries have a common need to protect the planet, though developed countries have both greater resources, and, in many respects, a greater responsibility for the damage has already been done. International agreements such as the **Kyoto Protocols** in 1999, the **World Summit on Sustainable Development** in 2002, and the **Paris Climate Agreement** in 2015, are all cited as important efforts made by the international community to actively limit damage to the environment.

Hands off theorists are, in general, skeptical of these points. Though laws limiting emissions and regulating industry sound like a good idea, they have tended to be highly ineffective. For example, the well known **Air Quality Act** of 1967 did succeed in reducing emissions in the United States, but it had virtually no effect on global emissions. High-emissions manufacturers, in many cases, simply moved their operations to countries with less stringent laws. Fifteen years after the

Air Quality Act, global carbon emissions were 15% higher than they were before. International agreements, the skeptics say, have likewise been ineffective. Since the Vienna Convention for the Protection of the Ozone Layer in 1987, there have been no fewer than twenty major global environmental conferences. Despite treaties and agreements among the world's largest countries, none of these international resolutions has been able to achieve anything more than a temporary drop in emissions. Many states (most notably the United States, following Donald Trump's withdrawal from the Paris Climate Accords in 2016) have simply refused to comply. Difficult as it may be to accept, the fact may be that "environmental responsibility" simply can't be legislated. At least not at the global level. Individual states, developed and developing, have no choice but to make their own decisions about their domestic industries and production practices. Though such a statement may sound like defeatism, anyone paying attention to the climate data over the past several decades has to acknowledge that there seems to be a great deal of truth in it.

Climate Conference	Global Tons of CO2
1985 Vienna convention for the Protection of the Ozone Layer	20,276,693,000
1988 Establishment of Intergovernmental Panel on Climate Change	21,195,418,000
1991 Madrid Protocol on Environmental Protection	22,591,041,000
1997 Kyoto Protocols	24,398,282,000
2009 Copenhagen Climate Conference	31,770,516,000
2015 Paris Climate Accords	35,631,078,000

Conclusion

As can be seen, both the hands on and the hands off have pros and cons. The hands on approach has the advantage of making a vigorous, centralized effort to fight injustice, yet it often risks creating long term instabilities, instituting ineffective policies, and creating bigger problems down the road. The hands off approach has the advantage of allowing for greater freedom and sovereignty yet it risks ignoring problems and allowing them to worsen and spread through casual passivity.

Does this mean there is no solution to the issues mentioned in this chapter? Should Euthyphro have answered "nothing" when Socrates asked him to define justice? Not at all. Remember, at the beginning of this book we defined politics as a "process." There is no "final state," no "utopia," no "once and for all" that will bring things to a consummation. If you've ever watched a dancer at a wedding, a juggler at a circus, or a surfer at the beach, you have a good idea of what it means for a process to be fluid and ever-changing. Likewise, in politics there are constant adjustments and counter-adjustments, corrections and re-corrections, visions and revisions, all making a perpetual way into, with any luck, a slightly better world.

Summing Up: Key Chapter Points

1) The question of "what is justice" has been an intractable philosophical issue since the time of Socrates.

2) In contemporary global politics, we can identify "hands on" approaches to justice, such as those articulated in the work of John Rawls, and "hands off" approaches such as those articulated in the work of Robert Nozick.

3) The "hands on" approach is characterized by active state intervention, robust institutions, and a concern for making life better for those at the bottom of the social hierarchy.

4) The "hands off" approach is characterized by not interfering with sovereignty and free choice, and decentralizing decision-making as much as possible.

5) Each approach emphasizes a different course of action in taking on global social justice issues such as poverty, climate change, global health, and violence.

6) Both approaches have advantages and disadvantages. Though no "ultimate" solution may be possible to these intractable problems, the political process is partly defined by the goal of making the world a better place.

GLOSSARY

30 Years War: (1618-1648) Major war during the European Wars of Religion. Possibly as many as one third of all people in the Holy Roman Empire were killed.

9/11: Terrorist attacks against the World Trade Center and Pentagon on September 11, 2001. Led to a major rethinking of American foreign policy.

Absolute Power: Power which is not dependent on any underlying source of authority, is not subject to challenge, and has the potential to pervade all aspects of society. Examples would be in an absolute monarchy or authoritarian state.

Act of supremacy: (1559) King Henry VIII's decision to break from the Roman Catholic Church, in so doing declaring the king to be the head of the Church of England. Represented a major shift in the norm of sovereignty and was one of the crucial events in the Protestant Reformation.

African National Congress: Led by Nelson Mandela, the ANC took power in the first free and fair election in South African history (1994), instituting majority rule. The election of Mandela was a major event in decolonization.

African slave trade: The inhumane importation of slaves from Western Africa to North and South America to be used as forced labor. The slave trade began in the 20th century and continued (despite a number of laws forbidding it) well into the 19th.

Age of Discovery: Term used to describe the voyages to the New World and far east by Portugal, Spain, and other European powers in the 15th and 16th centuries.

Age of Revolutions: Term used to describe the period between 1776 and 1848 in which almost all major countries in Europe and the Americas experienced political revolutions.

Agency: Term used to describe individual "decision making" embedded in a sense of "self-ownership." In social constructivist theory, agency is frequently opposed to "structures."

Agriculture: The invention of agriculture in ancient Sumer is typically thought of as the founding of international orders.

Albert of Prussia: (1490-1568) Prince of Prussia known for being the first ruler to convert to Protestantism.

Alienation: In Marxist theory, the sense of loss experienced by a worker as a result of having the products of his labor appropriated by the bourgeoisie.

American Revolution: (1776-1783) The North American colonies of Great Britain broke away from the crown, establishing a government based on the principle of popular sovereignty.

Amour de soi: Jean Jacques Rousseau's term for "the love of self." Along with "compassion," self-love, according to to Rousseau, was all that was needed for social harmony.

Amour propre: Jean Jacques Rousseau's

term for "the love of prestige." Created with the invention of property *amour propre*, for Rousseau, as at the root of many social evils.

Amsterdam stock exchange: Founded in 1602 in part due to the voyages of discovery, the Amsterdam stock exchange is one of the earliest examples of institutional changes in response to the rise of global capitalism.

Anarchy: In realist theory, anarchy is the idea that there is no "world police" or higher power that enforces right and wrong among political actors.

Anglo-German Arms Race: (1898-1912) Naval competition between Great Britain and Germany leading up to World War I.

Anglo-Maratha War: A series of 3 wars fought between 1775 and 1819 leading to the United Kingdom consolidating control over much of India.

Anticolonialism: A movement during the late 19th century criticizing imperial powers (notably Belgium) for cruelty and advocating for national self-determination.

Appeasement: Early European policy responding to Hitler's aggression in the mid 1930's. Now widely believed to have been too passive.

Arab Spring: (2010-2012). A series of protests and revolutions in multiple countries in the Arab world. While some were successful in instituting regime change and others were relatively minor and inconsequential, several led to the outbreak of civil war and violent reprisals by the government.

Archduke Franz Ferdinand: Heir to the throne of the kingdom of Austria-Hungary, his assassination in 1914 is one of the key causes of World War I.

Arms Race: A period of military competitions in which one or more states attempt to gain a competitive advantage over a rival.

ASEAN: Association of South Eastern Nations, founded 1967 to create economic cooperation and collective security.

Astell, Mary (1666-1731) British enlightenment rationalist philosopher, usually recognized as one of the earliest feminists.

Atlantic Charter: (1941) Document signed by FDR and Winston Churchill affirming that the post World War II international order would emphasize national self-determination, free trade, and interdependence. Often viewed as one of the founding documents of the United Nations.

Austin, John: (1790-1859) An important legal thinker in the tradition of positivism.

Authority: According to Max Weber, power is expressed in terms of three different types of authority: traditional (derived from common social custom), charismatic (derived from leadership qualities), and rational (derived from procedural organization).

Axis of Evil: George W. Bush's term for North Korea, Iran, and Iraq just prior to the War on Terror.

Bandwagoning: According to realist theory, the way small states achieve security by aligning with larger ones.

Banking, invention of: The establishment of banking in the 17th century was important in establishing a close connection between the royal families and private wealth. It is also connected to the development of capitalism during the period following the first voyages of discovery.

Base and Superstructure: According to Marxist theory, the economic base of society (the means and relations of production) condition the cultural superstructure, which, in turn, maintains the base.

Battle of Plassey: (1757) Decisive British victory during the Seven Year War, led to Great Britain taking control over all of the Bengal region of India.

Bay of Pigs: (1961) The CIA's failed attempt to invade Cuba with an army of trained refugees and expats. One of the great American failures of the Cold War.

Beggar thy neighbor: Attempting to gain an economic or political advantage at the expense of another political actor.

Benedictine monasteries: Catholic communities first founded in the early 5th Century C.E. which were instrumental in book-making, education, religious life, and other forms of administration.

Benthem, Jeremy (1748-1832) Utilitarian philosopher who was instrumental in early theories of liberal institutionalism.

Berlin Airlift: (1948-1949) Deceive event at the beginning of the Cold War. After a military blockade of West Berlin instituted by the Soviet Union, the United States and Great Britain airlifted essential supplies into the city.

Berlin Conference: (1885) Conference leading up to the Scramble for Africa, in which the major European powers essentially agreed to divide the uncolonized regions of Africa among themselves.

Bill of Rights: (1688) Following the Glorious Revolution William III and Mary agreed to abide by the Bill of Rights, guaranteeing certain basic freedoms and limiting the power of the monarchy. Marked the start of constitutional government in Great Britain.

Bosnian Crisis (1908) Major diplomatic crisis in Europe precipitated when Austria-Hungary annexed Bosnia and Herzegovina. Major factor in the lead-up to World War I.

Bourbons: One of the largest European dynasties. Founded in the 15th century, at its height, the house of Bourbon ruled over all of Spain, France, and much of Italy.

Bourgeoisie: In Marxist theory, the owners of the means of production.

Brazilian Gold Rush: (1690~1830) The discovery of gold in Brazil brought rapid settlement and colonization during much of the 18th century, leading to displacement of indigenous populations.

Bretton Woods Conference: 1945. Post World War II economic conference. Established the institutions that would structure the postwar economic order.

Brezhnev Doctrine: The USSR version of the "Truman Doctrine." The USSR decreed that it would stop its satellite states, by force if necessary, from adopting capitalism. Viewed as the justification for the invasion of Czechoslovakia in 1962.

BRICS: Brazil, Russia, India, China, and South Africa. According to some theorists, these five countries will be essential in a post-American international order.

Brinksmanship: The act of taking political positions to dangerous extremes, as, for example, during the Cold War.

British Conquest of Ireland: (1649-1653) Frequently described as a genocide, the conquest of Ireland was led by Cromwell's armies during the Wars of Religion.

British East India Company: A state-supported and militarized trading company operating in China and India, the company, employing mercenaries, conquered much of the subcontinent.

Bureaucracies: A major factor in the industrial revolution was the establishment of various "offices" for organizing and managing increased economic activity. These bureaucracies relied on rules, experts, hierarchy, and accountability.

Bush War: (1959-1974) Also known as the "War of Zimbabwean Liberation, the guerilla war between the white settlers of Rhodesia and the majority black Zimbabweans.

Bush, George W: President of the United States from 2000-2008. His presidency was defined as a shift towards unilateralism, embodied in the War on Terror.

Calvinists: Followers of John Calvin, these Protestants were a significant faction in the Wars of Religion. Many fled Europe for the New World.

Capitalism: An economic and political system based on private ownership of the means of production in which goods and services are produced for profit.

Casas, Bartoleme de las (1474-1566) Spanish priest, author of *A Short Account of the Destruction of the Indes*, widely regarded as the first work of anti-colonial literature.

Catholic Church: The dominant institution in Europe prior to the Protestant reformation. The Catholic Church was involved in nearly all aspects of European life and politics and was one of the first "supra-national" institutions in western history.

Century of Humiliation: Consisted of the Opium Wars between Great Britain and China, the unequal treaties, and the Boxer Rebellion. The climax of the Century of Humiliation was when Japan invaded China in 1935.

Christianity: The dominant religion in Europe and North America, Christianity was at the core of almost all political and social institutions prior to enlightenment secularization.

Christopher Colombus: (1451-1506) An

Italian explorer who was financed by Queen Isabella of Spain to find new sea routes to India and China. He is the man that history credits to "discovering" the Americas.

Clans: Groups of people who are related by family or have a perceived kinship.

Class Struggle: In Marxist theory, the dominant "dialectical" force in history which leads, over time, to revolutions in which a new economic base gives rise to a new superstructure and, with it, "entirely different social relations."

Clausewitz, Karl von: German general and military theorist who said that "war is a continuation of politics by other means."

Clausewitz's Trinity: Clausewitz's characterization of warfare as an interplay between passion, chance, and reason.

Clinton, William J: President of the United States from 1992 through 2000 whose foreign policy was defined by multilateralism.

Coercive: Power that involves force.

Code of Hammurabi: Ancient system of laws that dealt with retributive justice, distributive justice, procedural or ceremonial justice, and hierarchy and privilege.

Cold War: Geographic hostility between the USSR and the United States of America, which were the two main hegemons at the time. The Cold War consisted of proxy wars instead of direct fighting between the two parties.

Collective Security: Networks of military cooperation among member countries, the sharing of intelligence, the establishment of joint military bases, and the positioning of weaponry, including nuclear missiles, strategically across borders. An attack on one member of the collective security was seen as an attack on all in the group. Some examples include the Warsaw Pact and NATO.

Colombian exchange: Flows of goods, diseases, and ideas between the New World and the Old World.

Command Economy: is when all production decisions are undertaken by the state.

Commodification: Products taken by the bourgeoisie and exchanged for money.

Commons: Locke's ideal of an "unclaimed" state of nature in which resources were free for the taking.

Communism: Economic and cultural system advocated by Karl Marx, communism entails common ownership of the means of production. In the Soviet Union and China, this took the form of a centrally planned economy.

Communist International: an international organization that promoted communism.

Congo Free State: was a former nation in Africa that was taken by Leopold II as a personal possession.

Conquest of the Desert: When the Argentinian military cleared almost all indigenous peoples from the territory of Patagonia, in the year 1870, killing 1000 and displacing 15000.

Constitution: a legal agreement restricting the power of rulers and setting conditions for the exercise of authority.

Containment: The goal of this policy was to prevent the spread of communism as an ideology and limit Soviet influence.

Core and periphery: The core represents wealthy nations which exploit poorer countries, also known as the periphery, for labor.

Country: a geographic territory that has sovereignty over its citizens.

Crusades: Over hundreds of years, Christian and Muslim forces would fight back and forth in southern Europe, northern Africa and the Levent.

Cryptocurrency: electronic currencies which use a computer code, known as "blockchain" to prevent forgery. Seen by many as an alternative to state-backed fiat currency.

Cuban Missile Crisis: Following the Soviet attempt to install nuclear missiles in Cuba, the United States instituted a naval blockade in a stand-off that very nearly led to war.

Decentralization: The transfer of power, influence, knowledge, or wealth from a small group of political actors to a broader, more diffuse group.

Declaration of Independence: (1776) Drafted by Thomas Jefferson, document declaring the independence of the United States from Great Britain. One of the most famous articulations of the liberal ideas of human rights, consent, legitimate government, and popular sovereignty.

Declaration of the Rights of Man and the Citizen: (1789) Drafted by the French National Assembly, one of the founding documents of the first French Republic, following the French Revolution. Articulates the principle of popular sovereignty.

Decolonization: The process of oppressed peoples attempting to gain independence from the state that colonized them.

Deism: A religion which posits that there is an impersonal God that does not interfere with human affairs.

Democracy, Aggregate: Democracy, in the aggregate sense, is simply a tool for calculating the preferences of the majority.

Democracy, Deliberative: A model of democracy in which what matters is the rational conversation among democratic actors.

Democracy, Direct: A democratic system in which voters vote on every single policy decision.

Democracy, Indirect: A democratic system in which voters vote for representatives.

Deng Xiaoping: Former leader of China that started reforms to modernize the Chinese economy.

Descriptive Theory: A Political theory that

attempts to depict how political relations actually exist in the world.

DeToqueville, Alexis: One of the greatest theorists on the idea of democracy in the 19th century. In his book *On Democracy*, he discusses the idea of "accountability." In a democratic society, government officials, no matter how incompetant, will have to serve the majority of the people, since their livelihood depends on it.

Dialectical Materialism: Analyzes historical development in economic terms, showing how the material base of a society conditions the superstructure.

Diplomacy: At its most basic level, diplomacy is the way different international political actors make decisions.

Discourse: Negotiations occur through language, both spoken and written. Society shapes political action during a long conversation among its members.

Disenchantment: Max Weber's term for the world imagined in terms of impersonal forces and material laws.

Divine Right: Belief, common in much of Europe, that the authority of the king came from God.

Division of Labor: This occurs as workers only produce part of the product while the bourgeoisie commodify it.

Doomsday Clock: The clock, which measured the likelihood of nuclear and environmental catastrophe, would indicate "doomsday" if it were to ever reach midnight.

Dreadnaught: A battleship with iron armor, swivelling guns, and long-range torpedoes, the dreadnought was an unprecedented weapon and solidified Great Britain's leadership over the oceans.

Dumberton Oaks Conference: August of 1944, the Allied Powers met in Dumberton Oaks, near Washington, and agreed upon the rough framework of what would become the United Nations.

Dutch Revolt: Religious revolt between Catholic Spain and Protestant Holland that lasted until the Peace of Westphalia.

Economic Community of West Afrian States: is a regional partnership for West African States that focuses on politics and the economy.

Edict of Milan: In 313, Emperor Constantine passed this edict which ended state persecution of Christians and allowed them to worship openly throughout the Roman Empire.

Edict of Thessalonica: In 380, the three co-emperors Theodosius I, Gratian, and Valentinian II passed the Edict of Thessalonica, which made Christianity the "official religion of the Empire."

Electricity: In 1663, the first "friction generator" was invented, creating controlled electric sparks.

Emancipation: The attempt at establishing freedom and rights for an oppressed or disenfranchised population.

Embedded Liberalism: After World War II, the Liberal International Order created an economic system known as "embedded liberalism" designed to ensure both free trade and full employment.

Empire: A large geographic area that contained many nation states, but was under the control of one sovereign.

Empirical Approaches: It reports on "the facts" of the postcolonial experience, often in order to point out continued imbalances between the west and the non-west.

Encomiendas: Agricultural settlements, many of which employed native Americans as slaves, and harvested commodities (such as corn and tobacco) which would be sold back in Europe.

End of History: In 1992, philosopher Francis Fukayama suggested that with the dissolution of the USSR, nothing would keep the United States and the West from achieving total global supremacy. The liberal international order would encompass the globe, and Western liberal democracy would become, as he put it, "universalized as the final form of human government."

English Civil War: (1642-1651) During the English Civil War, many British political thinkers questioned the need for a king and advocated for democracy, equality, and religious toleration.

Enlightenment: Following the Peace of Westphalia, Europe entered an age of scientific advancement and secularization known as the Enlightenment.

Espionage and Sedition Acts: These acts, passed by Woodrow Wilson, were ostensibly designed to prevent spying on behalf of Germany. These laws essentially made it illegal to support any form of communism.

Eurocentrism: The tendency to emphasize European perspectives while ignoring those of other peoples and nations.

European Union: In 1992, twelve European states--including the United Kingdom, Spain, Portugal, France, Italy, Germany (the largest and most powerful countries in western Europe) signed the Maastricht Treaty, the official "start" of the European Union.

Euthyphro Problem: Socrates' Euthyphro Problem explores how difficult it is to define justice.

Exchange Value: The value of an object in terms of what it can be traded for.

Exploitation: The process of unjustly using the services of another for personal gain.

External Balancing: When a small country joins alliances with other small countries, in order to protect itself from a large and powerful country.

Fascism: An ideology that stems from nationalism and demands that only certain groups of people are allowed to belong to the nation state.

Feminism: Both a political theory and a

form of advocacy, feminism draws attention to the historical oppression of women and leads political actors to fight against it.

Feudalism: Under feudalism, the king would grant land to a local "lord" to rule as he saw fit. In exchange, the lord promised to provide horses and soldiers to the king in the event of war. The ordinary citizens, living under the lord, were granted small plots of land to farm on their own, under the condition that they likewise would go to war if and when their lord needed them.

Fiat Currency: Money that is not backed by a commodity.

Fragmentation: The breaking up of larger political units into smaller ones.

Franco-Prussian War: In 1870, Prussia (soon to be Germany) defeated France and seized the territories of Alceste and Lorraine. This defeat humiliated France and made it eager to attack Germany at the beginning of World War I.

Free trade: Free trade consists of opening the seas and ports for unrestricted commerce.

French Revolution: (1789-1799) The revolution was led by the "national assembly," the French "third estate" rose up against the French monarchy and its aristocratic leaders. As a result of the revolution, the idea of a "nation of equal citizens" took hold in much of Europe.

French Wars of Religion: (1562-1598) Catholic French leaders drove Protestant Heugonots from the country. The wars concluded with the Edict of Nantes and as many as 4,000,000 dead.

Fukayama, Francis: A philosopher who predicted that "western liberal democracy" would spread all over the world and that the liberal international order would become the final, universalized world system.

Gaza Strip: The Gaza Strip is part of occupied Palestine and has gained some measure of political autonomy but remains under Israeli military control.

Gender Gap: empirical data showing the ways women are still politically and economically unequal to men.

Gender Imperialism:

General Will: Part of the social contract by the thinker Rousseau where each individual in the community must freely agree to live in accordance with laws which are formed to reflect "the general will" or the common good.

Glasnost: Ghorbachev's policy of openness in the USSR.

Global north: The wealthy and developed countries of North America, the EU, and some parts of Southeast Asia.

Global south: The poorer and less developed countries of South America, Africa, and Asia.

Globalism: Interconnectedness between societies through the converging of politics, economies, and societies.

Glorious Revolution: (1688) Supporters of King Charles II's Protestant great-nephew William of Orange and his wife Mary II, succeeded in bringing the two to the throne in a "bloodless" coup. William and Mary were required to respect consent of parliament, regular elections, and free speech.

Gold Standard: Currency that can be traded for gold.

Government of India Act: The British Crown annexed India from the British East India Company in 1858.

Great Depression: A severe, world wide economic depression that lasted from 1929-1933.

Great divergence: Where Western society grew in power and wealth compared to the rest of the world. This growth in power can be traced back to the Voyages of Discovery in the 16th century and the Age of Imperialism in the 19th century.

Great Powers: Great Britain, Germany, France, Russia, Austria-Hungary, and the Ottoman Empire. The Great Powers dominated Europe and much of the globe.

Great Schism: The division of the Christian Church, in 1054, into the western Catholic and eastern Orthodox branches.

Gregorian Mission: Pope Gregory I launched a series of "missions" designed to convert the remaining non-Christians in Europe and to harmonize the organization

of the church.

Grotius, Hugo: (1538-1645) A theorist in the tradition of natural law. Though many natural law philosophers based their ideas on religion, Grotius believed that right and wrong could be discovered through human reason.

Gulf Cooperation Council: A regional partnership of the Gulf States which consists of Bahrain, Kuwait, Oman, Qatar, Saudi Arabia, and the United Arab Emirates.

Habsburg-Valois Wars: A war of religion that took place in Italy between 1494-1559.

Habsburgs: A royal German dynasty that held all of Spain, bits of Italy, and a good chunk of present day Germany.

Hart-Fuller Debate: A debate on whether morality and law are separate or inclusive. Herbert Hart sided with positivist thinking where the action is immoral, but not illegal. Lon Fuller argued natural law which relies on moral dimensions.

Hatian Revolution: (1791-1804) One of the most striking revolutions in world history, the Hatian Revolution began as a slave revolt. Led by Toussaint Louverture, former slaves fought off the French army and established Haiti as the "first black republic" of the Americas.

Hegemon: A major power such as Great Britain or the United States.

Herz, John: A 20th century realist who wrote a book entitled *Political Realism and*

Political Idealism. In the book, he coined the term security dilemma to describe the reason why politics always seems to be on the edge of violence.

Hessian Wars: (1567-1648) A war between House of Hesse vs House of Hesse-Cassel in the Holy Roman Empire. The outcome of this war resulted in 1,000,000 dead.

Hierarchy: A ranking of people based on categories.

Hinduism: A polytheistic religion concentrated in the Indian subcontinent with 1.2 billion adherents.

Hobbes, Thomas: A philosopher who deemed that human freedom was not "good" but chaotic. A strong government, Hobbes argued, was more important than individual choice.

Holism: the idea that structures are the explanation of individual units and that individual units cannot be understood in the absence of structures.

Holocaust: (1939-1945) A genocide where the Nazi German Party killed over six million Jews and other racial and minority groups.

Holy Roman Empire: The Holy Roman Empire (not to be confused with the ancient Roman Empire) was a multi-ethnic kingdom located, roughly, in present day Germany.

Homogeneity and heterogeneity: Homogeneity entails sharing a common set of values and beliefs while heterogeneity entails broad cultural, ideological, and religious groups.

Huguenots: Calvinist Protestants

Human rights: Universal rights that are supposed to belong to all humans.

Identity: Qualities or beliefs of a person, place, or thing.

Indian Civil Service: Officers who held political authority during the period of British Raj.

Indian Rebellion of 1857: The Indian Rebellion of 1857 saw forces from the former Mughal empire, private civilians and local "sepoys" rise up against the East India Company rule. The war went disastrously for the Indians.

Indian Removal Act: The Indian Removal Act of 1830 was the first of several official laws forcing Native Americans out of their homelands.

Indigenous Peoples: People native to their respective lands.

Industrial Revolution: A period of rapid growth in technology and economic productivity.

Institution: Roughly speaking, an institution is the way in which a society shapes behavior and creates trust.

Institutional Feminism: A theory that explains the way feminists attempt to reconstruct institutions to make them more equitable.

Institutionalism, Liberal: A process of gradual unification based on shared principles and beliefs.

Internal Balancing: A small country attempting to gain power in order to defend itself from a larger and more powerful country.

International Bank for Reconstruction and Development: An international bank offering loans to countries for post-war rebuilding and anti-poverty measures. The IBDR would allow countries to invest in their own economies without resorting to economic isolationism.

International Monetary Fund: An institution designed to regulate currency in order to prevent manipulation and other beggar-thy-neighbor policies. Nations would be required to link their currency to the United States dollar, which, in turn, would be pegged to gold at a fixed rate. This would prevent countries from arbitrarily changing the value of their currency

International Order: Common sets of rules amongst nation states that are recognized to be sovereign.

Iranian Hostage Crisis: In November 1979, Iranian protesters stormed and occupied the American embassy in Tehran, taking 52 American diplomats hostage. The hostages were freed in January 1981.

Iron Curtain: Winston Churchill's term for the Soviet presence in Europe.

Isaac Newton: Though Newton himself was a devout Christian, many intellectuals of the time used his and similar ideas in order to critique the Christian traditionalism which had dominated Europe for centuries. Toward the end of the 17th and the beginning of the 18th century, there were numerous books and pamphlets arguing that the world was best apprehended through ideas and reasons and not through divine revelation.

Islam: A monotheistic religion that is heavily concentrated in the Arabic Peninsula and Northern Africa with 1.8 billion adherents.

Islamophobia: Prejudice against followers of Islam.

Isolationism: A reluctance to interfere in international affairs.

John Lloyd Dunlop: (1887) Inventor of the air filled tire.

John Locke: Locke believed human beings were made in the image of God and, as such, were innately free and equal. He also believed that humans in the state of nature would still be governed by natural law, a basic sense of right and wrong.

Judaism: A monotheistic religion that is heavily concentrated in Israel and has 14 million adherents.

Just War Theory: A theory that attempts to describe the circumstances in which war is permitted. Their ideas of a just war involved two specific "categories" of justification: **jus ad bellum** (or, a just *cause* to go to war) and **jus in bello** (or, just actions within war).

Justice: Fair treatment of individuals.

Kant, Immanuel: 18th century German philosopher that is noted for his vision of "perpetual peace".

Kellog-Briand Pact: A pact created in 1928 that officially "outlawed war" and mandated that diplomacy be used to solve international agreements.

Keynes, John Maynard: British economist. Beginning in the 1930's, his ideas became highly influential in establishing an economic order in which the government was responsible for intervening in markets.

Keynesianism: A theory named after John Maynard Keynes that aimed for governments to use spending to increase employment in their economies.

King Charles I: King Charles I (1625-1649) was a firm believer in the Divine Right of Kings. His attempt to rule without the cooperation of parliament led to the English Civil War (1642-1651)

King Leopold: King Leopold of Belgium (1900) was remembered as one of the great villains of his time due to the barbarity of the Belgian-controlled "Congo Free State."

Kingdom of the Kongo: A kingdom in West Africa that established a close rapport with the Portuguese.

Kingship: The concentration of political authority in the hands of one leader with near absolute power.

Korean War: (1950-1953) After the communist north invaded the nationalist south, the United States intervened sending 300,000 soldiers to the Korean peninsula. After the Chinese intervened on the communist side, the war ended in a stalemate along the 38th parallel.

Labor movement: A series of political strikes and protests in the 19th century aimed at increasing wages, reducing work-hours, and ensuring safe conditions in factories. Women were instrumental in many of these protests.

Labor Theory of Value: The idea that value and ownership of something is a reflection of work. Karly Marx would define the value of a commodity in terms of the amount of "socially necessary labor time" to produce it.

Law: Written agreements establishing, in contractual terms, the actions which society requires or prohibits.

Law, international: Affairs outside of a state.

Laws of Burgos: (1512) A set of laws that dictated that Spanish settlers were forbidden from abusing the native populations

League of Nations: A democratic association, formed after WWI, that preceded the United Nations.

Legitimacy: When something is deemed credible or acceptable by other actors.

Leviathan: Hobbes' term for the state, suggesting its absolute power to keep people in "a state of awe."

Levellers: A group, during the English Civil War, that called for civil rights, democratically elected governments, and broad social freedoms.

Liberal International Order: The post World War II effort to ensure peace through rules and collaboration.

Liberalism: A political tradition emphasizing individual rights, free choice, and equality.

Locarno Treaty: The treaty, created in 1925, set post-war borders in an effort to ensure peace between Germany and newly independent Poland.

Lord Palmerston: Prime Minister of Great Britain from 1830-1865 who oversaw a period of imperialist expansion.

Maastricht Treaty: The 1992 agreement formally establishing the European Union.

Machiavelli, Niccolò: An Italian diplomat who wrote *The Prince*, which advanced a theory of government based on power, manipulation, and fear.

Mahatma Gandhi: (1869-1948) Leader of the Indian independence movement.

Mandela, Nelson: A revolutionary who rose up against the Apartheid goverment in South Africa.

Manifest Destiny: The belief that America was "destined" to settle and develop the land between the Atlantic and Pacific oceans.

Market Economy: The market determines prices in the economy.

Marshall Plan: The American policy of sending economic aid to western Europe in order to rebuild after the war and prevent the appeal of communism.

Martin Luther: Founder of the Protestant Reformation. In 1517, Luther nailed his "95 theses" to the door of the church in Wittenberg Germany, touching off the greatest split in the history of Christianity.

Marx, Karl: German philosopher whose theory suggested that capitalism was exploitative and that the proletariat would overthrow the bourgeoisie.

Marxism: A theory named after the philosopher Karl Marx that focuses on class conflict and material forces.

Mary II: The wife of William of Orange, who alongside her husband agreed to respect the Bill of Rights.

Mau Mau Uprising: (1952-1960) An uprising, started by the Kikuyu in Kenya, against British colonialism.

Maxim Gun: An early machine gun that allowed European armies to achieve decisive victories over native tribes, even with relatively small armies.

Melian Dialogue: Often taken to be the first example of the political philosophy called realism.

Meliorative Theory: A theory that is concerned with ways society might be improved to become more just or humane.

Mill, John Stuart: A thinker that saw the state of nature as violent, archaic, and governed by indifferent natural laws. Nonetheless, he believed that the natural pursuit of happiness and utility would lead to the creation of civil societies which, in turn, would establish social justice and safeguard freedom.

Modernism: The view that the idea of "the nation" is dependent on economic, technological, and political changes which have occured over the past 200 years.

Monarchy: A form of government where the ruler is the head of state until they face death or abdicate their throne.

Monopoly on violence: Max Weber's idea that in modern societies, the state is allowed to use force (i.e. the police and the military) while private actors, including citizens are not.

Moscow Conference: In October 1943, the allied Powers affirmed their belief in the necessity of an international organization to replace the League of Nations.

Mott, Lucretia: (1848) She co-organized the Seneca Falls Conference on women's rights.

Mugabe, Robert: Former president of Zimbabwe that was active in the struggle for African liberation.

Multilateralism: Having alliances with multiple countries in order to work towards a common goal.

Munich Agreement: (1938) An agreement made between Germany, Italy, Britain, and France, where the Sudetenland was given to Germany.

Mutually assured destruction: Both the United States and the Soviet Union would retain enough nuclear weapons to destroy each other in the event of war.

Nation: Refers to the people of a nation-state and their common identity.

Nation-state: Organizations in a country that give order to society.

National Assembly: In June of 1789, the Third Estate elected the National Assembly, a group of statesmen who were charged with representing the will of the people.

National interest: Policies that are done in the best interest of the country.

National self-determination: The right of each national group to have its own state and shape its own sovereign destiny.

Nationalism, Civic: Membership in a nation is a reflection of willingness to obey the law and participate in civic society.

Nationalism, Conservative: A form of nationalism that tends to emphasize the power and authority of the state.

Nationalism, Elite: Powerful political leaders in a country use the language of "the nation" in order to achieve political goals.

Nationalism, Ethnic: Membership in a nation is determined by race or ethnicity.

Nationalism, Liberal: A style of politics that focuses on the expansion of civil rights and liberties for members of the national community.

Nationalism, Popular: The "common people" define the character of the nation.

Nationalism, State Opposing: Loyalty to and identification with a particular "people" accompanied by opposition to the institutions of state power which govern them. State opposing nationalism may seek to reform the state or separate from it. Occasionally, it may seek to unify with another nation-state or to form a new nation-state.

Nationalism, State Supporting: Loyalty to and identification with a particular "people" accompanied with support of the institutions of state power which govern them. State supporting nationalism occasionally seeks to strengthen the power of the state or to "purify" it from the intrusion of "outsiders."

Nationalization: The process whereby the governing institutions of the state are transformed to represent the entire community. Often involves the unification of many smaller political units into one national community.

NATO: The United States and the countries of western Europed formed the North Atlantic Treaty Organization (NATO), a mutual defense agreement in which member countries agreed to defend one another in the event of a Soviet attack.

Natural Law: A law is legitimate if and when it aligns with the moral order. A law isn't a law because it is a *command* but because it's *right*.

Neoliberalism: The reforms in the 1980's which reduced taxes and regulations in order to stimulate the economy.

New Deal: Social welfare reforms implemented by FDR to help jump start the economy after the Great Depression.

Nixon, Richard: He was elected president in 1968 and instituted a shift in American policy towards the Soviet Union that was marked by a gradual reduction in tensions, which was known as detente.

Noble Savage: The pure and uncorrupted person who lived prior to modern institutions.

Norms: Certain legitimate and accepted patterns of behavior.

Obama, Barrack: (2008-2016) Former president of the United States that included a mix of multilateralism and unilateralism in foreign policy decisions.

Odoacer: A German army officer who launched a rebellion in 476 C.E. and captured the city of Rome in addition to holding King Romulus hostage.

Oligarchy: When the decisions of a nation-state are in the hands of a small number of people.

Oliver Cromwell: A Puritan general who won the English Civil War and held a military dictatorship from 1649-1660.

Ottoman Empire: It was a powerful state in the Middle East that held power for more than 600 years. It stretched from Central Asia to the gates of Vienna, along the North African coast all the way to Spain

Palestine: A geographic area that contains the West Bank and the Gaza Strip.

Parliamentarians: Supporters of Parliament during the English Civil War.

Partition of India: This partition enabled Muslim and Hindu populations to have independent states.

Passion, Chance, Reason: Three aspects included in Clausewitz's "trinity of war". Passion is what motivates and rallies both soldiers and civilians to engage in the war effort. Chance reflects the fact that anything can happen in a battle. Reason represents the "intellectual" or "calculated" aspects of warfare.

Pax Britannica: A period where lasting peace allowed Great Britain to become a hegemon.

Peace of Augsburg: (1555) The treaty established the principle of *cuius regio eius religio* (Latin for "whose realm, his religion"). Put simply, each ruler in the Holy Roman Empire had the right to establish the religion for his people.

Peace of Westphalia (1648) Principle of territorial sovereignty was established and states agreed to allow monarchs to choose the religion of their states.

Perestroika: Ghorbachev's policy of economic restructuring in the USSR.

Perpetual Peace: Kant's vision for a peaceful and harmonious international order.

Pied-noirs: Those who migrated from Algeria and Tunisia back to France following the French wars of decolonization.

Ping-Pong diplomacy: When China invited American table tennis players to exhibition matches in 1971.

Polarization: Tensions between nation-states.

Political Actor: Political actors can be "anything that acts politically" from an individual human being to a state.

Politics: Is a process which organizes "who gets what, when, and how" in society.

Portuguese Colonial War: Mozambique, Angola, and Guinea Bissau rose up against and succeeded in winning their independence from Portugal.

Positivism: Laws are simply the orders (what is "posited") from people authorized to give orders.

Postcolonialism: A theory that reports on "the facts" of the postcolonial experience, often in order to point out continued imbalances between the west and the non-west.

Potosi Silver Mines: In 1545, the Spanish established the Potosi silver mines in present-day Argentina, which, along with other mines in South America, quickly began to produce large quantities of the precious metal.

Potsdam Conference: (July 1945) The United States, Great Britain and the Soviet Union decide upon the partition of Germany and the fate of occupied territories. The Soviet Union promises to allow free and fair elections in the territories under its control.

Power: The ability to make people do things that they otherwise would not do.

Prague Spring: The 1968 Soviet invasion of Czechoslovakia in response to the "liberal" reforms of the Dubcek government.

Price revolution: The price revolution in the European economy led to the establishment of modern banking systems, which helped to regulate currencies and which funded both public and private projects.

Primordialism: The view, popular in the 19th century, that "the nation" is ancient and fundamental and that each nation has its eternal qualities.

Prince, The: A treatise written by Niccolo Machiavelli in 1532.

Principality: A state governed by a prince.

Principia: (1687) Articulated Isaac Newton's three famous laws of motion.

Printing Press: The printing press, invented in Germany in 1453, was utilized more and more widely, leading to the increasingly rapid dissemination of information and ideas.

Private Power: Describes economic actions that private citizens or businesses may take.

Privilege: Exceptions granted to a select group of people.

Process: Politics is a "process" in that it does not have a definite beginning or end. It changes continuously as the political body evolves and develops.

Proletariat: The "working class" that sells its labor to the bourgeoisie for a wage.

Protectorate: A name associated with Oliver Cromwell's military dictatorship.

Protestant Reformation: A religious split in Christianity which, in a few short years, would divide the faith into Catholic traditionalists and Protestant reformers.

Protofeminist: Early writings exploring themes and concerns which would be expanded on in later years.

Proxy War: An indirect war in which two larger nations arm and support smaller nations who then fight one another on their behalf.

Public good: Objectives that benefit society as a whole.

Public Power: Economic actions that governments can take.

Public Sphere: The mutually acknowledged

"reality" of terms, arguments, and perspectives through which democratic conversation is made possible.

Puritan: Religious reformers who advocated for a kind of half-republican, half-theocratic sort of government. They viewed the established English church as corrupt and hoped to institute a stricter, more rigorously Protestant national church which would "purify" British Christianity from Catholic influence.

Putin, Vladimir: Current leader of Russia whose leadership allowed Russia to become governed by a class of oligarchs who repressed political freedom and undid many liberal reforms.

Queen Victoria: (1819-1901): Monarch at the height of the British Empire.

Quit India Movement: A movement launched by Mahatma Gandhi in 1942 to end British rule in India.

Raison d'etat: French for "the purpose of the state."

Rapprochement: Reestablishing friendly relations between states.

Rashidun Caliphate: (632-661) A caliphate that consolidated the gains of Mohammad and took control of much of Persia and northern Africa.

Realism: Is the political philosophy that might makes right. Power, and little else, is what matters in politics.

Red Scare: Following the communist revolution in Russia, the United States enacted a series of anti-communist policies at home.

Regional integration: When neighboring nations enter into agreements with each other.

Regulation: A process that shapes how things should operate.

Relative: Varying according to time and place.

Relative Power: Concerns having more power relative to other states.

Republic: A state with a representative government.

Restoration: In 1660, Charles II, son of Charles I, returned to the throne and restored the monarchy in England.

Revanchism: Germany's deep-seated feeling of humiliation, bitterness, and desire for revenge against the allies, following the Treaty of Versailles.

Rhodesia: A state in southern Africa that is now known as Zimbabwe.

Rights: Freedoms that the state guarantees its citizens.

Roman Empire: Political authority, concentrated in Rome, which extended over almost all of Europe and North Africa.

Roman Empire, Fall: The "decline" of Rome was due to many factors: the economic strain of managing a large territory, the political instability created by rival factions, and the growing power of the many non-Roman peoples, particularly to the north.

Romulus Augustus: The last ruler of the Roman Empire before it fragmented.

Ronald Reagan: (1981-1989) 40th president of the United States who adopted a more confrontational foreign policy.

Roosevelt, Franklin Deleanor (FDR): He was the 32nd president of the United States and saw the country through the Great Depression and World War II.

Rousseau, Jean Jacques: (1712-1778) A French philosopher who argued in favor of liberal reforms. According to Rousseau, institutions are only fair when they reflect the "general will."

Royal Houses: The families of kings and queens, which often controlled territory in multiple "countries" at once.

Royalists: Supporters of the king during the English Civil War.

Russian Financial Crisis: (1998) Russia defaulted on its loans and President Yeltsin was forced to resign. In turn, Vladimir Putin took his place.

Russian Revolution: (1917) The revolution ended czarist rule and the Bolsheviks, winners of the revolution, ended up becoming the Communist Party in the USSR.

Rwandan Genocide: (1994) The majority Hutu tribe kill over a million of the minority Tsutsis, following the assassination of the

Rwandan president.

SALT: The first 'Strategic Arms Limitation Treaty' signed by the United States and the Soviet Union in 1972.

Schmalkaldic League: (1531) A military alliance designed to protect Protestant states' religious rights from the Catholic states in the Holy Roman Empire.

Scientific Racism: The effort to establish European superiority on the grounds of biology.

Scramble for Africa: European powers entered and colonized virtually all of Africa.

Secularism: The loss in church power that began to occur during the enlightenment along with the gradual establishment of a more "religion-free" social space.

Security Council: Made up of the most powerful nations who would be responsible for using their military might to maintain the peace and prevent conflict.

Security Dilemma: The term "security dilemma" describes the way that states, pursuing their own security, paradoxically continue to create the conditions of war.

Self-help: Accumulating strength for one's own state to gain a competitive advantage over others.

Seneca Falls Conference: (1848) The first conference in the world explicitly dedicated to the problem of women's rights.

Separate Domains: The government, it was

argued, makes decisions about two things: military affairs and industrial ones. Since women did not participate in either of these, it was inappropriate for them to exercise power over things they had no experience in.

Separation of Powers: In other words, separate branches of government would prevent power from becoming too concentrated in any one group.

Seven Day War: In 1967, fearing that the Arab states were planning another attack, Israel launched a preemptive strike against Egypt and Jordan, which started the Seven Day War.

Seven Years War: (1756-1763) War caused by tensions between Austria, Prussia, Britain and France over succession to the Austrian throne and territorial disputes in the New World between French Canada and the British colonies.

Ship of Fools: Plato's comparison to democracy.

Silk Road: A trade route that connected important centers of commerce in the ancient world.

Sino-Soviet Split: In 1969, a border disagreement between China and the Soviet Union led to a brief military skirmish in which dozens of soldiers were killed on both sides.

Social Contract: A common agreement to give up the freedom found in the state of nature and live under government for the sake of greater safety.

Social Constructivism: The idea that politics is best understood as the relationship between decision-makers (agents) and social conditions(structures).

Social Fact: Social facts are formed by common consensus. They often underlie norms, which, in turn, structure political institutions.

Social justice: Justice that deems all social groups deserve to have the same access to resources.

Socrates: Greek philosopher who questioned the nature of justice.

Sovereignty: Who has the right to control institutions.

Sovereignty, Popular: The notion that political power comes from "the people."

Sovereignty, Territorial: The idea that political authority extends over a certain area of land. Within that land the government has supreme legal authority. Political actors outside of that land, those in other land, have no right to meddle with external affairs.

Spanish American War: (1898) War between Spain and America in which Spain lost some of its colonies and America gained some of their own.

Spanish Armada: In Spain, there was the 1588 Spanish Armada, an attempt to invade England in order to restore Catholic leaders to the throne.

Spirit of reform: Spirit of reform was energized by technologies of communication which made the conditions of colonized peoples apparent to a broader public.

Spiritual Power: Power centered on religion and the social institutions and practices which religion helped organize.

St. Bartholomew's Day Massacre:(1572) Catholic mobs around Paris killed roughly 10,000 Protestants, wiping out entire villages and assassinating many religious leaders.

Stag Hunt: The stag hunt is a thought experiment about cooperation, trust, and the difference between relative and absolute gains.

Standard of Civilization: Presupposes Europe to be the "standard of civilization" to which all other cultures ought to rise.

Stanton, Elizabeth Cady: A co-organizer of the Seneca Falls Conference.

State: Organizations by which nations organize their societies.

State of Nature: Hobbes' term for a world without government. It inevitably led to a "war of all against all."

State-Building: European states grew more centralized and powerful due to the pressures of warfare. Increased tax revenue, expanded bureaucracies, and the growth of "experts" led to states that were well-organized and efficient.

Stateless Nation: A nation who does not have their own state.

Statism: Individual states exist with one another in a *competitive arena* where the pursuit of power is of primary importance.

Steam engine: (1712) Allows individuals to release the steam-energy stored in simple bricks of coal. Is often taken to mark the "official start" of the industrial revolution, a period of rapid growth in technology and economic productivity.

Stirrup: A stirrup gives a rider better balance and control of the horse, and, in the days when horses were used in battle, allowed cavalry soldiers more efficient use of thrusting and shooting weapons.

Sun Tzu: A Chinese general of the Zhou Kingdom, in the 5th century B.C., "Master Sun" divided war into five key elements: "the moral law, heaven, earth, the commander, and discipline:".

Supply Side Economics: The belief that taxing and regulating producers ("suppliers") leads to a decrease in the production of goods, and, correspondingly, that minimizing interference with producers leads to a maximum of production.

Suppression of the monasteries: Henry VIII dissolved the 900 monasteries in England, confiscating their funds, destroying many of their buildings, and executing many Catholic leaders.

Surplus: Having more of an object than is needed.

Survival: Survival, for rulers, depends first and foremost on military might.

Sykes-Picot Agreement: (1916) The agreement divided the territory formerly controlled by the Ottoman Empire into British, French, and Italian zones of administration.

Systemic Problem: Problems that are rooted deep within the foundations of society.

Tariffs: A tax on goods that are being imported from another country.

Taxes: Charges that are placed upon citizens by their government.

Technological Determinism: This idea posits that technology, which is often developed for the purpose of battle, drives political development.

Temporal Power: The authority of kings, on the other hand, was temporal power: power over the material resources of the land and people which they ruled.

Theory: An intellectual perspective which allows us to explain social phenomena.

Tiananmen Square Incident: (1989) The Chinese military dispersed protestors, imposing martial law on much of Beijing.

Tillich, Paul: A theologian that defined religion as "the state of being grasped by an ultimate concern, a concern which qualifies all other concerns as preliminary and which itself contains the answer to the question of the meaning of life."

Toussaint Louverture: Leader of the Haitian Revolution.

Trade: It establishes the ideas of "fairness" and "reciprocity" that bind communities together. Historically, it has been the basis for international cooperation, interdependence, and trust.

Trading post empire: European states held posts in colonies that gave them control of the ports and allowed them to influence the local economies.

Trail of Tears: The forced relocations of over 100,000 Native Americans that led to the deaths of perhaps as many as 10,000, many through malnutrition and disease.

Transaction: Exchanges among the global political actors that recognize one another as independent.

Triangular Trade: The trade sent slaves to the Americas, raw materials to Europe and manufactured goods to Africa.

Tribes: Communities that are related by family or that live in the same relative location.

Truman Doctrine: The goal of this policy was to prevent the spread of communism as an ideology and limit Soviet influence.

Trump, Donald: 45th president of the United States who ran on a "Make America Great Again" agenda.

Tyranny of the majority: John Stuart Mill's observation that the needs of the majority would be placed above the needs of the minority.

U-boat: A deadly underwater submarine.

Umayyad Caliphate: During the Umayyad Caliphate (661-750), Islamic conquest reached its high point, conquering Spain and parts of southern France.

Unequal Treaties: Treaties that the British forced the Chinese to sign after the Opium Wars.

Unilateralism: Sole action of a political entity.

United Nations: Successor of the League of Nations.

Use Value: The value of an object in terms of what it is "used" for.

Utilitarianism: A philosophical movement in which the concern was with understanding the principles which would maximize human happiness.

Utility: How useful something is.

Vietnam War: (1955-1975) The United States invaded Vietnam to support the South Vietnamese government in a civil war between it and the communist north.

Voyages of Discovery: They were intended to increase the wealth of European kingdoms through international trade and colonial development.

Wallerstein, Immanuel: In the later twentieth century, American sociologist Immanuel Wallerstein developed world-systems theory.

Waltz, Kenneth: American political scientist who suggested that balances of power form spontaneously as states seek "safety first."

War: Violence between political actors.

War of All Against All: Hobbes' reference to anarchy.

War of Austrian Succession: (1740-1748) The war resulted in the House of Habsburg maintaining control of Austria. Both sides lost nearly 500,000 soldiers. Prussia also became a dominant state in the Holy Roman Empire.

War of Spanish Succession: (1701-1714) A major loss for the Spanish Habsburgs as control of Spain falls to the House of Bourbon.

War on Terror: A series of military operations targeting "state sponsors of terror" as well as individuals affiliated with terrorist groups.

War, Civil: Wars that happen between rival factions *within* a state, often in order to gain control of the government or establish political independence.

War, Interstate: When one country battles another to settle a political dispute.

War, Limited: A war fought for a lesser goal than the survival of the state.

War, Total: A war in which the entire population and all of the resources of a nation are mobilized or otherwise involved in the war effort.

Wars of Religion: More than 30 extended military conflicts connected to conflicts between Catholics and Protestants, engulfed

Europe for close to one hundred and fifty years.

Warsaw Pact: A collective security agreement signed in 1956 between the Soviet Union and its satellite states. The "counter" to NATO.

Washington Consensus: An economic "recipe" that includes low taxes, low regulations, low spending, free trade, and private property rights. Often making the adoption of the Washington Consensus a condition for economic aid, the United States argues that the sooner developing nations adopt neoliberal principles, the faster they'll achieve economic growth.

Washington Naval Treaty: (1921) A promise made among major military powers to limit the sizes of their navies in order to ensure the balance of power.

Washington-Moscow Hotline: In June of 1963, a special communication device, the Washington-Moscow Hotline was installed in both the White House and the Kremlin. The device used "teletype," a precursor to the fax machine, in order to link the two offices.

Weber, Max: (1864-1920) A German sociologist that explained the operation of power in terms of three different *sources of authority*.

Welfare state: a system in which the government attempts to ensure full employment and economic stability through anti-poverty and regulatory measures.

West Bank: An area in occupied Palestine.

Westphalian Sovereignty: Equivalent to Territorial Sovereignty.

White man's burden: Imperialism was an act of tiresome but necessary charity through which the rest of the world would be brought up to the European standard of civilization.

William of Orange: In the Glorious Revolution, the protestant William of Orange invaded England, on religious grounds, to take the throne from the Cathlolic James II.

Wilson, Woodrow: The 28th president of the United States known for his Fourteen Points proposal which included national self-determination, the League of Nations, and economic interdependence.

Wollstonecraft, Mary: In 1792, Mary Wollstonecraft published *Vindication of the Rights of Women*, one of the greatest feminist works of the 18th century.

World Systems Theory: A model of understanding global relationships in terms of the unequal exchange of labor, materials, and manufactured goods.

Yalta Conference: (February 1945) The United States, Great Britain, and the Soviet Union made preliminary plans for post-war Germany.

REFERENCES

Figure 1.1
World Map of Pomponius Mela as reconstructed by K. Miller (1898)
Karl Miller
https://commons.wikimedia.org/wiki/File:Karte_Pomponius_Mela_rotated.jpg
License: United States Public Domain

Figure 1.2
United States Constitution, Constitutional Convention
License: United States Public Domain

Figure 1.3
Institutions
Copyright: Jeremy Penna, 2021

Chapter 2

Figure 2.1
Map of Mesopotamia
Nordnordwest
https://commons.wikimedia.org/wiki/File:Karte_Mesopotamien.png
License: Creative Commons Attribution 3.0 Unported

Figure 2.2
Guilio Rosati
Camp in the Desert
https://commons.wikimedia.org/wiki/File:Giulio_Rosati_5.jpg
License: United States public domain

Figure 2.3
Ancient ziggurat at Ali Air Base Iraq
Hardnfast
https://commons.wikimedia.org/wiki/File:Ancient_ziggurat_at_Ali_Air_Base_Iraq_2005.jpg
License: Creative Commons Attribution 3.0 Unported

Figure 2.4
Gilzai Nomads in Afghanistan
James Rattrai
https://commons.wikimedia.org/wiki/File:Ghilzai_nomads_in_Afghanistan.jpg
License: United States public domain

FIgure 2.5
Cylindrical Seal of Shulgi
Louis de Clerq

https://commons.wikimedia.org/wiki/File:Cylinder_seal_of_Shulgi.jpg
License: United States public domain

Figure 2.6
Still life with glass bowl of fruit and vases
Pompeian painter, circa 70 C.E.
https://commons.wikimedia.org/wiki/File:Pompejanischer_Maler_um_70_001.jpg
License: Public domain

Figure 2.7
Die Porta praetoria des Kastells Pfünz
Mediatus
https://commons.wikimedia.org/wiki/File:Porta_Praetoria_Kastell_Pf%C3%BCnz.jpg
License: Creative Commons Attribution 3.0

Figure 2.8
China Map 260 BCE Warring States Period
Philg88
https://commons.wikimedia.org/wiki/File:EN-WarringStatesAll260BCE.jpg
License: Creative Commons Attribution 3.0

Figure 2.9
Roman Empire Trajan
Tataran
https://en.wikipedia.org/wiki/File:Roman_Empire_Trajan_117AD.png
License: Creative Commons Attribution 3.0

Figure 2.10
Six major protectorates during Tang Dynasty
SY
https://commons.wikimedia.org/wiki/File:Tang_Protectorates.png
License: Creative Commons 4.0 Share Alike

Figure 2.11
Mediterranean Europe
Roki
https://commons.wikimedia.org/wiki/File:Europe_mediterranean_1190.jpg
License: United States Public Domain

Figure 3.1
Western and Eastern Roman Empires
https://commons.wikimedia.org/wiki/File:628px-Western_and_Eastern_Roman_Empires_476AD(3).PNG
License: Creative Commons SSA 3.0

Figure 3.2

Romulus Augustus
Classical Numismatic Group
https://commons.wikimedia.org/wiki/File:RomulusAugus-
tus.jpg
License: Creative Commons SSA 3.0
Figure 3.3
Napoli, Castel Del'ovo
Martin Belam
https://commons.wikimedia.org/wiki/File:Napoli-cas-
teldell%27ovo02.jpg
License: Creative Commons SSA 2.0

Figure 3.4
Political division in Europe, North Africa and Near East
after the end of the Western Roman Empire in 476 AD
Guriezous
https://commons.wikimedia.org/wiki/File:Europe_and_
the_Near_East_at_476_AD.png
License: Creative Commonns SSA 4.0

Figure 3.5
Monte Cassino
Radomil
https://commons.wikimedia.org/wiki/File:Monte_Cassi-
no_Opactwo_1.JPG
License: Creative Commons Attribution 3.0

Figure 3.6
Royal Vincent of Beauvais
Medieval Scribe
https://commons.wikimedia.org/wiki/File:BL_Royal_Vin-
cent_of_Beauvais.jpg
License: Public Domain

Figure 3.7
Catholic Hierarchy
Jeremy Penna

Figure 3.8
St. Gall Plan
Malcom Farmer
https://commons.wikimedia.org/wiki/File:St_gall_plan.jpg
License: United States Public Domain

Figure 3.9
Culture of Europe 1250
Mandramunjak
https://commons.wikimedia.org/wiki/File:Culture_of_Eu-
rope_in_1250.png
License: Public Domain

Figure 3.10
Karl Leo

https://commons.wikimedia.org/wiki/File:Karel_Leo.jpg
License: Public Domain

Figure 4.1
Middle Europe during the time of Staufer
Ricard Andee
https://commons.wikimedia.org/wiki/File:Mitteleuropa_
zur_Zeit_der_Staufer.svg
License: Creative Commons Attribution 4.0 Share Alike

Figure 4.2
Holy Roman Empire 1618, modified
Ziegelbrenner
https://commons.wikimedia.org/wiki/File:HolyRomanEm-
pire_1618.png
License: GNU free documentation license

Figure 4.3
Morning at the door of the Louvre
Edouard Debat Ponsan
https://commons.wikimedia.org/wiki/File:Debat-Pon-
san-matin-Louvre.jpg
License: Public Domain

Figure 4.4
Defenestration of Prague
Johan Philip Abelinus
https://commons.wikimedia.org/wiki/File:Prager.Fenster-
sturz.1618.jpg
License: Public Domain

Figure 4.5
Holy Roman Empire in 16th Century
Friederick Putzgern
https://commons.wikimedia.org/wiki/File:Deutschland_
im_XVI._Jahrhundert_(Putzger).jpg
License: Public Domain

Figure 4.6
Europe, 1740
Bryan Rutherford
https://commons.wikimedia.org/wiki/File:Europe_1740_
en.png
License: Creative Commons Attribution 4.0 Share alike

Figure 4.7
Swearing of the treaty of munster
Gerard ter Borsch
https://upload.wikimedia.org/wikipedia/commons/8/8a/
Westfaelischer_Friede_in_Muenster_%28Gerard_Ter-
borch_1648%29.jpg
License: Public Domain

Figure 4.8
The Tax Office
Peter Brughel
https://commons.wikimedia.org/wiki/File:Pieter_
BRUEGHEL_Ii_-_The_tax-collector%27s_office_-_Goo-
gle_Art_Project.jpg
License: Public Domain

Figure 4.9
16th Century Portuguese Spanish Trade Routes
World Topography
https://commons.wikimedia.org/wiki/File:16th_centu-
ry_Portuguese_Spanish_trade_routes.png
License: Public Domain

Figure 4.10
Sealing of the Bank of England Charter
Lady Jane Lindsay
https://commons.wikimedia.org/wiki/File:Bank_of_En-
gland_Charter_sealing_1694.jpg
License: Public Domain

Figure 4.11
Henry VIII
Hans Holbein
https://commons.wikimedia.org/wiki/File:After_Hans_
Holbein_the_Younger_-_Portrait_of_Henry_VIII_-_Goo-
gle_Art_Project.jpg
License: Public Domain

Figure 4.12
Roche Abbey
JohnArmagh
https://commons.wikimedia.org/wiki/File:RocheAbbey-
SouthYorkshire.JPG
License: Creative Commons Attribution 4.0 Share Alike

Figure 4.13
Luther's 95 Theses
Julius Hubner
https://commons.wikimedia.org/wiki/File:Der_Anschlag_
von_Luthers_95_Thesen.jpg
License: Public Domain

4.14
Holy Roman Empire
https://commons.wikimedia.org/wiki/File:HolyRomanEm-
pire_1618.png
Ziegelbrenner
License: Creative Commons Share Alike 4.0

Figure 5.1

Letter Concerning Toleration
John Locke
https://commons.wikimedia.org/wiki/File:Letter_Concern-
ing_Toleration.jpg
License: Public Domain

Figure 5.2
William III Gives his Royal Assent to the Toleration Act
John Cassell
https://commons.wikimedia.org/wiki/File:P588_William_
III._giving_his_royal_assent_to_the_toleration_act.jpg
License: Public Domain

Figure 5.3
Chelsea Pensioners Reading Waterloo Dispatch
David Wilkie
https://commons.wikimedia.org/wiki/File:David_Wilkie_
Chelsea_Pensioners_Reading_the_Waterloo_Dispatch.jpg
License: Public Domain

Figure 5.4
European Output of Printed Books 145-1800
Tentotwo
https://commons.wikimedia.org/wiki/File:European_Out-
put_of_Printed_Books_ca._1450%E2%80%931800.png
https://commons.wikimedia.org/wiki/File:European_Out-
put_of_Printed_Books_ca._1450%E2%80%931800.png
License: Creative Commons 3.0 Share Alike

Figure 5.5
Huygens Pendulum Clock
Christian Huygans
https://commons.wikimedia.org/wiki/File:Huygens_first_
pendulum_clock.png
License: Public Domain

Figure 5.6
Holz Influence Machine
https://commons.wikimedia.org/wiki/File:Holtz_influ-
ence_machine.jpg
Nordisk Familjebok
License: Public Domain

Figure 5.7
Charles I of England
Anthony Van Dyke
https://commons.wikimedia.org/wiki/File:King_
Charles_I_after_original_by_van_Dyck.jpg
License: Public Domain

Figure 5.8
Session of Long Parliament
17th Century Print

Qtd from Irish Times
https://www.irishtimes.com/news/science/how-nonhuman-life-forms-can-change-the-course-of-history-1.3482814

Figure 7.1
Steam Engine
Jacob Leopold
https://commons.wikimedia.org/wiki/File:Jacob_Leupold_Steam_engine_1720.jpg
License: Public Domain

Figure 7.2
Spinning Jenny
Clem Rutter
https://commons.wikimedia.org/wiki/File:Spinning_Jenny_improved_203_Marsden.png
License: Public Domain

Figure 7.3
Leyden Jar
Jerome Harrison
https://commons.wikimedia.org/wiki/File:Early_Layden_jar.png
License: Public Domain

Figure 7.4
Printing Press
Daniel Chodwiecki
https://commons.wikimedia.org/wiki/File:Chodowiecki_Basedow_Tafel_21_c_Z.jpg
License: Public Domain

Figure 7.5
Smallpox Vaccine
Earnest Board
https://commons.wikimedia.org/wiki/File:Jenner_phipps_01.jpg
License: Public Domain

Figure 7.6
Major Royal Houses
Copyright, Jeremy Penna, 2021

Figure 7.7
War of Spanish Succession
Francois Gerard
https://commons.wikimedia.org/wiki/File:Recognition_of_the_Duke_of_Anjou_as_King_of_Spain.png
License: Public Domain

Figure 7.8
Battle of Fontenoy
Pierre L'enfant

https://commons.wikimedia.org/wiki/File:Battle_of_Fontenoy_1745.PNG
License: Public Domain

Figure 7.9
Seven Years War
Richard Knoetel
https://commons.wikimedia.org/wiki/File:Erstes_pr._Bataillon_Leibgarde_in_Schlacht_bei_Kollin.jpg
License: Public Domain

7.10
Battle of Lexington
William Wollen
https://commons.wikimedia.org/wiki/File:The_Battle_of_Lexington.jpg
License: Public Domain

Figure 7.11
Freedom, leading the people
Eugene Delcroix
https://commons.wikimedia.org/wiki/File:Eug%C3%A8ne_Delacroix_-_Le_28_Juillet._La_Libert%C3%A9_guidant_le_peuple.jpg
License: Public Domain

Figure 7.12
Toussant Louverture
Unknown
https://commons.wikimedia.org/wiki/File:Toussaint_L%27Ouverture.jpg
License: Public Domain

Figure 7.13
Exodus from Caracas
Casas de Bolivar
https://commons.wikimedia.org/wiki/File:%C3%89xodo-deCaracasen1814.jpg
License: Public Domain

Figure 7.14
Palermo Insurrection
Tancredi Scaparelli
https://commons.wikimedia.org/wiki/File:Palermo_insurrection_of_1820.jpg
License: Public Domain

Figure 7.15
Belgian Revolution
Gustave Wrappers
https://commons.wikimedia.org/wiki/File:Gustave_Wappers_-_%C3%89pisode_des_Journ%C3%A9es_de_septembre_1830_sur_la_place_de_l%27H%C3%B4tel_de_Ville_

al-Pflanzen-179.jpg
Franz Kohler
License: Public Domain

Figure 8.14
Telegraph Lines
Stielers Hand Atlas
https://commons.wikimedia.org/wiki/File:1891_Telegraph_Lines.jpg
License: Public Domain

Figure 8.15
Steamship
William Talbot
https://commons.wikimedia.org/wiki/File:SS_Great_Britain_by_Talbot.jpg
License: Public Domain

Figure 8.16
Dunlop on bicycle
https://commons.wikimedia.org/wiki/File:John_Boyd_Dunlop_(c1915).jpg
License: Public Domain

Figure 8.17
Scramble for Africa
https://commons.wikimedia.org/wiki/File:ColonialAfrica.png
Eric Kstartis
License: GNU free documentation License

Figure 8.18
Indian Reservations in United States
Presidentman
https://commons.wikimedia.org/wiki/File:Indian_reservations_in_the_Continental_United_States.png
License: Creative Commons Attribution 4.0 Share Alike

Figure 8.19
White Man's Burden
Victor Gillam
https://commons.wikimedia.org/wiki/File:%22The_White_Man%27s_Burden%22_Judge_1899.png
License: Public Domain

Figure 8.20
Races and Skulls
https://commons.wikimedia.org/wiki/File:Races_and_skulls.png
License: Public Domain

Figure 8.21
King Leopold

https://commons.wikimedia.org/wiki/File:Leopold_ii_garter_knight.jpg
License: Public Domain

Figure 8.22
Mutilated Children from Congo
Alice Harris
https://commons.wikimedia.org/wiki/File:MutilatedChildrenFromCongo.jpg
License: Public Domain

Figure 8.23
Map of Empires in 1914
Andrew0921
https://creativecommons.or/licenses/by.30deed.en
License: Creative Commons Attribution 3.0

Figure 9.1
Queen Victoria
National Portrait Gallery
https://commons.wikimedia.org/wiki/File:Queen_Victoria_by_Bassano.jpg
License: Public Domain

Figure 9.2
Mahatma Gandhi
Eliot & Fry
https://commons.wikimedia.org/wiki/File:Mahatma-Gandhi,_studio,_1931.jpg
License: Public Domain

Figure 9.3
German Confederation
Ziegelbrenner
https://commons.wikimedia.org/wiki/File:Deutscher_Bund.svg
License: Creative Commons Attribution 3.0 Share Alike

Figure 9.4
German Empire
Ziegelbrenner
https://commons.wikimedia.org/wiki/File:DR_Fields_of_Law.png
License: Creative Commons Attribution 3.0 Share Alike

Figure 9.5
Dreadnought
US Navy
https://commons.wikimedia.org/wiki/File:HMS_Dreadnought_1906_H61017.jpg
Public Domain

Figure 9.6

U-boat
Paul Adams
https://commons.wikimedia.org/wiki/File:U534.jpg
Public Domain

Figure 9.7
Map of Europe 1914
Histoiricaire
https://commons.wikimedia.org/wiki/File:Map_Europe_alliances_1914-en.svg
License: Creative Commons Attribution 2.5 Share Alike

Figure 9.8
Assassination of Archduke Franz Ferdinand
Achille Beltrame
https://commons.wikimedia.org/wiki/File:DC-1914-27-d-Sarajevo-cropped.jpg
License: Public Domain

Figure 9.9
Step into your place
London Parliamentary Recruiting Committee
https://digital.library.temple.edu/digital/collection/p16002coll9/id/2910/
License: Public Domain

Figure 9.10
Machine Gun
Hohum
https://commons.wikimedia.org/wiki/File:WWImontage.jpg
License: Public Domain

Figure 9.11
Women in munitions factory
Unknown
https://commons.wikimedia.org/wiki/File:Arbeiten_zur_inneren_Ausr%C3%BCstung_der_Gasmasken_-_CH-BAR_-_3241297.tif
License: Public Domain

Figure 9.12
Gassed
John Singer Sargent
https://en.wikipedia.org/wiki/File:Sargent,_John_Singer_(RA)_-_Gassed_-_Google_Art_Project.jpg
License: Public Domain

Figure 9.13
League of Nations
Allard Postman
https://commons.wikimedia.org/wiki/File:League_of_Nations_Anachronous_Map.PNG
License: Creative Commons Attribution 3.0 Share Alike

Figure 9.14
Adolf Hitler
Unknown
https://commons.wikimedia.org/wiki/File:Hitler_portrait_crop.jpg
License: Creative Commons Attribution 3.0 Share Alike

Figure 9.15
Emperor Hirohito
Unknown
https://commons.wikimedia.org/wiki/File:Emperor_Showa_in_dress.jpg
License: Public Domain

Figure 9.15
Benito Mussolini
Unknown
https://commons.wikimedia.org/wiki/File:Mussolini_biografia.jpg
License: Public Domain

Figure 9.16
Francisco Franco
Unknown
https://en.wikipedia.org/wiki/File:RETRATO_DEL_GRAL._FRANCISCO_FRANCO_BAHAMONDE_(adjusted_levels).jpg
License: Public Domain

Figure 10.1
Hiroshima
George Caron
https://commons.wikimedia.org/wiki/File:Atomic_bombing_of_Japan.jpg
License: Public Domain

Figure 10.2
Buchenwald Conecentration Camp
https://en.wikipedia.org/wiki/File:Buchenwald_Slave_Laborers_Liberation.jpg
Private H Miller
License: Public Domain

Figure 10.3
Bombing of Dresden
https://commons.wikimedia.org/wiki/File:Lancaster_I_NG128_Dropping_Blockbuster_-_Duisburg_-_Oct_14,_1944.jpg
Unknown
License: Public Domain

References

Figure 10.4
FDR and Churchill aboard the Prince of Wales
https://commons.wikimedia.org/wiki/File:Prince_of_
Wales-5.jpg
U.S. Navy
License: Public Domain

Figure 10.5
Atlantic Charter
https://commons.wikimedia.org/wiki/File:Atlantic_Char-
ter_(color).jpg
Winston Churchill
License: Public Domain

Figure 10.6
John Manyard Keynes
https://commons.wikimedia.org/wiki/File:Keynes_1933.jpg
Unknown
License: Public Domain

Figure 10.7
Social Security Poster
https://commons.wikimedia.org/wiki/File:SocialSecurity-
poster1.gif
Unknown
License: Public Domain

Figure 10.8
USA Tarriff Rates
https://commons.wikimedia.org/wiki/File:Average_Tar-
iff_Rates_in_USA_(1821-2016).png
James4
License: Creative Commons Attribution 4.0 Share Alike

Figure 10.9
Churchill, Roosevelt, Stalin
https://en.wikipedia.org/wiki/File:Yalta_Conference_
(Churchill,_Roosevelt,_Stalin)_(B%26W).jpg
U.S. Government
License: Public Domain

Figure 10.10
Mount Washington Hotel
https://commons.wikimedia.org/wiki/File:Mt._Washing-
ton_Hotel.jpg
Rickpilot_2000
License: Creative Commons Attribution 2.0 Share Alike

Figure 10.11
Partition of India
https://commons.wikimedia.org/wiki/File:Partition_of_In-
dia.PNG

McMullen
License: Public Domain

Figure 10.12

Decolonization of Africa
https://commons.wikimedia.org/wiki/File:British_Decolo-
nisation_in_Africa.png
The Red Hat of Pat Ferrick
License: Public Domain

Figure 11.1

Russian Civil War
https://commons.wikimedia.org/wiki/File:Russian_Civ-
il_War_montage.png
CapLiber
License: Creative Commons Attribution 4.0 Share Alike

Figure 11.2
Russian Menace
https://commons.wikimedia.org/wiki/File:Satirical_map_
of_Europe,_1877.jpg
Frederick Rose
License: Public Domain

Figure 11.3
American Under Communism
https://commons.wikimedia.org/wiki/File:Is_this_tomor-
row.jpg
Unknown
License, Public Domain

Figure 11.4
Don't Patronize Reds
https://commons.wikimedia.org/wiki/File:Anticommu-
nist_Literature_1950s.png
Anticommunist Literature
License: Public Domain

Figure 11.5
American Warships
https://commons.wikimedia.org/wiki/File:Arizo-
na_(BB39)_Port_Bow,_Underway_-_NARA_-_5900075_-
_1930.jpg
Unknown
License: Public Domain

Figure 11.6
Korean War
https://commons.wikimedia.org/wiki/File:Chaffees_at_

Portuguese Civil War
https://commons.wikimedia.org/wiki/File:Guerra_Colonial_Portuguesa.jpg
SSGH
License: Public Domain

Figure 12.4
Congo Crisis
https://commons.wikimedia.org/wiki/File:Congo_Crisis_collage.jpg
Lindy Beetle
License: Creative Commons Attribution 1.0 Share Alike

Figure 12.5
Mau Mau Uprising
https://commons.wikimedia.org/wiki/File:Patrol_Kenya.jpg
UK Ministry of Defense
License: Public Domain

Figure 12.6
Non Aligned Movement
https://commons.wikimedia.org/wiki/File:Non-Aligned_Movement_by_Date_Joined.svg
Ahtenaken0
License: Creative Commons Attribution 4.0 Share Alike

Figure 12.7
Robert Mugabe
https://commons.wikimedia.org/wiki/File:Mugabe_1979_a.jpg
Koen Suyk / Anefo
Creative Commons Attribution 3.0 Share Alike

Figure 12.8
Nelson Mandella
https://commons.wikimedia.org/wiki/File:Nelson_Mandela_1994.jpg
John Mathew Smith 2001
License: Creative Commons Attribution 2.0 Share Alike

Figure 13.1
Francis Fukayama
https://commons.wikimedia.org/wiki/File:Francis_Fukuyama_2015_(cropped).jpg
Gabierno de Chile
License: Creative Commons Attribution 2.0 Generic

Figure 13.2
End of History
https://commons.wikimedia.org/wiki/File:The_End_of_History_and_the_Last_Man.jpg

Unknown
License: Public Domain

Figure 13.3 and 13.4
Expansion of NATO
Copyright Jeremy Penna, 2021

Figure 13.5
Rubles
https://commons.wikimedia.org/wiki/File:%D0%9E%D0%B1%D1%8B%D1%87%D0%BD%D1%8B%D0%B5_%D1%80%D0%BE%D1%81%D1%81%D0%B8%D0%B9%D1%81%D0%BA%D0%B8%D0%B5_%D0%B1%D0%B0%D0%BD%D0%BA%D0%BD%D0%BE-%D1%82%D1%8B_2020_%D0%B3.jpg
Unknown
License: Creative Commons Attribution 4.0 Share Alike

Figure 13.6
Vladamir Putin
https://commons.wikimedia.org/wiki/File:Vladimir_Putin_(2018-03-01)_03_(cropped).jpg
Unknown
Creative Commons Atribution 4.0

Figure 13.7
Ethnic Russians
https://www.washingtonpost.com/world/ethnic-russians-in-the-former-soviet-republics/2014/05/17/25298b4e-de19-11e3-8009-71de85b9c527_graphic.html
Washington Post
Fair Use

Figure 13.8
Chechnyan War
https://commons.wikimedia.org/wiki/File:Evstafiev-helicopter-shot-down.jpg
Mikhail Evstafiev
License GNU Free Documentation

Figure 13.9
Communist Party
https://commons.wikimedia.org/wiki/File:18th_National_Congress_of_the_Communist_Party_of_China.jpg
Dong Fau
License: Public Domain

Figure 13.10
ASEAN
https://commons.wikimedia.org/wiki/File:Association_of_Southeast_Asian_Nations_(orthographic_projection).svg
Addicted04
License: Creative Commons Attribution 3.0 Unported

Figure 13.11
Arab Spring
Copyright Jeremy Penna, 2021

Figure 13.12
Islamaphobia
https://commons.wikimedia.org/wiki/
File:IV%C4%8CRN_14-03-2015_2.JPG
Venca24
License: Creative Commmons Attribution 4.0 Share Alike

Figure 13.13
Sykes Picot
https://commons.wikimedia.org/wiki/
File:IV%C4%8CRN_14-03-2015_2.JPG
Unknown
License: Public Domain

Figure 13.14
Israel Palestine
https://commons.wikimedia.org/wiki/File:Occupied_Palestinian_Territories.jpg
Wickney-ni
License: Creative Commons Attribution 4.0 Share Alike

Figure 13.15
BRICS
https://commons.wikimedia.org/wiki/File:Informal_meeting_of_the_BRICS_during_the_2019_G20_Osaka_summit.jpg
Alan Santos
License: Creative Commons Attribution 2.0 Generic

Figure 14.1
Sparta and Athens
https://commons.wikimedia.org/wiki/File:Melos_Sparta_and_Athens_416_BCE.svg
Kurzon
License: Creative Commons Attribution 3.0 Share Alike

Figure 14.2
Greek Warrior
https://commons.wikimedia.org/wiki/File:Achilles_fighting_against_Memnon_Leiden_Rijksmuseum_voor_Oudheden.jpg
Jonah Lendering
License: Public Domain

Figure 14.3
Niccolo Machiavelli
https://commons.wikimedia.org/wiki/File:Portrait_of_Niccol%C3%B2_Machiavelli_by_Santi_di_Tito.jpg

Santi di Tito
License: Public Domain

Figure 14.4
Destruction of Florence
https://commons.wikimedia.org/wiki/File:Totila_fa_dstruggere_la_citt%C3%A0_di_Firenze.jpg
Unknown
License: Public Domain

Figure 14.6
Guillotine Execution
https://commons.wikimedia.org/wiki/File:Ex%C3%A9cution_de_Marie_Antoinette_le_16_octobre_1793.jpg
Unknown
License: Public Domain

Figure 14.7
Leviathan
https://commons.wikimedia.org/wiki/File:Destruction_of_Leviathan.png
Gustave Dore
License: Public Domain

Figure 14.8
Leviathan, Hobbes
https://commons.wikimedia.org/wiki/File:Leviathan_by_Thomas_Hobbes.jpg
Thomas Hobbes
License: Public Domain

Figure 14.9
Bomber
https://commons.wikimedia.org/wiki/File:8th_AF_Bombing_Marienburg.JPEG
Unknown
License: Public Domain

Figure 14.10
Copyright Jeremy Penna 2021

Figure 15.1
An Arrow Against Tyrants
Own Reproduction
License: Public Domain

Figure 15.2
Charles I
https://commons.wikimedia.org/wiki/File:King_Charles_I_after_original_by_van_Dyck.jpg
Anthony Van Dyke
License: Public Domain

References

Figure 15.3
English Civil War
https://commons.wikimedia.org/wiki/File:Battle_of_Naseby.jpg
Unknown
License: Public Domain

Figure 15.4
Oliver Cromwell
https://commons.wikimedia.org/wiki/File:Oliver_Cromwell_by_Samuel_Cooper.jpg
Samuel Cooper
License: Public Domain

Figure 15.5
Charles II
https://commons.wikimedia.org/wiki/File:King_Charles_II_by_John_Michael_Wright_or_studio.jpg
John Michel Wright
License: Public Domain

Figure 15.7
John Locke On Government
Own Reproduction
License: Public Domain

Figure 15.8
John Locke
https://commons.wikimedia.org/wiki/File:John_Locke.jpg
Godfrey Kneller
License: Public Domain

Figure 15.9
Seven Years War
https://commons.wikimedia.org/wiki/File:The_Victory_of_Montcalms_Troops_at_Carillon_by_Henry_Alexander_Ogden.JPG
Henry Ogden
License: Public Domain

Figure 15.10
Louis XV
https://commons.wikimedia.org/wiki/File:LouisXV-Rigaud1FXD.jpg
Hyacinth Gerund
License: Public Domain

Figure 15.11
Liberty Leading the People
https://commons.wikimedia.org/wiki/File:Eug%C3%A8ne_Delacroix_-_Le_28_Juillet._La_Libert%C3%A9_guidant_le_peuple.jpg
Eugene Delacroix

License: Public Domain

Figure 15.12
Jean Jacques Rousseau
https://commons.wikimedia.org/wiki/File:Jean-Jacques_Rousseau_(painted_portrait).jpg
Maurice Latour
License: Public Domain

Figure 15.13
Thomas Paine: Common Sense
Own Reproduction
License: Public Domain

Figure 15.14
Notre Dame Cathedral
https://commons.wikimedia.org/wiki/File:Cath%C3%A9drale_Notre-Dame_de_Paris,_3_June_2010.jpg
Sacremento-4
License: Creative Commons Share Attribution 4.0 Share Alike

Figure 15.15
Noble Savage
https://commons.wikimedia.org/wiki/File:Benjamin_west_Death_wolfe_noble_savage.jpg
Benjamin West
License: Public Domain

Figure 15.16
John Stuart Mill
London Steroscopic Company
License: Public Domain

Figure 15.17
Chaos
https://commons.wikimedia.org/wiki/File:Assistants_and_George_Frederic_Watts_-_Chaos_-_Google_Art_Project.jpg
George Frederic Watts
License: Public Domain

Figure 15.18
Liberty Leading the People
https://commons.wikimedia.org/wiki/File:Eug%C3%A8ne_Delacroix_-_Le_28_Juillet._La_Libert%C3%A9_guidant_le_peuple.jpg
Eugene Delacroix
License: Public Domain

Figure 15.19
Declaration of Independence

ba_Anguissola.jpg
Sofonisba Anguissola
License: Public Domain

Figure 17.2
Louise Labe
https://commons.wikimedia.org/wiki/File:Louise_
Lab%C3%A9.png
Pierre Woeioriot
License: Public Domain

Figure 17.3
Arabella Stuart
https://commons.wikimedia.org/wiki/File:Lady_Arabel-
la_Stuart.jpg
Robert Peake the Elder
License: Public Domain

Figure 17.4
Jean D'Albret
https://commons.wikimedia.org/wiki/File:Jeanne-albret-na-
varre.jpg
National Library of France
License: Public Domain

Figure 17.5
Isabella I of Spain
https://commons.wikimedia.org/wiki/File:IsabellaofCas-
tile03.jpg
Unknown
License: Public Domain

Figure 17.6
Queen Elizabeth I
https://en.wikipedia.org/wiki/File:Darnley_stage_3.jpg
National Portrait Gallery
Unknown
License: Public Domain

Figure 17.7
Matchstick Girls
https://commons.wikimedia.org/wiki/File:Women_work-
ing_in_a_match_factory.jpg
The National Arhicve
License: Public Domain

Figure 17.8
Suffragette
https://commons.wikimedia.org/wiki/File:Suffragette1913.
jpg
William Henry Chandler
License: Public Domain

Figure 17.9
Gloria Steinem Ms. Magazine
https://commons.wikimedia.org/wiki/File:Ms._magazine_
Cover_-_Spring_1972.jpg
Liberty Media for Women
License: Creative Commons Attribution 4.0 Share Alike

Figure 17.10
US Army Sharp
https://commons.wikimedia.org/wiki/File:US_Army_
SHARP_Sexual_Harassment_and_Sexual_Assault_Preven-
tion_Poster.jpg
US Army
License: Publc Domain

Figure 17.11
Wadjda Film Cover
Copyright Razor Films
Fair Use

Figure 18.1
Hand
https://commons.wikimedia.org/wiki/File:Hand_INC.svg
Furfur
Creative Commons Attribution 3.0 Unported

Figure 18.2
Michel Foucault
Unknown
https://commons.wikimedia.org/wiki/File:Michel_Fou-
cault_1974_Brasil.jpg
License: Public Domain

Figure 18.3
Jacques Derrida
Unknown
https://en.wikipedia.org/wiki/File:Jacques_derrida_pardon-
ner_limpardonnable_et_limprescriptible_22.jpg
License: Fair Use

Figure 18.4
Spider
John Richfield
https://commons.wikimedia.org/wiki/File:Palystes_super-
ciliosus_female_ventral_annotation_numbers.JPG
License: Creative Commons Attribution 4.0 Share Alike

Figure 18.5
Taxonomy
Peter Bochman
https://commons.wikimedia.org/wiki/File:Spindle_dia-
gram.jpg
License: Public Domain

graph_of_Hindustan_Times_Newspaper_when_India_got_
its_Independence_from_Britishers..!!.jpg
HIndustrani Times
License: Public Domain

Figure 19.12
Africa Poster
https://en.wikipedia.org/wiki/File:Africa_cs_poster.jpg
Unknown
License: Fair Use

Figure 20.1
War Witch
https://en.wikipedia.org/wiki/File:Rebelle_(2012_film).jpg
Copyright Metropole Films
License: Fair Use

Figure 20.2
Turtles Can Fly
https://en.wikipedia.org/wiki/File:Turtles_Can_Fly_poster.
jpg
Copyright Mij Film Co.
License: Fair Use

Figure 20.3
Bashu, the Little Stranger
https://en.wikipedia.org/wiki/File:BashutheLittleStranger.
jpg
Copyright: Bashram Baizai
License: Fair use

Figure 20.4
Egyptian Tank
https://commons.wikimedia.org/wiki/File:Egyptian_Mili-
tary_Police_in_Alexandria.jpg
Gigi Ibrahim
License: Creative Commons Attribution 2.0 Share Alike

Figure 20.5
World War II poster
https://commons.wikimedia.org/wiki/File:Herbert_Mat-
ter_World_War_II_poster.jpg
Herbert Matter
License: Public Domain

Figure 20.6
This is the enemy
https://commons.wikimedia.org/wiki/File:US_propagan-
da_Japanese_enemy.jpg
United States War Department
License: Public Domain

Figure 20.7
Uncle Sam
https://commons.wikimedia.org/wiki/File:I_Want_You_
for_U.S._Army.jpg
US Government
License: Public Domain

Figure 20.8
Stirrup
https://commons.wikimedia.org/wiki/File:Gaya_Confeder-
acy_Iron_Stirrups_(17378457343).jpg
Gary Todd
License: Creative Commons 1.0 Universal Public Domain

Figure 20.9
Battle of Tours
https://commons.wikimedia.org/wiki/File:Charles_Mar-
tel_at_Battle_of_Tours,_Great_Chronicles_of_France_
(27686528435).jpg
Raman Ramishivilli
License: Public Domain

Figure 20.10
Carolingian Empire
https://commons.wikimedia.org/wiki/File:Francia_814.svg
Alpaton
License: Creative Commons Attribution 4.0 Share Alike

Figure 20.11
Map of France
https://commons.wikimedia.org/wiki/File:Map_
France_1477-fr.svg
Ziguener
License: GNU Free Documentation License

Figure 21. 1
Map of India
https://commons.wikimedia.org/wiki/File:Map_of_India.
webp
Karehvhv
License: Creative Commons Attribution 4.0 Share Alike

Figure 21.2
Saudi Arabia
https://commons.wikimedia.org/wiki/File:Ka_Saudi_Ara-
bia_map.png
Giorgi13
License: Creative Commons Attribution 4.0 Share Alike

Figure 21.3
Peace of Westphalia
https://commons.wikimedia.org/wiki/File:Europe_
in_1648_(Peace_of_Westphalia).jpg
Robtert H Labsteron

References

Own work
License: Public Domain

Figure 21.22
African American Civil War Memorial, US National Park
Own Reproduction
License: Public Domain

Figure 22.1
British East India Company
https://commons.wikimedia.org/wiki/File:Destroying_Chinese_war_junks,_by_E._Duncan_(1843).jpg
Edward Duncan
License: Public Domain

Figure 22.2
Railroad
Modified From
https://commons.wikimedia.org/wiki/File:The_How_and_Why_Library_019.jpg
Ealeanor Stackhouse
License: Public Domain

Figure 22.3
Model T
https://commons.wikimedia.org/wiki/File:1925_Ford_Model_T_touring.jpg
ModeltMitch
Creative Commons Attribution 4.0 Share Alike

Figure 22.4
Computer
https://commons.wikimedia.org/wiki/File:ThinkCentre_S50.jpg
dno1967b
License: Creative Commons Attribution 2.0 Share Alike

Figure 22.5
Bartering
Olaus Magnus
https://commons.wikimedia.org/wiki/File:Olaus_Magnus_-_On_Trade_Without_Using_Money.jpg
License: Public Domain

Figure 22.6
King Darius Coin
Modified from
https://commons.wikimedia.org/wiki/File:Achaemenid_coin_daric_420BC_front.jpg
License: Public Domain

Figure 22.7
Roman Denarius

https://commons.wikimedia.org/wiki/File:Denarius-Domitilla-RIC_0137.jpg
Unknown
License: Creative Commons Attribution 2.0
Figure 22.8
Chinese Currency
https://commons.wikimedia.org/wiki/File:MENG_CHIANG_BANK_5_CHIAO_1938.jpg
Meng Chiang Bank
License: Public Domain

Figure 22.9
Wiemar Republic Coin
https://commons.wikimedia.org/wiki/File:5milmkbk.jpg
John Allen Elison
Creative Commons Attribution 3.0 Unported

Figure 22.10
Bolivar
https://commons.wikimedia.org/wiki/File:1998_2000_bolivares_obverse.jpg
Adamant cause
License: Creative Commons Attribution 4.0 Share Alike

Figure 22.11
Ronald Reagan
https://commons.wikimedia.org/wiki/File:Official_Portrait_of_President_Reagan_1981.jpg
Unknown
License: Public Domain

Figure 22.12
Margaret Thatcher
https://commons.wikimedia.org/wiki/File:Margaret_Thatcher_stock_portrait_(cropped).jpg
Thatcher Estate
License: With Permission

Figure 22.13
Wilt Chamberlain
https://commons.wikimedia.org/wiki/File:Wilt_Chamberlain_1967.jpeg
Unknown
Public Domain

Figure 23.1
Ship of Fools
Albrecht Durher
https://commons.wikimedia.org/wiki/File:Wheel_of_fortune.png
License: Public Domain

Figure 23.2

License: Public Domain

Figure 24.8
James Frazer
https://commons.wikimedia.org/wiki/File:JamesGeorge-Frazer.jpg
Unknown
License: Public Domain

Figure 24.9
Clifford Geertz
https://en.wikipedia.org/wiki/File:Clifford_Geertz.jpg
Institute of Advanced Study
Fair Use

Figure 24.10
Huston Smith
https://en.wikipedia.org/wiki/File:Huston_Smith.jpg
Ellis408
License: Public Domain

Figure 24.11
Caliphate Map
https://commons.wikimedia.org/wiki/File:Map_of_expansion_of_Caliphate.svg
Diebuche
License: Public Domain

Figure 24.13
Caliphate
https://commons.wikimedia.org/wiki/File:Muhammad-%27s_widow,_Aisha,_battling_the_fourth_caliph_Ali_in_the_Battle_of_the_Camel.jpg
Unknown
License: Public Domain

Figure 24.14
Dome of the Rock
https://en.wikipedia.org/wiki/File:Jerusalem-2013(2)-Temple_Mount-Dome_of_the_Rock_(SE_exposure).jpg
Godot13
License: Creative Commons Attribution 4.0 Share Alike

Figure 24.16
Cult of the Supreme Being
https://commons.wikimedia.org/wiki/File:F%C3%AAte_de_l%27Etre_supr%C3%AAme_2.jpg
Pierre DeMachy
License: Public Domain

Figure 24.17
French Republican Calendar
https://commons.wikimedia.org/wiki/File:Calendrier-re-

publicain-debucourt2.jpg
Philbert DeCourt
License: Public Domain

Figure 24.18
First Ammendment Enscription
https://commons.wikimedia.org/wiki/File:First_Amendment_inscription.JPG
Robert Klien
License: Creative Commons Attribution 3.0 Share Alike

Figure 24.19
Attack on the Wall of Separation
https://commons.wikimedia.org/wiki/File:The_attack_on_our_outer_ramparts_-_first_the_house_of_refuge_-_then_the_public_schools_-_then_-_the_Constitution!_LCCN2011661440.jpg
Puck Magazine
License: Public Domain

Figure24.20
Hijab Protest
https://commons.wikimedia.org/wiki/File:Jakarta_farmers_protest39.jpg
Jonathan Macintosh
Creative Commons Attribution 2.5 Generic

Figure 24.21
Obama Innauguration
https://commons.wikimedia.org/wiki/File:US_President_Barack_Obama_taking_his_Oath_of_Office_-_2009Jan20.jpg
Cecilio Recardo
License: Public Domain

Figure 24.22
House Church
https://commons.wikimedia.org/wiki/File:People_singing_chant.JPG
Huang Jinhui
License: Creative Commons Attribution 4.0 Share Alike

Figure 24.23
Grand Mosque
https://en.wikipedia.org/wiki/File:Sheikh_Zayed_Mosque_view.jpg
Wikimirati
License: Creative Commons Attribution 4.0 Share Alike

Figure 25.1
Stele of Hammurabi
https://commons.wikimedia.org/wiki/File:P1050763_Louvre_code_Hammurabi_face_rwk.JPG

Index

Made in the USA
Las Vegas, NV
26 January 2023